BEYOND
DISCRIMINATION

BEYOND DISCRIMINATION

Racial Inequality in a Postracist Era

Fredrick C. Harris and
Robert C. Lieberman,
editors

Russell Sage Foundation
New York

The Russell Sage Foundation

Library of Congress Cataloging-in-Publication Data

Beyond discrimination : racial inequality in a postracist era / edited by Fredrick C. Harris, Robert C. Lieberman.
    pages cm
  Includes bibliographical references and index.
  ISBN 978-0-87154-455-1 (pbk. : alk. paper) — ISBN 978-1-61044-799-7 (ebook :
alk. paper)   1. Minorities—United States—Social conditions—21st
century.   2. Minorities—United States—Economic conditions—21st
century.   3. Equality—United States.   4. Racism—United States.   5. Postracialism—United States.   6. United States—Race relations.   I. Harris, Fredrick
C., author, editor of compilation.   II. Lieberman, Robert C., 1964– author, editor
of compilation.
  E184.A1B47 2013
  305.800973—dc23   2012048237

Text design by Genna Patacsil.

RUSSELL SAGE FOUNDATION
112 East 64th Street, New York, New York 10065
10 9 8 7 6 5 4 3 2 1

Contents

Tables and Figures |

Contributors

FREDRICK C. HARRIS is professor of political science and director for Research in African-American Studies at Columbia University.

ROBERT C. LIEBERMAN is professor of political science and provost at The Johns Hopkins University.

ANTHONY S. CHEN is associate professor of sociology and political science at Northwestern University, where he is also faculty fellow at the Institute for Policy Research.

RICHARD P. EIBACH is assistant professor in social psychology at the University of Waterloo.

DEVIN FERGUS is associate professor of African American and African Studies at The Ohio State University and senior fellow at Demos.

PHILIP ATIBA GOFF is assistant professor of psychology at the University of California, Los Angeles, and executive director of research for the Consortium for Police Leadership in Equity.

RODNEY E. HERO is professor in the Department of Political Science and is the Haas Chair in Diversity and Democracy at the University of California, Berkeley.

DESMOND KING is Andrew W. Mellon Professor of American Government at the University of Oxford.

NAA OYO A. KWATE is associate professor in the departments of human ecology and Africana studies at Rutgers University.

MORRIS E. LEVY is Ph.D. candidate in the Department of Political Science at the University of California, Berkeley.

DEVAH PAGER is professor of sociology and public affairs and codirector of the Joint Degree Program in Social Policy at Princeton University.

VALERIE PURDIE-VAUGHNS is assistant professor in social psychology at Columbia University and research fellow at the Columbia University Institute for Research on African-American Studies (IRAAS).

BENJAMIN RADCLIFF is professor in the Department of Political Science at the University of Notre Dame.

LISA M. STULBERG is associate professor of sociology of education and director of the Sociology of Education Program at the Steinhardt School of Culture, Education, and Human Development at New York University.

DORIAN T. WARREN is associate professor of political science and public affairs and codirector of the Program on Labor Law & Policy at Columbia University.

VESLA M. WEAVER is assistant professor of African American studies and political science and faculty affiliate of the Institution of Social and Policy Studies at Yale University.

Acknowledgments

THIS BOOK BEGAN life as a series of intense conversations during and after the 2008 presidential election. Barack Obama's stirring campaign and dramatic election seemed to signal at once the maturation of a new pattern of American politics, in which a serious racial barrier to achievement had been shattered, and a new attentiveness to questions of race and inequality in American politics and society. But as Obama's presidency began to unfold, questions arose about the persistence of racial inequality in this new era. We especially thank Dorian Warren for his contributions to these discussions and his help in framing the animating questions that motivate this volume.

These reflections prompted us to convene a small conference in May 2010, generously funded and hosted by the Russell Sage Foundation with additional funding from the Center for African-American Politics and Society and the School of International and Public Affairs at Columbia University. The participants were drawn from across the social sciences, all of them outstanding scholars who have, in a variety of ways, tackled some of the key empirical and analytical challenges of explaining the persistence of racial inequality in the post–civil rights era, drawing on a wide range of theoretical traditions and methodological approaches, all of which are represented in the chapters that follow.

At the conference, Christina Greer, Kimberley Johnson, Olati Johnson, Samuel Roberts, and Carla Shedd participated as discussants, and Ira Katznelson also joined much of the discussion. Their contributions enriched the conversation over two days in New York City, and their comments helped sharpen the focus of the discussion and improved the papers. The conference was opened by a public roundtable, Racial Inequality in the Age of Obama, which framed the themes and challenges that the ensuing conference and this volume take up. For their participation in the roundtable, we are grateful to William Julius Wilson, Charles M. Blow of the *New York Times,* and Ira Katznelson. Kate Krimmel provided exemplary organizational support.

At Russell Sage, we are especially grateful to Eric Wanner for his support of the project and to Suzanne Nichols for her patient guidance through the publication process. Several anonymous reviewers provided tough but helpful comments that improved the book.

Introduction | Beyond Discrimination: Racial Inequality in the Age of Obama

Fredrick C. Harris and Robert C. Lieberman

CONTEMPORARY RACIAL INEQUALITY in the United States poses a dual challenge for social scientists and policy analysts. It is, first, a serious policy problem. Nearly half a century after the peak of the civil rights movement, racial identity remains a significant predictor of class status and life chances. Across a wide range of social and economic domains—income, wealth, employment, education, housing, health, criminal justice, and others—African Americans and other minority groups consistently lag behind whites, with severe consequences not only for the well-being of disadvantaged group members but also for the health of American democracy (Wilson 1999; Hochschild and Weaver 2007). Second, racial inequality in the post–civil rights era poses an analytical challenge for scholars of American politics and society. In the wake of the civil rights revolution of the 1950s and 1960s, the most obvious barriers to racial equality—state-sponsored and state-sanctioned segregation, explicit discrimination, and widespread racism among the white public—have declined dramatically as factors in American life. Moreover, the antidiscrimination regime created by the civil rights laws of the 1960s, especially the Civil Rights and Voting Rights Acts, has been comparatively successful at rooting out the most egregious practices of racial exclusion and institutionalizing racial integration as a widespread public policy goal.

But these changes, while they have dramatically improved life chances for many members of racial and ethnic minority groups, have not closed the gap entirely, and multiple sources of inequality—residency, education, employment, income, wealth, among others—still overlap and reinforce

1

one another. Moreover, as labor-market and income inequality have grown and hardened in recent decades, the racial gap has become more acute, not less. In short, to adapt T. H. Marshall's (1964) terminology, while the transformations of the mid and late twentieth century may have conferred civil and political rights on African Americans and other minorities, broad-based social rights remain elusive. This general puzzle—the persistence of racial inequality in a world in which overt racial hostility does not carry the same meaning and weight as it did in the past—is both a profound challenge for American politics and a fundamental question for scholars of American society, and it is the central conundrum that the authors assembled in this collection seek to address.

The civil rights revolution removed the most visible and blatant means of producing and reproducing racial inequality from American society. But beneath the surface of racism and discrimination lay another layer of institutions and processes that have made racial inequality persist. These subterranean mechanisms have not been fully exposed or explored, and they remain poorly understood; identifying and analyzing these mechanisms is critical to understanding and ameliorating racial inequality, and that is the central task that we and our colleagues in this volume undertake.

BARACK OBAMA AND THE DECLINING SIGNIFICANCE OF RACISM

To many observers, the election of Barack Obama seemed to punctuate the long civil rights struggle and mark the dawn of a new era in American politics in which race would no longer stand as a barrier to opportunity or achievement. Obama himself embraced this imagery, beginning with his Democratic National Convention speech in 2004 ("There is not a black America and a white America and Latino America and Asian America—there's the United States of America") and continuing through his speech on race during the 2008 campaign, at the moment when his association with an outspoken black preacher threatened to derail his campaign ("Barack Obama's Remarks to the Democratic National Convention," *New York Times*, July 27, 2004). In his race speech, which he titled "A More Perfect Union" and delivered at the National Constitution Center in Philadelphia ("Barack Obama's Speech on Race," *New York Times*, March 18, 2008), Obama at once acknowledged the history of racial division and conflict in the American past, envisioned a future in which racial distinctions would blur and ultimately fade into insignificance, and projected himself as an avatar of that future (Sugrue 2010, 118–24).

In keeping with these themes, Obama defied his opponents' attempts to identify him as a "black" candidate of limited and parochial electoral appeal (a dynamic most starkly apparent in the reaction to Bill Clinton's remarks around the time of the South Carolina primary in January 2008, first dismissing Obama's claims to have been a consistent opponent of the Iraq war as "a complete fairy tale" and then comparing Obama's campaign to Jesse Jackson's much more pointedly racialized presidential campaigns in 1984 and 1988) (Heilemann and Halperin 2010, 185–86, 196–201, 209–15; Remnick 2010, 510–12). Even African Americans were slow to embrace his candidacy for the Democratic nomination. For his part, Obama carefully straddled two political worlds, embracing (albeit uneasily) his African American identity and connecting himself with the legacy of the civil rights struggle as a member of the "Joshua generation" while methodically building a political career on the basis of cross-racial coalition building and electoral appeals (Obama 2007; Remnick 2010; Lizza 2008; Fredrick C. Harris, "The Price of a Black President," *New York Times*, October 27, 2012).

There is also ample electoral evidence that Obama reached beyond race more effectively than other candidates for office in recent American history. In the post–civil rights era, no Democratic nominee for president has received a majority (or even a plurality) of the white vote in the general election, and Obama was no exception to this trend. But he did better among white voters than any Democrat in recent memory. Obama got 43 percent of the white vote in 2008, more than John Kerry in 2004 or Al Gore in 2000 (41 percent each). In fact, only Jimmy Carter in 1976 (47 percent) and Bill Clinton in 1996 (43 percent) got so large a share of the white vote since the 1960s. Although Obama's share of the white vote fell to 39 percent in 2012, he won reelection with an impressively cross-racial coalition.[1] Moreover, as Valerie Purdie-Vaughns and Richard Eibach argue in our collection, the election of the first black president held important symbolic power for Americans across racial lines.

But although it seems clear that race is still a meaningful political category and racial inequality remains one of the defining features of American life, it is also clear that the racial landscape has shifted dramatically between the mid-twentieth and early twenty-first centuries. The United States, it seems, has entered what we might call a "postracist" era in which the role race plays in American society is more subtle and hidden from view than in earlier periods, when explicit racial beliefs and antagonisms underlay an open and explicit racial order.[2] Racial attitudes among white Americans have been substantially transformed over the past fifty years. Mass belief in biological or sociological theories of race that imply the superiority of some racial groups and the inferiority of others has almost vanished, and the expression of explicit racial prejudice has been rendered largely illegitimate in American political discourse. Americans broadly accept, at least rhetorically, the basic premises of legal, social, and political equality across racial lines and recognize the value of diversity and integration in many arenas—workplaces, schools, public settings—where it was once rare, if not expressly forbidden. As Desmond King and Rogers Smith (2011) have argued, these trends indicate the apparent political triumph of a color-blind racial policy alliance, a collection of actors and institutions that promote policies rooted in individualism, without reference to racial identities.

But the transformative, even revolutionary, change of recent decades in the American racial terrain has also left behind a puzzling, not to say disastrous, residue of stability in patterns of racial inequality. Color blindness in American politics is multilayered and complex, and as King and Smith also point out, the contemporary color-blind racial alliance is composed largely of those who are at best indifferent (and at worst hostile) to claims for substantive racial equality, suggesting that the transformation of American race politics is far from complete. Nearly five years into the Obama era, the realities of economic crisis, war, and deeply polarized politics define the political moment. The nearly giddy enthusiasm of the campaign and election has subsided and with it, perhaps, the hope that the politics of race would recede into the background.

Moreover, Obama's candidacy and election may have themselves generated a racial backlash. In the 2008 general election, Obama outperformed the 2004 Democratic nominee, Senator John Kerry, in every area of the country except for the areas of the South corresponding to the old Black Belt, the cotton-growing region that formed the core of the segregationist, white-supremacist South of the twentieth century, where racial tension and resentment remain politically salient, a result that tends to belie recent suggestions that race was declining as a factor in Southern electoral politics (Gelman 2010, 190–92; Key 1949; Shafer and Johnston 2006). And the extreme right-wing reaction to the Obama administration exemplified by the Tea Party movement, while certainly motivated by genuine discontent with the drift of American politics and policy, seems to embody a certain amount of discomfort with Obama's racial and ethnic identity, as suggested by the obsessive focus on Obama's alleged Muslim background and foreign birth (a distortion that persists despite all evidence to the contrary). The commonly voiced Tea Party slogan, "Take back our country," conveys a message resonant with racial overtones (Zernike 2010; Barreto et al. 2011; Skocpol and Williamson 2012). Take back the country from whom? Indeed, antiblack and anti-Latino sentiments increased from 2008 to 2012, even though Obama had spoken less publicly on racial issues during his first two years of office than any Democratic president since the early 1960s ("AP Poll: A Slight Majority of Americans Are Now Expressing Negative Views about Blacks," *Washington Post*, October 27, 2012; Harris 2012).

These contradictions and ambiguities of America's postracist present—continuity in the midst of change—underscore the central question with which the authors in this collection grapple, individually and collectively. The postracist notion resonates not because it describes contemporary American society in any important particulars but because it evokes our sense that the ways in which race matters in American public life have changed, upending both commonsense understandings and social-scientific theories of race's place in American society. The key empirical puzzles that we investigate revolve around the analytical meaning of a *postracist* America and the "stickiness" of race in the postracist era. In the pre–civil rights era of blatant prejudice, legally sanctioned segregation, and explicit discrimination, explanations for racial inequality and the subordinate position of African Americans and other racially and ethnically defined minority groups were relatively easy to grasp. Prejudice has since declined, Jim Crow has been dismantled, and discrimination is illegal, and yet racial inequality remains stubbornly resilient at least in some areas, although declining in others (Hochschild 1999; Brown et al. 2003). If so much has changed in American politics and society, if so many of the barriers to racial equality have crumbled, why is there so much dispiriting continuity in the contours of racial inequality? Why and how does race still matter as a marker of inequality and a predictor of life chances? In the absence of the more easily legible patterns of the past, what are the mechanisms that reproduce and reinforce racial inequality in contemporary American life?

BEYOND INDIVIDUALISM

The key methodological implication of the postracist puzzle is that we need to move away from the inference that racial inequality is exclusively the consequence of factors that operate at the individual level. Across the social sciences, accounts of the causes of racial inequality have long focused primarily on racial attitudes (particularly those of whites), explicit acts of discrimination (particularly those by whites against African Americans and members of other minority groups), and the individual characteristics of African Americans and other minorities themselves. For much of the twentieth century, white prejudice was the dominant racial attitude in American society. For Gunnar Myrdal (1944), white prejudice lay at the core of the "American dilemma," the tension between American ideals of equality and universal rights and the subordinate status of American blacks. In his wide-ranging study of race relations in the United States, Myrdal found that the belief among whites in black inferiority was widespread, a finding that was corroborated by newly emergent survey and experimental research across the social sciences. As a corollary, white Americans tended to support segregation and to oppose policies aimed at breaking down barriers and breaching color lines in settings such as workplaces, neighborhoods, and schools. Over time, as racial injustice increasingly came under assault in the middle third of the twentieth century, these attitudes began to change, and white Americans came to accept, at least rhetorically, principles of equality and integration (Page and Shapiro 1992, 68–81; Schuman et al. 1997).

More recently, however, some observers have argued that racial prejudice still dominates the racial beliefs of white Americans and that the express desire to exclude African Americans and other minorities accounts for the persistence of racial inequality (Bell 1992; Hacker 1992). More subtle versions of what we might call the "racism thesis" suggest that even though explicit expressions of racial prejudice are frowned on, racial stereotypes remain a powerful framing device that can shape social and political behavior and policy debates, often in ways that remain hidden behind a norm of color-blind equality (Kinder and Sanders 1996; Gilens 1999; Mendelberg 2001). Others suggest that racial prejudice per se is less important than other kinds of beliefs in shaping white Americans' opinions about policies such as affirmative action and others that are targeted at minorities (Sniderman and Piazza 1993; Sniderman and Carmines 1997; Sniderman, Crosby, and Howell 2000).

What these perspectives share, despite their disagreements about the prevalence of certain kinds of racist beliefs, is the view that what matters in creating and sustaining racial inequality is prejudice, whether overt or latent. Whatever the degree of prejudice that remains in American society, it is unquestionably less widespread and virulent than it once was, making it hard to attribute the persistence of inequality entirely to it. The more or less overt prejudice of an earlier era has largely been overwritten by a rhetoric of color blindness and an acceptance, if not a celebration, of diversity as a fundamental maxim, although as we suggest these categories are rather double edged.

A second approach to racial inequality centers on discrimination, the deliberate differential treatment of individuals based on their race or other characteristics. Along with racial prejudice, discrimination in politics, education, employment, and other domains of American life was the norm for much of the twentieth century. Sanctioned by the United States Supreme Court in 1896, the systematic exclusion of African Americans from schools, jobs, and neighborhoods reserved exclusively for whites was a core feature of American life—not only in the South, where segregation and white supremacy thoroughly structured politics, economy, and society, but also in the North, where public policy, group mobilization, and institutional structure conspired to exclude African Americans from opportunity and mobility (Plessy v. Ferguson, 163 U.S. 537 (1896); Key 1949; Jackson 1985; Wilson 1987; King 1995; Sugrue 1996). African Americans, moreover, were widely excluded from voting rights in the South, depriving them of political power and further reinforcing broad patterns of discrimination (Keyssar 2000; Valelly 2004).

Over the course of the twentieth century, African Americans waged a battle on multiple fronts against discrimination in education, employment, public accommodations, and the ballot box. The war against discrimination was engaged in multiple theaters—in states and at the national level; in both North and South; in the courts, Congress, the executive branch, and the streets—and by the 1960s it had met with broad success. The Supreme Court reversed its constitutional sanction of discrimination, state governments took action against discrimination, the civil rights movement toppled Jim Crow in the South, and Congress passed the Civil Rights and Voting Rights Acts, outlawing discrimination in education, employment, and at the ballot box (Brown v. Board of Education of Topeka et al., 347 U.S. 483 [1954]; Chen 2009; Johnson 2010; Sugrue 2008).

As a consequence of this mid-twentieth-century transformation of law and policy, overt discrimination in realms such as employment, education (especially higher education), housing, government contracting, and voting declined dramatically. This decline in discrimination resulted partly from state action in the wake of the core civil rights legislation of the 1960s: the Civil Rights Act of 1964, the Voting Rights Act of 1965, and the Fair Housing Act of 1968. State enforcement of these acts has been variable. In employment, the United States developed a comparatively strong enforcement regime, characterized by affirmative action practices and diversity norms that have come to be widely shared among private and public employers alike, braced by the federal courts, federal and state administrative authority, and private litigants (Lieberman 2005; Dobbin 2009; Farhang 2010). The legal protection of voting rights for African Americans as well as Latinos and other minority groups has similarly dramatically transformed the American electorate and expanded minority political empowerment (Davidson and Grofman 1994; Harris, Sinclair-Chapman, and McKenzie 2006).

At the same time, antidiscrimination enforcement in education has been somewhat less vigorous, from the Supreme Court's admonishment that desegregation of public schools should proceed "with all deliberate speed" to the court's denial of remedies such as metropolitan busing that might have more effectively overcome the limitations of residential segregation and the local control of schools (Brown v. Board of Education of Topeka et al., 349 U.S. 294, 301 [1955]; Milliken v. Bradley, 418 U.S. 717 [1974]). Similarly, antidiscrimination efforts in housing have achieved limited success as federal efforts to integrate neighborhoods have been caught between local resistance and bureaucratic lassitude at the federal level (Bonastia 2006; Sugrue 1996; Massey and Denton 1993).

From their highpoint in the 1970s, all of these formal efforts to desegregate American social and economic life have come under challenge in both the political arena and the courts, and these rollback attempts have also met with varying success. Liberal principles of equality frequently collided with politics as local communities resisted policy attempts to integrate schools and neighborhoods (Hochschild 1984; Sugrue 1996; Hochschild and Danielson 2004). Federal courts have limited the use of race-conscious desegregation measures in public primary and secondary education (Hopwood v. Texas, 78 F.3d. 932 [5th Cir. 1996]; Parents Involved in Community Schools v. Seattle School District No. 1, 551 U.S. 701 [2007]) and in government contracting (City of Richmond v. J. A. Croson, 488 U.S. 469 [1989]; Adarand Constructors, Inc., v. Peña, 515 U.S. 200 [1995]) but thus far, at least, protected them in higher education (Grutter v. Bollinger, 539 U.S. 306 [2003]).

The Florida state legislature enacted Governor Jeb Bush's proposal to end the use of affirmative action by state government, including public universities. Referendums banning affirmative action have passed in California, Michigan, and Nebraska, while more far-reaching efforts to prohibit the collection of race statistics (on the French model) have failed thus far. States have responded with creative efforts to work around these legal proscriptions of explicitly race-based diversity efforts, seeking to achieve integration by apparently color-blind means—an ironic strategic reversal of Justice Harry Blackmun's admonition that "in order to get beyond racism, we must first take account of race. There is no other way. And in order to treat some persons equally, we must treat them differently" (Regents of the University of California v. Bakke, 438 U.S. 265, 407 [1978]; Peterson 1995; Sabbagh 2007).

At the same time, the enforcement of antidiscrimination law has clearly worked to reduce racial and ethnic gaps in important economic outcomes. The economist James Heckman has documented the early impact of the Civil Rights Act in black employment and wages in the South in the 1960s and 1970s (Heckman and Payner 1989; Heckman 1990; Donohue and Heckman 1991). Affirmative action has in fact had a nontrivial, if modest, impact on the educational and employment opportunities, wages, and socioeconomic status of people of color and women, with significant spillover effects for the broader society (Burstein 1985; Bowen and Bok 1998; Holzer and Neumark 2006). More recently, Roland Fryer (2011) has shown that although racial gaps in economic and social outcomes (such as employment, health, and incarceration) remain robust, the share of those gaps that can be attributed directly to discrimination (rather than to gaps in education outcomes—which may themselves result from discrimination)—has fallen dramatically in recent decades.

Moreover, many large and influential public and private organizations—including corporations, universities, and the military—have thoroughly internalized the goals of diversity (along many dimensions, not restricted to race) and adopted a standard set of personnel practices that embody at least a version of antidiscrimination law (Dobbin 2009; Karabel 2005).[3] To be sure, discrimination is still a substantial barrier to economic success, especially in employment and particularly for young inner-city black men, who are frequently the targets of stereotyping about what William Julius Wilson (2009) summarizes as "ghetto behavior" (Neckerman and Kirschenman 1991; Goldsmith, Hamilton, and Darity 2006; Pager 2007). But despite the persistence of explicit discrimination, it is increasingly difficult to sustain the argument that the deliberate discriminatory actions of individuals alone can account for contemporary patterns of racial inequality.

BEYOND DISCRIMINATION

The persistence of racial inequality in an era when explicit, intentional racial discrimination has declined, if not entirely disappeared, frames the central puzzle we address in this volume. We have entered an era in which racial attitudes by themselves are no longer sufficient to account for patterns of racial inequality. This transformation gives rise to three key questions, which our contributors address in turn. First, when and how did this historical transformation occur, from a period in which racism and overt discrimination shaped American society to the contemporary postracist moment? Second, what role do racial attitudes play in the postracist era? The absence of the explicit racist expression of an earlier period does not imply that individual beliefs about racial difference are no longer consequential for social relations and collective outcomes, merely that they are expressed differently and act through different pathways. Several of our authors address the consequences of racial attitudes in this new world. Finally, what other institutional and structural mechanisms operate to perpetuate and shape racial inequality in the postracist world?

History and Context

The historical transformation of the landscape of racial inequality motivates the first group of contributions to the collection. How and when did the shift occur, from inequality visibly created and maintained by explicit and legally codified racial beliefs to today's more hidden and recondite structures? The Obama era, which frames the work of all the contributors, denotes a distinctive historical configuration of factors that shape the questions we ask and the arguments we fashion—the confluence of the post–civil rights, postracist moment we have already described with an era of conservative, deregulatory politics and rising economic inequality, punctuated recently by severe financial crisis and the longest and deepest recession since the Great Depression (see Pierson and Skocpol 2007). Locating our key analytical theme—the racially unequal consequences of facially racial-neutral institutions—in history's flow helps further to identify and analyze the role that these more macro-level historical conditions play in shaping and constraining the processes that produce racial inequality and to question the portability—across time, place, and context—of our propositions about the mechanisms that generate and reproduce racial inequality. Not all the chapters in the volume are themselves geared toward this kind of historical inquiry, but returning briefly to the distinctive characteristics of this historical moment allows us at least to ask key questions about the role of the broader political, economic, and social context and the generalizability of our perspective.

Historical inquiry is important also because we seek not a static portrait of racial inequality at a single moment but an account of how racial inequality has unfolded over time. It is a commonplace observation that racial inequality in the United States is pervasive and persistent because of the country's distinct history of slavery, segregation, and white supremacy. But this observation raises important questions about how racial inequality is transmitted over time, an issue that is usually elided in discussions of racial inequality. Scholars have suggested a range of processes that might account for the "stickiness" of racial inequality over time—psychological, sociological, economic, cultural, and political. An alternative set of arguments suggest that history has no bearing on racial inequality and minimizes the causal weight of such means by which inequality might reproduce itself over time, instead preferring to ascribe contemporary inequality to contemporary ills of politics, policy, and society (Thernstrom and Thernstrom 1997). Nevertheless, the mechanisms by which racial inequality is transmitted across time remain contested and obscure (Bleich 2005; Lieberman 2008; see generally Pierson 2004). Although few of the essays in this volume address the question explicitly, as a collection they focus precisely on a range of causal mechanisms by which racial inequality can be said to be built into American institutions, offering an innovative window onto this issue and allowing us to pose questions about processes as they develop over time in an analytically useful way.

Thinking about racial inequality as something that evolves over time also sheds light on a conspicuous choice that the editors and contributors made in developing the volume: the almost exclusive focus on black-white inequality. With a few exceptions, the contributions to the book address the contours and causes of inequality regarding African Americans and do not address the expanded meaning of race in American politics and society that has followed the opening up of the country's borders to immigration from the non-European world. We offer several justifications for this choice, while fully acknowledging that we miss a great deal of important nuance and variation in contemporary racial inequality. For most of American history, the black-white color line has been the defining axis of inequality in American society. Our contributors focus almost exclusively on black-white inequality in American institutions, structures, and processes, and the mechanisms that generate and reproduce inequality that we uncover have evolved around that feature of American life. Analytically, then, a historical focus on black-white inequality can reveal much about the contours and processes of American racial inequality more generally.

Racial and ethnic diversity in the United States has indeed proliferated in the past half century. Latinos (counted together) now constitute the largest minority group in American society, and Asian Americans also account for a fast-growing segment of the population. These groups, increasingly constructed as racially and ethnically distinct, have emerged in a society whose political institutions, markets, and civil society have been organized largely around the black-white divide (King and Smith 2005). The position of nonblack minority groups, too, has been largely defined in relation to the black-white color line, through what Claire Jean Kim (1999) has described as a process of "triangulation." Issues of inequality across this expanded panoply of racially defined groups have essentially been overlain across already existing patterns and mechanisms of black-white inequality.

Thinking in this way about the unfolding of broader patterns of racial inequality in a more multiracial context might lead us to consider racial inequality in light of recent advances in the theory of institutional change, invoking mechanisms such as layering, drift, and conversion that tend to occur when multiple institutional systems interact (Hacker 2004; Thelen 2004; Mahoney and Thelen 2010). These kinds of approaches have proved particularly fruitful in thinking about systems in which continuity and change intermingle and in which change comes about through unexpected and often imperceptible means, an apt description of the conundrum of contemporary racial inequality. The studies collected here suggest that this could be a powerful approach not only to understanding the history of racial inequality in the United States but also to assessing our contemporary condition in a world of greater diversity and complexity in race relations.

The first group of chapters begins to address some of these questions, by describing some key moments in the historical trajectory of racial equality and analyzing some of the key historical processes that drove the shifting political economy of racial inequality. Rodney Hero begins by describing the contemporary landscape of racial inequality and parsing the postracist moment, setting it in historical context. Dorian Warren's chapter situates the transformation of racial inequality in the broader evolution of the American political economy and offers a novel periodization scheme that links politics, economics, and race. Building both on King and Smith's (2005) argument about racial orders in American political development and on Charles Tilly's (1998) framework for understanding durable inequality, Warren reveals the deeply racialized structure of the American labor market over time and suggests that racial ascription and class dynamics are coequal forces in shaping markets and distributing economic opportunity (see also Warren 2010). He shows, moreover, how the twinned politically structured forces of racial exclusion and economic organization have shifted over time to create a series of distinct racial and economic orders that define both the mechanisms that tend to perpetuate racial and class inequality and the opportunities for mobilization to challenge inequality.

In his chapter, Desmond King questions why and, pertinently, when racial inequality becomes an especially salient issue in American politics. Under what historical conditions do American policymakers perceive racial inequality as a problem worthy of attention, and what kind of responses are they likely to construct? King builds on his earlier collaborative work (King and Smith 2005, 2011; King and Lieberman 2009) to show how the apparatus of the American state is situated within a system of competing racial policy alliances that perpetually contend for dominance and largely structure American politics. For much of American history, the dominant racial alliances were hostile to (or at best neglectful of) racial equality. In the mid-twentieth century, with the pro-equality forces momentarily dominant, the weight of federal policy shifted toward the protection of rights and the promotion of racial equality, and King's chapter focuses on the civil rights moment of the 1960s as a key pivot in the state's role in shaping America's racial terrain, but one that was produced in often surprising and unexpected ways. King's essay elicits from this history a configuration of conditions that seem to be necessary for the state to take on the challenge of racial inequality and then maps those same conditions onto some of the very limitations of state power that have vexed analysts and advocates ever since.

Anthony Chen and Lisa Stulberg similarly view the 1960s as a pivotal moment in the transformation of the terrain of racial inequality. They explore the origins of affirmative action in selective universities and challenge the conventional view that the violent urban unrest of the 1960s was primarily responsible for the opening up of university admissions policies in the ensuing years. Rather, they find that internal organizational forces and not external threats of disruption were primarily responsible for the rise of racially attentive admissions practices aimed at expanding opportunities for minority students and diversifying the population of schools that had been bastions of white privilege. Like King, in his exploration of the American state's capacity to challenge racial inequality, Chen and Stulberg probe a set of historical conditions under which selective universities, a key cog in the machinery of rigid privilege and exclusion and of economic mobility and opportunity in the American political economy, might act either to perpetuate or challenge racial inequality.

Finally, considering history and context provides a window onto another important thread that runs through the volume, the changing status and meaning of the rhetoric of color blindness. The concept of color blindness has a long and varied career, and we cannot do full justice to its intellectual genealogy here (see Thomas 2002; Haney López 2007). Nevertheless, we can observe that its meaning and valence have changed dramatically in recent decades, from a liberal aspiration in the era of Jim Crow segregation to a conservative rhetorical device frequently mobilized to evade collective responsibility for the persistence of racial inequality and to oppose policies, such as affirmative action, designed to tackle racial inequality head on.

Chen and Stulberg's argument about the origins of affirmative action in higher education also highlights this transformation, showing how the organizational imperatives of elite institutions in the 1960s led to the recognition that color blindness in admissions was insufficient to achieve equality, revealing an ideological context quite distant from a more current setting, where the rhetoric and appearance of color blindness often mask the race-laden processes of contemporary American life, some of which our contributors chronicle. More generally, the temporal arc of all the essays in the volume starkly frames this generational political and ideological transformation and offers a powerful answer to the tendentious claim—all too often accepted as self-evident—that color blindness is a timeless liberal virtue that inherently produces fairness and equality (Appiah and Gutmann 1996). Our central analytical theme, the unequal consequences of apparently racially neutral institutions, helps to puncture this mythology of color blindness, which has become central to American political discourse, never more so than in the Obama era.

The Role of Attitudes

The persistence of racial inequality in this postracist era, when explicit racism and intentional racial discrimination have declined, if not entirely disappeared, frames our central puzzle and suggests the need to reframe long-standing questions and conclusions about the role of attitudes in shaping racial inequality. One inference that has become increasingly common in recent decades is that the absence of discrimination implies a newly level playing field and that, in a new era of "meritocracy," continuing racial gaps must therefore reflect actual deficiencies of "merit" on the part of those who are less successful (Lemann 2000).

As the sociologist Lawrence Bobo (Bobo, Kluegel, and Smith 1997; Bobo and Smith 1998) has documented, since the civil rights breakthroughs of the 1960s many white Americans have come to presume that the end of state-sponsored legal segregation and the prohibition of discrimination have created a truly color-blind public sphere, making it seem reasonable to infer that inequality results neither from racism nor from structural barriers to minority achievement but from the incapacity of minorities themselves—a phenomenon that Bobo calls laissez-faire racism. Similarly, Martin Gilens (1999) has shown that similar beliefs about chronic poverty and the apparent undeservingness of the black poor, reinforced by specific cultural beliefs held by whites about African Americans (that blacks are lazy and lack a work ethic, for instance), undermined support for the New Deal welfare state in the decades following the 1960s, paving the way for the welfare reforms of the 1990s, which have had disproportionately punitive effects on people of color (Soss et al. 2001; see also Katz 1989).

A parallel version of this approach focuses on the self-destructive patterns of life in the ghettos and barrios of American inner cities—joblessness, broken families, welfare dependence, drugs, crime, and violence, among others. To some analysts, these characteristics of inner-city poverty reflect a set of pathological cultural and behavioral traits of minority groups that have been abetted by public policies that encourage dependency and isolation, particularly the welfare programs associated with the War on Poverty of the 1960s (Sowell 1978, 1994; Murray 1984). In the extreme, this argument takes on a biological cast, from the pseudoscience of Richard Herrnstein and Charles Murray (1994; see Gould 1996) to debates about the existence of race in the shadow of the Human Genome Project (Risch et al. 2002; Cooper, Kaufman, and Ward 2003; Foster and Sharp

2004). However, other scholars, such as William Julius Wilson (1996), have portrayed those attributes of inner-city life not as group traits that are somehow innate but as cultural adaptations to a political economy that has left those neighborhoods and their residents behind, with poor education, few jobs, and no reasonable economic prospects (Anderson 1999; Venkatesh 2006). Wilson's response suggests that such explanations for racial inequality, which attribute inequality to individual or collective pathologies of minorities themselves without setting those cultural patterns in a structural context, amount to nothing more than a canard.

Attitudinal and cultural explanations of these kinds tend to look for cause-and-effect relationships between the beliefs and behavior of individuals—whites, blacks, or other minorities—and outcomes, so that a series of individual decisions and actions cumulate into macro-level patterns of racial inequality. But given the growing gap between the individual-level indicators of intentionality, prejudice, and discrimination, on one hand, and societal patterns of inequality, on the other, such explanations are no longer tenable in isolation. By contrast, explanations rooted in structural features of the society or political economy can help us probe how racially imbalanced outcomes are possible even in the absence of racial intentions and can result even from the most scrupulously color-blind of objectives. One common critique of post–civil rights race policy has been that in the absence of explicit discrimination or prejudice, the emphasis on race-targeted policies that seek to confer advantages to African Americans and other minorities are the culprit in the persistence of inequality because they undermine the fundamental liberal commitments to color blindness and equality (Thernstrom and Thernstrom 1997; Sleeper 1997).

These views fail to consider that ostensibly race-neutral policies and processes often have the effect of perpetuating and reinforcing racial inequalities in the normal course of their operations and even if none of the people involved acts with racially biased intent (see Lieberman 2005). Moreover, this view places inordinate faith in the dominance and beneficence of American liberalism as a force for racial equality. But history does not bear this faith out. As Rogers Smith (1997) has shown, American liberalism has perpetually contended with alternative political traditions that do not share the liberal commitment to equality across racial lines. And liberalism itself has been prone to a racially exclusionary outlook. In the contemporary era, when explicit defenses of white supremacy are generally outside the bounds of acceptable political discourse (even for the right, which used to embrace such arguments openly), the liberal rhetoric of color blindness that animated the civil rights revolution has been increasingly appropriated by an antigovernment, promarket conservative political culture that is at best indifferent (and at worst hostile) to demands for racial equality (Morgan 1975; Horton 2005; King and Smith 2005; Steele 1990; MacLean 2006).

Several of our contributors take on the challenge of describing the new terrain of racial attitudes and mapping the changing and increasingly complex connection between attitudes and inequality. Phillip Goff directly addresses a fundamental conundrum of the contemporary era, which he calls the "attitude-inequality mismatch": the persistence of racial inequality, especially in criminal justice policy and policing behavior, in the face of declining racial prejudice. Goff observes both that racial prejudice is inherently hard to measure, especially in the postracist context, and that the notional relationship between individual prejudice and collectively unequal outcomes is hard to observe. Like the laissez-faire racism construct, this somewhat muddled field creates the impression that in the absence of explicit racial prejudice, apparently racially biased policing is simply the natural consequence of neutral procedures and thus reflects real underlying differences in levels of criminality between, say, blacks and whites. Goff shows, by contrast, that a range of attitudes about identity and circumstance can lead to police behavior that cumulates into manifestly unequal patterns of treatment across racial groups.

Valerie Purdie-Vaughns and Richard Eibach approach this set of questions from the opposite perspective. They explore the impact of public events on the construction of attitudes through the identification of an "Obama effect," the impact of the symbolism of Obama's status as the first black president on the social construction of African American identity. Building on important work in social and cognitive psychology, Purdie-Vaughns and Eibach focus on schools as a key setting where cognitive development and political socialization occur and connect processes of attitude formation with broader societal and political development. Their study identifies Barack Obama's election as a source of racial pride for young African American schoolchildren, and they explore its possible connection both to rising academic achievement and to a declining sense of urgency around a policy agenda focused on issues of racial equality. Purdie-Vaughns and Eibach zero in on some of the critical micro-level underpinnings that converge in complex ways to shape patterns of racial inequality. These chapters suggest, however, that though attitudes remain important to the reproduction and texture of racial inequality, they are far from sufficient to account for patterns of inequality. Not only have race-laden attitudes themselves changed but also the connection between attitudes and outcomes is no longer as linear and apparently straightforward as it once was. The next section of the collection focuses on the institutional and structural factors that bend this connection in new ways.

Institutional Mechanisms

In his most recent book, *More Than Just Race,* William Julius Wilson (2009) argues passionately and compellingly that the choice often posed between culture and structure as explanations of persistent racial inequality is a false one, that these two kinds of causes have reinforced one another, and that neither the cultural nor material hypotheses of previous generations of scholarship are sufficient to account for contemporary patterns of racial inequality. But even Wilson's persuasive deconstruction and reconstruction of the roots of racial inequality leaves open questions of the mixture of structural and cultural causes that lie behind the persistent racial gap that remains in American society, the precise mechanisms that underlie these causal relationships, and the conditions under which these mechanisms do and do not operate to produce and perpetuate racial inequality.

We need, then, an account of what the sociologist Eduardo Bonilla-Silva (2003) has called "racism without racists": the ways in which social relations, political institutions, and other features of American society often advance the interests of whites and thus reproduce existing patterns of inequality (see also Williams 2003; Katznelson 2005). Here is the central puzzle of the postracist society: how do institutions that are, on their face, scrupulously racially neutral have systematically racially imbalanced consequences, resulting over time in the replication of old lines of racial inequality or the construction of new ones, even as still others seem to dissolve? Earlier studies have documented the deeply race-laden character of much of American politics, its tendency to divide the population along racial lines without saying so explicitly. But the notion of race-laden policy goes beyond the merely incidental unintended consequences of ostensibly neutral arrangements to suggest that there might be more systematic sources of racial bias built into the structure of political, social, and economic structures and processes and that these structures might reflect more hidden racially structured power arrangements—class conflicts, party coalitions, political institutions, markets, political and social attitudes, and the like—whose characters are shaped by racial distinctions. Moreover, such arrangements can be expected to affect whites and people of color differently in the course of their normal operations, whether or not the people who designed them or inhabit them intend that result (Lieberman 1998; King and Smith 2005).

This perspective reverses the distorting presumption of color blindness that has come to dominate the American understanding of racial inequality and suggests that we cannot always take the appearance of color blindness at face value. American history is, in fact, full of instances of apparently color-blind arrangements that mask deeply racially unequal consequences. Jim Crow voting restrictions, for example, such as poll taxes, literacy tests, and the "grandfather clause," were adopted precisely because they were facially race neutral (and so did not violate the Fifteenth Amendment to the Constitution, which prohibits race-based voting qualifications) but could be applied to limit black registration (Valelly 2004). Moreover, as Melanie Springer (forthcoming) shows, other kinds of voting rules had similar effects over the course of the twentieth century, limiting black ballot access despite the appearance of neutrality. The Voting Rights Act of 1965 recognized precisely this feature of voting restrictions by requiring certain states to submit any change in voting or registration procedure, no matter how apparently trivial, for preclearance by the Justice Department. This procedural hurdle essentially places the burden of proof on the states to show that its voting procedures will not work to the detriment of minority voters, rather than expecting disadvantaged voters to demonstrate bias after the fact.

A parallel example is the role of occupational testing in employment discrimination law. Many employers use aptitude tests to screen job applicants and candidates for promotions, and many such tests generate biased results: white applicants tend to score higher than minorities, making the preponderance of whites in higher-ranking positions inside organizations appear to be the natural result of qualities than make them better fit for these jobs. But after the Civil Rights Act of 1964 outlawed employment discrimination, the Supreme Court held that occupational tests that have a "disparate impact" on white and nonwhite applicants should be presumed to be discriminatory unless the employer can show that passage of the test is a "bona fide occupational qualification" for the position, once again turning around the burden of proof and puncturing the complacent syllogism of color blindness (Griggs v. Duke Power Co., 401 U.S. 424 [1971]).[4] These examples and many others (some of which are addressed in this book) point toward a research agenda that moves beyond discrimination, understood as a set of intentional acts rooted in attitudinal prejudice, and understands racial inequality as the consequence of social, political, and economic structures as much as the agency of whites.

This outlook is reminiscent of an older tradition of identifying institutional racism in American political life. Stokely Carmichael, who coined the phrase in the late 1960s, distinguished between "individual racism" and "institutional racism." While the former referred to overt acts of discrimination and prejudice, the latter "originates in the operation of established and respected forces in the society, and thus receives far less public condemnation than the first [individual] type" (Carmichael and Hamilton 1967, 4; see also Knowles and Prewitt 1969; Katznelson 1971, 1972). But social scientists did not take up the challenge of institutional racism in a concerted way. In the wake of urban unrest of the 1960s and the economic decline of cities in the 1970s, debates about racial inequality came to focus on the urban "underclass" and its apparent pathologies, a line of inquiry that directed scholars away from the underlying structural sources of inequality (Wilson 1987; Katz 1993). But like the heyday of the institutional-racism thesis in the late 1960s and early 1970s, the Obama era is a moment when hope for progress mingles with anxiety over unfulfilled promise. The postracist puzzle of contemporary American society, the stubborn stickiness of racial inequality despite the decline of the factors that apparently accounted for it in the past, calls us back to the institutional-racism perspective and its distinction between overt and covert—individual and structural—sources of racial bias still has something to offer.

In its earliest formulation, the institutional-racism perspective tended to be descriptive (and even a bit polemical). But in the intervening decades, new analytical tools and methods have evolved in the social sciences that are oriented toward addressing precisely the challenge that institutional racism addresses: how do we expose, model, and test the subterranean effects of race in contemporary American society? Political scientists and sociologists have shown how various kinds of institutions—from formal governing arrangements and organizations to taken-for-granted cultural understandings—shape and constrain patterns of human behavior and interaction and help construct social identities and define political rationality. Social psychologists have shown how patterns of interaction between individuals and their surroundings can influence behavior. And historians have now begun to integrate the writing of social, cultural, and political history to show how lived human experience both shapes and responds to the world of politics and policy. Although the contributors to this volume represent a broad range of disciplines, methods, and analytical orientations, they share the conviction that we need to move beyond discrimination to understand how racial inequality can result from the ordinary workings of American society. Armed with this new repertoire of social-scientific approaches, analytical tools, and methodological techniques, they address some of the most pressing arenas of racial inequality, from education and employment to criminal justice and health.

The State   Several key institutional settings frame the contributions to this volume. The American state, first, is a key site of race-laden policy. The close connection between racial inequality and the state is not, of course, a novel observation; many scholars have documented the role that race has played in building and shaping the American state (Lieberman 1998; Marx 1998; King and Smith 2005; King and Lieberman 2009). For most of Amer-

ican history, the state protected and enforced segregation and white supremacy, as in race-based immigration restriction and the segregation of
the federal workforce (to say nothing of its protection of slavery), but more
recently it has become a powerful, if selective, force for racial equality
(King 1995, 2000). What is clear is that the state is closely linked to patterns
of racial identity and inequality; to paraphrase Charles Tilly (1975, 42),
race makes the state and the state makes race.

What remains relatively unexplored and unexplained, however, is how
to account for variation in the state's capacity and inclination to protect
civil rights and promote racial equality—over time, across policy domains,
and across geography, among other sources of variability. Some of the
mechanisms by which the American state's ability to enforce racial equality are well known: federalism, administrative fragmentation, and institutional rules. But the recent gathering legitimation crisis of the American
state that a number of observers have noted has implicated other kinds of
often-hidden mechanisms that affect the way American politics and policy
address the challenges of racial inequality: growing economic and ideological polarization, extreme sensitivity to organized interests, the repur-
posing of color-blind rhetoric to challenge civil rights policies, and the
growing prominence of a variety of private, subterranean, and obfuscating
means of exerting public authority (Jacobs and King 2009; Mettler 2011;
Morgan and Campbell 2011; Horton 2005; Clemens 2006; Lieberman 2009).
This crisis of the state has been especially acute in response to economic
crisis under conditions of extreme political polarization, but as Lawrence
Jacobs and Desmond King (2009) point out, it has been brewing for a long
time and is particularly deeply rooted in racial antagonism. These mechanisms of state action and their consequences for racial equality are among
the most compelling questions in the study of race in American society,
and the first group of chapters in this volume begin to address pressing
questions about how the American state shapes the politics of race.

King's chapter in particular connects recent advances in the study of the
American state to the challenges of racial inequality. How and when, he
asks, does the state mobilize its strong coercive apparatus behind efforts to
ameliorate racial inequality, and how can the variation in the state's efforts
be accounted for? King identifies the 1960s as a pivotal moment in the
development of the state's potential capacity to address racial inequality,
laying the groundwork for the political analysis that follows in subsequent
chapters. By illuminating the rare circumstances under which racial inequality in the United States has come out of the shadows and presented
itself as a problem worthy of concerted effort and overt policy, King un-
derscores the importance of probing the features of the state that ordinarily
tend to limit its scope as a force for racial equality.

More often, however, the state and its policies have the effect of generating and reproducing inequality despite their apparently race-neutral intentions, and a number of chapters examine the workings and effects of some of these policies. These contributions invoke and illustrate an important set of causal pathways for the reproduction and even hardening of racial inequality through the action of the state and the operation of public policies. State institutions and public policies can shape and reinforce attitudes, create economic incentives for market behavior, affect patterns of political organization, and interact with other social and economic forces to shape and constrain future possibilities for reform. These pathways correspond closely to the mechanisms of policy feedback that have received a great deal of recent attention in the historically oriented social sciences: the means by which policies enacted at one point in time can shape and reshape politics over time (Pierson 1993; Hacker 2002; Campbell 2003; Mettler and Soss 2004). Many of the contributions to this volume usefully employ this framework and show how it can help unravel knotty and seemingly intractable puzzles of cause and effect. As an analytical approach that is centered on examining the unfolding of political and social processes over time and exploring how causal patterns can become embedded, and even hidden, in the everyday workings of politics, society, and the economy, policy feedback seems especially well suited to further explorations of the politics of racial inequality and the "stickiness" of race.

One particularly important thrust of the policy feedback approach in recent years has emphasized the role that public policies themselves play in reshaping the political terrain, with unintended and often poorly understood consequences. The observation that policies shape politics is an old one, dating back to foundational works in political science by Theodore Lowi (1964) and E. E. Schattschneider (1935) before him. More recent work has extended this theme to consider the variety of ways that policies can themselves structure the politics of inequality by shaping opportunities for political action, creating group interests, and defining ideological and cognitive categories (Pierson 2006; Hacker, Mettler, and Soss 2007). But the impact of public policies as a form of state action also occurs in interaction with other social and economic forces, and these interactions and their consequences form the core of the analyses collected here; this is a key theme of Warren's chapter, which situates the American state in a "racialized political economy" in which state and labor-market institutions interact to structure politics along racial lines.

Vesla Weaver's contribution is a case in point. She shows how criminal justice policies have evolved over time to produce and sustain the mass incarceration of African Americans, particularly young black men. In large measure, as Weaver has documented elsewhere, the tremendous increase in the number of black men in jail is the result of a deliberate and racially motivated law-and-order political strategy that conservative policy makers deployed to undermine the civil rights gains of the 1960s (see also Weaver 2007; Weaver and Lerman 2010). But here she documents not just how policy makers framed criminal justice deliberately as a reaction to the civil rights revolution but also, and more precisely, how a set of policy enactments interacted with structural transformations of the economy that produced social dislocation and extreme black male joblessness in American cities. Overlaying this social and economic background, state action created self-reinforcing feedback effects that have not only solidified but also deepened racialized patterns of policing and incarceration.

In a related chapter, Devah Pager documents the consequences of mass incarceration, showing how severely felony convictions handicap black men in the labor market by fueling and reinforcing racial stereotypes that find expression in hiring behavior that can appear race neutral, thereby contributing to the stickiness of racial disparities in employment. For Pager, the key mechanisms at work are similarly at the intersection of criminal justice policies that result in disproportionately high criminalization among African American men and patterns of attitudes and behavior and in the labor market so that, as she puts it, "criminal records serv[e] as a principal mechanism for the sorting and stratifying of opportunities." The carceral state that Weaver describes affects not just the incarceration of young black men but also spills over, through the operation of the labor market, to shape broader patterns of racial stratification and inequality.

Similarly, Devin Fergus shows how a seemingly obscure set of tax and insurance policies penalize residents of disproportionately minority residential neighborhoods, amounting to a "ghetto tax" that imposes severe economic handicaps on poor blacks and Latinos. Again, these policies reinforce racial inequality without being overtly racially drawn, and they operate through the layering of public policies on top of a configuration of economic and social conditions—in this case, severe residential segregation by race—that channel and shape the consequences of state action. Like criminal justice policies, the ostensibly race-neutral commercial policies that Fergus depicts both invoke and reinforce the assumption that as long as markets are free of overt discrimination, unequal racial outcomes of these policies must at best be incidental and at worst constitute evidence of the incapacities of minorities themselves. But these chapters deflate this view and show that the racial consequences of these policies are stable, systematic, and predictable.

Markets   The market economy is a second race-laden institutional arena that our contributors take up. Economic inequality—whether measured

by income, wealth, employment, or nearly any other economic indicator—is particularly acute across racial lines, suggesting that Americans of
color, particularly African Americans and Latinos, fare poorly in markets.
Economic inequality has been rising steadily in the United States since the
1970s, and its causes and political and social consequences have increasingly been a focus of some of the most important and innovative research
in the social sciences in recent years (Piketty and Saez 2003; McCarty,
Poole, and Rosenthal 2006; Soss, Hacker, and Mettler 2007; Bartels 2008;
Gelman 2010; Hacker and Pierson 2010). The Occupy Wall Street protests
of 2011 and their offshoots and imitators around the country (and the
world) focused widespread attention on economic inequalities and on the
economic stagnation of the American middle class and brought the plight
of "the 99 percent" into the American political vocabulary.

But this body of research has not generally addressed the critical racial
component of inequality in the United States, and while the Occupy movement brought ample attention to the universal and cross-racial challenges
of economic crisis, it also reignited a common and perpetually unresolved
tension on the American left between class and identity politics (Lowndes
and Warren 2011). For one thing, its focus on the growth of inequality over
the past few decades has occluded the relatively stable racial gap in economic outcomes that have been a persistent feature of the American political economy for decades regardless of the overall level of inequality. In the
years immediately after World War II, median black family income was
nearly twice that of white families. That ratio declined steadily but slowly
over the postwar decades but has remained at roughly 1.6:1 since the mid-
1990s. (Latino incomes have actually shown the opposite pattern since the
Census Bureau began reporting them in the early 1970s: relative to whites,
the median Latino family income declined through the 1990s and has been
relatively stable since then.)[5]

On top of this relative stagnation of minority incomes, the Great Recession that began in 2008, which wreaked havoc on the American working
class generally, has been especially catastrophic for African Americans and
Latinos, for whom unemployment rates have risen to depression-like levels in many metropolitan areas (Austin 2011a, 2011b). Certain features of
the recent economic crisis, and the limited federal policy response—in particular, the collapse of state and local government finance and the mortgage and foreclosure crisis—have fallen especially sharply on already precarious minority communities (Johnson 2011). Moreover, the convergence
of economic and political polarization that has coincided with the growth
of inequality also coincides with racial cleavages in American politics and
society, rendering it difficult to disentangle race from class to declare one
or the other category more fundamental as an organizing framework for

the polity (King and Smith 2011). In his contribution here, Rodney Hero shows that racial inequality constitutes a large proportion—in many states, the lion's share—of overall class inequality, further underscoring the importance of connecting concerns of race and class and considering the role of markets in defining racial inequality.

Like the state, the market affects patterns of racial inequality not in isolation but in interaction with other structural forces in the American political economy. The relationship between economic inequality and racial inequality is largely a function of the structure and operation not just of various interconnected markets but also of the relationship between market forces and other political arrangements and social forces, as Pager and Fergus observe in their chapters. A recurring theme in the volume, then, is the political economy of racial inequality—the variety of ways in which these interconnected forces tend to systematically exclude people of color from the high end of successful, dynamic markets and connect then instead to broken or dysfunctional markets. These contributions, in turn, emphasize another recurring theme, the importance of a cross-disciplinary approach to understanding racial inequality and the limits of more specialized studies (in both disciplinary and substantive terms) that tend to obscure important configurations of causal forces that are essential to squaring the circle of racial inequality in the contemporary postracist era. Dorian Warren's chapter emphasizes precisely the political embeddedness of markets. Markets are, he shows, sites where the public and private sectors interact to shape human behavior and societal outcomes. Warren's contribution brings markets into an analytical framework for explaining racial inequality and shows how markets and politics interact to create particular patterns of inequality.

The interaction of markets with politics and a range of other social forces is central to a number of other contributions. Devin Fergus, for example, chronicles the adoption and consequences of a California law allowing ZIP-code profiling of risk for auto insurance underwriting, which had the effect of sorting black and Latino drivers into higher-risk, and therefore more expensive, insurance categories. Mirroring neighborhood-based redlining in real estate, ZIP-code profiling provides a powerful example of a politically constructed market mechanism with profound racial consequences (see Jackson 1985). Fergus (along with Devah Pager, who highlights the link between criminal justice policy and the labor market) shows that the market does not work by itself but rather filters the effects of public policy and other kinds of state action and social forces.

Similarly, Naa Oyo Kwate shows how apparently neutral and apolitical market forces such as the advertising and marketing of products such as fast food and alcohol are effectively targeted at minority urban neighborhoods, exposing poor residents to social and economic forces that exploit both race and class inequalities and result in degraded health outcomes. Markets thus interact with a variety of other forces of social and racial exclusion, such as patterns of unionization, industrial organization, and geographical isolation as well as public policies and structures of political power, to create powerful forces of inequality embedded in the American political economy. As with the emphasis on the state and public policy, our contributors help to puncture the common illusion that markets are inherently racially neutral as long as they are not explicitly discriminatory, a common conceit in neoclassical models of the economy (Becker 1971). In contrast, our contributors emphasize the embeddedness of markets in political, legal, and social structures and suggest a variety of pathways through which market forces shape racial inequality—particularly the way markets are shaped by legal and political forces and the ways their effects can be systematically augmented and redirected by geography.

BEYOND STATE AND MARKET

Beyond the state and markets, a range of other institutional settings and processes have been found to be particularly influential in shaping patterns of racial equality and inequality. The voluntary sector has been an important venue, both reinforcing patterns of segregation and inequality and providing minority communities with critical organizational and social resources to challenge segregation and inequality (Skocpol, Liazos, and Ganz 2006). The church has also been a key institution that has influenced the incorporation of African Americans into American politics and society and contributed to the contours of racial equality and inequality (Verba, Schlozman, and Brady 1995; Harris 1999). And, as several of our contributors point out, education has long been a central platform for struggles over racial equality in American society.

Education is, of course, a key element of what T. H. Marshall (1964) called social citizenship, which offers an important potential counterweight to patterns of economic inequality in a market-based society. Education has also been a key arena of the struggle for racial equality and inclusion in the United States, from the long legal battles over segregation to confrontations in Little Rock and on Southern university campuses, to conflicts over busing and other policy schemes designed to integrate American schools and provide equal opportunity. Education has been at the frontier of the political conflict over affirmative action in American politics and law, from Bakke (which established the diversity rationale for affirmative action) to the University of Michigan cases (which affirmed it) to Fisher v. Texas (in which it is coming under challenge once again) (Regents of the University of California v. Bakke, 438 U.S. 265 [1978]; Fisher v. University of Texas at Austin 631 F.3d 213 [5th Cir. 2011]). And racial inequality in education outcomes—especially the gap in standardized test scores—has long been an important area of research and policy concern (Jencks and Philips 1998; Fryer and Levitt 2004; Card and Rothstein 2007).

But beyond these direct struggles over integration and equality, education is also an arena where a variety of forces combine to influence inequality in often hidden and indirect ways, and our contributors examine several aspects of education and again consider a range of mechanisms that contribute to racial inequality in this sector. Several contributions focus on education as a key sector in their accounts of racial inequality. For Chen and Stulberg, higher education is embedded in a complex institutional setting that touches state, market, and civil society. Exploring the forces that led selective universities to challenge their own racial exclusivity provides yet another angle of vision on the question of mechanisms by which racial inequality can be both perpetuated and, at times, challenged, bringing questions of organizational structure and culture to the center of our inquiry (see Dobbin 2009). Similar questions about organizational setting animate other contributions as well: Dorian Warren on patterns of mobilization and organization around the proposed opening of Walmart stores in low-income neighborhoods in Chicago, or Purdie-Vaughns and Eibach's account of the Obama effect.

Education necessarily stands in here for a wide swath of American society that is shaped by, but not identical to, states, markets, and the political economy. Across a wide range of sectors of society and political economy, policy domains, and analytical frames, the work collected here shares the common aspiration to move beyond discrimination in accounting for the stubborn persistence of racial discrimination. Our contributors identify a range of casual mechanisms—cognitive, organizational, political, and economic, among others—that plausibly underlie that puzzle in all its grim particulars. We have deliberately sharpened and exaggerated the distinctions among levels of analysis, disciplinary origin, and varieties of causation that our colleagues deploy to sample the kinds of models that can fruitfully be brought to bear on this fundamental question. These mechanisms, of course, do not operate separately and independently in the world, as the richness and catholicity of the chapters that follow clearly demonstrate.

Collectively, this collection seeks to catalogue some of these mechanisms. But perhaps more important, it also aims to build the foundation of an analytical vocabulary that cuts across disciplines, sectors, and policy domains—precisely in order to locate some of these areas of overlap—and will afford more precise understanding of when and how racial bias can occur without its most common antecedents, prejudice and discrimination.[6] Progress toward this analytical goal will help us begin to explore how these mechanisms might shape outcomes and to suggest guidelines both for future research and for evaluating and designing policy instruments that might help ameliorate racial inequality in the same subterranean way.

The remainder of the volume is organized around these themes. The first section explores the historical setting of the postracist era. The chapters by Hero, King, and Chen and Stulberg, and Warren consider the historical specificity of the contemporary era and examine some of the important historical forces that have produced the distinctive configuration of politics, economics, and society that defines racial inequality in the twenty-first century. The following sections focus on these key factors that continue to shape racial inequality in new ways: attitudes and individual behavior in part 2 (Goff and Purdie-Vaughns and Eibach), politics and the state in part 3 (Weaver and Pager), and economics and markets in part 4 (Fergus and Kwate). Taken together, this collection of essays helps us to understand and unravel the processes that sustain racial inequality in the postracist era of American race relations.

NOTES

1. Data are from exit polls and the American National Election Study. Exit polls as reported at cnn.com/election; ANES at electionstodies.org.
2. We adapt this concept from Ira Katznelson, who analyzed it in a public panel discussion at Columbia University that opened the conference at which these papers were presented. "Inequality in the Age of Obama," A Roundtable Discussion, May 20, 2010, School of International and Public Affairs, Columbia University.
3. In the University of Michigan affirmative action cases of the early years of this century (Gratz v. Bollinger, 539 U.S. 244 [2003]; Grutter v. Bollinger, 539 U.S. 306 [2003]), more than sixty amicus curiae briefs were filed in support of the university's admissions policies, which used race in a variety of ways to achieve a diverse student body. Among the filers were nearly ninety major private and public universities and law schools, sixty-eight major corporations, and fourteen active and retired military leaders (including several former secretaries of defense and members of the Joint Chiefs of Staff). Compiled from material posted by the University of Michigan at www.umich.edu/~urel/admissions/legal/amicus.html.
4. In 2009 the Supreme Court revisited, but did not fully overturn, this ruling in a case involving the New Haven, Connecticut, Fire Department, which discarded a carefully designed promotion test after it was administered when the

results revealed that only white firefighters passed. The Court ordered New Haven to reinstate the test and promote the white firefighters despite the disparate impact. The case became a flashpoint of controversy in the confirmation hearings of Justice Sonia Sotomayor, who had ruled the opposite way when the case came before her as an appeals court judge (Ricci v. DeStefano, 557 U.S. 557 [2009]).

5. Income data are from the U.S. Census. Reported at www.census.gov/hhes/www/income/data/historical/families

6. At the same time, we acknowledge that the collection skirts an equally pressing analytical question: When do these mechanisms *not* produce racially biased outcomes? Further progress in sorting out the causes of persistent racial inequality will have to address this selection issue.

REFERENCES

Anderson, Elijah. 1999. *Code of the Street: Decency, Violence, and the Moral Life of the Inner City.* New York: W. W. Norton.

Appiah, K. Anthony, and Amy Gutmann. 1996. *Color Conscious: The Political Morality of Race.* Princeton, N.J.: Princeton University Press.

Austin, Algernon. 2011a. "High Black Unemployment Widespread Across Nation's Metropolitan Areas." Issue Brief 315. Washington, D.C.: Economic Policy Institute.

———. 2011b. "Hispanic Unemployment Highest in Northeast Metropolitan Area." Issue Brief 314. Washington, D.C.: Economic Policy Institute.

Barreto, Matt A., et al. 2011. "The Tea Party in the Age of Obama: Mainstream Conservatism or Out-Group Anxiety?" In *Rethinking Obama, Political Power, and Social Theory,* Vol. 22, edited by Julian Go, pp. 105–137. Bingley, UK: Emerald Group Publishing Limited.

Bartels, Larry M. 2008. *Unequal Democracy: The Political Economy of the New Gilded Age.* Princeton, N.J.: Princeton University Press.

Becker, Gary S. 1971. *The Economics of Discrimination.* 2d ed. Chicago: University of Chicago Press.

Bell, Derrick. 1992. *Faces at the Bottom of the Well: The Permanence of Racism.* New York: Basic Books.

Bleich, Erik. 2005. "The Legacies of History? Colonization and Immigrant Integration in Britain and France." *Theory and Society* 34(2): 171–95.

Bobo, Lawrence, James R. Kluegel, and Ryan A. Smith. 1997. "Laissez-Faire Racism: The Crystallization of a Kinder, Gentler Anti-Black Ideology." In *Racial Attitudes in the 1990s: Continuity and Change,* edited by Steven A. Tuch and Jack K. Martin. Westport, Conn.: Praeger.

Bobo, Lawrence, and Ryan A. Smith. 1998. "From Jim Crow Racism to Laissez-Faire Racism: The Transformation of Racial Attitudes." In *Beyond Pluralism: The*

Conception of Groups and Group Identities in America, edited by Wendy F. Katkin, Ned Landsman, and Andrea Tyree. Urbana: University of Illinois Press.

Bonastia, Christopher. 2006. *Knocking at the Door: The Federal Government's Attempt to Desegregate the Suburbs*. Princeton, N.J.: Princeton University Press.

Bonilla-Silva, Eduardo. 2003. *Racism Without Racists: Color-Blind Racism and the Persistence of Racial Inequality in the United States*. Lanham, Md.: Rowman and Littlefield.

Bowen, William G., and Derek Bok. 1998. *The Shape of the River: Long-Term Consequences of Considering Race in College and University Admissions*. Princeton, N.J.: Princeton University Press.

Brown, Michael K., et al. 2003. *Whitewashing Race: The Myth of a Color-Blind Society*. Berkeley: University of California Press.

Burstein, Paul. 1985. *Discrimination, Jobs, and Politics: The Struggle for Equal Employment Opportunity in the United States since the New Deal*. Chicago: University of Chicago Press.

Campbell, Andrea Louise. 2003. *How Policies Make Citizens: Senior Political Activism and the American Welfare State*. Princeton, N.J.: Princeton University Press.

Card, David, and Jesse Rothstein. 2007. "Racial Segregation and the Black-White Test Score Gap." *Journal of Public Economics* 91(11–12): 2158–84.

Carmichael, Stokely, and Charles V. Hamilton. 1967. *Black Power: The Politics of Liberation in America*. New York: Random House.

Chen, Anthony S. 2009. *The Fifth Freedom: Jobs, Politics, and Civil Rights in the United States, 1941–1972*. Princeton, N.J.: Princeton University Press.

Clemens, Elisabeth. 2006. "Lineages of the Rube Goldberg State: Building and Blurring Public Programs, 1900–1940." In *Rethinking Political Institutions: The Art of the State*, edited by Ian Shapiro, Stephen Skowronek, and Daniel Galvin. New York: New York University Press.

Cooper, Richard S., Jay S. Kaufman, and Ryk Ward. 2003. "Race and Genomics." *New England Journal of Medicine* 348(12): 1166–70.

Davidson, Chandler, and Bernard Grofman, eds. 1994. *Quiet Revolution in the South: The Impact of the Voting Rights Act, 1965–1990*. Princeton, N.J.: Princeton University Press.

Dobbin, Frank. 2009. *Inventing Equal Opportunity*. Princeton, N.J.: Princeton University Press.

Donohue, John J., III, and James Heckman. 1991. "Continuous Versus Episodic Change: The Impact of Civil Rights Policy on the Economic Status of Blacks." *Journal of Economic Literature* 29(4): 1603–43.

Farhang, Sean. 2010. *The Litigation State: Public Regulation and Private Lawsuits in the United States*. Princeton, N.J.: Princeton University Press.

Foster, Morris W., and Richard R. Sharp. 2004. "Beyond Race: Towards a Whole-Genome Perspective on Human Populations and Genetic Variation." *Nature Review: Genetics* 5(10): 790–96.

Fryer, Roland G., Jr. 2011. "Racial Inequality in the 21st Century: The Declining Significance of Discrimination." In *Handbook of Labor Economics* 4B, edited by Orley Ashenfelter and David Card, pp. 855–971. Amsterdam: Elsevier.

Fryer, Roland G., Jr., and Steven D. Levitt. 2004. "Understanding the Black-White Test Score Gap in the First Two Years of School." *Review of Economics and Statistics* 86(2): 447–64.

Gelman, Andrew, with David Park, Boris Shor, and Jeronimo Cortina. 2010. *Red State, Blue State, Rich State, Poor State: Why Americans Vote the Way They Do.* Expanded ed. Princeton, N.J.: Princeton University Press.

Gilens, Martin. 1999. *Why Americans Hate Welfare: Race, Media, and the Politics of Antipoverty Policy.* Chicago: University of Chicago Press.

Goldsmith, Arthur H., Darrick Hamilton, and William Darity Jr. 2006. "Shades of Discrimination: Skin Tone and Wages." *American Economic Review* 96(2): 242–45.

Gould, Stephen Jay. 1996. *The Mismeasure of Man.* Rev. and expanded ed. New York: W. W. Norton.

Hacker, Andrew. 1992. *Two Nations: Black and White, Separate, Hostile, Unequal.* New York: Charles Scribner's Sons.

Hacker, Jacob S. 2002. *The Divided Welfare State: The Battle over Public and Private Social Benefits in the United States.* Cambridge: Cambridge University Press.

———. 2004. "Privatizing Risk Without Privatizing the Welfare State: The Hidden Politics of Social Policy Retrenchment in the United States." *American Political Science Review* 98(2): 243–60.

Hacker, Jacob S., Suzanne Mettler, and Joe Soss. 2007. "The New Politics of Inequality: A Policy-Centered Perspective." In *Remaking America: Democracy and Public Policy in an Age of Inequality,* edited by Joe Soss, Jacob S. Hacker, and Suzanne Mettler. New York: Russell Sage Foundation.

Hacker, Jacob S., and Paul Pierson. 2010. "Winner-Take-All-Politics: Public Policy, Political Organization, and the Precipitous Rise of Top Incomes in the United States." *Politics and Society* 38(2): 152–204.

Haney López, Ian F. 2007. "'A Nation of Minorities': Race, Ethnicity, and Reactionary Colorblindness." *Stanford Law Review* 59(4): 985–1063.

Harris, Fredrick C. 1999. *Something Within: Religion in African-American Political Activism.* Oxford: Oxford University Press.

———. 2012. *The Price of the Ticket: Barack Obama and the Rise and Decline of Black Politics.* Oxford: Oxford University Press.

Harris, Fredrick C., Valeria Sinclair-Chapman, and Brian D. McKenzie. 2006. *Countervailing Forces in African-American Civic Activism, 1973–1994.* Cambridge: Cambridge University Press.

Heckman, James J. 1990. "The Central Role of the South in Accounting for the Economic Progress of Black Americans." *American Economic Review* 80(2): 242–46.

Heckman, James J., and Brook S. Payner. 1989. "Determining the Impact of Federal Antidiscrimination Policy on the Economic Status of Blacks: A Study of South Carolina." *American Economic Review* 79(1): 138–77.

Heilemann, John, and Mark Halperin. 2010. *Game Change: Obama and the Clintons, McCain and Palin, and the Race of a Lifetime.* New York: Harper.

Herrnstein, Richard J., and Charles Murray. 1994. *The Bell Curve: Intelligence and Class Structure in American Life.* New York: Free Press.

Hochschild, Jennifer L. 1984. *The New American Dilemma: Liberal Democracy and School Desegregation.* New Haven, Conn.: Yale University Press.

———. 1999. "You Win Some, You Lose Some: Explaining the Pattern of Success and Failure in the Second Reconstruction." In *Taking Stock: American Government in the Twentieth Century,* edited by Morton Keller and R. Shep Melnick. Washington, D.C.: Woodrow Wilson Center Press.

Hochschild, Jennifer, and Michael N. Danielson. 2004. "The Demise of a Dinosaur: Analyzing School and Housing Desegregation in Yonkers." In *Race, Poverty, and Domestic Policy,* edited by C. Michael Henry. New Haven, Conn.: Yale University Press.

Hochschild, Jennifer, and Vesla Weaver. 2007. "Policies of Racial Classification and the Politics of Racial Inequality." In *Remaking America: Democracy and Public Policy in an Age of Inequality,* edited by Joe Soss, Jacob S. Hacker, and Suzanne Mettler. New York: Russell Sage Foundation.

Holzer, Harry J., and David Neumark. 2006. "Affirmative Action: What Do We Know?" *Journal of Policy Analysis and Management* 25(2): 463–90.

Horton, Carol A. 2005. *Race and the Making of American Liberalism.* Oxford: Oxford University Press.

Jackson, Kenneth T. 1985. *Crabgrass Frontier: The Suburbanization of the United States.* New York: Oxford University Press.

Jacobs, Lawrence R., and Desmond King. 2009. "The Political Crisis of the American State: The Unsustainable State in a Time of Unraveling." In *The Unsustainable American State,* edited by Lawrence Jacobs and Desmond King. Oxford: Oxford University Press.

Jencks, Christopher, and Meredith Phillips, eds. 1998. *The Black-White Test-Score Gap.* Washington, D.C.: Brookings Institution.

Johnson, Kimberley. 2010. *Reforming Jim Crow: Southern Politics and State in the Age Before Brown.* Oxford: Oxford University Press.

Johnson, Olatunde C. A. 2011. "Stimulus and Civil Rights." *Columbia Law Review* 111(1): 154–205.

Karabel, Jerome. 2005. *The Chosen: The Hidden History of Admission and Exclusion at Harvard, Yale, and Princeton.* Boston, Mass.: Houghton Mifflin.

Katz, Michael B. 1989. *The Undeserving Poor: From the War on Poverty to the War on Welfare.* New York: Pantheon.

———, ed. 1993. *The "Underclass" Debate: Views from History.* Princeton, N.J.: Princeton University Press.

Katznelson, Ira. 1971. "Power in the Reformulation of Race Research." In *Race, Change, and Urban Policy,* edited by Peter Orleans and William Russell Ellis Jr. Beverly Hills, Calif.: Sage Publications.

———. 1972. "Comparative Studies of Race and Ethnicity: Plural Analysis and Beyond." *Comparative Politics* 5(1): 135–54.

———. 2005. *When Affirmative Action Was White: An Untold History of Racial Inequality in the Twentieth Century.* New York: W. W. Norton.

Key, V. O., Jr. 1949. *Southern Politics in State and Nation.* New York: Alfred A. Knopf.

Keyssar, Alexander. 2000. *The Right to Vote: The Contested History of Democracy in the United States.* New York: Basic Books.

Kim, Claire Jean. 1999. "The Racial Triangulation of Asian Americans." *Politics and Society* 27(1): 105–38.

Kinder, Donald R., and Lynn M. Sanders. 1996. *Divided by Color: Racial Politics and Democratic Ideals.* Chicago: University of Chicago Press.

King, Desmond. 1995. *Separate and Unequal: Black Americans and the U.S. Federal Government.* Oxford: Oxford University Press.

———. 2000. *Making Americans: Immigration, Race, and the Origins of the Diverse Democracy.* Cambridge, Mass.: Harvard University Press.

King, Desmond, and Robert C. Lieberman. 2009. "Ironies of State Building: A Comparative Perspective on the American State." *World Politics* 61(3): 547–88.

King, Desmond S., and Rogers M. Smith. 2005. "Racial Orders and American Political Development." *American Political Science Review* 99(1): 75–92.

———. 2011. *Still the House Divided: Race and Politics in Obama's America.* Princeton, N.J.: Princeton University Press.

Knowles, Louis L., and Kenneth Prewitt, eds. 1969. *Institutional Racism in America.* Englewood Cliffs, N.J.: Prentice Hall.

Lemann, Nicholas. 2000. *The Big Test: The Secret History of the American Meritocracy.* New York: Farrar, Straus and Giroux.

Lieberman, Robert C. 1998. *Shifting the Color Line: Race and the American Welfare State.* Cambridge, Mass.: Harvard University Press.

———. 2005. *Shaping Race Policy: The United States in Comparative Perspective.* Princeton, N.J.: Princeton University Press.

———. 2008. "Legacies of Slavery? Race and Historical Causation in American Political Development." In *Race and American Political Development,* edited by Joseph Lowndes, Julie Novkov, and Dorian T. Warren. New York: Routledge.

———. 2009. "Civil Rights and the Democratization Trap: The Public-Private Nexus and the Building of American Democracy." In *Democratization in America: A Comparative-Historical Analysis,* edited by Desmond King et al. Baltimore, Md.: Johns Hopkins University Press.

Lizza, Ryan. 2008. "Making It: How Chicago Shaped Obama." *New Yorker,* July 21, pp. 48–65.

Lowi, Theodore J. 1964. "American Business, Public Policy, Case-Studies, and Political Theory." *World Politics* 16(4): 677–715.

Lowndes, Joe, and Dorian Warren. 2011. "Occupy Wall Street: A Twenty-First Century Populist Movement." *Dissent,* Oct. 21. Available at: www.dissentmaga

zine.org/online_articles/occupy-wall-street-a-twenty-first-century-populist -movement (accessed April 3, 2013).

MacLean, Nancy. 2006. *Freedom Is Not Enough: The Opening of the American Workplace.* New York: Russell Sage Foundation.

Mahoney, James, and Kathleen Thelen. 2010. "A Theory of Gradual Institutional Change." In *Explaining Institutional Change: Ambiguity, Agency, and Power,* edited by James Mahoney and Kathleen Thelen. Cambridge: Cambridge University Press.

Marshall, T. H. 1964. "Citizenship and Social Class." In *Class, Citizenship, and Social Development.* Garden City, N.Y.: Doubleday.

Marx, Anthony W. 1998. *Making Race and Nation: A Comparison of South Africa, the United States, and Brazil.* Cambridge: Cambridge University Press.

Massey, Douglas S., and Nancy A. Denton. 1993. *American Apartheid: Segregation and the Making of the Underclass.* Cambridge, Mass.: Harvard University Press.

McCarty, Nolan, Keith T. Poole, and Howard Rosenthal. 2006. *Polarized America: The Dance of Ideology and Unequal Riches.* Cambridge, Mass.: MIT Press.

Mendelberg, Tali. 2001. *The Race Card: Campaign Strategy, Implicit Messages, and the Norm of Equality.* Princeton, N.J.: Princeton University Press.

Mettler, Suzanne. 2011. *The Submerged State: How Invisible Government Policies Undermine American Democracy.* Chicago: University of Chicago Press.

Mettler, Suzanne, and Joe Soss. 2004. "The Consequences of Public Policy for Democratic Citizenship: Bridging Policy Studies and Mass Politics." *Perspectives on Politics* 2(1): 55–73.

Morgan, Edmund S. 1975. *American Slavery, American Freedom: The Ordeal of Colonial Virginia.* New York: W. W. Norton.

Morgan, Kimberly J., and Andrea Louise Campbell. 2011. *The Delegated Welfare State: Medicare, Markets, and the Governance of Social Policy.* Oxford: Oxford University Press.

Murray, Charles. 1984. *Losing Ground: American Social Policy, 1950–1980.* New York: Basic Books.

Myrdal, Gunnar. 1944. *An American Dilemma: The Negro Problem and Modern Democracy.* New York: Harper and Brothers.

Neckerman, Kathryn M., and Joleen Kirschenman. 1991. "Hiring Strategies, Racial Bias, and Inner-City Workers." *Social Problems* 38(4): 433–47.

Obama, Barack. 2007. "Selma Voting Rights March Commemoration." Available at: http://barackobama.com/2007/03/04/selma_voting_rights_march_comm .php (accessed September 10, 2012).

Page, Benjamin I., and Robert Y. Shapiro. 1992. *The Rational Public: Fifty Years of Trends in Americans' Policy Preferences.* Chicago: University of Chicago Press.

Pager, Devah. 2007. *Marked: Race, Crime, and Finding Work in an Era of Mass Incarceration.* Chicago: University of Chicago Press.

Peterson, Paul E. 1995. "A Politically Correct Solution to Racial Classification." In

Classifying by Race, edited by Paul E. Peterson. Princeton, N.J.: Princeton University Press.

Pierson, Paul. 1993. "When Effect Becomes Cause: Policy Feedback and Political Change." *World Politics* 45(4): 595–628.

———. 2004. *Politics in Time: History, Institutions, and Social Analysis.* Princeton, N.J.: Princeton University Press.

———. 2006. "Public Policies as Institutions." In *Rethinking Political Institutions: The Art of the State,* edited by Ian Shapiro, Stephen Skowronek, and Daniel Galvin. New York: New York University Press.

Pierson, Paul, and Theda Skocpol, eds. 2007. *The Transformation of American Politics: Activist Government and the Rise of Conservatism.* Princeton, N.J.: Princeton University Press.

Piketty, Thomas, and Emmanuel Saez. 2003. "Income Inequality in the United States, 1913–1998." *Quarterly Journal of Economics* 118(1): 1–39. Available, with updated data, at: http://elsa.berkeley.edu/~saez (accessed April 3, 2013).

Remnick, David. 2010. *The Bridge: The Life and Rise of Barack Obama.* New York: Alfred A. Knopf.

Risch, Neil, et al. 2002. "Categorization of Humans in Biomedical Research: Genes, Race and Disease." *Genome Biology* 3(7):1–12.

Sabbagh, Daniel. 2007. *Equality and Transparency: A Strategic Perspective on Affirmative Action in American Law.* New York: Palgrave Macmillan.

Schattschneider, E. E. 1935. *Politics, Pressures, and the Tariff.* New York: Prentice-Hall.

Schuman, Howard, et al. 1997. *Racial Attitudes in America: Trends and Interpretations.* Revised ed. Cambridge, Mass.: Harvard University Press.

Shafer, Byron E., and Richard Johnston. 2006. *The End of Southern Exceptionalism: Class, Race, and Partisan Change in the Postwar South.* Cambridge, Mass.: Harvard University Press.

Skocpol, Theda, Ariane Liazos, and Marshall Ganz. 2006. *What a Mighty Power We Can Be: African American Fraternal Groups and the Struggle for Racial Equality.* Princeton, N.J.: Princeton University Press.

Skocpol, Theda, and Vanessa Williamson. 2012. *The Tea Party and the Remaking of American Conservatism.* Oxford: Oxford University Press.

Sleeper, Jim. 1997. *Liberal Racism.* New York: Viking.

Smith, Rogers M. 1997. *Civic Ideals: Conflicting Visions of Citizenship in U.S. History.* New Haven, Conn.: Yale University Press.

Sniderman, Paul M., and Edward G. Carmines. 1997. *Reaching Beyond Race.* Cambridge, Mass.: Harvard University Press.

Sniderman, Paul M., Gretchen C. Crosby, and William G. Howell. 2000. "The Politics of Race." In *Racialized Politics: The Debate about Racism in America,* edited by David O. Sears, Jim Sidanius, and Lawrence Bobo. Chicago: University of Chicago Press.

Sniderman, Paul M., and Thomas Piazza. 1993. *The Scar of Race.* Cambridge, Mass.: Harvard University Press.

Soss, Joe, Jacob S. Hacker, and Suzanne Mettler, eds. 2007. *Remaking America: Democracy and Public Policy in an Age of Inequality.* New York: Russell Sage Foundation.

Soss, Joe, et al. 2001. "Setting the Terms of Relief: State Policy Choices in the Devolution Revolution." *American Journal of Political Science* 45(2): 378–95.

Sowell, Thomas. 1978. "Three Black Histories." In *Essays and Data on American Ethnic Groups,* edited by Thomas Sowell. Washington, D.C.: Urban Institute.

———. 1994. *Race and Culture: A World View.* New York: Basic Books.

Springer, Melanie J. Forthcoming. *The Rules We Vote By: The Evolution of Electoral Institutions and Voter Turnout in the American States.* Chicago: University of Chicago Press.

Steele, Shelby. 1990. *The Content of Our Character: A New Vision of Race in America.* New York: St. Martin's Press.

Sugrue, Thomas J. 1996. *The Origins of the Urban Crisis: Race and Inequality in Postwar Detroit.* Princeton, N.J.: Princeton University Press.

———. 2008. *Sweet Land of Liberty: The Forgotten Struggle for Civil Rights in the North.* New York: Random House.

———. 2010. *Not Even Past: Barack Obama and the Burden of Race.* Princeton, N.J.: Princeton University Press.

Thelen, Kathleen. 2004. *How Institutions Evolve: The Political Economy of Skills in Germany, Britain, the United States, and Japan.* Cambridge: Cambridge University Press.

Thernstrom, Stephan, and Abigail Thernstrom. 1997. *America in Black and White: One Nation, Indivisible.* New York: Simon and Schuster.

Thomas, Kendall. 2002. "Racial Justice: Moral or Political?" In *Looking Back at Law's Century,* edited by Austin Sarat, Bryant Garth, and Robert A. Kagan. Ithaca, N.Y.: Cornell University Press.

Tilly, Charles. 1975. "Reflections on the History of European State-Making." In *The Formation of National States in Western Europe,* edited by Charles Tilly. Princeton, N.J.: Princeton University Press.

———. 1998. *Durable Inequality.* Berkeley: University of California Press.

Valelly, Richard M. 2004. *The Two Reconstructions: The Struggle for Black Enfranchisement.* Chicago: University of Chicago Press.

Venkatesh, Sudhir Alladi. 2006. *Off the Books: The Underground Economy of the Urban Poor.* Cambridge, Mass.: Harvard University Press.

Verba, Sidney, Kay Lehman Schlozman, and Henry E. Brady. 1995. *Voice and Equality: Civic Voluntarism in American Politics.* Cambridge, Mass.: Harvard University Press.

Warren, Dorian T. 2010. "The American Labor Movement in the Age of Obama:

The Challenges and Opportunities of a Racialized Political Economy." *Perspectives on Politics* 8(3): 847–60.

Weaver, Vesla. 2007. "Frontlash: Race and the Development of Punitive Crime Policy." *Studies in American Political Development* 21(2): 230–65.

Weaver, Vesla M., and Amy E. Lerman. 2010. "Political Consequences of the Carceral State." *American Political Science Review* 104(4): 817–33.

Williams, Linda Faye. 2003. *The Constraint of Race: Legacies of White Skin Privilege in America.* University Park: Pennsylvania State University Press.

Wilson, William Julius. 1987. *The Truly Disadvantaged: The Inner City, the Underclass, and Public Policy.* Chicago: University of Chicago Press.

———. 1996. *When Work Disappears: The World of the New Urban Poor.* New York: Alfred A. Knopf.

———. 1999. *The Bridge over the Racial Divide: Rising Inequality and Coalition Politics.* Berkeley: University of California Press.

———. 2009. *More Than Just Race: Being Black and Poor in the Inner City.* New York: W. W. Norton.

Zernike, Kate. 2010. *Boiling Mad: Inside Tea Party America.* New York: Times Books.

PART I | The Political Development of Racial Inequality

Chapter 1 | The End of "Race" as We Know It? Assessing the "Postracial America" Thesis in the Obama Era

Rodney E. Hero and Morris E. Levy, with
Benjamin Radcliff

IN HIS HIGHLY influential analysis of democracy in America, Alexis de Tocqueville ([1848] 1966, 475–76) contended that "democratic . . . peoples' passion for equality is ardent, insatiable, eternal and invincible." On the other hand, he also recognized the profound importance of and problems posed by race in American society. Tocqueville emphasized America's liberal and civic republican political values. But his qualification for race identified what has recently been recognized as a powerful inegalitarian or hierarchical normative tradition that has provided justifications for racial-ethnic and other social differentiation, indeed stratification and inequality, in American politics (Smith 1997).

It has been argued, on the other hand, that the post–civil rights era, especially as embodied and crystallized in the election of the first African American president, Barack Obama, has, in essence, ended race as we know it. Although this claim has been made especially forcefully in the presidential electoral arena, one of its general implications is that a broader displacement or replacement of the predominant role of race in American society by other factors or phenomena has occurred. Such other bases of social division are commonly viewed as fundamentally less averse than racial ones to core American values. This chapter complements scholarship addressing the alleged declining importance of race in other arenas of

American politics but also advances such research in a distinctive way and brings unique evidence to bear.

The major welfare reform legislation of 1996 (the Personal Responsibility and Work Opportunity Reconciliation Act), for example, was, in President Clinton's words, supposed to have "end[ed] welfare as we know it," (Vobejda 1996, A01) and maybe it did. But part of the reason for reforming welfare was a subtext of race: the existing policy (Aid to Families with Dependent Children) was linked, in the minds of the reform proponents, with race. According to one scholarly analysis, the "poor became black" with the fuller inclusion of blacks in receipt of welfare benefits following civil rights legislation of the 1960s (Gilens 2003). The attainment of increased legal and formal equality for blacks regarding various governmental services was presumably an indicator of black advancement.

However, that attainment, and more black inclusion as welfare beneficiaries, engendered a racialization of this policy, which had previously been viewed as largely nonracial in nature. Over time, there was a growing perception that blacks were disproportionately represented, and implicitly undeserving, beneficiaries of welfare; thus their heightened legal status was accompanied by attitudinal resentment toward them. Research on welfare from the 1960s up to the 1996 reforms consistently showed that states with larger black populations spent less on welfare, and research on the 1996 welfare legislation demonstrated that the reform did not remove the impact of racial factors long associated with this redistributive policy (Soss et al. 2001). The finding that ending welfare as we know it hardly diminished the influence of racial factors offers lessons for and suggests further reason to question claims that the 2008 election substantially changed, much less ended, race as we know it.

The election of Obama and the various developments leading up to it have already generated an enormous amount of commentary and media attention, including blog discussions, editorials, articles, books, and so on. We can only begin to imagine how much more, and what, will be written, debated, and otherwise discussed about these and a host of related issues in the near and long-term future. Early on, the word *postracial* was popularized as a description of the rise and election of Obama (compare Lee 2011). Although its origins are a bit murky and its substantive accuracy dubious, the sheer frequency of its mention is striking. This prominence merits further reflection—and of a different sort from that it has already received. Here, we consider the postracial notion from two different vantage points: the role of race in elections and racial inequality in the economic sphere.

Earlier scholarship that considers and conceptualizes the role of race in elections also illustrates the vagueness in the contemporary meaning and use of the concept "postracial." The concept probably conflates or confuses as much as or more than it clarifies, but assessing its applicability to contemporary American society is significant nonetheless. In some ways, directly engaging the notion of a postracial society makes us complicit in reinforcing, then confronting, something of a straw man, because the basic claim often seems doubtful if interpreted broadly or taken to its logical conclusion and even when considered on narrower terms. Yet the idea seems to have attained sufficiently widespread use and popularity that engaging it is worthwhile. When analyzed critically, what appears to some to be a straw man may nonetheless have enough resonance and plausibility among the public, and even in public intellectual circles, that it should not and cannot be dismissed out of hand. (Indeed a quick Google search indicates almost 92 million listings regarding the word "postracial.")

In a society that may be postracial (even if only in limited respects), we might expect that race would become decreasingly consequential for voting behavior and for economic outcomes and social position. We might also expect that social forces other than race would become increasingly strong determinants over time, particularly class. Class is generally thought to embody several significant social dimensions that may broadly define yet also divide a society and polity and be a major sources of inequality, as much as or more than race.

MEANING OF POSTRACIAL

When invoking Obama's election to argue for a strong trend toward and achievement of substantial diminution of the impact of race in American politics and economic opportunity, people usually make one of two arguments. Focusing on politics, they claim that Obama's election demonstrates the willingness of many whites to vote for a black candidate (at least when the incumbent party is widely blamed for bad economic times). Some then go on to assert that the election of a black person to the nation's highest office is emblematic of—or even clear evidence of—the dramatic lowering of racial barriers to social advancement in America. The first argument takes Obama's election to be evidence that race plays a greatly reduced role in American electoral politics. The second interprets Obama's personal achievement as at least an indication that race plays a greatly reduced role in the structure of American social mobility.

We can characterize an idealized postracial society as one in which race was once a significant and substantial predictor of various behavioral patterns and life outcomes but in which race has ceased to have much if any predictive power in these respects. America becomes more postracial as it evolves to be closer to this ideal.

In the electoral arena, we take postracial to mean that the race of neither voters nor candidates remains predictive of voting behavior or campaigning strategy. Thus in a truly postracial society, blacks and whites would not exhibit distinct voting patterns, nor would the candidate's race influence either group's vote choices. A number of years ago, Charles Bullock III and Bruce Campbell (1984) drew a distinction between racial and racist voting in American cities' mayoral elections. Racial voting was defined as the strong tendency to vote for a candidate of one's own race, one who is "like me (or you, or oneself)," unless there are strong reasons to do otherwise. On the other hand, racist behavior meant voting against a candidate based on race alone or at least primarily, even if the policy positions of the candidate of the other race are highly consistent with one's own. This potentially important distinction may not apply equally to voting in presidential elections, which are more visible and where there is a broader array of other relevant factors. And it leaves open other conceptual issues as well. Nonetheless, this distinction between racial and racist, made years ago, may also be useful in assessing a weaker version of what postracial might mean in the contemporary context and whether it is plausible even within the electoral arena.

In the economic arena, we take an ideal version of postracial to mean that race is no longer predictive of income or occupation. Other measures of economic well-being, such as wealth accumulation, could certainly also be considered. If anything, a rebuttal of the postracial thesis would probably be easier were one to emphasize individuals' or households' net worth rather than income and occupation. Vast racial disparities in household net worth are well known and appear to have grown more dramatic in the wake of the 2008 and 2009 economic recession. In 2004 the median white household net worth was approximately ten times that of the median black household nationwide, whereas in 2009 the gap grew to approximately forty-five times (Washington 2011).

Still, the disparities in wealth accumulation existing today are arguably more direct legacies of earlier eras in American history that could not reasonably be alleged to have been postracial. Of course income and occupation disparities are also, in part, legacies of earlier discrimination. But one might expect those measures to indicate narrowing of racial inequality before wealth accumulation would, so that if the United States were approaching rather than arriving at a postracial era, this trend would be observed in income and occupation convergence before wealth convergence. As a result, emphasizing income and occupational status seems a fairer, indeed, a quite conservative, test of the postracial thesis. Thus in a true postracial society, blacks and whites would have the same income distributions and would be equally represented in the more desirable occupational strata. It could be argued that Obama's election signals more equalization of economic opportunity among blacks and whites, which does not necessarily translate into equality of economic success. However, if the expansion of opportunity is real, it could reasonably be expected to result in at least some dampening of actual between-race economic gaps in outcomes.

THE PERSISTENCE OF RACE IN AMERICAN ELECTORAL POLITICS

Some have attributed a part of white voters' support for Obama to class trumping race in bad economic times. Even if that were the case to some degree, it still seems questionable not to see some substantial level of racial (rather than postracial) impact if one defines racial voting as described earlier: the general tendency to vote for or against the candidate who is racially "like me" (or not) in the absence of reasons to vote otherwise. The overall racial-ethnic group pattern of voting in the 2008 election, with whites, particularly in southern states, voting so strongly against Obama (or for McCain?), seems inconsistent with general postracial assertions. Additionally, the postracial view does not seem to necessarily identify or attempt to identify alternative explanations for presidential voting (or other political processes and outcomes, for that matter). Indeed, such a view overlooks a plausible alternative possibility that Obama was elected despite the impact of race or racial factors because of the way the American electoral college aggregates votes; that is, overall increased racial negativity in one or more states need not be fully matched by increased support for a candidate's vote in another set of states to substantially affect the outcome in these states or overall.

Obama's substantial vote share among whites could be taken as evidence of a move toward postracial electoral politics since it indicates that other factors may well have trumped racial considerations for many voters; however, there is important countervailing evidence. Indeed, though the interpretation of Obama's victory in the 2008 election as a sign of transition toward a postracial society has been widespread, the very exit polls that ostensibly signaled the momentous result also told a story of a persistent and perhaps even growing racial voting divide. Moreover, in only a few states did whites support Obama in 2008 at higher levels than they did John Kerry in 2004, despite the economic collapse and the ongoing unpopularity of the two wars initiated by the previous administration. It is difficult to determine, as some scholars have tried to do, how much of a race penalty Obama suffered among white voters, and there is some evidence that Obama's race benefited him among some white voters (see, for example, Tesler and Sears 2010). But regardless of how various white voters reacted to Obama with respect to his race or how many black voters were more enthusiastic, the overall deep split in racial voting patterns across the states belies the notion that electoral politics has reached or is rapidly approaching a postracial era.

America may have become increasingly postracist, but, whether through the racial partisan divide or other channels, black and white Americans vote in increasingly different ways. Hence, even if one seeks to give the postracial interpretation its due—which we interpret to be the relatively narrow claim that the outcome of the 2008 presidential election demonstrates a trend toward a postracial reality—evidence that contradicts it is as substantial as that which supports it. Figure 1.1 shows the magnitude and persistence of the gap for the twenty-five states with reliable exit polling results for vote by race in both 2004 and 2008, and appendix table 1A.1 shows the data for all states. The evidence indicates that in general the racial divide was larger in 2008 than in the 2004 elections in most states, albeit with a few, though important, exceptions. There are more states in which the black-white gap in voting for Obama in 2008 increased relative to the 2004 vote for the Democratic nominee, John Kerry.

Overall, the cross-state correlation of the black-white ratio in Democratic vote share in the two elections is .91 (N = 25), suggesting that the cross-state structure of the racial electoral divide was similar in the two elections. Casting further doubt on the claim that the 2008 presidential election signals the emergence of a postracial electoral politics, the mean increase in this ratio across these twenty-five states between 2004 and 2008 was 0.4. The mean is so high in part owing to the especially large increase in the ratio in Alabama, Louisiana, and Mississippi,[1] but the median increase is close to 0.1, and eighteen of the twenty-five states saw an increase in the black-white Democratic vote share ratio while only seven saw a decrease. Even if some of the divide has its roots in socioeconomic differences between racial groups, the persistence of such large differences and the fact that Obama did not outperform Kerry among whites in most states, in an election year in which macro factors indicated that the Democratic candidate should have, suggest that race continues to play an independent role.

RACIAL INEQUALITY IN THE ECONOMIC SPHERE

Our evidence on race and inequality in the economic sphere includes several indicators from each of two census surveys: about a decade before the 2008 election of Obama (2000) and the period after the election (2010). We

Figure 1.1   Black-White Ratio in Democratic Vote for President, Selected States, 2004 and 2008 (N=25)

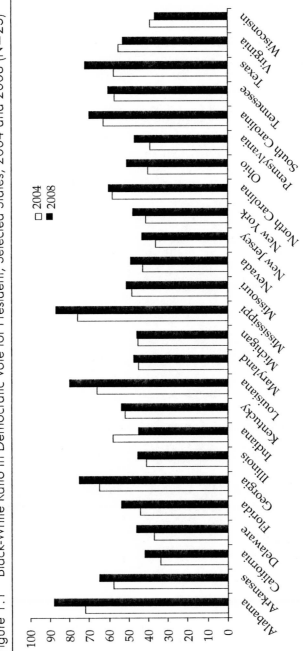

Source: Authors' compilation based Roper Center (2004, 2008).

seek to ascertain the extent of inequality in the two periods and, more important, how much (if at all) and in what directions racial inequality changed over the period to assess whether there has been improvement— that is, a decline—in racial inequality. In general, the findings show relative persistence and some increase in the black-white racial divide with respect to various indicators of economic inequality over the period. Even though general economic inequality has increased at a fast clip as well during the time considered, race has become (on average) a modestly larger component of total inequality. Ironically, the ongoing significance of race is made difficult to discern only because other dimensions of inequality have increased in relevance in tandem.

Since our reasons for examining states in analyzing economic inequality are perhaps not as apparent as why we would choose to examine them in assessing voting divergence in elections whose basis for aggregation is state vote shares, it is important that we explain this decision. We examine the American states, specifically, because they are core institutions and have constitutionally uniform legal status and authority within the American federal system of government. Also, it makes sense to consider inequality within the states to capture its variation in these diverse governmental and economic contexts frequently overlooked in aggregate analyses of groups at the national level. Other prominent subnational governments, cities in particular, have a different legal standing vis à vis their own state governments in the specific breadth and nature of their formal authority, their geographic boundaries, and a host of other attributes that vary considerably within and across the states, and they have other unique limits (Peterson 1981). They also have little legal or constitutional standing in relation to the national government. For these and other reasons they have shortcomings for present analytical purposes. Moreover, states have been examined in numerous instances with respect to issues of economic and political inequality (for example, Hill and Leighley 1992; Key 1949; Hero 1998; Barrilleaux, Holbrook, and Langer 2002; Radcliff and Saiz 1995; Putnam 2000).

The notion of states' rights has been influential in American history, advanced as grounds or justification for strong, sometimes exclusive, state government authority in numerous policy domains, some of which have been associated with racial inequality. States play a major role in domestic policy in areas in which they have primary legal authority, such as public education, which is often argued to be the linchpin of equality (of opportunity) in American politics. And states share in the decision making and implementation of federal programs, including major redistributive ones such as welfare, Medicaid, and others that are key policies intended to address economic inequality. Furthermore, states figure prominently in the processes of presidential selection, as the domains of the party nomination primaries and through the Electoral College, the entity designated in the Constitution to aggregate the popular vote.

As has been found elsewhere (Hero 1998), the implications of race have some commonalities across the political system, but the race effect also varies across states, affected by their distinctive histories, differences in the aggregate size and configurations of the racial-ethnic population, and economic and class dynamics and other aspects of the social and governmental system. We found high standard deviations on the percentage change in various indicators of inequality, which suggests that states followed a range of widely divergent patterns over the period (and indicates at least that sampling error has precluded identification of any singular trend, especially in smaller states or states with small black populations). Although these nuances are worthy of further consideration, we focus our discussion on larger trends among and across states because the identification of these trends permits the best way of assessing claims of substantial progress toward the postracial ideal.

Comparisons of differences in median income of whites and blacks overall, the relative presence of whites and blacks in the professional class, and the differential or relative income of whites and blacks within classes suggest both the depth and breadth of inequality and thereby give a sense of the scope of inequality. Considering the share of total income inequality that can be attributed to between-race disparities also gives a sense of the breadth of black-white inequality. Both of these perspectives are relevant to understanding inequality particularly because we can sometimes overlook deep inequality when it is concentrated in a small minority population (compare Hero 1998).

Several points about data and measurement are important to note. The data are drawn from the 2000 Census and 2009–2011 American Community Survey (ACS) public use files (IPUMS 2000, 2009) The first year defines the earlier period, and the second the period around Obama's election and early presidency. A three-year period was used with the ACS to obtain larger samples and more reliable measurements of black representation in the professional class and median black income in states with small black populations or small populations overall.

All respondents identifying as any race other than white, black, or black and some other race were dropped from the analysis, and all respondents identifying black as at least one of their racial categories were classified as black. Only male heads of household between the ages of nineteen and sixty-five were included in the analysis. Respondents who reported having no income from any source were also dropped from the analysis, though they constitute only a small portion of the total respondents. Income figures refer to the respondent's total income from all sources, including government transfer payments. If anything, this should bias our results toward finding greater equality than exists with respect to wages and salaries.[2] Those unemployed or otherwise out of work at the time of each survey were included, as long as they reported some income from some source, including government benefits. This is because differential rates of unemployment and labor force participation figure prominently in the level of racial economic inequality. Medians are most often reported to avoid a strong influence of outliers and to mitigate problems inherent in top-coding practices.[3] Top-coding will, however, most likely exert some influence on the computation of Theil indexes discussed later in this chapter.

The analyses that control for class or assess racial representation within classes are based on a modified, two-class version of the Goldthorpe schema proposed by Robert Erikson, John Goldthorpe, and Lucianne Portocarero (1979) and subsequently elaborated on and refined by Goldthorpe and his collaborators (most notably, Goldthorpe and Mueller 1982; Goldthorpe 1987; Erikson and Goldthorpe 2002). The conceptual core of the Goldthorpe schema is its emphasis on the individual's structural position in the labor market, which is most affected by the individual worker's relationship to the employer. The resulting hierarchical classification depends on two principal factors: the ability or the inherent difficulty that employers have in monitoring the employee's job performance, which in effect amounts to the degree of autonomy and self-direction individuals enjoy in the workplace, and the skill level of the employee. Thus the least privileged class, unskilled manual laborers such as textile sewing machine operators, whose lack of specialized skills, coupled with the ease by which their labor is monitored and directed by superiors, are clearly under both the wage and supervisory thumb of their employer. At the other end of the class hierarchy are professionals (college professors, physicians, etc.) and managers or administrators (who supervise large number of employees), who enjoy both the autonomy that is part of the nature of their work and the ability to negotiate terms of employment consistent with their specialized skill sets. In between, there are simply gradations along this continuum.[4]

Most scholars using the Goldthorpe approach have simplified the number of classes, most typically relying on either a four- or two-class categorization, rather than Goldthorpe's simplest seven-part typology.[5] We adopt the two-class model, because it has a long pedigree within social science in general and political economy in particular. Most telling from the perspective of American politics, it is the point of view adopted, explicitly or otherwise, as part of the American political tradition of dualism, by the political parties and most other political entrepreneurs. More narrowly, the two-class model is also that implicitly adopted by those studying inequality within the literature on American politics since V. O. Key (1949) introduced the terminology of the haves and the have-nots (also see, for example, Wolfinger and Rosenstone 1980; Hill and Leighley 1992, 354; Brown 1995). This study relies on the operationalization and refinement of the Goldthorpe class schema suggested by Stephen Morgan and Mark McKerrow (2004), using their class 1 as our professional class and their classes 2 to 7 as our working class.

EXAMINING THE EVIDENCE

We compare the class situation of blacks and whites in the economic structure of the American states on several dimensions, presenting basic data as well as simple descriptive statistics. With such evidence we initially assess continuity and change and whether class and racial inequality vary significantly eight years preceding the election of Obama (2000) and in the immediate aftermath of his election (2010). Expansions in the between-race differences in various indicators of economic well-being could be interpreted as suggesting that racial inequality in most states has become more pronounced. We also interpret modest change in ratios of white to black income and presence in the professional class as indicating that any growth has continued to be apportioned among the races in essentially the same unequal proportions during the time leading up to the second measurement period (2010) as it had been before the first (2000).

Although both ratios and differences are informative, we most often present and focus on the ratio measures and leave tabulations of the absolute differences to the appendix tables. Looking only at absolute differences in medians might wrongly suggest that inequality is higher in states with overall higher median incomes. For example, in the later period, the median absolute differences in incomes between races were lower in Louisiana ($21,300) than New Jersey ($24,699). However, the ratio of white to black income was much higher in Louisiana (1.8 vs. 1.6) because both black and white incomes in New Jersey were higher. However presented, the evidence indicates the continuing importance of race in American society beyond the political realm into the economic.

Overall White-Black Differences in Income

We first consider, in figure 1.2, general white-black difference in median incomes by state, for all states for which reasonably reliable samples could be derived for blacks from Census and ACS public use data. The tabulation (appendix table 1A.2) shows that, in most cases, the gap widened, and in some cases by quite a bit, though the limitations especially in small states or states with small black populations should be treated with caution in this and subsequent results. Of the thirty-seven states included, thirty-two had at least some increase in the differences, and most had quite a lot. The overall median degree of change between the two periods is an increase in inequality of 12 percent.

The median change in the ratio is an increase of 8 percent, indicating approximately no racial convergence and more modest divergence in incomes. As Obama won and occupied the presidency, white populations in each state accrued, on average, roughly $1.50 per individual in additional real income for each $1.00 per individual accrued by black populations, a slight uptick from the $1.40 per $1.00 reflected in the data for the earlier period.[6]

Within-Class Racial Differences in Income

Having indicated general differences in income, we are also interested in white-black differences within the professional and working classes because it is important to see whether the overall differences seem more or less attributable to income differences within one class or the other (or both). Looking within classes also provides a conservative measure of racial inequality because it tests whether racial inequality exists even with respect to the incomes of blacks and whites of roughly similar occupational status. It may well be that some of this persistent inequality results from the tendency for blacks to hold lower status jobs (with respect to the Goldthorpe formulation) within each of the two class categories. To the extent that is so, one could argue that we are identifying "presence" inequality (see below) rather than simple income inequality. In either case, however, the conclusion is the same: racial gaps are large and persistent.

Looking within occupational class, the evidence indicates that the gap between races in median income persists in almost all states and has increased in many. Figure 1.3 shows the ratio in each period for the professional class, and figure 1.4 for the working class (data on differences are presented in tables 1A.3 and 1A.4). (It should again be noted, however, that all estimates—and especially those for the black professional class—must be interpreted with caution owing to small sample sizes, and high levels of sampling variability are clear.)

The figures indicate that between-race inequality is not confined to either class and is not only the result of overrepresentation of blacks in lower-earning occupations (at least based on the dichotomous class formulation). The trajectory of racial income inequality within each class differs. The median professional-class change in terms of racial income differences

Figure 1.2   White-Black Median Income Ratios, Selected States, 2000 and 2010 (N=37)

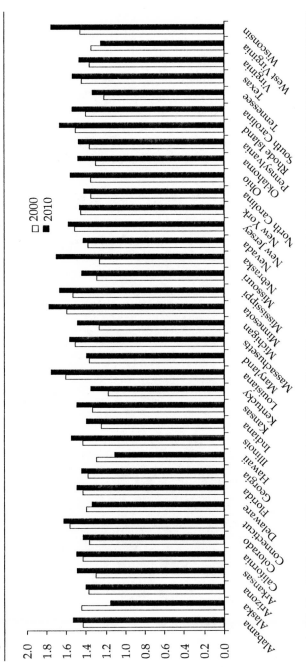

Source: Authors' compilation of Census 2000 and 2010 IPUMS Microdata (U.S. Census Bureau n.d.).

Figure 1.3   White-Black Median Professional-Class Income Ratio, Selected States, 2000 and 2010
(N=37)

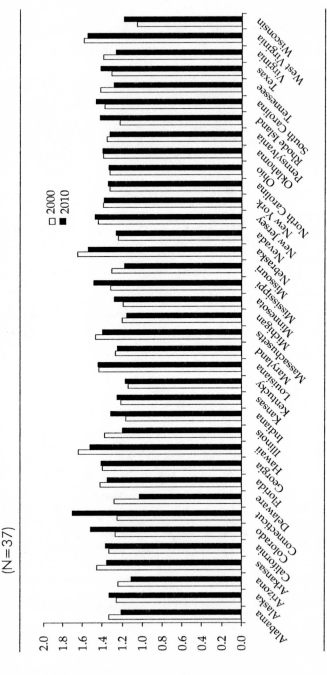

Source: Authors' compilation of Census 2000 and 2010 IPUMS Microdata (U.S. Census Bureau n.d.).

Figure 1.4   White-Black Median Working-Class Income Ratio, Selected States, 2000 and 2010 (N=37)

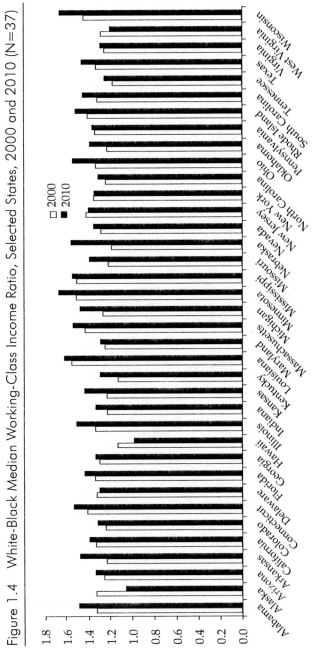

Source: Authors' compilation of Census 2000 and 2010 IPUMS Microdata (U.S. Census Bureau n.d.).

was a 1 percent increase, and the same for the working class was a 12 percent increase. Ratio changes tell a similar story, with a 1 percent median increase in the professional class white-black income ratio and an 8 percent median increase in racial inequality in the working class. Another way of looking at the result is that over the period in question, nineteen of the thirty-seven states examined had an increase in the ratio of white to black professional-class income while seventeen saw a decrease, and thirty-two of the thirty-seven had an increase of this ratio in the working class while five saw a decrease.

The Presence of Whites and Blacks within Classes

The data on within-class racial inequality do not necessarily tell the whole story; inequality may be manifested in the relative presence of each race within each occupational stratum, as well as in income disparities. It is one thing for the members of a racial group to receive more or less equal income to those of another group in a social class, but their presence or distribution within and across classes is another issue. Simply looking within classes at racial income disparities understates the full amount of racial inequality because a substantially smaller share of blacks than whites achieves professional-class employment.

Figure 1.5 shows the ratio of the percentage of all whites in a state who are in the professional class to the percentage of all blacks in the state who are in the professional class; the higher the number, the greater the "over-representation" of whites (and underrepresentation of blacks) in the professional class (a score of one indicates representational parity). For example, in Alabama in 2000, the ratio of 2.8 reflects the fact that approximately 18.9 percent of whites and only 6.7 percent of blacks in the state are in the professional class (and 18.9 divided by 6.7 rounds to 2.8). By 2010, this ratio had declined slightly to 2.2 because now 9.0 percent of blacks were in the professional class, compared to 20.4 percent of whites (appendix table 1A.5).

In almost every state, whites are overrepresented in higher-income occupations, usually by more than 2:1. Though the percentage change in the white-black presence ratio indicates some decline in this overrepresentation (see figure 1.5), the raw numbers suggest persistence. Twenty-five out of the thirty-seven states analyzed show a drop in the ratio of white-to-black representation in the professional class. Yet, for all intents and purposes, the median ratio remained constant at 2.0, meaning the white share of the professional class roughly continues to double the black share in the median state. Moreover, in only fourteen states did the difference between

Figure 1.5   Group Presence: Ratio of Percentage of Whites in Professional Class to Percentage of Blacks in Professional Class, Selected States, 2000 and 2010 (N=37)

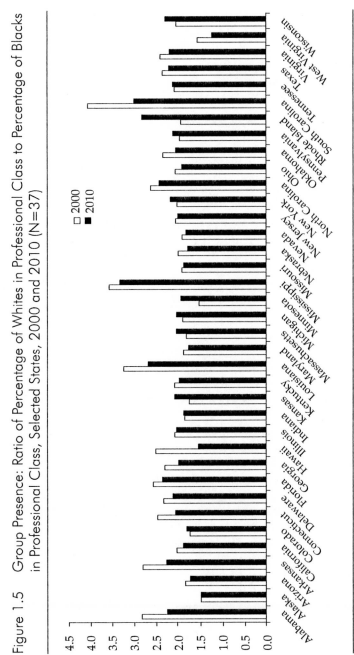

Source: Authors' compilation of Census 2000 and 2010 IPUMS Microdata (U.S. Census Bureau n.d.).

the percentage of whites and blacks in the professional class diminish, compared to twenty-two in which it increased. The discrepancy here is due to the fact that the professional class grew as a share of both races during this period. Whites continued to find their way into the professional class at a faster pace than blacks, but the racial gap in rates of entry to the professional class shrank modestly.

Income Inequality as Measured by the Theil Index

It is well known that income inequality in the United States generally has increased steadily since the 1980s (see, for example, Hacker and Pierson 2010). Figure 1.6 uses the Theil index to measure income inequality; the Theil index measures the extent to which groups or individuals have income shares in excess of their population shares (for the data, see appendix table 1A.6). For present purposes, the advantage of the Theil over the often-used Gini coefficient is that it can be decomposed into between-group components so that we may assess how much inequality across a given social division (in this case, black versus white) contributes to total inequality in society's incomes. The evidence in this figure indicates that the general trend of increased income inequality applies across states, though it also indicates substantial variation in its growth across the states.

There are four reasons that the median increase we find might appear smaller than those uncovered in national analyses. First, our summary metrics do not weight the states according to population, so that the 11 percent increase in inequality in New York, for example, might outweigh similarly large decreases in a number of smaller states when measures are aggregated to the national level. Second, top coding in Census products might limit the extent to which growth in inequality owing to increases in the highest incomes can influence our results. And it should be noted that several scholars (for example, Hacker and Pierson 2010) emphasize that income growth at the highest levels of income (such as the top 0.1 percent) has been clearly the most striking development in income inequality in America over the past several decades. Third, our analysis considers only blacks and non-Latino whites, so that any contribution to overall inequality generated by increased immigration and differential fertility rates would not affect our calculations. Fourth, our analysis considers only income inequality trends within states, whereas between-state incomes may also contribute to the national growth in income inequality. Nevertheless, we do find that twenty-seven states experienced an increase in their Theil

Figure 1.6 Total Income Inequality as Measured by Total Theil Index, Selected States, 2000 and 2010 (N = 37)

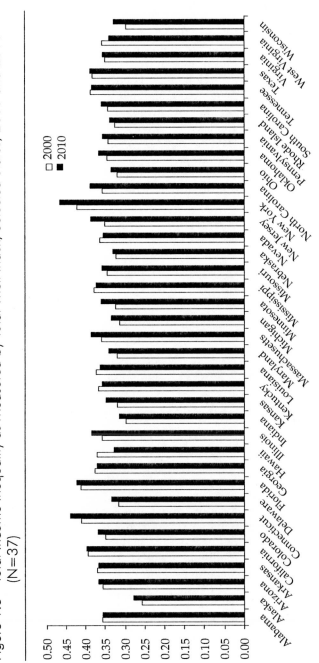

Source: Authors' compilation of Census 2000 and 2010 IPUMS Microdata (U.S. Census Bureau n.d.).

index, while only nine experienced a decrease, resulting in a median increase of approximately 3.8 percent.

As noted, the advantage of the Theil index as a measure of income inequality is its decomposability into between- and within-group components (for an accessible discussion of the Theil and its properties, see Conceicao and Ferreira 2000). We may gauge the breadth of racial inequality by asking what share of total income inequality among blacks and whites in each state can be accounted for by the income disparities between them. This gives a sense of racial inequality's breadth and whether it has kept pace with rising inequality overall.

It turns out that between-race inequality since 2000 has risen at a faster rate than inequality overall—that is, by 2010 between-race inequality had become a larger percentage of total income inequality among whites and blacks than it was in 2000 (see figure 1.7). Only three of the thirty-seven states we analyze register declines in the share of total income inequality that can be accounted for by between-race income disparities, while thirty-four of the thirty-seven register increases. In some states the increases exceed a percentage point. As shown in table 1A.7, the median state in our analysis shows an increase of more than half a percentage point in the share of all income inequality that is due to black-white income differentials.

These data call into question the postracial thesis more than any other we have presented. As income inequality overall has increased dramatically in the U.S., its racial component more than kept pace. Though rising total inequality may make ongoing racial inequality less distinctive than it once was, the persistence of race as a deep socioeconomic divide cannot be gainsaid.

CONCLUSION

The election of Barack Obama in 2008 was clearly a profound landmark in American social and political history. A striking legacy of the civil rights movement, this outcome suggests a postracist society, and some have gone even further, claiming the Obama election heralds a postracial social and political system. This chapter has considered possible meanings of the concept postracial while acknowledging that few (if any) scholars have accepted the specific or general accuracy of such claims. Yet the term has been widely and frequently used in public discourse and should not be discounted out of hand.

When assessed first in simple terms of vote choices of whites and blacks in the 2008 election itself, the postracial assertion is at least somewhat du-

Figure 1.7   Between-Race Theil as Percentage of Total Theil (Percentage of Total Income Inequality Attributable to Black-White Income Disparity), Selected States, 2000 and 2010 (N=37)

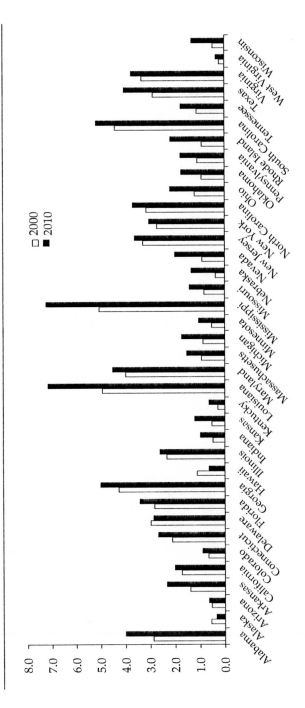

Source: Authors' compilation of Census 2000 and 2010 IPUMS Microdata (U.S. Census Bureau n.d.).

bious. And analysis of the 2010 congressional elections indicates a larger racial divide in voting patterns than in 2008 (Abramowitz 2011). We also undertook an extensive analysis of race and class distributions and equality as evident in fundamentally important political and social entities, the American states, and over a ten-year period. As part of our larger effort to understand the presumably evolving role of race in American society, we deemed it important to identify and consider contours and patterns of continuity and change in these more structural indicators of inequality and what they might suggest about possible lessening of the impact of race.

The evidence is not altogether simple or straightforward and may look somewhat different depending on the specific dimensions examined (and how they are measured, whether as ratios or in raw terms or others). On the whole, however, there is little definitive or consistent evidence of a decline in racial or overall economic inequality between 2000 and 2010. If anything, both of these forms of inequality remained similar or increased across states. Overall income inequality growth may have made between-race inequality more difficult to discern. Yet the relative racial portion of inequality increased nevertheless. Even the peculiar vision of a postracial society in which growing class inequality drowns out persistent racial disparity appears unfounded.

The possible decline in attitudinal racial bias that some believe is occurring, as manifested in voting decisions, within a broader context of continuing racial inequality regarding class and an upsurge in general economic inequality often referred to as the "great divergence" (Krugman 2007) is substantively remarkable and calls for careful analysis. There is thus a need to further conceptualize key terms, such as the ideas of race and postracial, among others, and to examine these systematically in their various dimensions and as they play out in various governmental arenas, including the states. Although the claims of a postracial society are patently questionable they nonetheless encourage us to reflect on how and why such assertions have attained such widespread use. The claims also impel us to examine race along with class in different political and social contexts. This is essential for better understanding the scope and evolving, though persistent, nature of social inequality in early twenty-first-century America, all the while acknowledging the profound importance of the election of its first black president.

Appendix: Data Used to Construct Charts

Table 1A.1 Black-White Gap in Democratic Vote for President, Selected States, 2004 and 2008

	2004				2008				2004–2008	
	White (%)	Black (%)	Difference (%)	Ratio	White (%)	Black (%)	Difference (%)	Ratio	Change in difference (%)	Change in ratio
Alabama	19	91	72	4.8	10	98	88	9.8	16	5.0
Alaska	33	n.a.	n.a.	n.a.	33	n.a.	n.a.	n.a.	n.a.	n.a.
Arizona	41	n.a.	n.a.	n.a.	40	n.a.	n.a.	n.a.	n.a.	n.a.
Arkansas	36	94	58	2.6	30	95	65	3.2	7	0.6
California	47	81	34	1.7	52	94	42	1.8	8	0.1
Colorado	42	87	45	2.1	50	n.a.	n.a.	n.a.	n.a.	n.a.
Connecticut	51	n.a.	n.a.	n.a.	51	93	42	1.8	n.a.	n.a.
Delaware	45	82	37	1.8	53	99	46	1.9	9	0.0
District of Columbia	80	97	17	1.2	86	97	11	1.1	-6	-0.1
Florida	42	86	44	2.0	42	96	54	2.3	10	0.2
Georgia	23	88	65	3.8	23	98	75	4.3	10	0.4
Hawaii	58	n.a.	n.a.	n.a.	70	n.a.	n.a.	n.a.	n.a.	n.a.
Idaho	29	n.a.	n.a.	n.a.	33	n.a.	n.a.	n.a.	n.a.	n.a.
Illinois	48	89	41	1.9	51	96	45	1.9	4	0.0
Indiana	34	92	58	2.7	45	90	45	2.0	-13	-0.7
Iowa	49	n.a.	n.a.	n.a.	51	93	42	1.8	n.a.	n.a.
Kansas	34	n.a.	n.a.	n.a.	40	n.a.	n.a.	n.a.	n.a.	n.a.
Kentucky	35	87	52	2.5	36	90	54	2.5	2	0.0
Louisiana	24	90	66	3.8	14	94	80	6.7	14	3.0

Table 1A.1 (Continued)

	2004				2008				2004–2008	
	White (%)	Black (%)	Difference (%)	Ratio	White (%)	Black (%)	Difference (%)	Ratio	Change in difference (%)	Change in ratio
Maine	53	n.a.	n.a.	n.a.	58	n.a.	n.a.	n.a.	n.a.	n.a.
Maryland	44	89	45	2.0	47	94	47	2.0	2	0.0
Massachusetts	59	n.a.	n.a.	n.a.	59	n.a.	n.a.	n.a.	n.a.	n.a.
Michigan	44	89	45	2.0	51	97	46	1.9	1	-0.1
Minnesota	50	87	37	1.7	53	n.a.	n.a.	n.a.	n.a.	n.a.
Mississippi	14	90	76	6.4	11	98	87	8.9	11	2.5
Missouri	42	90	48	2.1	42	93	51	2.2	3	0.1
Montana	39	n.a.	n.a.	n.a.	45	n.a.	n.a.	n.a.	n.a.	n.a.
Nebraska	33	n.a.	n.a.	n.a.	39	n.a.	n.a.	n.a.	n.a.	n.a.
Nevada	43	86	43	2.0	45	94	49	2.1	6	0.1
New Hampshire	50	n.a.	n.a.	n.a.	54	n.a.	n.a.	n.a.	n.a.	n.a.
New Jersey	46	82	36	1.8	49	92	43	1.9	7	0.1
New Mexico	43	n.a.	n.a.	n.a.	42	n.a.	n.a.	n.a.	n.a.	n.a.
New York	49	90	41	1.8	52	100	48	1.9	7	0.1
North Carolina	27	85	58	3.1	35	95	60	2.7	2	-0.4
North Dakota	35	n.a.	n.a.	n.a.	42	n.a.	n.a.	n.a.	n.a.	n.a.
Ohio	44	84	40	1.9	46	97	51	2.1	11	0.2

Oklahoma	29	72	43	2.5	29	n.a.	n.a.	n.a.	n.a.	n.a.
Oregon	50	n.a.	n.a.	n.a.	57	n.a.	n.a.	n.a.	n.a.	n.a.
Pennsylvania	45	84	39	1.9	48	95	47	2.0	8	0.1
Rhode Island	57	n.a.	n.a.	n.a.	58	n.a.	n.a.	n.a.	n.a.	n.a.
South Carolina	22	85	63	3.9	26	96	70	3.7	7	-0.2
South Dakota	37	n.a.	n.a.	n.a.	41	n.a.	n.a.	n.a.	n.a.	n.a.
Tennessee	34	91	57	2.7	34	94	60	2.8	3	0.1
Texas	25	83	58	3.3	26	98	72	3.8	14	0.4
Utah	24	n.a.	n.a.	n.a.	31	n.a.	n.a.	n.a.	n.a.	n.a.
Vermont	58	n.a.	n.a.	n.a.	68	n.a.	n.a.	n.a.	n.a.	n.a.
Virginia	32	87	55	2.7	39	92	53	2.4	-2	-0.4
Washington	52	73	21	1.4	55	n.a.	n.a.	n.a.	n.a.	n.a.
West Virginia	42	83	41	2.0	41	n.a.	n.a.	n.a.	n.a.	n.a.
Wisconsin	47	86	39	1.8	54	91	37	1.7	-2	-0.1
Wyoming	28	n.a.	n.a.	n.a.	32	n.a.	n.a.	n.a.	n.a.	n.a.
Mean (unweighted)	41	86	48	2.5	44	95	54	3.0	5	0.4
Median	42	87	45	2.0	45	95	50	2.1	7	0.1
Standard deviation (unweighted)	12	5	14	1.1	14	3	16	2.1	6	1.2
N	50	30	30	30	50	27	27	27	25	25
Correlation									.93	.91

Source: Authors' compilation of data from Roper Center (2004, 2008).

Table 1A.2   White-Black Gap in Median Income, Selected States, 2000 and 2010

	Difference			Ratio		
	2000 (dollars)	2010 (dollars)	Change (%)	2000	2010	Change (%)
Alabama	13,197	15,450	17	1.4	1.5	8
Alaska	17,931	8,077	−55	1.5	1.2	−20
Arizona	13,526	14,065	4	1.4	1.4	2
Arkansas	8,901	12,066	36	1.3	1.5	15
California	19,092	20,473	7	1.4	1.5	5
Colorado	14,190	15,372	8	1.4	1.4	5
Connecticut	23,478	24,377	4	1.6	1.6	4
Delaware	15,480	13,214	−15	1.4	1.3	−4
Florida	14,190	15,000	6	1.4	1.5	4
Georgia	14,448	15,442	7	1.4	1.4	4
Hawaii	11,404	5,200	−54	1.3	1.1	−14
Illinois	17,338	18,665	8	1.4	1.5	8
Indiana	9,675	12,203	26	1.3	1.4	12
Kansas	11,610	15,191	31	1.3	1.5	12
Kentucky	6,063	10,017	65	1.2	1.4	15
Louisiana	17,196	21,300	24	1.6	1.8	9
Maryland	16,770	18,412	10	1.4	1.4	2
Massachusetts	19,866	21,393	8	1.5	1.6	4
Michigan	11,610	14,816	28	1.3	1.5	17
Minnesota	19,350	21,344	10	1.6	1.8	11
Mississippi	14,577	16,349	12	1.5	1.7	9
Missouri	10,062	12,656	26	1.3	1.5	12
Nebraska	9,056	17,537	94	1.3	1.7	34
Nevada	14,190	15,191	7	1.4	1.4	4
New Jersey	23,220	24,699	6	1.5	1.6	5
New York	17,802	17,278	−3	1.5	1.5	1
North Carolina	11,610	12,689	9	1.3	1.4	6
Ohio	12,900	15,634	21	1.4	1.6	15
Oklahoma	9,417	13,213	40	1.3	1.5	14
Pennsylvania	13,145	15,043	14	1.4	1.5	8
Rhode Island	17,415	20,416	17	1.5	1.7	11
South Carolina	12,900	15,047	17	1.4	1.5	10
Tennessee	7,482	10,000	34	1.2	1.3	10
Texas	16,383	18,678	14	1.4	1.5	6
Virginia	14,190	18,093	28	1.4	1.5	7
West Virginia	9,411	7,341	−22	1.4	1.3	−7
Wisconsin	15,480	19,153	24	1.5	1.8	20
Mean	14,177	15,705	14	1.4	1.5	7
Median	14,190	15,372	12	1.4	1.5	8
Standard deviation	4,096	4,443	26	0.1	0.1	9
N	37	37	37	37	37	37
Correlation			0.76			0.57

Source: Authors' compilation of Census 2000 and 2010 IPUMS Microdata (U.S. Census Bureau n.d.).

Table 1A.3   Black-White Gap in Median Professional-Class Income, Selected States, 2000 and 2010

	Difference			Ratio		
	2000 (dollars)	2010 (dollars)	Change (%)	2000 (dollars)	2010 (dollars)	Change (%)
Alabama	19,866	14,179	−29	1.3	1.2	−9
Alaska	17,415	21,345	23	1.3	1.3	6
Arizona	15,609	7,985	−49	1.3	1.1	−11
Arkansas	21,285	17,452	−18	1.5	1.4	−7
California	24,510	26,191	7	1.3	1.4	2
Colorado	18,060	28,312	57	1.3	1.5	20
Connecticut	19,350	41,251	113	1.3	1.7	37
Delaware	19,092	3,038	−84	1.3	1.0	−20
Florida	23,336	20,057	−14	1.4	1.4	−5
Georgia	24,510	24,601	0	1.4	1.4	1
Hawaii	31,734	28,170	−11	1.6	1.5	−7
Illinois	24,252	14,452	−40	1.4	1.2	−13
Indiana	11,610	17,378	50	1.2	1.3	12
Kansas	13,739	15,551	13	1.2	1.3	3
Kentucky	9,701	10,164	5	1.2	1.2	1
Louisiana	22,962	24,800	8	1.4	1.4	0
Maryland	19,737	20,000	1	1.3	1.3	−2
Massachusetts	29,025	26,658	−8	1.5	1.4	−5
Michigan	14,267	10,736	−25	1.2	1.2	−3
Minnesota	12,900	17,478	35	1.2	1.3	7
Mississippi	16,641	23,377	40	1.3	1.5	13
Missouri	17,415	11,148	−36	1.3	1.2	−10
Nebraska	27,735	24,882	−10	1.7	1.6	−6
Nevada	15,196	16,000	5	1.3	1.3	1
New Jersey	32,250	33,673	4	1.5	1.5	2
New York	25,800	25,645	−1	1.4	1.4	−1
North Carolina	19,350	19,098	−1	1.3	1.3	1
Ohio	19,350	19,044	−2	1.3	1.3	1
Oklahoma	19,350	20,581	6	1.4	1.4	1
Pennsylvania	21,414	20,256	−5	1.4	1.3	−2
Rhode Island	15,480	24,307	57	1.2	1.4	15
South Carolina	21,414	24,348	14	1.4	1.5	6
Tennessee	23,220	16,148	−30	1.4	1.3	−9
Texas	20,640	26,716	29	1.3	1.4	8
Virginia	25,800	20,770	−19	1.4	1.3	−9
West Virginia	25,155	25,435	1	1.6	1.6	−2
Wisconsin	3,870	11,433	195	1.1	1.2	13
Mean	20,082	20,342	8	1.3	1.3	1
Median	19,737	20,256	1	1.3	1.3	1
Standard deviation	5,941	7,420	47	0.1	0.1	10
N	37	37	37	37	37	37
Correlation			0.55			0.52

Source: Authors' compilation of Census 2000 and 2010 IPUMS Microdata (U.S. Census Bureau n.d.).

Table 1A.4   White-Black Gap in Median Working-Class Income,
             Selected States, 2000 and 2010

	Difference			Ratio		
	2000 (dollars)	2010 (dollars)	Change (%)	2000 (dollars)	2010 (dollars)	Change (%)
Alabama	9,546	12,660	33	1.3	1.5	12
Alaska	12,513	3,050	−76	1.3	1.1	−20
Arizona	8,720	10,127	16	1.3	1.3	6
Arkansas	6,450	10,520	63	1.2	1.5	20
California	12,745	14,179	11	1.3	1.4	5
Colorado	9,030	10,164	13	1.2	1.3	6
Connecticut	15,609	18,295	17	1.4	1.5	9
Delaware	11,868	10,261	−14	1.3	1.3	−2
Florida	10,320	11,647	13	1.3	1.4	7
Georgia	10,320	10,056	−3	1.3	1.3	2
Hawaii	5,289	−800	−115	1.1	1.0	−14
Illinois	12,771	15,354	20	1.3	1.5	13
Indiana	8,385	9,656	15	1.2	1.3	8
Kansas	7,740	12,000	55	1.2	1.4	16
Kentucky	4,167	7,512	80	1.1	1.3	14
Louisiana	14,706	16,357	11	1.6	1.6	4
Maryland	10,320	11,181	8	1.3	1.3	2
Massachusetts	15,480	17,475	13	1.4	1.5	8
Michigan	10,315	12,502	21	1.3	1.5	16
Minnesota	15,480	16,727	8	1.5	1.7	10
Mississippi	12,900	12,623	−2	1.5	1.5	3
Missouri	7,043	10,128	44	1.2	1.4	14
Nebraska	6,192	13,736	122	1.2	1.6	31
Nevada	10,320	11,731	14	1.3	1.4	5
New Jersey	17,222	15,902	−8	1.4	1.4	−1
New York	12,900	11,738	−9	1.3	1.3	0
North Carolina	7,740	8,811	14	1.2	1.3	6
Ohio	11,223	13,559	21	1.3	1.5	15
Oklahoma	6,708	10,034	50	1.2	1.4	13
Pennsylvania	10,965	10,656	−3	1.3	1.4	2
Rhode Island	13,003	14,840	14	1.4	1.5	8
South Carolina	9,804	11,668	19	1.3	1.4	10
Tennessee	5,805	7,000	21	1.2	1.3	6
Texas	11,223	14,275	27	1.3	1.5	9
Virginia	9,030	10,127	12	1.3	1.3	3
West Virginia	7,353	5,279	−28	1.3	1.2	−7
Wisconsin	13,803	16,016	16	1.4	1.7	15
Mean	10,406	11,542	14	1.3	1.4	7
Median	10,320	11,668	14	1.3	1.4	7
Standard deviation	3,221	3,908	38	0.1	0.1	9
N	37	37	37	37	37	37
Correlation			0.70			0.64

Source: Authors' compilation of Census 2000 and 2010 IPUMS Microdata (U.S. Census Bureau n.d.).

Table 1A.5   Group Presence: Ratio of Percentage of Whites in Professional Class to Percentage of Blacks in Professional Class, Selected States, 2000 and 2010

	Difference (%)			Ratio		
	2000	2010	Change (%)	2000	2010	Change (%)
Alabama	12	11	–8	2.8	2.2	–21
Alaska	7	7	10	1.5	1.5	1
Arizona	12	11	–2	1.8	1.7	–7
Arkansas	10	10	1	2.8	2.3	–20
California	15	14	–5	2.0	1.9	–8
Colorado	12	13	12	1.7	1.8	4
Connecticut	18	16	–8	2.5	2.1	–17
Delaware	14	14	–3	2.3	2.1	–9
Florida	14	14	1	2.6	2.3	–8
Georgia	14	13	–4	2.3	2.0	–14
Hawaii	14	9	–39	2.5	1.5	–39
Illinois	13	13	3	2.1	2.0	–2
Indiana	8	9	12	1.8	1.9	1
Kansas	9	11	29	1.7	2.1	19
Kentucky	8	8	7	2.1	2.0	–5
Louisiana	14	13	–4	3.2	2.7	–17
Maryland	15	15	3	1.9	1.8	–6
Massachusetts	13	16	23	1.8	2.0	12
Michigan	10	11	12	1.9	2.0	7
Minnesota	7	11	53	1.5	1.9	27
Mississippi	13	14	12	3.6	3.3	–6
Missouri	9	9	6	1.9	1.9	–1
Nebraska	9	9	–3	2.0	1.8	–11
Nevada	9	9	–4	1.9	1.8	–5
New Jersey	15	15	0	2.0	2.0	–3
New York	12	14	14	2.0	2.2	7
North Carolina	13	14	8	2.6	2.4	–7
Ohio	10	10	–3	2.0	1.9	–7
Oklahoma	10	10	–2	2.3	2.0	–13
Pennsylvania	10	12	22	1.9	2.1	9
Rhode Island	11	16	53	1.9	2.8	47
South Carolina	15	15	–3	4.1	3.0	–27
Tennessee	10	11	13	2.1	2.1	1
Texas	15	16	4	2.3	2.2	–5
Virginia	16	17	7	2.4	2.2	–9
West Virginia	4	3	–41	1.5	1.2	–20
Wisconsin	10	11	18	2.0	2.3	12
Mean	12	12	5	2.2	2.1	–4
Median	12	12	3	2.0	2.0	–6
Standard deviation	3	3	18	0.5	0.4	15
N	37	37	37	37	37	37
Correlation			0.83			0.76

Source: Authors' compilation of Census 2000 and ACS 2010 IPUMS Microdata (U.S. Census Bureau n.d.).

Table 1A.6   Total Income Inequality as Measured by Total Theil Index,
Selected States, 2000 and 2010

	2000	2010	Change (%)
Alabama	0.36	0.36	−1
Alaska	0.26	0.28	9
Arizona	0.36	0.37	3
Arkansas	0.37	0.37	−1
California	0.40	0.40	1
Colorado	0.35	0.37	6
Connecticut	0.41	0.44	7
Delaware	0.32	0.34	6
Florida	0.42	0.43	2
Georgia	0.38	0.37	−1
Hawaii	0.37	0.33	−12
Illinois	0.36	0.39	7
Indiana	0.30	0.31	5
Kansas	0.32	0.35	9
Kentucky	0.37	0.36	−2
Louisiana	0.37	0.36	−3
Maryland	0.32	0.34	6
Massachusetts	0.36	0.39	8
Michigan	0.31	0.34	7
Minnesota	0.32	0.36	12
Mississippi	0.38	0.37	−2
Missouri	0.35	0.36	4
Nebraska	0.32	0.33	2
Nevada	0.36	0.36	−2
New Jersey	0.35	0.39	10
New York	0.42	0.47	11
North Carolina	0.36	0.39	8
Ohio	0.32	0.34	4
Oklahoma	0.35	0.37	6
Pennsylvania	0.35	0.36	4
Rhode Island	0.33	0.34	3
South Carolina	0.34	0.36	5
Tennessee	0.39	0.39	0
Texas	0.38	0.39	1
Virginia	0.35	0.36	1
West Virginia	0.36	0.34	−5
Wisconsin	0.30	0.33	11
Mean	0.35	0.36	3.5
Median	0.36	0.36	3.8
Standard deviation	0.0	0.0	5.0
N	37	37	37
Correlation			0.87

Source: Authors' compilation of Census 2000 and 2010 IPUMS Microdata (U.S. Census Bureau n.d.).

Table 1A.7   Between-Race Theil as Percentage of Total Theil (Percentage of Total Income Inequality Attributable to Black-White Income Disparity), Selected States, 2000 and 2010

	2000 (%)	2010 (%)	Change (percentage points)
Alabama	2.9	4.0	1.1
Alaska	0.5	0.4	–0.2
Arizona	0.5	0.7	0.1
Arkansas	1.4	2.3	0.9
California	1.7	2.0	0.3
Colorado	0.7	0.9	0.3
Connecticut	2.1	2.7	0.5
Delaware	3.0	2.9	–0.1
Florida	2.8	3.4	0.6
Georgia	4.3	5.0	0.7
Hawaii	1.1	0.7	–0.5
Illinois	2.3	2.6	0.3
Indiana	0.5	1.0	0.5
Kansas	0.5	1.2	0.7
Kentucky	0.3	0.6	0.3
Louisiana	4.9	7.1	2.2
Maryland	4.0	4.5	0.5
Massachusetts	0.9	1.5	0.6
Michigan	0.9	1.7	0.9
Minnesota	0.5	1.0	0.5
Mississippi	5.0	7.2	2.2
Missouri	0.8	1.4	0.6
Nebraska	0.4	1.4	0.9
Nevada	0.9	2.0	1.1
New Jersey	3.3	3.6	0.3
New York	2.7	3.0	0.3
North Carolina	3.1	3.7	0.5
Ohio	1.2	2.2	1.0
Oklahoma	0.9	1.7	0.8
Pennsylvania	1.1	1.8	0.6
Rhode Island	0.9	2.2	1.2
South Carolina	4.4	5.2	0.8
Tennessee	1.1	1.8	0.6
Texas	2.9	4.0	1.2
Virginia	3.3	3.7	0.4
West Virginia	0.3	0.3	0.1
Wisconsin	0.5	1.3	0.8
Mean	1.9	2.5	0.6
Median	1.1	2.0	0.6
Standard deviation	1.4	1.7	0.5
N	37	37	37
Correlation			0.96

Source: Authors' compilation of Census 2000 and 2010 IPUMS Microdata (U.S. Census Bureau n.d.).

NOTES

1. This is partly a result of large decreases in Democratic vote share among whites and increases among blacks in those states but also attributable to the extremity of ratios in both years in those states, as ratios are particularly sensitive to changes that result in a very small denominator becoming smaller (in this case, the white vote for the Democratic candidate).
2. We do not consider wealth, an indicator on which black-white differences are dramatically higher.
3. The Bureau of Labor Statistics assigns a particular high value (a top code) to any income whose level, compared with others in the same geographic area, might allow the precise determination of the respondent's identity.
4. It is important to note that terms of employment relate not merely to salary or wages but to the general conditions of work. What is at stake in such noncompensatory issues is not only safety and comfort but, in many instances, individuals' sense of dignity, that is, their belief that they are both valued and treated fairly by their employers. One need not ruminate too long over differences in the workplace experiences of college professors and sewing machine operators to see the relevance of this point.
5. A full description of this typology is available in any of Goldthorpe's works cited here. Briefly, the seven categories are ordered in this way: class 1, higher-grade professionals, administrators, and officials; managers in large industrial establishments; and proprietors of large businesses; class 2, lower-grade professionals (for example, medical technicians); class 3, routine non–manual service employees (for example, secretaries); class 4, proprietors of small businesses, artisans, and farmers; class 5, lower-grade technicians (for example, dental hygienists); class 6, skilled manual workers (for example, tool and die makers); and class 7, semiskilled and unskilled manual workers (for example, lathe machine operators).
6. Throughout this section, it is important to recognize that our averages across states do not weight for population size within states. Thus our descriptive statistics refer to trends in the median welfare of black and white populations across states rather than to overall trends in income gaps within the whole United States.

REFERENCES

Abramowitz, Alan I. 2011. "The 2010 Midterm Elections: Aberration or Return to Normal?" *Extensions: A Journal of the Carl Albert Congressional Research and Studies Center*, Summer: 12–18.

Barrilleaux, Charles, Thomas Holbrook, and Laura Langer. 2002. "Electoral Competition, Legislative Balance, and American State Welfare Policy." *American Journal of Political Science* 46(2): 415–27.

Brown, Robert. 1995. "Party Cleavages and Welfare Effort in the American States." *American Political Science Review* 89(1): 23–33.

Bullock, Charles S., III, and Bruce Campbell. 1984. "Racist or Racial Voting in the 1981 Atlanta Municipal Elections." *Urban Affairs Review* 20(2): 149.

Conceicao, Pedro, and Pedro Ferreira (2000). "A Young Person's Guide to the Theil Index: Suggestive Intuitive Interpretations and Exploring Analytical Applications." University Texas Inequality Project Working Paper No. 14.

Early, Gerald L. (2008). "The End of Race as We Know It." *The Chronicle Review* 55(7): B11. Available at: www.chronicle.com/article/The-End-of-Race-as-We -Know-It/3343 (accessed January 10, 2013).

Economic Policy Institute. 2011. *Ten Facts about the Recovery*. July 6.

Erikson, Robert, and John H. Goldthorpe. 2002. "Intergenerational Inequality: A Sociological Perspective." *Journal of Economic Perspectives* 16(3): 31–44.

Erikson, Robert, John H. Goldthorpe, and Lucianne Portocarero. 1979. "Intergenerational Class Mobility in Three Western European Societies: England, France, and Sweden." *British Journal of Sociology* 30(4): 415–30.

Gilens, Martin. 2003. "How the Poor Became Black." In *Race and the Politics of Welfare Reform*, edited by Sanford F. Schram, Joe Soss, and Richard C. Fording. Ann Arbor: University of Michigan Press.

Goldthorpe, John H. 1987. *Social Mobility and Class Structure in Britain*. 2nd ed. Oxford: Clarendon Press.

Goldthorpe, John H., and Walter Mueller. 1982. *Social Mobility and Class Formation in Industrial Nations: Proposal for a Comparative Research Project*. Oxford: Mannheim.

Hacker, Jacob S., and Paul Pierson. 2010. *Winner-Take-All Politics: How Washington Made the Rich Richer and Turned Its Back on the Middle Class*. New York: Simon and Schuster.

Hero, Rodney E. 1998. *Faces of Inequality: Social Diversity in American Politics*. New York: Oxford University Press.

Hill, Kim Quaile, and Jan E. Leighley. 1992. "The Policy Consequences of Class Bias in State Electorates." *American Journal of Political Science* 36(2): 351–65.

Key, V. O., Jr. 1949. *Southern Politics—in State and Nation*. Knoxville: University of Tennessee Press.

Krugman, Paul. 2007. "The Conscience of a Liberal." *New York Times*. Available at: Krugman.blogs.nytimes.com/2007/09/18/introducing-this-blog.com (accessed January 28, 2013).

Lee, Taeku. 2011. "Somewhere Over the Rainbow? Post-Racial & Pan-Racial Politics in the Age of Obama." *Daedalus* 140(2): 136–50.

Morgan, Stephen L., and Mark W. McKerrow. 2004. "Social Class, Rent Destruction, and the Earnings of Black and White Men, 1982–2000." In *Inequality: Struc-*

tures, Dynamics, and Mechanisms: Essays in Honor of Aage B. Sorensen. Research in Social Stratification and Mobility, Volume 1. Amsterdam: Elsevier.

Peterson, Paul E. 1981. *City Limits.* Chicago: University of Chicago Press.

Putnam, Robert D. 2000. *Bowling Alone: The Collapse and Revival of American Community.* New York: Simon and Schuster.

Radcliff, Benjamin, and Martin Saiz. 1995. "Race, Turnout, and Public Policy in the American States." *Political Research Quarterly* 48(4): 775–94.

Roper Center. 2004, 2008. National Election Pool Exit Polls. University of Connecticut. Accessed April 19, 2012.

Smith, Rogers M. 1997. *Civic Ideals: Conflicting Visions of Citizenship in U.S. History.* New Haven, Conn.: Yale University Press.

Soss, Joe, et al. 2001. "Setting the Terms of Relief: Explaining State Policy Choices in the Devolution Evolution." *American Journal of Political Science* 45(2): 378–95.

Tesler, Michael, and David O. Sears. 2010. *Obama's Race: The 2008 Election and the Dream of a Post-Racial America.* Chicago: University of Chicago Press.

Tocqueville, Alexis de. (1848) 1966. *Democracy in America.* Edited by J. P. Mayer. New York: Harper & Row.

U.S. Census Bureau. n.d. 2000 Census and 2009–2011 American Community Survey. Microdata assembled by Steven Ruggles, J. Trent Alexander, Katie Genadek, Ronal Goeken, Matthew B. Schroeder, and Matthew Sobek. Integrated Public Use Microdata Series: Version 5.0 (Machine-Readable Database). Minneapolis: University of Minnesota.

Vobejda, Barbara. 1996. "Clinton Signs Welfare Bill Amid Division." *Washington Post*, August 23, A01.

Washington, Jesse. 2011. "The Disappearing Black Middle Class," *Chicago Sun Times*, July 10. Available at: www.suntimes.com/business/6397110-420/the-disappearing-black-middle-class.html (accessed September 20, 2012).

Wolfinger, Raymond, and Steven J. Rosenstone. 1980. *Who Votes?* New Haven, Conn.: Yale University Press.

Chapter 2 | The American State as an Agent of Race Equity: The Systemic Limits of Shock and Awe in Domestic Policy

Desmond King

THE HISTORICAL INFIRMITY of the American state in ameliorating the nation's searing racial inequalities is notable. It is even more striking when set against the same state's gargantuan military, fiscal, cultural, ideological, and political capacities, which have enabled the United States to dominate modern affairs since the Second World War and to maintain legitimacy at home. These raw capacities are described in this chapter as "shock and awe," a shorthand for the set of formidable policy measures and resources the U.S. political executive draws on to set the agenda and sometimes to achieve policy priorities (Weir and Skocpol 1985; Posner and Vermeule 2010, 11–12). The announcement may be more dramatic than the execution, but the aura of massive policy attack is irrefragable. Such engagements as Harry Truman's Hiroshima, Lyndon Johnson's War on Poverty, and George W. Bush's "war" on terrorism exemplify what James Scott (1998) memorably terms "seeing like a state," with its implied allocation of state power.

Yet this American state rarely sees profound race inequality as a priority for national action. The multiple material inequalities documented in this volume and elsewhere (Cohen 2010; Smith and King 2009) in African American housing and education opportunities and encounters with the criminal justice system, for instance, are grounds for a national restorative policy, but none is forthcoming. These unequal patterns are not construed as crises by the American state at present. Historically, it is the exclusion of

73

African Americans from equality instead of ameliorating inequities that attracts state support (Katznelson 2005). The American state's ample resources to intervene in U.S. society were deployed from the 1880s to the 1950s to maintain race inequity in the separate-but-equal governance institutions.

In the mid-1960s, in the wake of the enactment of the Civil Rights Act, President Lyndon Johnson's adviser, the Harvard professor Daniel Patrick Moynihan, wrote a famous report declaring that legal equality for African Americans was crucial but needed immediately to be followed with a plan of "national action" to destroy material legacies of America's history of slavery and Jim Crow segregation (Moynihan 1965). Moynihan's imperative reached President Johnson. In his Howard University commencement speech, "To Fulfill These Rights," drafted by Moynihan and delivered in June 1965, Johnson conceded that freedom is not enough to rectify the searing damage of centuries of race inequality and systemic discrimination: "In far too many ways American Negroes have been another nation: deprived of freedom, crippled by hatred, the doors of opportunity closed to hope." National action, in Moynihan's view, meant at least a guaranteed family allowance, a massive employment program guaranteeing jobs, proper adoption and family planning services, and education and housing initiatives (Johnson 1965).

Moynihan's call for national action and Johnson's admission about the feeble policy response to enduring material inequities followed the culmination of decades of protests, which produced the Civil Rights Act of 1964. Johnson's and Moynihan's entreaties predated by a couple of months' enactment of the Voting Rights Act of 1965. Combined, these two laws created the potential for a postracial America, establishing equal rights of legal and democratic citizenship; however, the persistence of entrenched discrimination and systemic inequality precluded this possibility. One less important explanation is the content and reception of the so-called Moynihan Report, published in 1965, entitled *The Negro Family: The Case for National Action* (Moynihan 1965). As is well known, the report, intended by its author Moynihan, who was then based in the U.S. Department of Labor, and President Johnson to formulate a comprehensive strategy for helping African Americans, became mired in controversy about its characterization of African American families. The report's apparent judgmentalism on African American family structures overshadowed its policy recommendations, and these latter rapidly receded from the pool of American state actions.

In understanding the challenge, Moynihan emphasized that the sudden granting of equal rights of citizenship could not be taken as equivalent to providing equal material income or future opportunity. But the sociological evidence he compiled while writing the report shifted his focus to the African American family structure and what he unhelpfully came to term the "tangle of pathology": "The Negro community has been forced into a matriarchical structure which, because it is so out of line with the rest of American society, seriously retards the progress of the group as a whole, and imposes a crushing burden on the Negro male and, in consequence, on a great many Negro women as well" (Moynihan 1965, 31). The report contained copious data about low wage rates, limited employment opportunities, poor education attainment, and numerous other factors that contributed to economic inequality facing African Americans and demonstrating a knowledge of major African American research findings such as W. E. B. Du Bois's (1996) work on Philadelphia and the writings of Kenneth Clark (1965) and Franklin Frazier (1939) (Patterson 2010). Nonetheless, Moynihan's conclusions focused primarily on the family crisis: "In a word, a national effort toward the problems of Negro Americans must be directed towards the question of family structure" (Moynihan 1965, 47).

Because of Moynihan's failure to attend to the overpowering significance of structural factors such as housing, schools, and proper jobs, the report became an easy target for African Americans, to whom the writer was an outsider, and for whom racism was not an academic issue. Moynihan was not presenting a simplistic cultural account of the issues, but his focus on the structure of African American families was curiously disconnected from the structural context of that structure. He did support a rigorous national program—the "national action" in the report's title—consistent with what came to be understood as affirmative action combined with family allowances, job schemes, and so forth. But this aspiration got drowned out in the negative response to other parts of his report (for a summary, see Patterson 2010, chap. 4).

What is interesting about the Moynihan controversy for this volume's thematic purposes is that from the mid-1950s, for a brief period of a decade and a half, the American state did see race inequity—at least, when inequality violated norms and formal rules of democratic citizenship—as a key priority and did bring to bear its shock-and-awe resources on the problem. The American state, in the exercise of concentrated policy initiative by the executive and its bureaucratic agencies such as the Department of Justice and the Equal Employment Opportunity Commission and with support from the Supreme Court, proved capable of mobilizing to address race inequities when a crisis strikes (and thereby to employ the shock-and-awe resources observable in other policy areas). Such executive engagement requires bypassing the institutional constraints on executive power embodied in both the separation of powers and in federalism. But why has this level of national action eluded advocates of a decisive response to material race inequalities of the scope and depth prerequisite to shifting to a postracist society?

These issues prompt a broader query. Why has the American state at certain times and under certain conditions taken direct measures to address race inequity? When does the U.S. state see race as an issue? This chapter focuses on the conditions that enabled the executive to respond to a crisis in race inequity in the 1950s and 1960s to analyze the conditions and circumstances under which such American state action occurs. Two factors are crucial to understanding the state activism of the 1950s and 1960s: First, the time and context—already much documented by scholars—shows the force of the civil rights movement in domestic politics and the international Cold War pressure (Morris 1984; Klinkner and Smith 1999; Dudziak 2000; McAdam 1982). Second, the denial of civil and voting rights had reached crisis proportions, and the opportunity and willingness of the executive to act was unusually high, especially because, unlike reform to material race inequities, civil rights required legal reform and enforcement rather than a massive exercise in economic redistribution.

SHOCK AND AWE: FROM FAIR EMPLOYMENT PRACTICES TO TROUBLED ASSETS RELIEF

From the late 1930s and through the Second World War years the crisis that race inequality posed in and for American democratic politics was explosive (Johnson 2010; Morris 1984; Myrdal 1944; Parker 2009). War mobilization did not just intensify the grassroots movement against race inequity and the segregationist racial order. It demonstrated the capacity of American state officeholders to use concentrated national authority and enforcement capacity significantly to advance the meaning of race equity (Kryder 2000). President Franklin D. Roosevelt's issuance of Executive Order 8802 in June 1941 establishing a Fair Employment Practices Committee responded to the threatened March on Washington organized by A. Philip Randolph (King 2007, 25, 74–75). Equipped with hesitant powers of implementation and denied permanent status by Congress in 1946, nonetheless the committee demonstrated the ability of the executive to marshal national American state resources toward the goal of reducing race inequality (Frymer 2004).

The Fair Employment Practices Committee set a trajectory that took an egregiously long period to mature (through such actions as desegregating the Armed Forces, the Brown decision in 1954, and civil rights legislation) but nonetheless proved to be the first step of an irreversible journey to enact equal rights of citizenship for African Americans. What is striking, however, is the enduring reluctance since mid-twentieth century to push this journey along with what I term the shock-and-awe tools used by the American state to resolve comparable crises in public order and challenges from social inequality in two respects: first, the slowness to pass civil rights laws and second, the reluctance to step beyond legal equality to the sort of national action, advocated, for instance, in Moynihan's 1965 report, required to abrogate material inequities. Thus while the misery of many New Orleanians' lives exposed by Hurricane Katrina prompted the president, George W. Bush, to call for the use of "greater federal authority" and "military resources" (Bush 2005, 1408) in addressing American society's ills, to many proponents of race equity the prior question ignored in Bush's remarks was important: Why have the American state's vast resources and capacities not been a greater tool of intervention toward this goal? It certainly has used these resources on other occasions.

Crises enable the political executive legitimately to mobilize otherwise fractious and conflicting centers of political power and interest, institutionalized in the separation of powers designed to constrain centralized authority, to set out priorities and agendas, to channel new resources through energized bureaucratic agencies, and to declare or delegate emergency powers. War is an obvious and often dramatic instance (the attack on Pearl Harbor in Hawaii ineluctably put the United States at war), but other domestic or international events have a comparable impact on the central state's authority and responsibility to act (Dudziak 2012; Sparrow 2011).

The power of crises has a further consequence. Crises may be contrived to empower the political executive to embark on a new initiative with the sort of concentrated policy focus familiar from warlike circumstances. For instance, declaring war on an inanimate target—such as poverty, illegal drugs consumption, crime, or even inflation—is a strategy to which many White House incumbents have resorted. The militarization of the U.S. border and domestic detention policy toward undocumented immigrants since the 1990s has the trappings of a war.

Although the extensive activist apparatus of taxing, spending, regulating, and standardizing continues—if somewhat imperceptibly for many Americans (Howard 1997, 2007; Mettler 2011)—historically, the American state is mobilized most forcefully and visibly in conditions of crisis rather than of routine politics. Social disorder, public health epidemics, financial system meltdown, war, or the threat of war elicit concentrated policy responses; indeed, crisis is such a powerful stimulus to executives wishing to mobilize state power that resorting to warlike or mimicking strategies is common.

Crisis is rarely an objective condition. The decades during which lynchings of African Americans often numbered more than a hundred a year did not prove a crisis of sufficient importance to warrant federal action in the

1920s and 1930s. This violent form of disorder elicited only failure in national institutions to enact antilynching laws, and after the failure of the Dyer bill in 1923 the issue disappeared as a congressional priority for two decades, despite the continuation of the murderous practice. George W. Bush did not perceive Hurricane Katrina as a crisis warranting federal action until the political fallout of failing to act made such action a matter of urgency.

But in contrast to Katrina, the American state's response to the post–September 2008 fiscal meltdown demonstrates its formidable resources and capacity to engage in massive policy attack. Faced, in the final months of his presidency, with an imminent global market implosion and liquidity crisis, George W. Bush delegated authority to his treasury secretary, Hank Paulson, who worked with the chairman of the Federal Reserve, Ben Bernanke, to prop up the collapsing U.S. banking sector. The American state response was substantial, beginning with the generous $700 billion Troubled Asset Relief Program and followed with almost daily government responses to the U.S. financial crisis in the fall of 2008. The American state was still hard at work on the fiscal crisis on March 18, 2009, when Bernanke announced the expenditure of $300 billion to purchase U.S. government debt, raising the Fed's balance sheet to more than $3 trillion, close to a third of the size of the U.S. economy.[1]

Commonly viewed as a stopgap to offset immediate distress, in fact pumping trillions of dollars in loans, buyouts, and guarantees into the U.S. economy to shore up the financial sector is the culmination of a half century of activist state expansion, an activism refined during wartime (Sparrow 2011). Since the 1950s the American state has become an activist and interventionist system of governance, in a process steered as much by Republican presidents such as George W. Bush as by Democrats such as Bill Clinton. This enlarged presence includes not just the reasonably observable changes in taxing, spending, and regulating in the United States—remaking the U.S. state, through "a great transformation," into an "activist state," according to the political scientist Paul Pierson (2007, 19)—but also the deployment of legitimate national authority to social policies such as education and for democratic nation building, defense, and struggles against internal if obscure "enemies" such as illegal drug users and illegal immigrants.

This expanded activism is mirrored in a scholarly literature on the idea and meaning of the U.S. state, commencing with Stephen Skowronek's *Building a New Administrative State* (1982) and the "bringing the state back in" research agenda orchestrated by Ira Katznelson and Theda Skocpol (see Evans et al. 1985). Scholars document the specificity and materiality of the American state (see Katznelson 2005; Mettler 2009, 2010) in studies that include Margaret Weir and Theda Skocpol's (1985) seminal comparative study of U.S., British, and Swedish state responses to the Great Depression in the 1930s and taken up in an impressive outpouring of articles and monographs by political scientists and historians (which includes Balogh 2009; Dobbin and Sutton 1998; Edling 2003; Frymer 2004; Johnson 2007, 2009; Katznelson 2005; Kryder 2000; Lieberman 2009; Novak 2008; Sheingate 2009; Skowronek 2009; Stears 2002, 2010; and Ward 2005).

Although comparatively the U.S. federal government or American state has access to exceptional resources (military, fiscal and economic, cultural, and bureaucratic), because of constitutionally divided power the deployment of a concentrated massive policy response is far from automatic and more infrequent than common. But as Adam Sheingate (2009, 2) remarks, this literature and other research finds that "what is distinctive about the American state, . . . is where, by whom and for what purpose public authority is exercised," not the exercise of that public authority itself. This exercise of public authority was practiced forcefully in response to the 9/11 terrorist attacks, as it has been in responding to earlier crises and is perceptible in America's escalation of quasi-military resources against illegal immigrants. And rarely has the raw content and scale of American state power and exercise of public authority been as pellucid as in the response to the post–August 2008 Great Recession.

This enhanced American state activism and use of public authority includes the legislative, judicial, and executive programs democratizing the race inequities in the United States in the 1950s and 1960s, inequities constitutive at the nation's founding (Smith 1993, 1997), maintained and reformulated in shifting racial orders with observable legacies in contemporary America (King and Smith 2005, 2011). Scholars now acknowledge the historical and contemporary importance of American state activity—or, on occasion, purposeful inactivity—in shaping patterns of race inequity.

THE AMERICAN STATE AND RACE: FROM OPPRESSOR TO REFORMER TO SPENT FORCE

The history of the American state's engagement with issues of race equity between the mid-nineteenth and mid-twentieth centuries is an unhappy one, illustrating the importance of how the state sees race. This is the era of the "segregated state, the decades during which the U.S. federal government not only failed to uphold equal rights but actively fostered segregated race relations in government departments and agencies (King 2007; Lieberman 1998). The federal government was part of a segregationist racial order, consolidated from the 1890s, when the Plessy (Plessy v. Ferguson, 163 U.S. 537 [1896]) ruling legitimated the "separate but equal" pretense, and in place until the 1960s (King and Smith 2005), through which all policies—such as the New Deal programs or wartime mobilization in addition to education and transport—were established on the premise of separate facilities for African Americans to parallel those for white Americans.

This arrangement was not merely about separate facilities but also about separate governance. As federal government activism grew from the 1930s, ushering in an era of New Deal programs, so the disproportionate (and often inferior) inclusion of African American citizens unfolded. Ira Katznelson (2005, x) succinctly dubs this era as one "when affirmative action was white" and writes that "policy decisions dealing with welfare, work, and war during Jim Crow's last hurrah in the 1930s and 1940s excluded, or differentially treated, the vast majority of African Americans. . . . Inequality, in fact, increased at the insistence of southern representatives in Congress, while their other congressional colleagues were complicit. As a result of the legislation they passed, blacks became even more significantly disadvantaged when a modern American middle class was fashioned during and after the Second World War." Thus as national policy makers used American state power to expand national capacities and intervention in society, they not only demonstrated the enhanced resources and capacities—the genesis of shock-and-awe powers—but did so in a way that purposefully exacerbated race inequity. For those discriminated against and disappointed in this process, the American state was anything but weak or invisible or "out of sight" as understood in the conventional understanding (Nettl 1968).

State segregation was not confined to employment programs, however; it pervaded departments of the federal government and their field offices in the North as well as the South. The principles of segregation imbued the development of federal housing policy to underwrite mortgages and mortgage insurance as it developed from the 1930s; this legacy endures in American cities' residential divisions.

The segregated state was not merely epiphenomenal on a segregated society. It was an active agent of the discriminatory policies. In the 1890s and 1900s, for instance, the U.S. Civil Service Commission regularly reported the employment of African American graduates from black colleges in the federal government; this practice ended in 1915 as civil service recruitment was modified to exclude African Americans. Another example comes from the work of the U.S. Bureau of Prisons, which from its establishment in 1930 monitored and enforced racial segregation in U.S. federal penitentiaries (Gottschalk 2006). This was not an instance of simply responding to societal pressures but involved embedding segregationist practices in institutional rules and procedures. It is notable how successful the American state proved as an enforcer of the segregationist racial order in the century to the 1960s. National action solidified race inequality by giving it state authority.

Inactivity in certain areas was equally a hallmark of the segregated state. Initiatives to get the executive and legislature to outlaw lynching, for instance, failed in the 1920s and was not implemented until several years after the Second World War. Voting rights violations gained little attention from the Justice Department until late in the 1950s, when, under the impetus of the civil rights movement, department officials began monitoring abuses and enforcing federal standards.

Then, in what appears historically as a remarkable transformation, the world of segregation imploded in the 1950s and 1960s, decisive reform legislation to establish civil and voting rights was enacted in the mid-1960s in a Congress energized by President Lyndon Johnson, and executive agencies were either enhanced or created to enforce the new democratic standards (Frymer 2004, 2005). The scope of these standards, however, is contested: even Justice Department enforcement of civil rights measures and monitoring of voting rights violations fluctuates with presidencies (this division was downgraded under the George W. Bush administration and revived by Obama under the auspices of his attorney general, Eric Holder). The need to address enduring material race inequities in housing, education, income, health care, and employment discrimination specifically gained recognition for a decade from 1957 but never became a national priority. These inequalities and the surge in African American incarceration rates strike many observers as crises (Alexander 2010; Barker 2009; Manza and Uggen 2006; Murakawa 2008; Simon 2007; Wacquant 2009; Weaver 2007; Western 2005; Western and Petit 2005), but not crises that have yet attracted significant American state policy engagement. Explaining this unevenness of American state activity and particularly the activism of the 1950s is my concern here.

AMERICAN STATE ACTIVISM FOR RACE EQUITY IN THE 1950S AND 1960S: A TYPOLOGY

Many scholars ponder the implications for policy implementation arising from the distinct bureaucratic structures of the American state. Civil servants spend careers in one department or agency rather than moving between them to create an elite cadre; the most senior appointments in these departments are party political rather than meritocratic (Carpenter 2001; Poggi 1990, 23; and see Novak 2008). In a recent paper Desmond King and

Robert Lieberman (2009) argue that these patterns give the American state comparatively distinct policy-making capacities. They identify five dimensions of the American state, including its role as a standardizer, that is, the task of setting and enforcing uniform standards within a given national territory such as democratic rights. On this view, standardization is not just a means of "seeing like a state," as James Scott's (1998) memorable phrase has it, it is a key aspect of being a state. The American state can thus be recognized, at least in part, by its efforts to standardize: efforts that range from engagement in measurement, census taking, and employment of statistics in the very early days of the Republic to enforcing patterns of and rights to democratic participation and attempts to engrain uniform moral beliefs across a diverse citizenry in the twentieth century (Desrosieres 1998, 188–209; Kelman 1987). But it is pertinent to reverse the focus and to ask what forces the American state to see race inequity as a pressing problem meriting action and policy response.

Achieving democratic standards to end race inequities is an important aspect of state legitimacy and presents a key activity for agents of the national state. In the United States, democratizing rights and representative institutions has been a comparatively agonizingly slow process because of the way in which state power was used until the middle of the twentieth century to curtail rather than to establish and enforce equal rights of citizenship (Katznelson 2005; Tuck 2009; Valelly 2004).

America's race inequities from the mid-twentieth century on have frequently presented as crises in national politics. Some of these eruptions are immediate—police attacks on civil rights marchers in Birmingham, Alabama, or the Little Rock standoff—and others slow burning—the decades' long build-up to declaring separate-but-equal segregation unconstitutional in Brown (1954), or the final enactment of voting rights enforcement powers by Congress, or the tortuous years of protest to get antilynching laws established. All constitute conditions which the state may wish to ignore but cannot, as disregarding the crisis merely permits and invites intensification of the underlying condition.

Three types of national action characterize the ways in which the American state has acted to address some of those race inequities as they explode into politics and elicit policy responses, whether the latter are designed merely to shore up the crisis or intended to provide long-term resolution: the state creates new standards; it uses coercive state power; and it initiates societal reform. Mobilization and enforcement of high levels of targeted policy activism are rendered institutionally complex by the fragmented American state: unlike centralized political systems exercising legitimate leadership, the U.S. political system requires unusual rather than routine circumstances. However, the American state can be effectively

Table 2.1   American State Responses to the Race Inequity Crises of the 1950s and 1960s

Response	Crisis	Does crisis overcome separated powers?	Is policy activism sufficient to end crisis?
Creating new state standards	Civil Rights Act of 1964; Voting Rights Act of 1965; Fair Housing Act of 1968	Yes	No
Coercive state power	Fair Employment Practices Commission, 1941; Little Rock, Arkansas, 1957; Public order in cities, 1965 and 1966; Attorney General Robert Kennedy and Alabama; Mississippi university education	Yes	Yes
State-led societal reform	School desegregation; housing desegregation	No	No

Source: Author's compilation.

mobilized in response to crises, including crises in race inequity and injustice. The resources and capacities available to the political executive means that the American state can deliver concentrated policy attacks. The content and success or failure of national policy initiatives turns on how, if at all, a new policy or heightened policy activism in response to a crisis is sufficient, first, to overcome the constraints of separated powers in the U.S. polity and second, relatedly, to resolve the crisis circumstances (table 2.1).

The major laws enacted in the 1960s, including the Civil Rights Act of 1964, the Voting Rights Act of 1965, and, to a lesser extent, the Fair Housing Act of 1968, are the prototype in creating new standards by which equal rights of citizenship and other measures are upheld. These new rights need not just to be promulgated but also to be enforced, which requires other types of American state activity. But the key aspect of this type of action is the creation of touchstone standards that citizens can look to the American state to provide. That it took almost two hundred years and a massive civil rights movement struggle to get the standards established is indicative of how precious they are for democratization.

Coercive state power involves speedy executive action in response to specific threats. The executive uses powers and resources it possesses independently of judicial or congressional challenges. Examples include President Franklin D. Roosevelt's executive order establishing a Fair Employment Practices Committee in 1941 and President Dwight Eisenhower's deployment of federalized national guards to Little Rock, Arkansas, in October 1957. This type of state power is designed to restrain disorderly behavior and above all to maintain public order.

Many changes require engaged processes of social and economic change. This is particularly apparent in such changes as the desegregation of housing and schools. These are state led in that new standards are institutionalized but the state pushes leadership for the changes onto societal actors, notably communities. Lacking a coercive edge and often enjoying judicial protection for the weakest version of the reform, communities and citizens mostly obfuscate, resist, and dilute the changes.

The three types are created by distinguishing between events that either succeed or fail in empowering the executive to overcome the constitutionally constraining separation of powers and between the levels of the policy response. The varying policy outcomes speak to the issue of the stubborn "stickiness" of racial inequality by showing that activism is greater for the short than long term. Inevitably, these categories are overdrawn and overlap in numerous ways. But the framework provides a starting point.

Crises vary. I allude mostly to significant breakdowns or threatened breakdowns in public order that local authorities either encourage or fail to control. In this context *crisis* alludes also to enduring issues of systemic discrimination and segregation. For example, the marches led by Martin Luther King Jr. to protest segregated housing prompted legislation in 1968 after King's assassination, but the underlying problem of discrimination was not resolved. These distinctions can be explained in part by the dynamics generating crises and by consideration of who in society is affected by the crisis.

DYNAMICS OF THE AMERICAN STATE AND RACE EQUITY CRISES

Six sorts of factors help differentiate the types of American state responses to crises over race inequity. Not every factor is manifest in each crisis, but several are, and how they interact helps determine the state's policy response. First, whether reforming legislation has been enacted affects the authority and legitimacy of American state policy enforcement. The Voting Rights Act of 1965 augmented the Justice Department's powers and legitimacy. Of course, legislation is no guarantee of legitimacy or effectiveness, as the tepid content of the Civil Rights Act in 1957 with respect to desegregation or weak antilynching laws shows, but it can be a firm point of minimum standards. Second, the willingness of the president to use executive orders to enforce agreed national policy has often proved critical to change over the long term, though its short-term effect is to stem rather than prevent a crisis (Howell 2003; Mayer 2001, 2009; Robinson 2001). Ordering the mobilization of national troops is a dramatic step to maintain order in an explosive situation but rarely resolves the underlying source of conflict. Third, and related, is the powers of enforcement used by the American state, distinguished by being either emergency powers (such as troops deployment) or routinized (such as referral to mediating bodies, which became common as enforcement of civil rights developed from the 1960s democratizing laws [Frymer 2005; Skrentny 2006]).

Fourth, the strength and violence or potential violence of local resistance to reducing race inequity is a key determinant of the scale and significance of American state responses. Historically, resistance is spread widely, with elected officeholders, law enforcement officials, and prosegregationist whites having the potential to mobilize separately or collectively toward a cumulative purpose (Kryder 1999; Simon 2007); routine politics can also dissipate the efforts of American state initiatives to address race inequity (Weir 2005). Governor Orval Faubus's failure to act in Little Rock, Arkansas, in 1957 encouraged police officers to ignore whites' thuggery toward African Americans. In Selma, Alabama, in 1965 the local sheriff assaulted local African Americans attempting to register to vote; and as the political scientist Richard Valelly (2004, 193) records, on February 18, 1965, "in the nearby town of Marion, the Alabama state police attacked reporters from NBC News and the *New York Times* and launched a frenzied attack on black citizens." But resistance to busing policy in the 1970s was orchestrated without such obvious law enforcement connivance. The greater the general opposition, the more robust any effective American state policy initiative needs to be.

Fifth, the power and influence of the civil rights movement's activists and reformers affects American state policy response to race inequity (Johnson 2010). Protest stretches from nonviolent demonstration and marching to political engagement directly with the White House (Harris 2006). These varied expressions of demand for the American state to act to address a crisis commonly interact with other pressures on the executive. Sixth, the international context of America's race inequity crises shapes executive action, even when the executive has wished to resist taking the initiative (Dudziak 2000; Klinkner and Smith 1999). President Kennedy's reluctant involvement in discrimination in housing and restaurants was forced on him by the complaints of African State ambassadors in Washington and even New York and on Maryland's Highway 40 (Dudziak 2000, 167–69). The American state feared the effect of images of African American civil rights activists being brutalized and mistreated beamed around the world.

Equally germane to these six factors are those actors who trammel the use of effective state power. In retrospect, the enforcement of integration and the attack on race inequality looks weak: when public order broke down or teetered on the edge of anarchy, national action was almost unavoidable and forthcoming, but using that action to ameliorate underlying issues and causes was rare. Furthermore, the American state did not face deep threats from corporate interests or threats of economic boycott to state revenues, suggesting that its timidity was about political unwillingness to use public authority for race equity. But effective action required sustained engagement either through the use of shock-and-awe resources, including military presence, or by fostering change by stealth with expanded fiscal resources to local institutions, such as universities, Justice Department personnel to counter rolling law suits, and national programs targeted on enduring material deprivations.

AMERICAN STATE RESPONSES IN ADDRESSING RACE INEQUITY: ILLUSTRATIONS

As table 2.1 sets out, there is a typology of national American state responses to racial inequality. In this section, I examine each type using examples from the 1950s and 1960s.

Creating and Enforcing New State Standards

A new statutory law with appropriate resources for enforcement is the most effective American state type of response to race inequity. In principle, it combines the branches of government through unitary action. Legislation can be passed—such as the 1957 and 1960 civil rights laws—bereft of appropriate powers of implementation, which postpones dealing with enduring problems. Or meaningful reform can be enacted but a lack of political will or public authority precludes American state enforcement. The state creates and enforces new state standards when the crisis forces a policy response of sufficient magnitude to overcome intransigence in one institution that is historically a hindrance to change. Thus the passage of the Civil Rights Act in 1964 and the Voting Rights Act in 1965 both benefited from a decisive White House incumbent—Lyndon Johnson, abandoning his segregationist origins—whose efforts defeated the traditionally obstructive role of the Congress, which had subverted numerous previous bills designed to achieve similar change.

Numerous of the six factors were at work compelling executive enforcement from the American state, including international reproach of Americans' tolerance of discrimination toward African American citizens, a galvanized and long-standing civil rights movement, a localized resistance opposition whose nastiness was captured on television, and executive commitment both in the White House and in agencies and departments, such as Justice, to fundamental reform.

Contingency mattered. The assassination of President John F. Kennedy undoubtedly helped to carve an opportunity for deeper reform, and the massive Democratic party victory in 1964 signaled a political mandate for national action. Neither effect was automatically translated into legislation, however. The civil rights bill passed the House in February 1964 with a strong majority (290–130), but the Senate filibustered for three months before a cloture motion passed on June 10 (71–29), permitting the legislation to gain a majority. Equally, the beatings of civil rights marchers in Alabama and the brutal killing of Jimmie Lee Jackson in Marion, Alabama, gave Johnson an opportunity to deliver his March 15, 1965, speech to a joint session of Congress galvanizing support for the voting rights bill, which was eventually passed and signed into law on August 6 (Valelly 2004; Keyssar 2000).

The Voting Rights Act of 1965 established federal capacity to intervene in voting registration practices, empowering the Department of Justice to monitor and override state and local agents. This was an instance of concentrated policy action supported in the short term with appropriate resources. The act was explicitly designed to end Jim Crow segregationist disenfranchisement. It suspended voting tests and systems in areas that had registration or turnout below 50 percent of the resident voting-age population in the 1964 elections. The act extended the federal presence in voting arrangements by requiring Justice Department "preclearance" of new voting rules. By proscribing long-standing techniques to prevent African Americans' voting and establishing mechanisms to enforce them, the act soon generated increases in black voter registration and voting (but not office holding in the short term) and was eventually made permanent after contested renewals and Supreme Court rulings. Preclearance was a bitter instrument for defenders of the segregationist order. But it survived judicial review and functions as a key mechanism for ensuring the achievement of standards-setting legislative enforcement by American state power. Yet even in this sphere of American state enforcement, numerous caveats about voting endure, including the at times dubious culling of names from voting registers, as in Florida in 2000, and the use of photo ID requirements to vote that critics charge affect minority voters disproportionately.

State legislative power changes relations in society and affects groups differently. New voting laws threatened white voters and white supremacist officeholders who discriminated against and violently opposed African American citizens trying to vote. The new state power did not challenge any corporate or powerful economic interests directly, which may have helped to get the state to act but in the instance of voting challenged the existing segregationist order in a fundamental way.

Coercive State Power

Coercive power is an expression of American state resources and capacities in circumstances of crisis. Its use by the executive in response to enduring race inequities is frequent. It signals the gravity of crisis for the state. Without action there will be a breakdown in social order or a collapse of vital services. It is very much a top-down state-led conception of crisis, however: the Little Rock resistance embarrassed the United States internationally, whereas lynching failed to garner such attention.

A key instrument of state coercive power is the executive order, which normally carries emergency powers of enforcement sufficient to control the short-term crisis. For the long-term resolution of a crisis executive orders often signal that the issue cannot be ignored, though how long this "long term" will be is hard to predict. Franklin D. Roosevelt's response to the threatened March on Washington by African American war workers in 1941, demanding some federal effort to ensure equality of employment opportunities in the defense industry, was to issue an executive order. Roosevelt simply bypassed the recalcitrant segregationist Congress to issue executive order 8802, "Reaffirming Policy of Full Participation in the Defense Program by All Persons Regardless of Race, Creed, Color or National Origin." The order created the Fair Employment Practices Committee to investigate cases of employment discrimination in war industries (any firm receiving federal procurement contracts directly or indirectly), government employment, and unions. The committee proved the precursor of post-1960s antidiscrimination laws, and thus a harbinger of the long term, but getting to that point was protracted as Congress refused to make the wartime agency permanent and deliberately obstructed proper monitoring of employment practices. But the Fair Employment Practices Committee was the first step toward a nondiscrimination policy and the first instance of the transformation in the federal government's role as a practitioner and defender of segregation into its critic and reformer. The response to the immediate crisis did not resolve the underlining injustice. But it marked more than a symbolic step toward its resolution.

Coercive power violated President Dwight Eisenhower's whole philosophy of how Americans should deal with race inequity and injustice. But Eisenhower was compelled to use this unilateral presidential action in 1957 to address the integration crisis at the high school in Little Rock, Arkansas; the presidential deployment of federal troops was a short-term solution only. Eisenhower's reluctant but decisive action trumped an uninterested Congress and staved off the short-term crisis in favor of upholding a federal judicial ruling—the Brown I (Brown v. Board of Education of Topeka et al., 347 U.S. 483 [1954]) and II (Brown v. Board of Education of Topeka et al., 349 U.S. 294 [1955]) decisions that schools should be integrated because segregation was unconstitutional. But the action was short term in focus.

The objective crisis centered on the enforcement of federal law. The Supreme Court ruled, in 1954, that all American schools should be desegregated and integrated. This outcome was predictably ignored in many districts throughout the country. In 1957 the school board and city mayor of Little Rock (following plans drawn up by the school district superintendent Virgil Blossom in May 1955) ruled that schools within its district should be desegregated and integrated from the academic year beginning in September. The high school authorities agreed, but the Arkansas governor, Orval Faubus, vowed strenuously to resist the planned integration.[2] The governor deployed 270 National Guard troops to Central High School to "protect" against social disorder. The nine African American pupils were discouraged from attending on the first day of term but did present themselves for classes on the second day, accompanied by two white ministers and two African American ministers.

As televised nationwide and around the world, the National Guard troops prevented them from entering the school, a reversal of the role many expected the forces of law and order would assume; the racist taunts and abuse endured by the courageous African American children shocked. And on September 20 a federal judge (following the Supreme Court ruling in May 1955 about enforcing desegregation) ordered Faubus to withdraw the National Guard troops in their role of preventing the African American children from enrolling and to permit integration to occur. The domestic and international political pressure on the White House to enforce federal authority was intense. Republican president Dwight Eisenhower had frequently expressed his doubts about imposing desegregation and was unwilling to assert federal authority through the deployment of federal troops. He now faced a crisis of such proportions that executive action was inevitable.

Nonetheless, for eighteen days after the initial retreat by the nine high school students the White House negotiated feverishly but pointlessly with the Arkansas governor (efforts that included a face-to-face meeting between the president and Faubus in Newport, Rhode Island), while the children were forced to stay at home because of the danger of attack and violence if they tried to attend Central High School. Eruption into violent public disorder was imminent. The chaperoning of the children into the school through a side entrance on September 23 incensed the white mob into generalized attacks on African Americans, unprotected by a disengaged local police force whose 150 members walked away from the violence with their badges removed. The scale of disorder and continued barring of the African American children from school (who were later sneaked out of the school) forced the city mayor to request federal support to maintain order; this request went straight to the White House. Hoping that the mob would disperse, Eisenhower prevaricated but was forced the next day, September 24, to deploy eleven hundred paratroopers to restore order and to federalize the Arkansas National Guard, whom Governor Faubus had used as his anti-integration force. No such employment of federal force to uphold the law and maintain public order because of a race inequity crisis had occurred since the collapse of Reconstruction in 1877. Predictably, Eisenhower defended his action as a means of restoring public order and not as an instrument of desegregation.

This American state action dealt with the crisis in the short term. Eisenhower issued executive order 10730 to deploy the units of the U.S. Army 101st Airborne Division and to federalize the Arkansas National Guard. In so doing, he demonstrated the president's power as commander-in-chief and ultimate arbiter of order. The resistance to integration and the arrival of a federal protection force became fodder for nightly television news worldwide. But the measure failed to overcome the separation of powers constraint on American state action: the paratroopers and federalized Guardsmen remained for a year outside Central High School, permitting eight of the nine African American students to attend, enduring unpleasantness throughout, as did the school principal, who received death threats. Some of the parents of the nine lost their jobs. Reelected as governor the following year, Orval Faubus closed all the schools in Little Rock to preclude desegregation. The 1954 Brown decision was followed up in 1955 by the Supreme Court's injunction that desegregation should proceed "with all deliberate speed," an unreachable prospect—in both the North and the South—without American national federal enforcement of the sort Eisenhower was unwilling to exercise.

The state's action directly challenged citizens, local law enforcement officers, and elected officeholders. It challenged the legitimacy of racists' use of federalism to protect racialist segregation. It did not directly intervene in local business practices (hiring and separated provision), but the implication that these racial arrangements would have to change was clear. Eisenhower's focus was on publicly funded school systems.

The U.S. attorney general during the John Kennedy administration (1961 to 1963), Robert Kennedy, was kept busy fielding a stream of logistical, constitutional, and political challenges rooted in America's segregationist order. His involvement provides another example of coercive state power. The attorney general had numerous exchanges with Alabama governor George Wallace about ending segregation in education (these exchanges occurred in the wake of James Meredith's entry to the University of Mississippi, Oxford, campus in September 1962, where rioting required President Kennedy to deploy federal troops). In April 1963 the following dialogue took place:

> MR. KENNEDY: Do you think it is so horrifying to have a Negro attend the University of Alabama?
>
> GOVERNOR WALLACE: I think it is so horrifying for the federal courts and the central government to rewrite all the law and force upon people that which they don't want.
>
> MR. KENNEDY: But Governor, it is not the central government. We are not rewriting the laws. It is the federal courts that have made a decision and a determination. . . .
>
> GOVERNOR WALLACE: The federal courts rewrote the law in the matter of integration and segregation. (Marshall Papers, 8)

Wallace denounced the 1954 Brown decision. Kennedy reminded the governor that "as well as being a citizen of the State of Alabama, Governor of Alabama you are also a citizen of the United States" (Marshall Papers, 9). Wallace was unmoved, restating, "I will never submit to an order of the federal court ordering the integration of the school system" (Marshall Papers, 17).

The crisis prompting this exchange followed the matriculation of James Meredith at the University of Mississippi six months earlier, an event that helped galvanize the national civil rights crisis. His attendance required federal marshals and troops to accompany him (an exercise in state coercive power) and provoked rioting in which two people lost their lives. Meredith entered the university under a court order asserting his right to attend. Mississippi governor Ross Barnett stood firm with the violent opponents of African American attendance at a university.

Governor Wallace blamed the courts and the Department of Justice for going against "the overwhelming majority [of the people who] are against the matter of integration. The Congress has passed no law regarding integration. It is not the law of the land. It is the law of the case" (Marshall Papers, 20–21). Attorney General Kennedy and Wallace discussed the discrimination against African Americans seeking to register to vote in Alabama, a contorted exchange during which the governor predictably threw back every charge of obstruction and regularly cited civil rights violations in Northern states, such as cities with statutes that excluded black Americans from living in parts of them. But Kennedy did not relent, telling Wallace that his department had a "responsibility" to enforce the law to maintain the "integrity of the courts" and "to that end . . . all of the force behind the Federal Government will be used." This last threat provoked an angry governor: "I know you are going to use all of the force of the Federal Government. In fact, that is what you are telling to me today, if it is necessary you are going to bring troops into Alabama" (Marshall Papers, 49). The threat of deploying federal troops infuriated Wallace, and a heated argument ensued; Kennedy reiterated his wish not to use troops. But the issue would not abate. Wallace replied,

> I am not trying to trick anybody, but of course we do know that troops were used in Mississippi, we know they were used in Arkansas, and we know that you took photographs of the University of Alabama, for what purpose I cannot comprehend other than the use of troop ingress and egress, and you did say, Mr. Kennedy, that you would make full use of the full power of the Federal Government to enforce the orders of the court and protect the integrity of the courts, and the full power of the government necessarily means military power" (Marshall Papers, 49).

The Justice Department and the Kennedy administration anticipated a repeat of the violence seen at the University of Mississippi on Alabama's campuses (Tuscaloosa and Huntsville) in June 1963, when two African American students—Vivian Malone and James Hood—were due to enroll. They were correct. Wallace led Alabama Highway Patrol officers and special deputies to bar the students. In July President Kennedy ordered the governor and his underlings to desist from obstructing desegregation at the state university. A federal court ruled in June 1963 that Malone and Hood had the right to attend the University of Alabama and should be admitted immediately. Governor Wallace disregarded this order and used gubernatorial powers to appoint himself as temporary university registrar. In this capacity he famously stood in the doorway of the main campus's administration building where the students should have registered. Just as local officials had intimidated and beaten African Americans when they tried to register to vote in Alabama, so the Alabama governor refused to let these two students register for university. President Kennedy was forced to follow the example of his republican predecessor Eisenhower and federalized the Alabama National Guard, who then mustered a hundred-strong unit to chaperone the two students into the registration building, Governor Wallace having been ordered to step aside. The conflicts to resist civil rights in both Alabama and Mississippi were sizable and often brutal, and many civil rights reformers were injured or killed.

To avert state failure the federal government used other measures—as part of a long-term state-enforced reform process—to shift race inequality in these states by giving additional grants to the university to strengthen administrators' resolve and getting the U.S. Civil Service Commission to monitor closely promotion and appointment patterns by race in state branches of federal departments such as the Post Office, the Internal Revenue Service, the Veterans Administration Hospital, and Social Security payment centers. These efforts complement the sort of state-led societal reform measures, the third type of state activity. These measures relied on initially very weak regulatory efforts.

But although the crisis at Mississippi and Alabama campuses forced the White House to exercise executive authority without the support of Congress to deploy troops, the convoluted processes and arguments deployed by the governors and their assistants in those states ensured that the process of ameliorating gross racial inequalities would be hindered for a decade. The governors exploited constitutional language and arrangements about states' rights to the full; only state-enforced reform could displace such purposeful resistance. The short-term crisis was absorbing and led to coercive state action.

The state lacked the resolve to go much further with direct intervention at that time. Rather, it settled on a long-haul but purposeful approach, emboldened by judicial decision. School integration, in the long term, required judicial rulings and direction (Swann v. Charlotte-Mecklenburg Board of Education 402 U.S. 1 [1970]) and continued federal enforcement.

State-Led Societal Reform

Dismantling segregated housing was a core aim of the civil rights movement and a cause repeatedly singled out by Martin Luther King Jr. in the 1950s and 1960s. He led marches for open housing. But in American cities the legacy of residential racial segregation is overwhelming. This is despite several landmark pieces of legislation, judicial rulings, enhanced powers of anti-discrimination given to the Department of Housing and Urban Development, and the almost complete eradication of the vestiges of the segregationist order that long informed Federal Housing Authority mortgage underwriting and mortgage insurance premiums (though minor aspects recurred in the subprime lending practices).

Both the passage of legislation and the enhancement of enforcement powers put housing policy into the third category of American state responses to race inequity: state-led societal reform. This is a case of state-led reform in that the resources to enforce fair housing and housing desegregation laws have at last been established in federal authority and agencies, in contrast to busing, which lacked any kind of federal statutory authority, no executive support except in Richard Nixon's Southern strategy, limited judicial authority, and little or no federal agency direct implementation power. Indeed, the Supreme Court blocked any meaningful metropolitan busing plans early on. But implementation of the anti–discriminatory housing powers is diluted the further from national authority one looks: implementation is weak because the state fails to make use of coercive power, including executive orders or material enforcement through, for instance, massive house building. Furthermore, the concentrated policy initiative required visibly to shift the contours of racial residential occupancy have not been forthcoming in American state measures; such sizable initiatives as urban renewal and social housing construction, remarkably, merely reinforced the segregationist patterns (Lamb 2005; Massey and Denton 1993; Mollenkopf 1983; King 2007).

Civil rights legislation was meant to mark an end to housing discrimination and a transformation in labor-market opportunities for African Americans. In practice, legislation agreed by Congress—thus passing the test of transcending the separation of powers—proved inadequate to the task. The 1968 Fair Housing Act lacked the enforcement powers necessary to implement measures capable of ending discrimination in housing (in renting and sales, mortgage evaluations, and insurance underwriting), and further legislation was necessary and was enacted over the next twenty years (indeed, given current levels of residential segregation, these additional measures are inadequate) (King and Smith 2011, 153–63). The 1968 legislation faced an uncertain future as a bill until the assassination of Martin Luther King Jr. on April 4, 1968, sent a signal about the significance of reform that Congress could not disregard; it was passed within several days of King's murder. One reason for American state legislative enactment was pressure from the civil rights movement, often conjoined with international commentary on U.S. cities' skewed residential patterns. King's murder accelerated these pressures, since Congress had failed to enact various fair housing bills introduced during the preceding two years and some of the urban disorders during the mid-1960s—such as the 1965 Watts or 1967 Detroit riots—were sparked in part by the crisis of inadequate affordable and nondiscriminatory housing for African Americans. Civil rights reformers expected the 1964 law to be a breakthrough for robust fair housing legislation, but in this expectation they were disappointed.

Since the temptation to local homeowners is to discriminate and practice segregation, unwittingly or wittingly, integrated housing necessitates federal standards and federal enforcement, a feature recognized by Nixon's housing secretary George W. Romney, whose plans to achieve desegregated housing nationally in the Open Communities project were undercut by the White House (Lamb 2005). Nixon's use of state power did not extend to shifting low-income families into suburban neighborhoods. He supported subsidized low-income housing. This position was articulated in Nixon's fair housing policy, issued on June 14, 1971. A more ambitious housing integration program—Secretary Romney's Operation Breakthrough—foundered. (A parallel race inequity manifesting characteristics of state-led societal reform is that of affirmative action and antidiscrimination in the labor market [Chen 2009].)

To achieve truly fair housing requires use of both the legal constraints against discrimination established in 1968 and robust enforcement mechanisms. These were not put in place until new legislation enacted in 1988, twenty years after the first antidiscrimination legislation. Without the latter, state-led societal reform fumbled, a deliberate outcome, given presidential party calculations and the unwillingness to deploy executive power such as executive orders. For these two decades complaints about housing discrimination mounted as the weakness of Housing and Urban Development's regulatory powers became plain. Indeed, the race inequity crisis in housing remains, and state-level enforcement continues to be weak.[3]

As with any government measures that induce substantive reform in race inequalities, some groups in society are likely to be affected detrimentally. In the case of housing, such ripples included not only obvious corporate interests such as real estate firms, builders, and politicians but almost all Americans, since residential housing is so widely segregated. This meant that designing and enforcing effective antidiscrimination measures was a huge task. But what the Nixon nonaction reveals is an unwillingness to use available state power to this end, in contrast to the rapid engagement of the Justice Department's active pursuit of voting violations under President Johnson.

The contrast between these three types of state action imply a dichotomy between race inequality, which leads to violations in democratic norms and therefore measurable government failure, and racial inequality, which is attributed by public officials to society in a very general sense and therefore not to government inaction and failure. This distinction—often implicit in discussions of America's segregated state—has limits, however. Housing discrimination clearly arises both from government action and societal practice. Nonetheless, the distinction might help to show that shock-and-awe tactics may work better in the former case—that is, in the presence of clear violations of the democratic rules of the game—than in the latter, where inequalities are ascribed to personal or societal sources. It is a thin line, however, since many government policies reinforce societal practice and, as noted earlier, often foster that practice (King 2007).

THE SOURCES OF STICKINESS: WHY AMERICAN STATE POLICY FAILS THE GOAL OF RACE EQUITY

The discussion in this chapter takes as a given that the problems of enduring material race inequities not only preclude use of the appellation "postracial" to the United States but also that these legacies move the problem beyond the level of individual behavior to one of systemic institutionalization. Even crises framed as rooted in societal interests ultimately require state action for resolution. The issues discussed here engage with two other themes identified by the editors: timing and stickiness. The American state has an arsenal of resources on an impressive scale deployable against the evil and sources of race inequity, but that the deployment of those resources is far from automatic. Although the evilness of race inequality was increasingly recognized from the 1930s and decisively so after the 1940s, this recognition did not elicit sufficient state action to excise inequality from democratic norms and social relations.

The three types of American state responses discussed here focus on a particular period in American history when domestic forces—principally the civil rights movement and a new generation of Democrats in Congress—and, to a lesser extent, international pressures—a new era of global politics that articulates human rights and exposes the United States to external scrutiny—constituted pressure for change. These pressures and the resultant changes, however, were far from automatic or ineluctable: the struggles and activism of the civil rights movement (broadly construed from protests to legal avenues) were lengthy and arduous. They were fought on the canvas of an American state whose substantial resources were historically dedicated both to maintaining the separate and marginalized governance of African Americans in the U.S. polity and to privileging affirmative action for whites.

The transformation in how the state came to see race inequality as an evil and a violation of democratic norms rather than as a public good for whites is the subject of substantial research focused on the civil rights movement and changes in the American state between the 1930s and 1960s, which I do not rehearse here. Suffice to say that the combination of a discrediting of so-called scientific doctrines about race hierarchies, acknowledgement of the partiality of U.S. democratic institutions, and the negative consequences of these legacies, concurrent with the sorts of inter-national and domestic factors outlined in this chapter, eventually forced such a shift. The presence of some key figures who adopted antisegrega-tionist rather than prosegregationist stances was crucial (King and Smith 2005). And crises, I have argued, were equally galvanic.

Thus the timing of these two types of state activity—creating new stan-dards and using coercive state power—was unusual, given that histori-cally the American state more commonly fails to address the issue of race inequity. This activism arose because of social order crises. Without the crises, the status quo would have been uninterrupted. For instance, Presi-dent Eisenhower would never have considered employing coercive power to address school integration if he had not been compelled to do so by circumstances beyond his control, and he did everything he could to avoid the eventuality; mere disobedience of the rule of law did not exercise na-tional leaders—it was how that disobedience translated into severe social order crises that mattered. But state reaction to crises driven by America's race inequalities were treated with policy directed at the surface rather than the deeper sources. The Wallace intransigence about integrated edu-cation succeeded in shaping the immediate crisis as public disorder and delaying the process of integration.

This latter pattern helps explain the timidity of the American state (and therefore the stickiness of inequality) in responding to gross unequal treat-ment of its citizens. The Moynihan report (1965), produced intentionally to influence policy makers to act, failed on its own terms because Ameri-can state officials were unwilling to use colossal resources in a case of na-tional action on the scale he proposed (full employment measures, exten-sive training and education, family support). Ignoring sources and focusing only on surface expressions of the inequalities ensured a limited response to real problems and legacies with which the United States still struggles, as the need for state-led societal reforms implies.

This stickiness is one reason that scholars correctly express reservations about any transition to a postracial society. Yes, there is historical change signaled by Barack Obama's election (Sugrue 2010), and this is a culmina-tion of changes enforced by the American state from the 1960s to make voting rights real; but the enduring material race inequities are too deep not to require targeted state policies (Cohen 2010; Smith and King 2009). The election marks a key development in the civil rights movement's agenda, developed from the 1940s, but not its fulfillment. The legacy of material race inequities in education, employment, housing, criminal jus-tice, and health care provision is profound, and truly to be modified neces-sitates a crisis-style declaration and level of resources policy. Historically, it is striking for what a brief period this allocation of state activism enjoyed, and this brevity is warning about the systemic limits on state activism.

The American State and Institutional Constraints

Race inequality and injustice crises exemplify the general problem that American state mobilization of resources and capacities is biased toward the short term rather than durable solutions. For instance, Lyndon Johnson's War on Poverty commenced with considerable concentrated resources applied to the issue and a military-like campaign by the president to get his legislation enacted and funded. But sustaining this initiative proved harder, and specifying criteria of success proved woefully undeveloped. The same problems affect the American state's quasi-wars on illegal drugs (which have contributed to the rise in male African American prison rates) and undocumented workers, where, despite expanding resource allocation for border patrols, detention, and deportation and expanded coordination with local enforcement authorities, the rates of illegal migration remain high.

The American state's response to Hurricane Katrina is an enduring example of inequality in the deployment of resources and capacities and clarity of purpose. Because the national political system is fragmented and executive authority to make policy mostly requires cooperation with other branches, policy making is biased toward stealth rather than direct measures. For instance, the outcomes of state-led societal reform have dogged efforts to use affirmative action to reduce race inequity in the labor market. Beginning with an unexpected commitment to a significant program of reform—the Philadelphia Plan (the scheme to require contractors to employ minority workers proportionate to their numbers in the local labor market) implemented by the Nixon administration—the scale of required change scared off American state officeholders. Thus reform has become a gradual and steady process achieved through particular agents in the state's bureaucracy (such as the Equal Employment Opportunity Commission and No Child Left Behind) rather than a highly visible one guided by clear quota goals and their enforcement (Dobbin 2010; Dobbin and Sutton 1998). The cost of this process is insufficient progress effectively to make the labor market fairer. Within the American state's systemic constraints, individual agencies do effect important reforms.

The American State and Racial Orders

The threefold typology of American state responses to race crises illuminates how important the definition of the crisis is to policy action and level

of resources applied to the issue. Crises rooted in dichotomous policy options—the right to vote or denial of the right to vote, for instance—or in
the breakdown of social order offer a clearer response (though with com-
plications, as discussed in the preceding pages) than a more general policy
goal of ending housing discrimination. In practice, even apparently un-
complicated aims such as establishing and enforcing the right to vote have
complex implications—for example, whether majority-minority voting
districts are necessary for previously excluded citizens to have effective
participation and representation (King and Smith 2008). But the general
point is that the way policy for race equality was defined in historic legislation enacted in the 1960s sets the issue as one of protecting constitutional
rights and entitlements, not ameliorating material inequities, although the
latter was a fundamental aim of the civil rights movement and its importance acknowledged nationally by President Lyndon Johnson and other
policy makers. This constitutionalism—cautiously supported in the first
and second types of state activism—meant that material inequities could
only be treated within a universal framework, not as part of a targeted
scheme. Crucially, such an effect was not a random outcome but a consequence of how race is constitutive of American politics and history.

   This pattern reflects the way racial orders have developed and endure
in American political development, I argue in collaborative work with
Rogers Smith (King and Smith 2005, 2011). Thus to grasp the potential and
limits of American state responses to the nation's recurring and enduring
race inequality crises requires that they be placed in their historically
shaped racial orders. President Barack Obama operates within a racial order that structures policy options dichotomously between color-blind or
race-targeted responses to these inequalities; thus while the sorts of inequalities in housing, education, criminal justice, and income levels might
well lead some reformers to advocate targeted policy, it is pretty clear that
the political and racial orders structuring the Obama presidency dictate
standards-inspired activism: a universalist response that can be justified in
general benefits and not particularistic ones—for example, the Federal
Protection and Affordable Care Act and the education program, Race to
the Top.

This chapter draws on research completed while the author held a *Lever-
hulme Trust Major Research Fellowship* (2005–09) and is also part of the racial
alliances collaborative project with Rogers M. Smith. For valuable comments
on an earlier version of this chapter the author is grateful to the participants
at the Russell Sage Foundation conference and at the APSA 2010 meetings

especially to Anthony Chen, Devin Fergus, Philip Goff, Fredrick Harris, Rodney Hero, Kimberley Johnson, Ira Katznelson, Robert Lieberman, Sid Milkis, Devah Pager, Dorian Warren, and Vesla Weaver, and to the two Russell Sage Foundation anonymous readers.

NOTES

1. By the time of this November announcement, the federal government had taken on close to $7.8 trillion of direct and indirect financial obligations, a sum equivalent to half of the U.S. GNP.
2. Hostility from parents of children in elementary schools led the school district to begin integration in high school in 1957, hoping to include the junior school in 1960 and the elementary school in 1963.
3. A parallel issue of race inequity that manifests characteristics of state-led societal reform is the use of affirmative action and antidiscrimination legislation in labor markets. The struggle to end discrimination in labor markets continues with the affirmative action measures enacted from the mid-1960s (including the Nixon-era quotas of the Philadelphia Plan), having made important inroads into employment opportunities for African Americans, but a pattern of material race inequity endures.

REFERENCES

Alexander, Michelle. 2010. *The New Jim Crow*. New York: New Press.

Balogh, Brian. 2009. *A Government Out of Sight: The Mystery of National Authority in Nineteenth-Century America*. New York: Cambridge University Press.

Barker, Vanessa. 2009. *The Politics of Imprisonment*. New York: Oxford University Press.

Bush, George W. 2005 "Address to the Nation on Hurricane Katrina Recovery from New Orleans, Louisiana," September 15. *Weekly Compilation of Presidential Documents, Administration of George W. Bush 2005*.

Carpenter, Daniel. 2001. *Forging Bureaucratic Autonomy*. Princeton, N.J.: Princeton University Press.

Chen, Anthony. 2009. *The Fifth Freedom*. Princeton, N.J.: Princeton University Press.

Clark, Kenneth B. 1965, new print 1989. *Dark Ghetto: Dilemmas of Social Power*. Middletown, Conn.: Wesleyan University Press.

Cohen, Cathy J. 2010. *Democracy Remixed: Black Youth and the Future of American Politics*. New York: Oxford University Press.

Desrosieres, Alain. 1998. *The Politics of Large Numbers*. Cambridge, Mass.: Harvard University Press.

Dobbin, Frank. 2010. *Inventing Equal Opportunity*. Princeton, N.J.: Princeton University Press.

Dobbin, Frank, and John R. Sutton. 1998. "The Strength of a Weak State: The Rights Revolution and the Rise of Human Resources Management Divisions." *American Journal of Sociology* 104(2): 441–76.

Du Bois, W. E. B. (1899) 1996. *The Philadelphia Negro: A Social Study.* Philadelphia: University of Pennsylvania Press.

Dudziak, Mary. 2000. *Cold War Civil Rights.* Princeton, N.J.: Princeton University Press.

———. 2012. *War Time.* New York: Oxford University Press.

Edling, Max M. 2003. *A Revolution in Favor of Government: Origins of the U.S. Constitution and the Making of the American State.* New York: Oxford University Press.

Evans, Peter, et al., eds. 1985. *Bringing the State Back In.* New York: Cambridge University Press.

Frazier, E. Franklin. 1939. *The Negro Family in the United States.* Chicago: University of Chicago Press.

Frymer, Paul. 2004. "Race, Labor, and the Twentieth Century American State." *Politics and Society* 32(4): 475–509.

———. 2005. "Racism Revisited: Courts, Labor Law, and the Institutional Construction of Racial Animus." *American Political Science Review* 99(2): 373–87.

Gottschalk, Marie. 2006. *The Prison and the Gallows.* Cambridge: Cambridge University Press.

Harris, Frederick. 2006. "'It Takes a Tragedy to Arouse Them': Collective Memory and Collective Action During the Civil Rights Movement." *Social Movement Studies* 5(1): 54–73.

Howard, Christopher. 1997. *The Hidden Welfare State: Tax Expenditures and Social Policy in the United States.* Princeton, N.J.: Princeton University Press.

———. 2007. *The Welfare State Nobody Knows.* Princeton, N.J.: Princeton University Press.

Howell, William G. 2003. *Power Without Persuasion: The Politics of Direct Presidential Action.* Princeton, N.J.: Princeton University Press.

Johnson, Kimberley S. 2007. *Governing the American State.* Princeton, N.J.: Princeton University Press.

———. 2009. "The First New Federalism and the Development of the Modern American State: Patchwork, Reconstitution or Transition?" in *The Unsustainable American State,* edited by Lawrence Jacobs and Desmond King. New York: Oxford University Press.

———. 2010. *Reforming Jim Crow: Southern Politics and State in the Age Before Brown.* New York: Oxford University Press.

Johnson, President Lyndon B. 1965. "To Fulfill These Rights." Commencement Address at Howard University, June 4, 1965. Available at: www.lbjlib.utexas.edu/johnson/archives.hom/speeches.hom/650604.asp (accessed June 16, 2011).

Katznelson, Ira. 2005. *When Affirmative Action Was White.* New York: W. W. Norton.

Kelman, Steven. 1987. "The Political Foundations of American Statistical Policy."

In *The Politics of Numbers*, edited by William Alonso and Paul Starr. New York: Russell Sage Foundation.

Keyssar, Alexander. 2000. *The Right to Vote: The Contested History of Democracy in the United States*. New York: Basic Books.

King, Desmond. 2007. *Separate and Unequal: African Americans and the U.S. Federal Government*. New York: Oxford University Press.

King, Desmond, and Robert C. Lieberman. 2009. "Ironies of State Building: A Comparative Perspective on the American State." *World Politics* 61(3): 547–88.

King, Desmond S., and Rogers M. Smith. 2005. "Racial Orders in American Political Development." *American Political Science Review* 99(1): 75–94.

———. 2008. "Strange Bedfellows? Polarized Politics? The Quest for Racial Equity in Contemporary America." *Political Research Quarterly* 61(4): 686–703.

———. 2011. *Still a House Divided: Race and Politics in Obama's America*. Princeton, N.J.: Princeton University Press.

Klinkner, Philip, and Rogers M. Smith. 1999. *The Unsteady March*. Chicago: University of Chicago Press.

Kryder, Daniel. 1999. "Democratizing Authority: The Multiple Motives Behind Black Police Appointments in the Twentieth Century United States." In *Democratization in America: A Comparative-Historical Analysis*, edited by Desmond King et al. Baltimore, Md.: Johns Hopkins University Press.

———. 2000. *Divided Arsenal*. New York: Cambridge University Press.

Lamb, Charles M. 2005. *Housing Segregation in Suburban America since 1960*. New York: Cambridge University Press.

Lieberman, Robert C. 1998. *Shifting the Color Line*. Cambridge, Mass.: Harvard University Press.

———. 2009. "Civil Rights and the Democratization Trap: The Public-Private Nexus and the Building of American Democracy." In *Democratization in America: A Comparative-Historical Analysis*, edited by Desmond King et al. Baltimore, Md.: Johns Hopkins University Press.

Manza, Jeff, and Christopher Uggen. 2006. *Locked Out*. New York: Oxford University Press.

Marshall Papers. Conversation Between Attorney General Robert F. Kennedy and Governor George Wallace, Montgomery, Alabama, April 25, 1963, 8. Transcript. Box 18, folder Meredith, University of Alabama. John F. Kennedy Presidential Library, Boston.

Massey, Douglas, and Nancy Denton. 1993. *American Apartheid*. Cambridge, Mass.: Harvard University Press.

Mayer, Kenneth R. 2001. *With the Stroke of a Pen: Executive Orders and Presidential Power*. Princeton, N.J.: Princeton University Press.

———. 2009. "Going Alone: The Presidential Power of Unilateral Action." In *The Oxford Handbook of the American Presidency*, edited by George C. Edwards III and William G. Howell. Oxford: Oxford University Press.

McAdam, Doug. 1982. *Political Process and the Development of Black Insurgency, 1930–1970*. Chicago: University of Chicago Press.

Mettler, Suzanne. 2009. "Promoting Inequality: The Politics of Higher Education Policy in an Era of Conservative Government." In *The Unsustainable American State*, edited by Lawrence Jacobs and Desmond King. New York: Oxford University Press.

———. 2010. "Reconstituting the Submerged State: The Challenges of Social Policy Reform in the Obama Era." *Perspectives on Politics* 8(3): 803–24.

———. 2011. *The Submerged State*. Chicago: University of Chicago Press.

Mollenkopf, John M. 1983. *The Contested City*. Princeton, N.J.: Princeton University Press.

Morris, Aldon D. 1984. *The Origins of the Civil Rights Movement: Black Communities Organizing for Change*. New York: Free Press.

Moynihan, Daniel Patrick. 1965. *The Negro Family: The Case for National Action*. Washington: U.S. Department of Labor. March.

Murakawa, Naomi. 2008. "The Origin of the Carceral Crisis: Racial Order as 'Law and Order' in Postwar American Politics." In *Race and American Political Development*, edited by Joseph Lowndes, Julie Novkov, and Dorian Warren. New York: Routledge.

Myrdal, Gunnar. 1944. *An American Dilemma*. 2 vols. New York: Knopf.

Nettl, J. P. 1968. "The State as a Conceptual Variable." *World Politics* 20(4): 559–92.

Novak, William J. 2008. "The Myth of the 'Weak' American State." *American Historical Review* 113(4): 752–72.

Parker, Christopher S. 2009. *Fighting for Democracy*. Princeton, N.J.: Princeton University Press.

Patterson, James T. (2010). *Freedom Is Not Enough*. New York: Basic Books.

Pierson, Paul. 2007. "The Rise and Reconfiguration of Activist Government." In *The Transformation of American Politics*, edited by Paul Pierson and Theda Skocpol. Princeton, N.J.: Princeton University Press.

Poggi, Gianfranco. 1990. *The State: Its Nature, Development, and Prospects*. Oxford: Polity.

Posner, Eric A., and Adrian Vermeule. 2010. *The Executive Unbound*. New York: Oxford University Press.

Robinson, Greg. 2001. *By Order of the President*. Cambridge, Mass.: Harvard University Press.

Scott, James C. 1998. *Seeing Like a State*. New Haven, Conn.: Yale University Press.

Sheingate, Adam. 2009. "Why Can't Americans See the State?" *Forum* 7(11): 1–14.

Simon, Jonathan. 2007. *Governing Through Crime*. New York: Oxford University Press.

Skowronek, Stephen. 1982. *Building a New American State: The Expansion of National Administrative Capacities, 1877–1920*. Cambridge: Cambridge University Press.

————. 2009. "Taking Stock." In *The Unsustainable American State*, edited by Lawrence Jacobs and Desmond King. New York: Oxford University Press.

Skrentny, John D. 2006. "Law and the American State." *Annual Review of Sociology* 32: 213–44.

Smith, Rogers M. 1993. "Beyond Tocqueville, Myrdal and Hartz: The Multiple Traditions in America." *American Political Science Review* 87(3): 549–66.

————. 1997. *Civic Ideals*. New Haven, Conn.: Yale University Press.

Smith, Rogers M., and Desmond S. King. 2009. "Barack Obama and the Future of American Racial Politics." *Du Bois Review* 6(1): 1–11.

Sparrow, James. 2011. *Warfare State*. New York: Oxford University Press.

Stears, Marc. 2002. *Progressives, Pluralists, and the Problems of the State: Ideologies of Reform in the United States and Britain, 1909–1926*. Oxford: Oxford University Press.

————. 2010. *Demanding Democracy: American Radicals in Search of a New Kind of Politics*. Princeton, N.J.: Princeton University Press.

Sugrue, Thomas J. 2010. *Not Even Past*. Princeton, N.J.: Princeton University Press.

Tuck, Stephen. 2009. "The Reversal of Black Voting Rights after Reconstruction." In *Democratization in America: A Comparative-Historical Analysis*, edited by Desmond King et al. Baltimore, Md.: Johns Hopkins University Press.

Valelly, Richard M. 2004. *The Two Reconstructions: The Struggle for Black Enfranchisement*. Chicago: University of Chicago Press.

Wacquant, Loic. 2009. *Punishing the Poor*. Durham N.C.: Duke University Press.

Ward, Deborah E. 2005. *The White Welfare State: The Racialization of U.S. Welfare Policy*. Ann Arbor: University of Michigan Press.

Weaver, Vesla. 2007. "Frontlash: Race and the Development of a Punitive Crime Policy." *Studies in American Political Development* 21(1): 230–65.

Weir, Margaret. 2005. "States, Race, and the Decline of New Deal Liberalism." *Studies in American Political Development* 19(1): 157–72.

Weir, Margaret, and Theda Skocpol. 1985. "State Structures and the Possibilities for 'Keynesian' Responses to the Great Depression in Sweden, Britain, and the United States." In *Bringing the State Back In*, edited by Peter B. Evans, Dietrich Rueschemeyer, and Theda Skocpol. Cambridge: Cambridge University Press.

Western, Bruce. 2005. *Punishment and Inequality in America*. New York: Russell Sage Foundation.

Western, Bruce, and Becky Petit. 2005. "Black-White Wage Inequality, Employment Rates, and Incarceration." *American Journal of Sociology* 111(2): 553–78.

Chapter 3 | Racial Inequality and Race-Conscious Affirmative Action in College Admissions: A Historical Perspective on Contemporary Prospects and Future Possibilities

Anthony S. Chen and Lisa M. Stulberg

THE RACIAL COMPOSITION of undergraduates attending American colleges and universities has experienced a far-reaching transformation over the past sixty years. At the midpoint of the twentieth century, most institutions of higher education were racially exclusive, whether by policy or custom. The overwhelming majority of students going to college were white—no matter where in the country they went to school. Of course, African Americans did go to college in modest numbers, but most of them attended historically black colleges and universities in border or southern states. A tiny handful of black students were enrolled in the predominantly white schools of the North, and even fewer could be seen on the campuses of public and private institutions in the South. Whether a capable person could obtain a college degree seemed more dependent on an accident of birth than anything else.

By the end of the century, undergraduate education had grown far more racially diverse. In 1998 more than 10 percent of full-time college students were black, and 80 percent of black college students were enrolled at predominantly white institutions (Clotfelter 2004, 154; see also Karen 1991).[1] The change in the racial composition of American undergraduates is even more pronounced when one takes a more fine-grained look at different types of selective institutions (table 3.1). At eleven selective private universities, black full-time enrollment rates went from an average of less than 1 percent in 1951 to an average of 7 percent in 1998. Similar average increases occurred at ten liberal arts colleges and four public universities, where the black full-time enrollment rate rose from 1 percent to 6 and 7 percent. The racial profile of American college students at the turn of the twenty-first century looked quite different than it had fifty years earlier.

Few policies are more responsible for breaking down the racial exclusion of undergraduate education than race-conscious affirmative action programs; namely, programs or practices that formally take race into account in some manner during the college recruitment or admissions process. To be sure, many other changes over the course of the past half century have made the incorporation of black students possible. The doctrine of separate-but-equal no longer enjoys constitutional sanction. Public schools around the country have taken a variety of steps to address racial imbalance in the composition of their student body, sometimes at the behest of the federal courts and sometimes of their own volition. There are federal statutes on the books that mandate nondiscrimination in housing, voting, employment, and many other areas of public and private life. For several successive decades, government contractors and private corporations took affirmative action to integrate their workforces by hiring black workers. Although it did not disappear, the black-white earnings gap shrank, making college financially viable for hundreds of thousands of African Americans. But no other policy has taken more direct aim at racial exclusion in higher education than race-conscious affirmative action in college admissions, and none has been more consequential, in the view of both critics and supporters.

During the early 1960s, racial segregation, inadequate school resources, and peer inequality combined to sharply limit the number of African Americans qualified to compete for admission to highly selective colleges and universities. Race-conscious affirmative action began when key numbers of college administrators were motivated by the mobilization of the civil rights movement to address such "pipeline" problems and bring meaningful levels of racial diversity (beyond tokenism) to college campuses. The first wave of affirmative action began in the early to mid-1960s, when liberal college administrators were inspired by the civil rights movement to integrate and diversify the student bodies at their own institutions. A second wave of affirmative action programs began during the late 1960s and early 1970s, when campus protests and urban uprisings led to the proliferation of such programs and the intensification of the emphasis given to race in the admissions process. A third wave of affirmative action, marked by the consolidation of policies that considered race in a more re-

Table 3.1   Average Percentage of Black Students Enrolled Full-Time at Selective Institutions, by Type of Institution, 1951 to 1998

Type of institution	1951	1967	1970	1976	1986	1998
Private universities (N = 11)	0.3	1.8	4.0	5.6	5.3	7.0
Liberal arts colleges (N = 10)	1.0	2.8	5.7	6.0	5.1	6.1
Public universities (N = 4)	1.0	1.4	2.8	3.9	4.8	6.6

Source: Authors' adaptation of Clotfelter (2004, 159).

Note: Private universities: Columbia, Duke, Emory, Northwestern, Princeton, Rice, Tufts, Tulane, University of Pennsylvania, Vanderbilt, and Yale. Private liberal arts colleges: Bryn Mawr, Denison, Hamilton, Kenyon, Oberlin, Smith, Swarthmore, Wellesley, Wesleyan, and Williams. Public universities: Miami of Ohio, Michigan, Pennsylvania State, and the University of North Carolina. For the year 1976, we report data from Clotfelter's column labeled "1976b." Further details on his exact sources are available in Clotfelter (2004, 159).

strained way, began in the years following the Supreme Court's 1978 Bakke decision, and it started to unravel only two decades later, when the Regents of University of California moved to ban affirmative action in the mid-1990s.

The unequal conditions in public education that originally spurred the establishment of race-conscious affirmative action are still very much with us today. Although recent critics continue to urge American colleges and universities to adopt a "color-blind" system of admissions, educational opportunities today are far from color blind. The legal and constitutional foundations of race-conscious affirmative action have been significantly undercut since it was initially established, but race continues to mark a distinctive form of inequality that pervades not just education but almost every other sphere of life in the United States. That is why taking race into account in undergraduate admissions remains a powerful and relevant way of adding diversity to the mix of experiences that admitted students bring with them to highly selective American colleges and universities. It is also why racial considerations in college admissions continue to have no real substitutes.

RACIAL INEQUALITY AND THE COLLEGE PIPELINE BEFORE AFFIRMATIVE ACTION

To understand and appreciate the underlying motivations of the college administrators who launched race-conscious affirmative action, one might begin with a simple but essential observation about the college pipeline at mid-century: American public education at every level was highly segregated and highly unequal, and segregation and inequality were strongly correlated. From the 1954 Brown v. Board of Education (347 U.S. 483 [1954]) decision to the passage of the Civil Rights Act of 1964 and the Voting Rights Act of 1965—years that bookended what Bayard Rustin called the "classical" phase of the civil rights movement (Rustin quoted in Hall 2005, 1234)—American public schools from kindergarten to high school were segregated, and predominately black schools were almost always the worst off, financially and educationally.

The overall pattern was most infamous and most visible in the South, where the overwhelming majority of black students were concentrated in segregated, majority-black schools. In 1968 four-fifths of black students in the South went to schools in which 90 percent or more of the students were from racial minorities (Orfield and Lee 2004, 20). By contrast, majority-white schools in the South enrolled a miniscule proportion of black students (Orfield and Lee 2004, 19). The quality of segregated black schools in the South was significantly lower than the quality of predominantly white schools, leading to a host of adverse education and economic outcomes for many black students. Among segregated black schools in the postwar South, student-teacher ratios were higher, the school year was shorter, and teacher salaries were lower—all of which contributed significantly to the black-white earnings gap (Card and Krueger 1992, 168; also see Margo 1986).[2]

A similar, if somewhat less pronounced, pattern prevailed elsewhere across the country, where high proportions of black students attended highly segregated, majority-black schools. In 1968 nearly 60 percent of black students in the Midwest, 50 percent of black students in the West, and 40 percent of black students in the Northeast attended schools in which students of color represented 90 percent or more of enrolled students (Orfield and Lee 2004, 20). In urban school districts in large, metropolitan areas in the North and Midwest—areas where the majority of black children in the region went to school—a degree of racial segregation rivaled, and in some cases exceeded, Southern segregation. The school systems of Detroit and Chicago, for instance, were severely segregated through the mid-1960s, leading to vastly different school experiences for African Americans and whites (see, for example, National Commission on Professional Rights and Responsibilities 1967, 34–35; Hauser 1964, 14–15). Like their counterparts throughout the South, highly segregated black schools in such areas were far from the equal of white schools, especially those in the surrounding suburbs. Although the devastating consequences of urban deindustrialization, joblessness, and middle-class flight were apparent to almost everyone by the 1980s, such trends were already fairly advanced by the early 1960s, and the students who attended urban schools were increasingly nonwhite children from low-income households (see, for example, Sugrue 1996). Such schools faced a lengthening list of serious challenges: overcrowding, growing class sizes, deteriorating finances, crumbling infrastructure, and shortages of qualified and experienced teachers (see, for example, Hauser et al. 1964; National Commission on Professional Rights and Responsibilities 1967).

Perhaps the most ubiquitous education inequality in the years after Brown was the black-white gap in academic achievement. The earliest systematic evidence of the achievement gap came with the publication of the Coleman Report in 1966. Based on tests administered to a sample of first, third, sixth, ninth, and twelfth graders in 1965, the sociologist James Coleman's data on educational achievement indicated that black students scored lower than white students on practically every type of test administered (Coleman 1966). Table 3.2 presents a selection of Coleman's findings on the black-white test-score gap in the sixth, ninth, and twelve grades. The gap is expressed in the number of standard deviations that the average black student fell below white students in the metropolitan Northeast (who scored the highest on all tests) as well as the number of grade levels that the average black student was behind the same group of white students. Coleman found that black students across the country were roughly one standard deviation below the reference group in their scores on verbal ability, reading comprehension, and math achievement. White students outside the metropolitan Northeast also fell below the reference group, but the gap was comparatively small, ranging from 0 to 0.3 standard deviations. What was even more concerning was Coleman's finding that in all regions the grade-level gap between black and white students was larger at higher grades, growing as students progressed through school. For example, on scores of verbal ability the average black sixth grader in the metropolitan Northeast was 1.6 grade levels behind the average white sixth grader from the same region, but the average black twelfth grader was 3.3 grade levels behind the average white twelfth grader.

The achievement gap and other racial inequalities were challenging problems in their own right, but their intrinsic severity was compounded by racial segregation, which adversely influenced the peer characteristics of students attending black schools. Just as racial segregation meant that neighborhood poverty rates were higher in black neighborhoods than in white neighborhoods (for example, Massey and Denton 1993), it also meant that students attending segregated, black schools were exposed to greater levels of poverty and lower levels of academic achievement among their peers than students at more racially integrated schools. Since a large fraction of black students attended racially segregated schools, black students tended to find themselves surrounded by peers whose socioeconomic and academic characteristics differed from the peers of white students.

Table 3.2   Black-White Achievement Gap at the Sixth, Ninth, and Twelfth Grades, Fall 1965, by Region

	Standard deviations below			Grade levels behind		
	6	9	12	6	9	12
Region	Verbal ability					
Northeast	1.0	1.1	1.1	1.6	2.4	3.3
Midwest	1.0	1.0	1.1	1.7	2.2	3.3
South	1.3	1.4	1.5	2.0	3.0	4.2
West	1.2	1.2	1.3	1.9	2.6	3.9
	Reading comprehension					
Northeast	0.8	0.9	0.8	1.8	2.6	2.9
Midwest	0.8	0.8	0.8	1.8	2.3	2.8
South	0.9	1.1	1.2	2.1	3.0	3.9
West	0.9	1.1	1.2	2.1	3.1	3.8
	Math achievement					
Northeast	1.1	1.0	1.1	2.0	2.8	5.2
Midwest	1.1	0.9	1.0	2.1	2.5	4.7
South	1.3	1.1	1.2	2.4	3.1	5.6
West	1.3	1.1	1.1	2.4	3.1	5.3

Source: Authors' compilation of data from Coleman (1966, 274–75).
Note: The reference group is whites living in the metropolitan Northeast.

This racial difference in peer characteristics was also amply evident in Coleman's data (table 3.3). Compared with the average white student, the average black student was surrounded by a lower proportion of peers whose mothers had received at least a high school education; a lower proportion of peers who lived with their biological fathers; and a lower proportion of peers whose households subscribed to a daily newspaper or had access to more than a hundred books. Clear measures of wages, earnings, and income were not available, but there was indirect evidence that the average black student was exposed to a higher proportion of low-income peers than the average white student. The average black student was less likely than the average white student to have peers who belonged to a household with a telephone, car, or vacuum cleaner. Finally, black students tended to be exposed to peers with higher drop-out rates and lower college attendance rates than white students.

Table 3.3 Peer Characteristics in Selected Metropolitan Areas, by Race and Level, Fall 1965 (percentage)

Peer characteristic	Northeast			Midwest			West		
	Black	White	B – W	Black	White	B – W	Black	White	B – W
Mother completed high school or more education									
Elementary	39	55	-16	36	49	-13	35	48	-13
Secondary	51	63	-12	49	58	-9	53	60	-7
Biological father living at home									
Elementary	68	82	-14	63	84	-21	60	75	-15
Schoolmates have following items in home									
Car									
Elementary	70	87	-17	77	95	-18	80	93	-13
Secondary	72	84	-12	88	97	-9	90	93	-3
Telephone									
Elementary	79	91	-12	79	90	-11	83	93	-10
Secondary	89	94	-5	93	94	-1	91	94	-3
Vacuum cleaner, secondary	78	90	-12	79	94	-15	82	88	-6
Household receives a daily newspaper									
Elementary	75	85	-10	70	84	-14	67	83	-16
Secondary	91	91	0	86	91	-5	81	83	-2
One hundred or more books in home, secondary	41	53	-12	36	43	-7	37	41	-4
Drop-out rate, secondary	23	10	13	19	7	12	12	5	7
College attendance rate of preceding year's graduating class	33	54	-21	33	41	-8	49	52	-3

Source: Authors' compilation of data from Coleman (1966: 188, 190, 196).
Notes: The data for whites are drawn from Coleman's "W/N" columns, which basically report information on white children living in counties with the highest concentration of black children. This has the tendency to understate any racial differences that may exist.

The cumulative and combined effect of racial segregation and racial inequality in all regions of the country was to narrow the stream of black students flowing through the college pipeline. As black students made their way from elementary school to high school, progressively fewer and fewer of them acquired the skills and credentials that qualified them to compete for admission to selective institutions. As a result, black students remained severely underrepresented at most selective undergraduate institutions, even at predominantly white colleges and universities outside the South that did not actively exclude them. Before the start of the Second World War, only 2 percent of full-time college students were black (Gordon 1976, 118). Fifteen years later, when the Supreme Court handed down the first Brown decision, they still made up only 3.9 percent of full-time college students (Clotfelter 2004, 154). Of the 63,000 black students who were attending college in 1954, more than 80 percent were attending historically black colleges and universities, which were typically located in border or southern states (Clotfelter 2004 150, 154). By 1964 black students still made up only 5 percent of college students in the United States (Gordon 1976, 118), and few of them were enrolled in predominantly white institutions.

FIRST-WAVE AFFIRMATIVE ACTION ON COLLEGE CAMPUSES

The paucity of black students at American colleges and universities became increasingly difficult to ignore, especially as the burgeoning civil rights movement moved racial issues to the fore of national consciousness after Brown. In the early 1960s, leaders in higher education began to argue that racial segregation and racial inequality in primary and secondary schooling were effectively barring black students with academic ability from attending college. In his widely discussed 1961 book, *Slums and Suburbs*, Harvard president James B. Conant noted that the "most important problem" for affluent parents of suburban school children is ensuring the "admission of their children to prestige colleges." For the educators leading such schools, managing parental expectations was perhaps their most "vexing" task. By contrast, principals and counselors at schools in "slums"—which, Conant noted, many commentators had taken to calling "culturally deprived" or "culturally different" neighborhoods—faced an altogether different set of tasks. Their main responsibility was preparing the vast majority of their students to find jobs and encouraging their students with "academic talent" to enter into the professions by obtaining further education (Conant 1961, 1–2, 7).

This seemed straightforward in the abstract, but the difficulties in real life were "appalling" (Conant 1961, 2). The challenge could be summarized in a simple observation: "In the suburb there is likely to be a spacious modern school staffed by as many as 70 professionals per 1,000 pupils; in the slum one finds a crowded, often dilapidated and unattractive school staffed by 40 or fewer professionals per 1,000 pupils" (Conant 1961, 3). The implication was hard to contest. "Slum" schools faced enormous hurdles in preparing their students for the workforce and qualifying their most talented students for college.

Conant's conclusions about the educational challenges faced by schools in "slum" neighborhoods were buttressed by extensive, firsthand observation of student experiences there. Under a grant from the Carnegie Corporation, Conant had visited schools in the impoverished neighborhoods of Chicago, Detroit, and St. Louis, and he was struck by what he had observed. Many students and their parents were recent migrants from the South, and there was a high turnover rate in the classroom population. Many students came from single-parent families, and few of their parents had completed high school or even elementary school. The schools were plagued by violence, often driven by gangs, and female students were vulnerable to harassment and assault. Schools were overcrowded and chaotic, students were tired and distracted (Conant 1961, 18–21, 23). It would have been a challenging environment for any student, even the ones most determined to make it to college.

Of course, Conant understood that school itself was only one piece of a complicated puzzle. What happened within schools was a reflection of the economic conditions in the larger community and the socioeconomic background of the families that made it up. Indeed, he argued that the "poor achievement" of children in "slum" schools "may be ascribed to their depressing cultural and socio-economic backgrounds" (Conant 1961, 30). But he did not want his readers—"many of whom live in wealthy suburbs"—to miss the stark "contrast between the lives and education of their children and the lives and education of the boys and girls in the neighborhoods I have been describing" (21). Much of the contrast stemmed from basic inequalities in resources, given the higher level of educational need at urban schools. Conant's recommendation was unequivocal. The answer was not "token" integration. Rather, "the answer to improving Negro education in the large Northwestern cities is to spend more money and to upgrade Negro schools" (146).

Conant was not alone among his peers in his concern about the impact of racial inequality in public education on the flow of capable black students through the college pipeline. Looking back at a graduation ceremony in the early 1960s, President Charles E. Odegaard of the University of Washington recalled that he had been profoundly struck by the small number of African American students who were participating (Stulberg and

Chen 2008, 57). The university had formally declared a nondiscrimination policy in 1959, codifying a long-time practice, but it still struggled to enroll and graduate black students—something not lost on Odegaard and several other leaders in higher education.

It was concern for racial inequality in public education and its contribution to the underrepresentation of black students in American colleges and universities—and not some vague commitment to remedying societal discrimination—that motivated a number of administrators to establish race-conscious affirmative action programs in college admissions during the early 1960s (Stulberg and Chen 2008). The men who led these schools came to realize that simply opening their doors was not enough. They believed that intellectually capable African Americans had been encumbered by their specific experience of segregated and unequal public education, and they came to believe that it was morally incumbent on selective institutions to identify black students who had been previously overlooked but who had the capacity to do college work, admit them with scholarships and financial aid if necessary, and prepare them to compete on equal terms with their white classmates (Greenland, Chen, and Stulberg 2010, 17–19).

The prevailing view on the advent of race-conscious affirmative action is somewhat different. According to the conventional wisdom, such programs first emerged in the late 1960s, primarily as a response to urban riots (after Watts in the summer of 1965) and campus protests by student radicals. In this view, this surge in disruption prompted college administrators to take a look at black underrepresentation and encouraged them to launch new initiatives and programs to address the situation. For instance, John D. Skrentny (2002, 166–67) argues that "black violence in the nation's cities," as well as violence (and the threat of violence) on college campuses, "fostered an interest among university administrators in affirmative admissions" and special admissions programs.[3] There is empirical evidence to support the prevailing view, and the strongest evidence comes from a comparative history of admissions practices at Harvard, Yale, and Princeton. Jerome Karabel's exhaustive archival research reveals that Yale and Princeton adopted race-conscious affirmative action only after riots in Watts, Detroit, and Newark and the "terrifying wave of riots in the wake of Martin Luther King's assassination" (Karabel 2005, 406–07). Even Harvard, which began to take race-conscious affirmative action earlier than Yale and Princeton, experienced a surge in black enrollment after the disruptions of the mid- to late 1960s.

But an examination of a broader set of schools reveals that the Big Three were not representative of other highly selective schools. Yale and Princeton especially were laggards in adopting race-conscious affirmative action, as were other socially exclusive schools—such as Amherst and Williams—that were historically identified with the Protestant elite (Stulberg and Chen 2008). The first race-conscious affirmative action programs were actually established in the early to mid-1960s at schools led by liberally minded northern administrators who were inspired by the example of the southern civil rights movement to remedy black exclusion from college education. Many of them believed that black underrepresentation in higher education was a direct outgrowth of broader social and economic inequalities in American life—specifically, racial inequality in public education. Although they were doubtless aware of the challenging conditions in education that black students in the South faced, they also were motivated by the racial character of urban-suburban inequalities in the larger metropolitan areas of the North. Where such administrators were relatively unconstrained by the countervailing demands of alumni, trustees, students, and other potentially powerful stakeholders, they seized the opportunity to institute race-conscious affirmative action programs (Stulberg and Chen 2008).

Perhaps the clearest example is Cornell University. Cornell's earliest race-conscious affirmative action program, known as the Cornell Opportunity Program, admitted an inaugural class of ten students in 1964, followed by thirty-seven students in the subsequent year. Most of the students had been recruited from predominantly black high schools across New York state (Greenland, Chen, and Stulberg 2010, 17–19). The program can be traced back to at least a year earlier, when the university's president, James Perkins, formed a university-wide committee to study how Cornell could facilitate the education of "qualified students" who had grown up in "disadvantaged" social, cultural, and economic backgrounds. The committee recommended that Cornell begin a scholarship program targeting the "culturally disadvantaged" student—by which it meant "students whose racial, social, or educational backgrounds" made it unlikely that they would be enrolled in a top university without special consideration (Greenland, Chen, and Stulberg) 2010, 17; see also Downs 1999, 46–54). It went on to note that the program should consider all types of disadvantage, though it would naturally focus on black students, who they believed experienced the most severe disadvantages in American society.

The committee also recommended that the scholarship program work out a new way of identifying and admitting students. This was because the committee—citing new research by Kenneth B. Clark and Lawrence Plotkin—believed that the "usual criteria" did not reliably predict how well disadvantaged students would do in school, and the Scholastic Aptitude Test (SAT) was especially problematic in this regard. If it relied on traditional criteria, the new program would run the risk of rejecting students who were perfectly capable of doing satisfactory work at a top university

(Committee on Disadvantaged Students, quoted in Greenland, Chen, and Stulberg 2010, 17–19). When the Cornell Opportunity Program eventually began recruiting students from predominantly black high schools throughout the state, test scores were given less weight than high school transcripts or counselors' recommendations (Greenland, Chen, and Stulberg 2010, 17–19).

What motivated Perkins to take race-conscious affirmative action? No riots or protests of much significance had roiled Cornell in 1963 or 1964, certainly none comparable in scale to the iconic disruptions that would erupt in the late 1960s. Perkins himself would credit the lawsuits, marches, and demonstrations of the southern-based civil rights movement. In a 1968 speech to the United Negro College Fund, he explicitly referred to the "Brown case in 1954 and the rise of a visible concern for the equal treatment of minority groups" as his central inspiration. The civil rights movement had "stirred" his conscience as well as the conscience of others at Cornell and elsewhere. It had led them to ask "why we really have so few Black students." What they concluded was that a "passive policy would only guarantee a continuation of de facto exclusion." It was necessary to experiment with new policies and challenging ideas, including the possibility that SAT scores were simply inadequate for assessing whether black and disadvantaged students were capable of succeeding in a rigorous academic environment (Perkins, quoted in Greenland, Chen, and Stulberg 2010, 20).

By the mid-1960s race-conscious affirmative action was initiated for similar reasons at some of the top public universities outside of the South. For example, affirmative action began at the University of Michigan under the leadership of Provost Roger W. Heyns, who in 1963 convened the Ad Hoc Committee on the Negro in Higher Education to explore how the university might increase the enrollment of "disadvantaged" students. In 1964, after receiving the committee's recommendations, Heyns announced the establishment of the Opportunity Awards Program, which recruited and admitted students from predominantly black schools in Detroit. The program enrolled seventy students in 1964. Of these students, sixty-eight were black and two white. It enrolled 110 students in 1965—ninety-two black students, sixteen white students, one Native American student, and one Asian American student (Opportunity Award Program 1968).

Michigan program students, like Cornell Opportunity Program students, were given a modest degree of preference at the point of admission. For instance, most students in the first Opportunity Awards Program cohort met university standards, but it was necessary to make exceptions for academic deficits in a number of cases (Greenland, Chen, and Stulberg 2010, 16). Heyns wanted to "increase the number of qualified Negro students enrolled" at Michigan because he felt that it was important to give "educational opportunities" to academically capable students whose socioeconomic backgrounds might act as a barrier in some way to their enrollment at the university. Moreover, he felt that Michigan, as a public university, also had a distinct responsibility to "participate appropriately in the national movement to improve the status of the American Negro in our society" (Heyns, quoted in Stulberg and Chen 2008, 52).

Michigan and Cornell were not the only schools that began taking race-conscious affirmative action in the early to mid-1960s. Other early adopters included a number of highly selective public and private universities across the country, such as Swarthmore, Wesleyan, Northwestern, Columbia, the University of Pennsylvania, Duke, and the University of California, Los Angeles. The program at UCLA, known as the Educational Opportunities Program, for instance, was also explicitly aimed at expanding opportunities for "disadvantaged" youth, targeting mainly racial minorities. Its first cohort included thirty-three students, three of whom were admitted under the 2 percent rule, which exempted 2 percent of students at the University of California from normal admissions standards (Stulberg and Chen 2008, 53).

Programs in this first wave of race-conscious affirmative action certainly varied in the ways they sought to increase black enrollment. Moreover, colleges and universities were experimenting with many different types of programs in the early to mid-1960s—not only admissions programs but also recruitment programs and compensatory education programs for promising high school students. However, these early programs generally had four characteristics in common. First, they combined both hard and soft forms of affirmative action. That is to say, they invoked racial considerations not only during the recruitment process (soft affirmative action) but also in the decision to admit (hard affirmative action).[4] For instance, both the Cornell Opportunity Program and the Opportunity Awards Program at Michigan targeted predominantly black schools to increase the number of black applicants, but they also granted special consideration to black applicants whose traditional credentials would not have earned them a coveted spot at a top college. Second, race was only one kind of "disadvantage" that was eligible for special consideration. To be sure, first-wave programs explicitly targeted racial minority enrollment. But others were also eligible for special consideration. As the figures from Michigan's program indicate, white applicants from the same schools and neighborhoods could enroll through the Opportunity Awards Program as well. Race was a key consideration, but it was one consideration among many. Third, first-wave programs had a strong and clear geographic focus. Both the Cornell Opportunity Program and Opportunity Awards Program (and perhaps even the Educational Opportunities Program at UCLA) targeted segregated urban high schools in northern metropolitan areas. The administrators who started such programs were concerned primarily with extending educational opportunity to capable students from specific disadvantaged communities in their own states and near their own campuses. Finally, first-wave programs granted only a modest degree of preference on the basis of race. Most students admitted under the programs at Cornell, Michigan, and UCLA appeared to have met university admissions standards, and only a small number of applicants were granted academic allowances of any significance.

BETWEEN WATTS AND BAKKE: THE SECOND WAVE

A second wave of race-conscious affirmative action emerged in the wake of the urban riots and campus protests of the mid- to late 1960s. This second wave was in some ways even more heterogeneous than the first. It included schools that had sat out the first wave but belatedly adopted race-conscious affirmative action in response to a growing sense of crisis. It also included early-adopting schools that expanded and broadened affirmative action programs they had started years earlier. The number of schools taking affirmative action rose, and the types of programs proliferated. What most of the second-wave programs had in common was the relatively strong degree of preference they gave to racial minority applicants. In general, these later programs leaned fairly heavily on racial considerations in taking affirmative action, particularly during the process of evaluating applicants.

Perhaps the two best-known examples of second-wave programs were implemented not at undergraduate institutions but rather at law and medical schools. As revealed in the DeFunis v. Odegaard ruling (416 U.S. 312 [1974]), the University of Washington Law School operated a separate-track affirmative action program in 1971. Applications to the law school were divided into two groups, one for whites and the other for applicants who self-identified as a member of a racial minority (that is, using the labels from the policy itself, black, Chicano, American Indian, or Filipino). If the applicant did not indicate minority status, then his or her application would go through the regular evaluation procedure. If the applicant did indicate minority status, then his or her application was sent to one of two subcommittees and evaluated apart from nonminority applications. Hence minority applications were evaluated on a separate track from others, and they were not judged competitively against the rest of the applicant pool.

The medical school at the University of California, Davis, also operated a separate-track program but combined it with a set-aside policy, as noted in the Bakke decision (Regents of the University of California v. Bakke, 438 U.S. 265 [1978]). For a period from 1971 to 1974, sixteen out of one hundred seats were set aside at the University of California, Davis, medical school for matriculants who had indicated that they were a member of a "disadvantaged" group—which was defined in practice as membership in a racial or ethnic minority group (438 U.S. 265 [1978]). No disadvantaged whites were admitted through the program, though many applied for consideration. Race was not just one of many criteria at either school; it was central to the structure of the admissions process.

During this period in the late 1960s and the early 1970s, a number of undergraduate programs also adopted affirmative action programs for the first time or increased the degree of consideration given to race in the admissions process. It remains unclear whether most of these programs categorically separated candidates through set-asides or separate tracks. Most did, however, involve a more aggressive program of recruiting students of color to increase the admissions pool and providing a degree of additional consideration to racial minorities, even taking some risk on candidates who were not considered to be traditionally qualified for admission. Swarthmore College, for example, was guided by a young, liberal admissions administrator, and it became an early affirmative action adopter in 1964. But it pursued a more aggressive policy after the campus faced substantial—though nonviolent—student protests in the year after Dr. King's 1968 assassination. Williams College, by contrast, adopted affirmative action for the first time in the late 1960s, prompted by student action after King's death (Stulberg and Chen 2008).

Despite the proliferation of affirmative action programs during the second wave—or perhaps because of their proliferation—the degree to which race could be considered in the admissions process was narrowed substantially in the late 1970s. Aggressive models of race-conscious affirmative action—including quotas, set-asides, and separate-track programs, which treated aspiring students in categorically different ways during the admissions process—were struck down by the Supreme Court in its famously fractured Bakke decision of 1978. In lieu of such models, after Bakke colleges and universities adopted programs that treated race as one of several "plus" factors that could enhance the competitiveness of a particular applicant. Schools also generally ceased justifying the operation of such programs on compensatory grounds. In keeping with the message of the Bakke ruling, they also emphasized that race-conscious affirmative action generated educational value for all students, who would benefit from the experience of belonging to a student body composed of people from varied backgrounds, abilities, and outlooks—and not just peers who had gotten the best grades and test scores (Lipson 2011).

Both changes in emphasis signaled how the scope of affirmative action had shrunk since the heyday of the second wave, but they also pointed to the manner in which schools could clear both prongs of strict scrutiny by the federal courts, which under Bakke would be directed to ask whether the programs they were running were narrowly tailored to serve a compelling state interest. Bakke was hence as much a beginning as an end. On one hand, it did little to resolve the fundamental conflicts over race-conscious policy making that had given rise to the lawsuit. On the other, it ushered in a third wave of race-conscious affirmative action, made up of a much more limited set of programs than in earlier years.

THE RETRENCHMENT OF AFFIRMATIVE ACTION AMID THE PERSISTENCE OF THE ACHIEVEMENT GAP

Despite the fairly stringent limits set by Bakke on race-conscious affirmative action, such programs continued to come under sustained political and legal attack through the 1980s. By the mid-1990s, opposition to affirmative action had gained traction and momentum, leaping into the realm of electoral politics through a 1995 decision of the University of California Regents to eliminate affirmative action at all University of California campuses and the subsequent passage of Proposition 209. This California ballot initiative essentially eliminated all race-conscious affirmative action operated by the state government, and voters in several other states seemed inclined to follow suit. By the end of the first decade of the twenty-first century, race-conscious affirmative action had been prohibited by ballot initiative in California, Washington state, Nebraska, and Michigan. It also had been retired in the public higher education system in Florida by Governor Jeb Bush (Pusser 2004; Espenshade and Radford 2009, 5) and struck down (though later reinstated) at the University of Texas by the 1996 appellate court in Hopwood v. Texas (78 F.3d 932 [5th Cir. 1996]) (Kurlaender and Flores 2005, 26).

The legal challenge to race-conscious affirmative action intensified in 2003, when the Supreme Court addressed race-conscious affirmative action for the first time since Bakke. In a pair of Supreme Court decisions involving the University of Michigan, Grutter v. Bollinger et al. (539 U.S. 306 [2003]) and Gratz et al. v. Bollinger et al. (539 U.S. 244 [2003]), race-conscious affirmative action was allowed to continue but was again further constrained by the Court. Grutter countenanced the flexible use of race in the context of an individualized, holistic review process of the kind followed by the University of Michigan Law School. But Gratz struck down the use of race at the University of Michigan's College of Letters, Science, and Arts, which featured a point system that was popular at large state schools with heavy application loads. The program awarded a fixed number of points to applicants from designated racial minority groups (see Ancheta 2005), a setup that the Court found too automatic and mechanical to be narrowly tailored.

In response to the prospect of declining racial minority enrollment—or actual declines in minority enrollment—some states tried alternative ways of achieving racial diversity on their campuses. Florida, California, and Texas moved to seemingly race-neutral "percent plans," which automatically admitted some proportion of the top high school graduates to the state college system. These plans relied on high school racial segregation to produce a racially diverse group of college applicants who qualified for admission (Espenshade and Radford 2009, 362).

But the elimination of race-conscious affirmative action had a consistent outcome almost everywhere in the country. The enrollment of underrepresented racial minorities fell at education institutions that no longer employed race-conscious affirmative action—even those with alternatives such as the percent plans. Thomas Espenshade and Alexandria Radford (2009, 5), citing a UCLA publication, note that in the first year that the University of California schools could no longer take race into consideration in admissions, the proportion of underrepresented students of color who entered UCLA as freshmen fell from 24.4 percent (in the fall of 1997) to 17.5 percent (in the fall of 1998). By the fall of 2006, the proportion of black students entering UCLA as freshmen had reached a thirty-year low of just 2 percent (Espenshade and Radford 2009, 5; Tamar Lewin, "Colleges Regroup after Voters Ban Race Preferences," *New York Times*, January 26, 2007, p. A1). At the University of Texas, after the Hopwood decision of 1996, the proportion of black freshmen at the flagship campus in Austin declined from 5 percent in 1995 to less than 3 percent two years later (Espenshade and Radford 2009, 361). In the first year after Michigan's Proposition 2 eliminated affirmative action in January 2007, even after some students already had been admitted under the old policies, the proportion of African American, Latino, and Native American students entering as freshmen in the fall of 2007 fell to 11.4 percent—from 12.7 percent the previous fall (Espenshade and Radford 2009, 5).

This development, not surprisingly, provoked further controversy and disagreement. Some observers interpreted the declines as evidence that race played a much more substantial role in the admissions process than defenders of affirmative action had been prepared to admit, while others saw the declines as strong proof that there was no workable substitute for racial considerations if the objective was achieving racial diversity. Whatever the case, selective colleges and universities found it far more difficult to maintain racial diversity wherever race-conscious affirmative action had been abolished.

Race-conscious affirmative action is now more limited in scope than it has ever been, yet the controversy over it shows no sign of abating. Even as college administrators and policy makers continue to grapple with the ongoing challenge of promoting racial diversity on their campuses, especially in areas of the country where affirmative action is no longer permissible, scholars and researchers continue to debate the merit, legitimacy, and future prospects of affirmative action policy.

Abigail and Stephan Thernstrom remain the most prominent, persistent, and influential critics of race-conscious affirmative action. They argue, in effect, that no race-conscious affirmative action programs are narrowly tailored. When race is considered in the application process, it overwhelms the influence of any other supplementary factor, overriding even basic measures of academic merit. For evidence of how heavily race has been weighed, they imply, it is necessary to do little more than compare the average SAT scores of black and white students at elite schools. In 1994, for instance, black undergraduates at Stanford had earned an average combined SAT score of 1,164, but the average white student arrived on campus with a score of 1,335. An even larger differential existed for black freshmen who entered Berkeley a few years earlier, in 1988. The average combined SAT score for black first-years was under 1,000, placing them 304 points below the average white first-year and 326 points below the average Asian first-year in the same year. In 1992 black-white SAT gaps of comparable magnitude could be found at many schools: Princeton (150), Cornell (162), Northwestern (180), Virginia (241), and Rice (271) (Thernstrom and Thernstrom 1997, 388, 406, 408).

The Thernstroms argue that overreliance on affirmative action in the admission of black college students does not help black students. Rather, it harms them by placing them in academic environments where they are not prepared to compete with their peers. Affirmative action programs, in other words, create a mismatch between black college students who are admitted under them and the academic demands of the selective institutions that they attend. The result, the Thernstroms argue, is an unusually high drop-out rate among black college students. In the end, they conclude, no program of race-conscious affirmative action can really be narrowly tailored. The magnitude of the black-white achievement gap is too great. The Thernstroms suggest that the solution to black underrepresentation at selective colleges and universities is not social policy but hard work by black students themselves (Thernstrom and Thernstrom 1997, 391–92, 405–09, 422).

The most influential response to the Thernstroms' critique of affirmative action has been mounted by the former Ivy League college presidents William G. Bowen and Derek Bok. In *The Shape of the River*, Bowen and Bok (1998) examine data from the College and Beyond database and reach very different conclusions from the Thernstroms. They argue that the black-white SAT gap at selective institutions is a poor measure of the weight accorded to race in the admissions process. This differential is simply a reflection of the fact that black students nationwide have lower SAT scores on average than white students. A more informative way to gauge the magnitude of racial preference would be to compare the academic credentials of black students who would have been rejected under a race-neutral policy with the academic credentials of black students who would have gained admission anyway. Bowen and Bok make the calculation for a subsample of schools in their database and discover that the difference between "retrospectively rejected" students and retained black students is small, amounting to 36 points on the SAT (Bowen and Bok 1998, 42–43).

Moreover, they find little evidence to support the mismatch hypothesis. Although black academic underperformance remains a genuine puzzle, black students at selective colleges graduate at higher rates than black students at less selective schools, even among black students with the lowest SAT scores. Bowen and Bok estimate the effect of a race-neutral policy on black enrollment at selective institutions and find that black enrollment would fall anywhere from 50 to 70 percent. The academic profile of black students at selective institutions would hardly improve under a race-neutral policy, but there would be far fewer black students on campus under such a policy regime. This finding is all the more significant because there does not appear to be a workable substitute for race-conscious affirmative action. Citing the work of Thomas Kane (1998), Bowen and Bok point out that there are simply too few low-income students of color with high test scores to make up the shortfall, and a program of affirmative action based on class would not do much for racial diversity (Bowen and Bok 1998, 47, 50–51).

Thernstrom and Thernstrom (1999) have responded to Bowen and Bok with their customary intensity, but our reading of the literature as it has developed is that most of Bowen and Bok's main conclusions have held up over time. To be sure, Espenshade and Radford (2009, 92) calculate the magnitude of racial preferences using new data from the National Study of College Experience, finding that black students at the surveyed schools receive a preference that is equivalent to 310 points on the SAT. This seems consistent with what Thernstrom and Thernstrom report. However, much in the spirit of Bowen and Bok, Espenshade and Radford (94) caution that the actual effect of race is probably much smaller because race is likely correlated with so many important unobservables.

At the same time, there remains little persuasive evidence to confirm the mismatch hypothesis at the undergraduate level. Several authors have examined other datasets using a variety of statistical methods, and all have reached the same conclusion as Bowen and Bok (Alon and Tienda 2005; Charles et al. 2009; Espenshade and Radford 2009). Espenshade and Radford (2009) also confirm in their analysis that eliminating race-conscious affirmative action would dramatically lower black shares of college enrollment. But perhaps the most important area of corroboration concerns the question of whether class is a serviceable proxy for race. Espenshade and Radford's further analysis (2009, 355–61) of data from the National Study of College Experience indicates that there is no substitute for race-conscious affirmative action that would enable college and university administrators to maintain current levels of racial diversity. Shifting from racial consideration to class consideration would still lead to a large drop in black enrollment.

If there is no substitute for race-conscious affirmative action, then it is mainly because many of the racial inequalities that motivated the establishment of such programs are still with us today—more than fifty years after Brown sought to address racial inequality in education. Indeed, more than half a century after Brown, many public schools remain highly segregated and unequal, and the pipeline of black students to selective colleges and universities is still tenuous and thin. This is the main continuity that connects now with then.

Evidence of current and persistent racial inequality in education is not difficult to muster. Schools across the country remain racially segregated (table 3.4). Of course, there has been improvement on some measures for some regions. Compared with their predecessors, far fewer black students in the South and the West attend schools that are 90 percent or more black. There also has been a substantial decline in the percentage of black students in the South who attend schools that are 50 percent or more black. But improvement has been slow for other regions. In 2001 nearly half of all black students in the Midwest were enrolled in schools that were highly segregated, just a few points down from 1968 and few points up from 1991. Schools in the Northeast have become even more segregated since 1968, with more than half of all black students attending highly segregated schools. Large majorities of black students all across the country still attend majority-black schools. Schools located in central-city neighborhoods

Table 3.4   Black Students Attending Segregated and Highly
            Segregated Schools, Various Years, 1968 to 2001
            (percentage)

Region	1968	1988	1991	2001
	50–100 percent minority			
South	80.9	56.5	60.1	69.8
Border	71.6	59.6	59.3	67.9
Northeast	66.8	77.3	75.2	78.4
Midwest	77.3	70.1	69.7	72.9
West	72.2	67.1	69.2	75.8
	90–100 percent minority			
South	77.8	24.0	26.1	31.0
Border	60.2	34.5	34.5	41.6
Northeast	42.7	48.0	49.8	51.2
Midwest	58.0	41.8	39.9	46.8
West	50.8	28.6	26.6	30.0

Source: Orfield and Lee (2004, 20), reprinted with permission.

of large metropolitan areas remain the most extremely segregated. Nearly 2.5 million black students were enrolled in such schools in 2001–2002. These schools, for the average black student, were overwhelmingly minority (Orfield and Lee 2004, 34–35).

Black students also exhibit higher exposure to poverty than their white counterparts. This is partly because black poverty rates are higher than white poverty rates, and racial segregation concentrates exposure to poverty in segregated black schools. The typical black student in 2005–2006 attended a school in which 59 percent of the students were poor, whereas the average white student went to a school in which 31 percent of the students were poor (Orfield and Lee 2007, 19). Moreover, black students are much more likely than white students to attend a high poverty or extreme poverty school (table 3.5). In 2005–2006, more than a million black students, or 13 percent of black students nationwide, attended extreme poverty schools, where the poverty rate among students was above 90 percent. A little more than a quarter of a million white students were enrolled in such schools, amounting to only 1 percent of the country's white students. Nearly two-thirds of all black students attended a school in which at least half of the students were poor, compared with less than a quarter of whites. Twenty percent of white students attended an extremely

Table 3.5   Percentage Distribution of Students at Schools of Varying
Poverty Levels, by Race, 2005 to 2006

Percentage poor students	White	Black
0–10	20%	5%
11–20	17	5
21–30	16	7
31–40	14	9
41–50	12	11
51–60	9	11
61–70	6	12
71–80	3	13
81–90	2	14
91–100	1	13

Source: Orfield and Lee (2007, 22) a portion of which is reprinted with permission.
Note: Poverty levels are measured by Orfield and Lee as the percentage of students receiving free or reduced-price lunch.

low poverty school, compared with 5 percent of black students (Orfield and Lee 2007, 22).

Although they have fluctuated somewhat in size over time, racial gaps in academic achievement continue to exist at every grade level. Data from the National Assessment of Educational Progress (NAEP) indicate that the black-white gap among seventeen-year-olds in reading and mathematics fell by roughly 0.5 standard deviations from the early 1970s to the late 1980s (Jencks and Phillips 1998, 3). But the gaps today are still substantial. The reading gap in 2009 for twelfth graders was 27 points, and the math gap was 30 points, which translates roughly into a difference of 0.8 standard deviations (National Assessment of Educational Progress 2009, 11, 27). This is comparable to the magnitude of the gaps identified in the Coleman Report. Perhaps most troubling from the perspective of college admissions is the continuing black-white gap in SAT scores (figure 3.1). The gap in verbal and math scores narrowed progressively from 1975 to 1990, but the gap for the period 2007 to 2008 is roughly 100 points on the verbal portion and 110 points on the math portion.

Racial differences in average performance can translate into large racial disparities in absolute numbers at the high end of the test score distribution. This disparity seems to exist. As noted by Krueger, Rothstein, and Turner (2006, 290), roughly 250 white students in 2000 attained a perfect score, compared with only 2 black students. Almost 22,000 white students earned a score of 1,400 or higher, compared with only 322 black students. These differences have serious implications for the competitiveness of

Figure 3.1   Black-White Gap in SAT Scores, 1975–1976 to
2007–2008

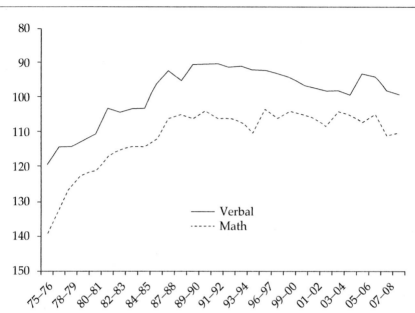

Source: Authors' compilation based on U.S. Department of Education (2009, 208, table 143); U.S. Department of Education (1996, 127, table 126).
Note: Figures for all years represent average black scores minus average white scores. Data are not available for 1976–1977, 1985–1986, 1995–1996, and 1997–1998.

black applicants to highly selective institutions, where 65 percent of all students who are admitted score 1,400 or higher on their SATs (Krueger, Rothstein, and Turner 2006, 290–92).

Racial segregation and racial inequality in public education remain highly correlated in numerous ways; moreover, racial segregation continues to ensure that the socioeconomic and academic composition of the peer group surrounding a typical black student is very different from the peer group of the typical white student. But several rigorous new studies provide the strongest evidence yet of a causal link between racial segregation and the achievement gap. David Card and Jesse Rothstein (2007) use College Board data on SAT scores to estimate the impact of metropolitan-level racial segregation on the black-white test-score gap. They find that the gap is larger in more heavily segregated cities, even when a rich set of individual-level, school-level, and metropolitan-level controls are included in their models. Examining panel data from a Texas administrative dataset, Eric A. Hanushek and Steven G. Rivkin (2009) find that high proportions of black students and "rookie teachers" at a school contribute to the achievement gap. The effect of racial segregation on black math scores is particularly acute for students in the upper parts of the initial achievement distribution. It appears that the highest achieving black students—precisely the ones with the potential to be accepted by a selective college—are the students who are most adversely impacted by having a high proportion of black peers in segregated schools. This suggests that reducing racial segregation and improving the quality of certain school inputs may help to reduce the achievement gap and increase the flow of black students into selective institutions.

But the possibility that the achievement gap is amenable to policy interventions is counterbalanced by the sobering observation that this gap appears very early in childhood and does not appear to fall as students progress through school (table 3.6). In studies that have now been carried out on a variety of large datasets, estimates of the raw black-white achievement gap for reading and math are fairly large across all grade levels, and there is evidence that the regression-adjusted gap increases from one grade to the next. In their analysis of the new Early Childhood Longitudinal Study, Roland Fryer and Steven Levitt (2004) do show that the observed gap among kindergarteners can be almost completely accounted for by using only a few variables, including measures of socioeconomic status, number of children's books in the home, birth weight, and teenage motherhood. But the gap grows over the first and second grades. As students reach the end of the third grade, it becomes difficult for Fryer and Levitt (2006) to explain the black-white test score gap with the characteristics they observe. What is most puzzling is that they are unable to find evidence supporting any explanation for the gap, including the measures of school quality available in their dataset.

Hence the fundamental sources of the achievement gap remain something of a mystery to researchers, and the subject continues to stimulate important research. What cannot be doubted is that racial segregation and racial inequality continue to be highly correlated in American public education today, and the pipeline to college admissions is still narrow, especially the flow of black students whose academic preparation and educational achievements have made them fully competitive for admission to highly selective colleges and universities. If it was difficult half a century ago for highly selective institutions to create a racially diverse student body without taking race-conscious affirmative action, it remains difficult today.

Table 3.6   Standardized Measures of the Black-White Achievement
             Gap in Selected Studies for Selected Grades

Grade	Study	Raw differences in means	
		Math	Reading
K (fall)	Fryer-Levitt (2006)	−0.66	−0.40
K	Fryer-Levitt (2006)	−0.73	−0.45
K	Murnane et al. (2006)	−1.00	−1.18
1	Fryer-Levitt (2006)	−0.76	−0.52
1	Bali-Alvarez (2004)	−0.55	−0.35
3	Fryer-Levitt (2006)	−0.88	−0.77
3	Hanushek-Rivkin (2009)	−0.70	
3	Clotfelter, Ladd, and Vigdor (2009)	−0.78	−0.71
4	Phillips-Chin (2004)	−0.90	−0.83
4	Bali-Alvarez (2004)	−0.50	−0.45
4	Clotfelter, Ladd, and Vigdor (2009)	−0.82	−0.76
5	Hanushek-Rivkin (2009)	−0.73	
5	Murnane et al. (2006)	−1.03	−1.09
5	Stiefel et al. (2007)	−0.81	−0.73
5	Clotfelter, Ladd, and Vigdor (2009)	−0.79	−0.77
8	Phillips-Chin (2004)	−1.06	−0.85
8	Hanushek-Rivkin (2009)	−0.76	
8	Stiefel et al. (2007)	−0.84	−0.78
8	Clotfelter, Ladd, and Vigdor (2009)	−0.81	−0.78

Source: Authors' compilation of data from Clotfelter, Ladd, and Vigdor (2009, 399, 402).
Notes: This table includes the gaps reported in Clotfelter, Ladd, and Vigdor (2009).

CONCLUSION

Colleges and universities have become substantially more racially diverse
since the 1950s. Yet the inequalities in K–12 education that prompted the
development of affirmative action in the early 1960s still stubbornly persist. Not surprisingly, this contributes to an enduring racial gap in four-
year college enrollment and graduation rates (Espenshade and Radford
2009, chap. 10; Kurlaender and Flores 2005, 26).

Given these persistent gaps, what is the future of race-conscious affirmative action? Has it reached the end of its usefulness as a policy to bring
true diversity to our nation's college campuses, or is it still necessary? Is it
still politically viable, or has the American public grown intolerant of policies that it perceives as insufficiently color blind in their application?

Despite their modesty by historical standards, current race-conscious
affirmative action programs remain hugely controversial. Affirmative ac-

tion persists today, but it is a far more restricted set of policies than it was in the years between the riots and protests of the mid- to late 1960s and the Bakke decision of the late 1970s. In certain respects, today's race-conscious affirmative action programs resemble the kind of programs that emerged during the first-wave of affirmative action, in the early 1960s. In many of these programs, race was only one of several nonacademic factors that could be taken into consideration during the admissions process, and it was not apparently given a fixed value. Sometimes the degree of preference was extremely small. Today's race-conscious affirmative action programs are similar in these respects; they are large in their ambitions but modest in their execution. Maybe we have come full circle.

In the 2003 Grutter decision, Justice Sandra Day O'Connor, who was writing for the majority, expressed the hope that "25 years from now, the use of racial preferences will no longer be necessary." At William Bowen's suggestion, Alan Krueger, Jesse Rothstein, and Sara Turner (2006) projected what the black-white test score distribution might look like twenty-five years from now, and they argue that "[e]conomic progress alone is unlikely to narrow the achievement gap" enough to achieve current levels of racial diversity in the admissions process without taking race into account. They go on to argue that even if we were to experience a convergence in test scores comparable to the one seen in the 1980s, racial diversity at the most selective institutions would still be lower than its current levels. While we hope that we are wrong, we share their skepticism that racial considerations in college admissions will no longer be necessary in twenty-five years. Race-conscious affirmative action programs were partly conceived of as a response to the achievement gap—along with the education inequalities that gave rise to it—and they will remain the only serviceable tool for constructing racially diverse college classes as long as the achievement gap remains large.

Twenty-five years is not a long time. The college students of Justice O'Connor's quarter century were born only a few years ago. As Espenshade and Radford (2009, 405) note, the children born in 2010 will belong to the collegiate class matriculating in 2028. This class will graduate twenty-five years after the Grutter decision. How these children fare in school over the next few years and whether they develop the same achievement gaps as the cohorts immediately ahead of them will tell us whether we should hold our breath—and whether we can really close the book on this legacy of the southern civil rights movement.

This chapter is based on a paper prepared for "Racial Inequality in a Post-Racial World?" conference, jointly sponsored by the Center on African-

American Politics and Society and the School of International and Public Affairs at Columbia University and by the Russell Sage Foundation. The research reported herein received grant support from the Spencer Foundation and financial support from the Robert Wood Johnson Scholars Program in Health Policy Research, New York University, Northwestern University, and the University of Michigan. The authors would like to thank Frederick C. Harris and Robert C. Lieberman for their enormous patience and skilled encouragement as well as Christina Greer and the other conference participants for their thoughtful comments. All errors and oversights are the responsibility of the authors.

NOTES

1. In fact, one study analyzing data from the National Educational Longitudinal Study (1988 to 1994) shows that black high school graduates were more likely than white high school graduates to enroll in any type of college, even when taking into consideration the large number of black students enrolling in historically black colleges and universities. However, this is true primarily for black high school students coming from disadvantaged socioeconomic backgrounds (Bennett and Xie 2003, 578).
2. Segregation appears to have had direct effects, as well. Studies on subsequent periods in American history suggest that racial segregation may have also contributed to a higher black drop-out rate (Guryan 2004) and lower rates of black educational attainment (Reber 2007) during the 1970s.
3. Skrentny is not alone in pointing to urban riots and campus protest as the prime mover of race-conscious affirmative action. See also Bowen and Bok (1998, 5–7), Wilkinson (1979, 262), Anderson (2004, 111), and many others.
4. We borrow the distinction between hard and soft affirmative action from our conversations with Jerome Karabel.

REFERENCES

Alon, Sigal, and Marta Tienda. 2005. "Assessing the 'Mismatch' Hypothesis: Differences in College Graduation Rates by Institutional Selectivity." *Sociology of Education* 78(October): 294–315.

Ancheta, Angelo N. 2005. "After *Grutter* and *Gratz*: Higher Education, Race, and the Law." In *Higher Education and the Color Line: College Access, Racial Equity, and Social Change*, edited by Gary Orfield, Patricia Marin, and Catherine L. Horn. Cambridge, Mass.: Harvard Education Press.

Anderson, Terry H. 2004. *The Pursuit of Fairness: A History of Affirmative Action.* New York: Oxford University Press.

Bali, Valentia A., and R. Michael Alvarez. 2004. "The Race Gap in Student Achieve-

ment Scores: Longitudinal Evidence from a Racially Diverse School District."
The Policy Studies Journal 32(3): 393–415.

Bennett, Pamela R., and Yu Xie. 2003. "Revisiting Racial Differences in College At-
tendance: The Role of Historically Black Colleges and Universities." *American Sociological Review* 68(August): 567–80.

Bowen, William G., and Derek Bok. 1998. *The Shape of the River: The Long-Term Consequences of Considering Race in College and University Admissions*. Princeton, N.J.:
Princeton University Press.

Card, David, and Alan Krueger. 1992. "School Quality and Black-White Relative
Earnings." *Quarterly Journal of Economics* 107(1): 151–200.

Card, David, and Jesse Rothstein. 2007. "Racial Segregation and the Black-White
Test Score Gap." *Journal of Public Economics* 91(11–12): 2158–84.

Charles, Camille A., et al. 2009. *Taming the River: Negotiating the Academic, Financial,
and Social Currents in Selective Colleges and Universities*. Princeton, N.J.: Princeton
University Press.

Clotfelter, Charles T. 2004. *After Brown: The Rise and Retreat of School Desegregation*.
Princeton, N.J.: Princeton University Press.

Clotfelter, Charles T., Helen Ladd, and Jacob L. Vigdor. 2009. "The Academic
Achievement Gap in Grades 3 to 8." *Review of Economic and Statistics* 91(2): 398–
419.

Coleman, James S. 1966. *Equality of Educational Opportunity*. Washington: U.S. Government Printing Office.

Conant, James B. 1961. *Slums and Suburbs: A Commentary on Schools in Metropolitan
Areas*. New York: McGraw Hill.

Downs, Donald Alexander. 1999. *Cornell '69: Liberalism and the Crisis of the American
University*. Ithaca: Cornell University Press.

Espenshade, Thomas J., and Alexandria Walton Radford. 2009. *No Longer Separate,
Not Yet Equal: Race and Class in Elite College Admission and Campus Life*. Princeton,
N.J.: Princeton University Press.

Fryer, Roland G., Jr., and Steven D. Levitt. 2004. "Understanding the Black-White
Test Score Gap in the First Two Years of School." *Review of Economics and Statistics* 86(May): 447–64.

———. 2006. "The Black-White Test Score Gap Through Third Grade." *American
Law and Economics Review* 8(2): 249–81.

Gordon, Milton A. 1976. "An Analysis of Enrollment Data for Black Students in
Institutions of Higher Education, from 1940–1972." *Journal of Negro Education*
45(2): 117–21.

Greenland, Fiona, Anthony S. Chen, and Lisa M. Stulberg. 2010. "Beyond the Open
Door: The Origins of Affirmative Action in Undergraduate Admissions at Cor-
nell and the University of Michigan." Paper presented to the Policy History
Conference, sponsored by *Journal of Policy History* and the Institute for Political
History. Columbus, Ohio, June 4, 2010.

Guryan, Jonathan. 2004. "Desegregation and Black Dropout Rates." *American Economic Review* 94(4): 919–43.

Hall, Jacquelyn Dowd. 2005. "The Long Civil Rights Movement and the Political Uses of the Past." *Journal of American History* 91(4): 1233–63.

Hanushek, Eric A., and Steven G. Rivkin. 2009. "Harming the Best: How Schools Affect the Black-White Achievement Gap." *Journal of Policy Analysis and Management* 28(3): 366–93.

Hauser, Philip M., et al. 1964. *Integration of the Public Schools—Chicago.* Chicago: Advisory Panel on the Integration of the Public Schools.

Jencks, Christopher, and Meredith Phillips, eds. 1998. *The Black-White Test Score Gap.* Washington, D.C.: Brookings Institution Press.

Kane, Thomas. 1998. "Racial and Ethnic Preferences in College Admission." In *The Black-White Test Score Gap*, edited by Christopher Jencks and Meredith Phillips. Washington, D.C.: Brookings Institution Press.

Karabel, Jerome. 2005. *The Chosen: The Hidden History of Admission and Exclusion at Harvard, Yale, and Princeton.* Boston/New York: Houghton Mifflin Harcourt.

Karen, David. 1991. "The Politics of Class, Race, and Gender: Access to Higher Education, 1960–1986." *American Journal of Education* 99(2): 208–337.

Krueger, Alan, Jesse Rothstein, and Sarah Turner. 2006. "Race, Income, and College in 25 Years: Evaluating Justice O'Connor's Conjecture." *American Law and Economics Review* 8(2): 282–311.

Kurlaender, Michal, and Stella M. Flores. 2005. "The Racial Transformation of Higher Education." In *Higher Education and the Color Line: College Access, Racial Equity, and Social Change*, edited by Gary Orfield, Patricia Marin, and Catherine L. Horn. Cambridge, Mass.: Harvard Education Press.

Lipson, Daniel. 2011. "The Resilience of Affirmative Action in the 1980s: Innovation, Isomorphism, and Institutionalization in University Admissions." *Political Research Quarterly* 64(1): 132–44.

Margo, Robert A. 1986. "Educational Achievement in Segregated Schools: The Effects of 'Separate-but-Equal.'" *American Economic Review* 76(4): 794–801.

Massey, Douglas, and Nancy A. Denton. 1993. *American Apartheid: Segregation and the Making of the Underclass.* Cambridge, Mass.: Harvard University Press.

Murnane, Richard J., John B. Willett, Kristen L. Bub, and Kathleen McCartney (January 2006). "Explaining Puzzling Patterns in Black-White Achievement Gaps." Harvard Graduate School of Education.

National Assessment of Educational Progress. 2009. *Grade 12: Reading and Mathematics, 2009.* Washington, D.C.: National Center for Education Statistics.

National Commission on Professional Rights and Responsibilities. 1967. *Detroit, Michigan: A Study of Barriers to Equal Education Opportunity in a Large City.* Washington, D.C.: National Education Association.

Opportunity Award Program. 1968. Draft report, December 9, Box 1, UM Vice

President for Research Records. Bentley Historical Library, University of Michigan.

Orfield, Gary, and Chungmei Lee. 2004. *Brown at 50: King's Dream or Plessy's Nightmare?* Cambridge, Mass.: Harvard Civil Rights Project.

———. 2007. *Historic Reversals, Accelerating Resegregation, and the Need for New Integration Strategies.* Cambridge, Mass.: Harvard Civil Rights Project.

Phillips, Meredith, and Tiffani Chin. 2004. "School Inequality: What Do We Know?" In *Social Inequality*, edited by Kathryn Neckerman. New York: Russell Sage Foundation.

Pusser, Brian. 2004. *Burning Down the House: Politics, Governance, and Affirmative Action at the University of California.* Albany: State University of New York Press.

Reber, Sarah J. 2007. "School Desegregation and Educational Attainment for Blacks." Working Paper 13193. Cambridge, Mass.: National Bureau of Economic Research.

Skrentny, John David. 2002. "Policy-Elite Perceptions and Social Movement Success: Understanding Variations in Group Inclusion in Affirmative Action." *American Journal of Sociology* 111(6): 1762–1815.

Stiefel, Leanna, Amy Ellen Schwartz, and Ingrid Gould Ellen. 2007. "Disentangling the Test Score Gap: Probing the Evidence in a Large Urban School District." *Journal of Policy Analysis and Management* 26: 7–30.

Stulberg, Lisa M., and Anthony S. Chen. 2008. "Beyond Disruption: The Forgotten Origins of Affirmative Action in College and University Admissions, 1961–1969." Working Paper 2007-001. Gerald R. Ford School of Public Policy, University of Michigan.

Sugrue, Thomas J. 1996. *The Origins of the Urban Crisis: Race and Inequality in Postwar Detroit.* Princeton, N.J.: Princeton University Press.

Thernstrom, Stephan, and Abigail Thernstrom. 1997. *America in Black and White: One Nation, Indivisible.* New York: Simon and Schuster.

———. 1999. "Reflections on *The Shape of the River*." *UCLA Law Review* 46(5): 1583–1632.

U.S. Department of Education. 1996. *Digest of Education Statistics, 1996.* Washington, D.C.: National Center for Education Statistics.

———. 2009. *Digest of Education Statistics, 2009.* Washington, D.C.: National Center for Education Statistics.

Wilkinson, J. Harvie, III. 1979. *From Brown to Bakke: The Supreme Court and School Integration.* New York: Oxford University Press.

Chapter 4 | Racial Inequality in Employment in Postracial America

Dorian T. Warren

How DO WE understand persistent racial inequality in employment in an era of increased African American and Latino political and social inclusion? This question is one of the most significant and enduring challenges in our current post–civil rights, postindustrial, and so-called postracial era: the issue of increasing economic inequality in communities of color. The broader structural transformations of the American economy coupled with the significant decline in union density over the past thirty years have shaped current levels of inequality and poverty in communities of color (Massey 2007). For example, before, during, and even after the Great Recession that began in the fall of 2008, African American workers saw heavier job losses than other workers, owing to the continued hemorrhaging of unionized manufacturing jobs, the deunionization and downgrading of building, food, and home care services, and the adverse effects of privatization of the public sector—all industries in which black workers have been concentrated since the Second World War (Milkman 2006; Parks 2010; Uchitelle 2005; Wilson 1996). Replacing this massive disappearance of quality employment have been low-wage, nonunion jobs in the service sector, creating what Steven Pitts calls the two-dimensional crisis of work in black communities: unemployment and bad jobs (Pitts 2007; Appelbaum, Bernhardt, and Murnane 2003; National Employment Law Project 2011. In addition, we know that patterns of racial discrimination exist in both the highest and lowest tiers of labor-market job ladders, limiting employment opportunities for African Americans and Latinos regardless of education (Pager, Bonikowski, and Western 2009).

RACIAL REGIMES IN AMERICAN
POLITICAL ECONOMY

The primary mechanisms creating "durable racial inequality" (Brown et al. 2003, 22) in the employment context are exploitation and opportunity hoarding (Tilly 1998; Brown et al. 2003; Massey 2007). Borrowing Charles Tilly's concepts from his classic *Durable Inequality*, Douglas Massey defines *exploitation* as one "social group expropriat[ing] a resource produced by members of another social group and prevent[ing] them from realizing the full value of their effort in producing it," while *opportunity hoarding* is defined as a social group's restricting "access to a scarce resource, either through outright denial or by exercising monopoly control that requires out-group members to pay rent in return for access" (Massey 2007, 6; Tilly 1998). In the case of employment in the U.S. context, the dominant social group's use of both exploitation and opportunity hoarding have been inescapably racialized. And there has been both continuity and change in these two mechanisms in creating durable racial inequality in economic outcomes.

To understand fully the historical legacies and contemporary processes of durable racial inequality in employment, an explicit account of the role of race in American political economy is necessary. The basic notion is this: politics structures both racial and economic orders, and these orders are mutually constitutive. This account is related to, yet distinct from, the voluminous work of economic sociologists and institutionally oriented political scientists seeking to reembed markets in society and political institutions.[1] Drawing on the "new institutionalism" in both sociology and political science, Tim Bartley's (2007, 336) recent contribution focused on the "political construction of market institutions" comes close to the concept I advance here. But for Bartley and the vast majority of this research, race is entirely absent (Krippner and Alvarez 2007).[2] These deracialized and ahistorical accounts of market institutions in the American context fail to explain the evolution of American political economy over time, as well as attempts to challenge and transform economic inequalities with specifically racialized effects. In contrast, I "bring race in" by combining these neo-Polanyian and institutional accounts of markets with American political development scholarship that places race at the center of political development (King and Smith 2005; Lowndes, Novkov, and Warren 2008). The central role of race in my account challenges much of this recent scholarship on market institutions and provides better analytical leverage through which to understand racial inequality in employment outcomes.

Similarly, the central role of political economy in my account challenges much of the recent scholarship on race in American politics that ignores the relationship between historically specific economic regimes and racial orders (King and Smith 2005; Dawson and Cohen 2002; McClain et al. 2009).[3] Indeed, in their seminal article on "racial orders in American political development," Desmond King and Rogers Smith say explicitly that their approach "analyzes the 'political economy' of American racial systems by stressing the 'political,' not the 'economy'" (King and Smith 2005, 75). Leaving the "economy" out of their framework presumes that economic regimes are conceptually and empirically separate from state institutions. In contrast, my conception here of the political construction of racialized markets provides analytical traction in explaining broad political and economic developments in the U.S. context over time, specifically the successes and failures of the black freedom movement and the American labor movement's efforts to confront them.

Two important Polanyian concepts have emerged from the three decades of work in economic sociology focused on the political construction of markets: the embeddedness of markets and the double movement (Polanyi 2001; Krippner and Alvarez 2007; see also Granovetter 1985). Sharon Zukin and Paul DiMaggio define *political embeddedness* as "the manner in which economic institutions and decisions are shaped by a struggle for power that involves economic actors and nonmarket institutions, particularly the state and social classes" (Zukin and DiMaggio 1990, 20). Similarly, Fred Block advances a neo-Polanyian theoretical framework describing the relationship between politics and markets in this way: "Labor markets, in short, are politically structured institutions in which the relative power of the participants is shaped by legal institutions that grant or deny certain baskets of rights to employers and employees. And this, in turn, generates an ongoing process of political contestation to shape and reshape these ground rules to improve the relative position of the different actors" (Block 2003, 6). The argument here is not about whether states are always involved in constructing and shaping labor markets; they are. Rather, the question becomes what kind of politically structured markets will exist, what are their consequences, and who gets to decide?

This is where Karl Polanyi's concept of the "double movement" comes in. The movement by free-market liberals and business interests to shape markets to their benefit via ideologies and practices of coerced labor, favorable rules and subsidies, deregulation, free trade, and privatization is expected to produce a countermovement to push for social protections for workers, whether through social welfare legislation, trade unions, organizations based on ascriptive categories, or other mechanisms (Polanyi 2001; Block 2003; Silver 2003). Yet these countermovements do not arise in a vacuum (whether business or worker organizations); the political construction of racial and economic orders directly shapes social groups' rights and the political opportunities they have to organize and mobilize. Zukin and DiMaggio (1990, 21) make this point clearly: "Political embeddedness is illustrated most clearly when power relations among economic actors are inscribed in, or prescribed by, the legal framework of the state." Without question, we know the legal framework of the state strongly shapes the development of countermovements as economic and political actors, but in racially specific ways in the case of the United States (Frymer 2008; Hattam 1993). But countermovements also always attempt to shape this legal framework to their advantage (Orren 1991); whether political elites offer inducements or constraints to labor movements, for instance, is also a function of the power of organized labor at any given historical moment (Collier and Collier 1979).

What role does race play in the political construction of markets? As the historian Thomas Holt reminds us, race is "embedded in political economies that are quite historically specific" (Holt 2000, 27–28). Borrowing Holt's tripartite categorization, I identify three discrete yet overlapping periods characterizing the development of a racialized American political economy: feudal-preindustrial, industrial, and postindustrial.[4] Although conceptually distinct, these three orders were not born anew; they each overlap with previous orders and are each politically contested regimes that evolve over time. The mechanisms of exploitation and opportunity hoarding are central, durable, and racialized across these three orders. What is key about each of these highly unequal racial and economic regimes is that they are politically constructed.[5] Citizenship laws have defined racialized groups as either eligible or not to make claims on political and market institutions, while state regulations governing employment relations have served the equivalent function in proscribing the rights and freedoms of workers across race.[6] The cumulative results of politically contested settlements over laws and regulations that define political membership, as well as the rules of the game of labor markets, shape unequal employment access, quality, and outcomes for racially marginalized groups.

Feudal-Preindustrial Regime

Our modern conception of race took root in the feudal-preindustrial racial and economic order.[7] Defined largely by a Southern agricultural plantation system based on the racially explicit exploitation of African slave labor, followed in the postemancipation period by the exploitation of Jim Crow sharecropper labor, this feudal-preindustrial era is the clearest example of political embeddedness or of the political construction of a racialized market economy. This order, in which "racial and labor regimes

were mutually dependent" (Holt 2000, 37), tied together ascriptive no-
tions of race and feudal labor relations within a hierarchy of civic status
(Reed 2002; see also Orren 1991; Nakano Glenn 2002). Simply put, no state
(and its attendant hierarchy of civic membership), no racialized economic
order. Ascriptive categorization based on race, exploitation of racialized
slave labor, exclusion of blacks from all political and social institutions,
and opportunity hoarding by free whites defined in relation to slaves constitute the multiple mechanisms at work in this first period of racial inequality.

One key aspect of this feudal-preindustrial racial and economic regime
is the place of black workers. Although they were excluded from political
membership, before emancipation, all blacks were included in this economic regime; racial slavery was a full-employment economic institution.
After emancipation the vast majority of the "free" black population was
still employed, albeit in conditions similar to slavery under a debt peonage
system whereby black workers never got out of debt. This harsh and feudal system of exploitation of African American workers was the core of
American political economy for more than a century. It would take structural, demographic, and political transformations starting in the late nineteenth and early twentieth centuries to begin the shift from a feudal-
preindustrial to an industrial racial and economic regime.

Industrial Regime

Emerging first in the American North with industrialization, the second—
industrial—regime radically reorganized the process and production of
work, the meaning and reproduction of race, and the possibilities for political mobilization. Often referred to as Fordism—named for the production process made most famous by Henry Ford's automobile factories in
Detroit—this mass production and mass consumption–based economy
was strongly shaped by state policy at the same time that the social dislocations of industrial workers in the new racialized wage-labor system produced a countermovement for social protections. The same mechanisms
of racial inequality are evident in this second racial and economic order as
in the first, albeit with some slight developments: the reproduction of ascriptive categorization of racial groups, continued exploitation of racialized but now officially "free" labor, opportunity hoarding by whites across
class, and sustained exclusion of racialized groups from political and social institutions.

From infrastructure investments in canals and railroads to the disciplin-
ing of unruly workers, the national state was deeply intertwined with the
rapid and vast industrialization of the American economy (Bensel 2000;

Dray 2010). This industrialization period during the late nineteenth century saw the emancipation of former black slaves, a short period of freedom, and a move toward racial equality during Reconstruction, followed by racial retrenchment by the turn of the century, whether through state-imposed black codes or the Supreme Court's 1896 Plessy v. Ferguson (163 U.S. 537 [1896]) decision reestablishing legal racial exclusion and segregation (Klinkner and Smith 1999). At the same time, the capaciousness of industrialization provoked the most bitter and bloody labor conflicts among white workers and newly powerful industrialists and their large corporations (Dray 2010). From former slaves to Chinese immigrants to white workers, political institutions again set the rules of the game governing the economy and determined the opportunities for marginalized groups to organize and mobilize. The federal as well as state governments denied workers any legal rights to organize and strike, while workers of color were still excluded from political institutions and full citizenship (Hattam 1993; Nakano Glenn 2002). Not coincidentally, the first Gilded Age of extreme inequality and the concentration of wealth emerged under this racial and economic regime.

This growing inequality would lead to the external shock of the Great Depression, which, combined with the social and economic effects of the Second World War, provided a political opportunity for a countermovement to achieve New Deal social reforms that gave birth to the uniquely "exceptional" American welfare state (Amenta 1998; Hacker and Pierson 2002; Lieberman 1998; Skocpol 1995). In addition, the postwar "labor accord" (Lichtenstein 2002) created a private welfare state for advantaged labor insiders, along with labor stability, rising productivity, and declining inequality throughout the regime (Gottschalk 2000; Lichtenstein 2002; Stone 2004). Yet we know that the vast social protections won in this industrial era were racially exclusive, a legacy of the path-dependent and causal effect of the previous racial-economic order (Lieberman 1998, 2008; Brown 1999; Williams 2003; Katznelson 2005; King and Smith 2005; Frymer 2008). As American political development scholarship explains, race and gender hierarchies and exclusions institutionalized ascriptive inequalities in social policy and citizenship laws, undermining the vitality of the American social welfare system and efforts at redistribution for all (Smith 1997; Lichtenstein 2002). For example, Robert Lieberman (1998, 26) shows how "race and class were mutually constitutive in the making and growth of the American welfare state," while Suzanne Mettler (1998) argues that the gendered nature of New Deal social welfare policy created "divided and unequal citizens" by race and gender throughout the polity (see also Skocpol 1995). The racialized and gendered structure and implementation of the American welfare state was consequential for the future trajectories and vulnerabilities of social welfare policies and for the differential inclusion of marginalized groups into the body politic.

But the major New Deal–era labor law reform—the 1935 National Labor Relations Act—though critically important for both the American labor movement and the black freedom movement, was racially exclusive (Frymer 2008). Prima facie race-neutral occupational exclusions for domestic and agricultural workers in the act, identical to the exclusions in other New Deal social policies, had the racialized effect of excluding the vast majority of black workers, who found themselves at the bottom of the feudal-preindustrial and industrial racial and economic regimes. Southern political elites' material and social incentives to maintain these orders explain the compromise between the Southern and Northern wings of the Democratic Party that led to this exclusion (Farhang and Katznelson 2005; Frymer 2008). But the racialized labor policy itself had long-term causal consequences for the development of both countermovements (Frymer 2008). The 1947 Taft-Hartley labor law reform left in place the racialized occupational exclusions while severely limiting the power and growth of organized labor across the South, just as the labor movement began seriously threatening the feudal and industrial racial and economic orders in the Jim Crow South.[8] Both the racially exclusive legacy of New Deal social policies and the severe curtailment of labor power embodied in Taft-Hartley were the effects of politically constructed racialized markets. Advanced by Southern Democrats intent on protecting their feudal-preindustrial and industrial racial and economic orders, these policy legacies would prove consequential for the claims and strategies advanced by the labor and black freedom movements aimed at transforming highly unequal racialized labor markets.

Postindustrial-Post–Civil Rights Regime

The third, postindustrial economic order is mutually constitutive with a post–civil rights racial order.[9] The transition to this regime involved two fundamental changes, one structural, one political. The structural shift from an industrial "General Motors" economy to a postindustrial "Walmart" economy (Lichtenstein 2006) was characterized by mass deindustrialization and a shift to a polarized service-based economy with job growth at the high and low ends of the labor market, high levels of job insecurity and volatility, mass consumption driven by consumer debt as a result of stagnant wages, and increasing income inequality, with the top 1 percent of Americans gaining a far larger share of national income (Atkinson, Piketty, and Saez 2011; Hacker and Pierson 2010). The second, political, change was one of democratic inclusion. The mid-twentieth-century civil rights movement brought about the triumphant end to formal de jure racial exclusion and discrimination and secured the political rights associated with citizenship in the American context (Sassen 1998; Cohen 1999; Reed 1999; Wright and Dwyer 2003; King and Rueda 2008; Stone 2004; Lichtenstein 2006).

The relationship between structural and political changes (in terms of democratic inclusion) during the shift between racial and economic regimes is not straightforward. Indeed, greater democratic inclusion often occurs in the midst of structural changes in the economy and either precedes or accompanies greater economic inequality writ large, blunting the impact of advances in political rights. We see this pattern during transitions from one racial and economic order to another. Writing of the end of Reconstruction, the first Gilded Age, and the transition between the feudal-preindustrial and industrial racial and economic orders, the social scientist and activist W. E. B. Du Bois writes in his autobiography,

> For the American Negro, the last decade of the 19th and the first decade of the 20th centuries were more critical than the Reconstruction years of 1868–1876. Yet they have received but slight attention from historians and social students. They were usually interpreted in terms of personalities, and without regard to the great social forces that were developing. This was the age of triumph for big business, for industry, consolidated and organized on a world-wide scale, and run by white capital with colored labor. The southern United States was one of the most promising fields for this development, with a fine climate, invaluable staple crops, with a mass of cheap and potentially efficient labor, with unlimited natural power and use of unequalled technique, and with a transportation system reaching all the markets of the world. (Du Bois 2003, 229)

Our current, second Gilded Age is similar in effect to the first one that Du Bois identifies. The last decade of the twentieth and first decade of the twenty-first centuries, arguably, were more critical than the Second Reconstruction years of 1954 to 1977 (Marable 2007). In our current historical moment of the postindustrial, post–civil rights economic and racial order, the "great social forces" of globalization and neoliberalism have combined to produce another triumph for industry "organized on a world-scale" with distinctly Southern roots: Walmart. Characterized by the historian Nelson Lichtenstein as the "template for 21st century capitalism," Walmart is the contemporary manifestation and representation of a postindustrial racial and economic order, characterized by racialized low-wage work, mass consumption, trade liberalization, global supply chains, and environmental degradation (Lichtenstein 2006, 3; 2009).

The racialized effects of globalization and structural changes in the political economy in this postindustrial transition have adversely affected workers, especially workers of color, over the past forty years. Focusing on the city of Chicago, the sociologist William Julius Wilson has drawn the most significant attention to the effects of urban economic restructuring and the emergence of postindustrial black America (Wilson 1978, 1996, 2009). Chicago used to be one of the many Rust Belt cities, located primarily in the industrial Northeast and Middle West, such as Detroit, Philadelphia, Toledo, Milwaukee, and Gary and, further west, Los Angeles (Sides 2004). These manufacturing cities were the bases for industrial capitalism in the United States during the Second World War and the postwar years. The industrial war economy, in particular, was a catalyst for the Second Great Migration of African Americans from the South to industrial cities of the North (Lemann 1992). The unionization of manufacturing industries, through the comparatively racially inclusive Congress of Industrial Organizations, led to stable employment, decent working conditions, greater racial equality at the workplace, and a path to the middle class for many African Americans (Zeitlin and Weyher 2001).

In contrast to this political-economic regime of industrialism, the current postindustrial era of globalization has ushered in deindustrialization, the restructuring of the economy, and a shift to a service-, information-, and technology-based economy (Wilson 1996; Holt 2000; Sassen 1998). As a result, many of the old Rust Belt cities have experienced devastating economic decline owing to the loss of hundreds of thousands of manufacturing jobs that have led directly to the deunionization of the workforce and increased unemployment. The effects of these changes on the urban political economy of Chicago, for example, have been most pronounced in African American communities, where work has literally disappeared (Wilson 1996). Indeed, "Black workers have borne much of the brunt of Chicago's job losses" according to one study (Squires et al. 1987, 29). Overall, manufacturing jobs in the city declined from a postwar high of 688,000 factory jobs in 1947 to 187,000 by 1992 (Abu-Lughod 1999). With this devastating loss of jobs has come growth in the low-wage service sector of the economy.

Before such rapid deindustrialization at the end of the century, the immediate post–Second World War period saw the emergence and victories of a countermovement challenging racial and economic inequality. The mobilization and civil disobedience of thousands of ordinary people in the civil rights movement who challenged explicit racial inequality in American economic, social, and political institutions and life led to extraordinary outcomes. Most important were the hard-fought legal and legislative victories, including most notably the 1964 Civil Rights Act, which banned racial discrimination in employment and public accommodations, and the 1965 Voting Rights Act, which finally secured the right to vote for black Americans. As a result, throughout the post–civil rights era (1965 to the present), thousands of black elected officials took office at all levels—local, state, and national. Black communities in large metropolitan areas (Atlanta, Cleveland, Gary, Chicago, Los Angeles, New York, Detroit, Newark, for example) were even able to elect black mayors. Yet we now know, as Adolph Reed and Phil Thompson have shown in their work on the structural constraints and policy consequences of black urban regimes, black working-class and black poor populations often benefited little from this triumph of black electoral power (Reed 1999; Thompson 2006). Racial democracy, as exemplified by black political empowerment, did create a new and expanded black middle class that still occupies an ethnic niche in public employment today, yet one that is quite precarious (Parks 2010).

The civil rights movement, as the primary political actor in the industrial "transformative egalitarian" (King and Smith 2005, 75) racial order, succeeded in the midst of the transition from an industrial to a postindustrial racialized economic order (King and Smith 2005, 2011). Unfortunately, one of the unintended consequences of these economic and political developments is that the assumptions that undergirded this countermovement against the prevailing industrial racial and economic order took for granted the permanence of this historically specific order. This is reflected in the civil rights movement's major employment-focused victories, including the 1964 Civil Rights Act, affirmative action, consent decrees, and the War on Poverty (McCall 2001; Stein 1998; Sides 2004). Aimed at reducing racial and gender inequality in the prosperous 1960s, the focus was on changing the composition of employment rather than its underlying structure. That is, most policy makers and activists assumed that an industrial America was here to stay and would continue to provide good jobs for working- and middle-class Americans, especially black and Latino Americans (Stein 1998; McCall 2001).

The dominant approaches of many scholars, policy makers, and activists to eradicating race and class inequalities were programs to make poor people and people of color "more employable" within the existing economy (O'Connor 2000). This included advocating for policies focused on increasing human capital through education and greater skill development and the creation of the legal tool in Title VII of the 1964 Civil Rights Act to eliminate racism in employment and in labor unions. Enforced by the newly created Equal Employment Opportunity Commission, notably separate from the National Labor Relations Board and the Department of Labor, Title VII would, it was assumed, finally allow African Americans and other racially marginalized workers to be integrated into unions and manufacturing industries (Frymer 2008). Unfortunately, according to Josh Sides (2004, 179), despite the good intentions of these approaches, "the great tragedy of the War on Poverty is not that it failed to eradicate poverty and unemployment among the black population but that it failed to recognize the new, as well as the old, causes." The "tragic irony of postwar African American history," he continues, is that the "decline in industrial employment began just as the civil rights movement was finally making headway in America's largest industries" (Sides 2004, 183). One of the new causes Sides alludes to was the rise of the service sector economy, characterized by a bipolar distribution of low- and high-skill work and having greater insecurity, volatility, and reductions in benefits and workplace standards (Wright and Dwyer 2003; Sassen 1998; Stone 2004).

Deindustrialization was not only the result of apolitical economic processes such as capital flight and increased global competition. Local, state, and national political decisions and policies were also causally consequential in reinforcing the co-constitutive relationship between state and market in the United States (Bluestone and Harrison 1982; Ranney 2002; Rast 1999). The political construction of a new, postindustrial racial and economic order also coincided with increasing political polarization, a rightward shift in American politics, and a decades-long countermovement by business against the social justice legacies of the labor and civil rights movements (McCarty, Poole, and Rosenthal 2006; Pierson and Skocpol 2007; Hacker and Pierson 2006; Bartels 2008). The ideological and political shift to the right in all branches of government—the executive, legislative, and especially a nonfavorable judicial and legal regime—have all directly shaped union and civil rights strategies under the current racial and economic order (Levi 2003).

Emerging in the 1950s and exploding in the 1960s and 1970s was another path to economic security and middle-class life for many black Americans (and women): the expansion of public sector employment—and the benefits from public sector unions specifically—as blacks created an ethnic niche in local, state, and federal employment (Johnston 1994; Parks 2010). Public sector employment is arguably as important a causal mechanism facilitating an equally important pathway for African American economic mobility and security in the late twentieth century as manufacturing was from the 1940s through the 1970s. Focusing on the empirical case of Chicago, the exemplary city analyzed in accounts of the effects of the rise and fall of manufacturing on blacks, Virginia Parks argues that "government, more so than manufacturing, served as black Chicagoans' most persistent and disproportionate sector of employment throughout the second half of the twentieth century—a singularly African American employment trend" (Parks 2010, 16).

Government, in its role as a direct employer, has the ability to hire directly, advance social equity goals such as affirmative action more effectively than the private sector, and remain more accountable to pressure from constituents, especially insofar as voters can replace their "bosses" every two or four years. Unlike the overall trend throughout the postindustrial, post–civil rights era, the relationship between greater racial inclusion into the polity and economic equality is linked, then, on this dimension of public sector employment. The election of greater numbers of African Americans to local-, state-, and national-level office as an expression of black political inclusion from the 1970s to the present did have a direct effect on black employment outcomes. And the public sector's role as the sole remaining ethnic niche for upwardly mobile African American workers is even more pronounced in comparison with the ravaging effects of deindustrialization on black communities that Wilson and others have long identified (Wilson 1978, 1996, 2009). Yet the hegemony of neoliberal discourses and policies of privatization of public goods and services, as well as conservative attacks on public sector collective bargaining rights, puts this niche at risk.

Both continuity and change in the mechanisms of racial inequality are evident in this third racial and economic order compared with the previous two. Racial categorization continues to be reproduced, but racialized groups are now officially included in political, social, and economic institutions. Opportunity hoarding continues, but in more complex ways. Whites continue to hoard the best jobs across classes and industries, yet black and Latino workers have been integrated in a range of occupations from which they were previously excluded. Exploitation of racialized labor is still a major mechanism of durable racial inequality in employment under this regime, but with a twist: In the previous two racial and economic orders, African American labor was perceived as serving a positive economic function: whether as slave labor at the heart of the plantation economy, or debt-peonage agrarian labor in the South and cheap industrial labor in the North, black labor was necessary to the American economic regime. Yet in our current postindustrial, post–civil rights racial and economic order, black labor is seen as expendable and for the first time is perceived as a serving a negative economic function in some cases (Wacquant 2001).[10]

FRAGMENTED COUNTERMOVEMENTS

Each of the three racial and economic orders shaped the possibilities and constraints for social groups mobilizing to seek protection and redistribution against the mechanisms of exploitation, exclusion, and opportunity hoarding produced by each regime (Jacobs and King 2010). For the American labor movement, race was the fundamental source of division and fragmentation throughout the first two regimes and well into the third (Gould 1977; Hill 1985; Zieger 2007). No single factor is more important for understanding the relative weakness of the U.S. labor movement. Although the feudal-preindustrial and industrial racial-economic orders produced other exclusionary divides—based on skill, gender, and geography—race, tied explicitly as it was to civic status and economic position, was the central divide. And though white workers arguably had little power to affect the "boundary-drawing strategies" of the state and of capital in creating racially segmented labor markets, they were, in fact, complicit in actively "constructing exclusionary class identities" based on whiteness (Silver 2003, 24; Roediger 1991). This took the form of explicit racial exclusions from American Federation of Labor craft unions during the feudal-preindustrial and industrial racial-economic regimes and of continued racial discrimination within more inclusive industrial unions during the industrial and postindustrial orders (Gould 1977; Hill 1985; Zieger 2007).

The political implications of these racial exclusions of workers of color from the labor movement would be far reaching for both organized labor and the black freedom movement and for American political development more broadly. W. E. B. Du Bois makes this path-dependent argument in his 1935 *Black Reconstruction*, discussing the failure of a racially united labor movement during and immediately after Reconstruction.

> It was not until after the period which this book treats that white labor in the South began to realize that they had lost a great opportunity, that when they united to disfranchise the black laborer they had cut the voting power of the labor class in two.... They realized that it was not simply the Negro who had been disfranchised in 1876, it was the white laborer as well.... The South, after the war, presented the greatest opportunity for a real national labor movement which the nation ever saw or is likely to see for many decades. Yet the labor movement, with but few exceptions, never realized the situation. It never had the intelligence or knowledge, as a whole, to see in black slavery and Reconstruction, the kernel and meaning of the labor movement in the United States. (Du Bois [1935] 1965, 353)

After the failure of Reconstruction, many hoped that the emergence of the twentieth-century civil rights movement and the Second Reconstruction it promised would solve both the labor and the race problem in American political development (Marable 2007; Draper 1994). But race would continue to divide the labor movement. At the same time, class would continue to divide the black countermovement. As a consequence, demands aimed at the economic transformation of the low-wage racialized labor market were overshadowed by other integrationist demands, centered on education and political rights, whose achievement became the major victories of the civil rights movement (Goluboff 2007).

CONCLUSION

Most accounts of the politics of economic inequality argue that businesses exert invariant power over local communities in the policy-making process. Whether through direct instrumental power over other political actors in the policy process or through the indirect structural power business exerts, often unintentionally, the overwhelming influence of corporate interests, especially in an era of neoliberal globalization, is rarely disputed. Indeed, it is only under exceptional circumstances, such as an exogenous shock like the Great Depression or the emergence of the civil rights movement, that the reigning racial and economic order is challenged.

Yet there have been numerous recent successes since the mid-1990s by a number of grassroots political actors in communities of color who challenged racial inequality in the contemporary postindustrial, post–civil rights racial and economic order. The most prominent policy victories of these actors have been the enactment of at least 140 living-wage ordinances around the country as of 2009. These policy successes raise questions about why, how, and under what conditions communities of color can impinge on the seemingly invariant power of business under normal circumstances to advance a racial and economic equity agenda. The policy twin of the living-wage movement is a new accountable development movement that demands that businesses give back to communities in visible and material ways in exchange for the privilege of operating within the city. Through the use of community benefits agreements mentioned earlier and their focus on high-road, quality jobs as a key component of urban development in communities of color, the accountable development movement brings racial inequality and redistribution claims to the center of contemporary African American and Latino politics. If these efforts can add up to more than the sum of their parts, they might potentially challenge and fundamentally transform the durably racially unequal low-wage labor market characteristic of the postindustrial, post–civil rights racial and economic order. It would not create a "postracial" American workplace, but certainly postinequality one.

NOTES

1. See, for example, Krippner and Alvarez (2007) for an overview of this vast literature. See also Hall and Soskice (2001).
2. Even Larry Jacobs and Joe Soss's (2010) otherwise excellent attempt to recenter a political economy framework within American politics fails to explicitly situate the role of race in American political economy.
3. See Jacobs and Soss (2010) for an argument about making political economy the center of American politics research.
4. This conceptualization overlaps with Katherine V. W. Stone's (2004) similar typology of artisanal, industrial, and digital production and Loic Wacquant's (2001) four "peculiar institutions." I include Jacobs and King's (2010) "finance capitalism" as constitutive of the third regime.
5. See King and Pearce (2010) for an overview of contentious politics and markets.
6. Smith (1997); Nakano Glenn (2002); Orren (1991). See also Pager, Bonikowski, and Western (2009) for empirical evidence of the role of "civil death" as a result of incarceration that contributes directly to racially unequal employment outcomes.
7. "Race" as the defining ascriptive characteristic of a social, political, and economic hierarchy of inequality did not take root immediately, as Barbara Fields (1982, 1990) reminds us.
8. See Farhang and Katznelson (2005) for an extended discussion.
9. See Cohen (1999) for her typology of categorical, integrative, advanced, and secondary marginalization. In this account, categorical marginalization overlaps with the feudal-preindustrial and industrial economic regimes, while integrative, advanced, and secondary marginalization all overlap with the industrial and especially the postindustrial regimes.
10. In Loic Wacquant's (2001) functionalist schema, the prison and "hyperghetto" now serve as the institutions housing such expendable labor. See also Alexander (2010).

REFERENCES

Abu-Lughod, Janet L. 1999. *New York, Chicago, Los Angeles: America's Global Cities.* Minneapolis: University of Minnesota Press.

Alexander, Michelle. 2010. *The New Jim Crow: Mass Incarceration in the Age of Colorblindness.* New York: New Press.

Amenta, Edwin. 1998. *Bold Relief: Institutional Politics and the Origins of Modern American Social Policy.* Princeton, N.J.: Princeton University Press.

Applebaum, Eileen, Annette Bernhardt, and Richard J. Murnane, eds. 2003. *Low-*

Wage America: How Employers Are Reshaping Opportunity in the Workplace. New York: Russell Sage Foundation.

Atkinson, Anthony B., Thomas Piketty, and Emmanuel Saez. 2011. "Top Incomes in the Long Run of History." *Journal of Economic Literature* 49(1): 3–71.

Bartels, Larry M. 2008. *Unequal Democracy: The Political Economy of the New Gilded Age.* New York: Russell Sage Foundation.

Bartley, Tim. 2007. "Institutional Emergence in an Era of Globalization: The Rise of Transnational Private Regulation of Labor and Environmental Conditions." *American Journal of Sociology* 113(2): 297–351.

Bensel, Richard F. 2000. *The Political Economy of American Industrialization, 1877–1900.* Cambridge: Cambridge University Press.

Block, Fred. 2003. "Karl Polanyi and the Writing of *The Great Transformation.*" *Theory and Society* 32(3): 275–306.

Bluestone, Barry, and Bennett Harrison. 1982. *The Deindustrialization of America.* New York: Basic Books.

Brown, Michael K. 1999. *Race, Money, and the American Welfare State.* Ithaca, N.Y.: Cornell University Press.

Brown, Michael K., et al. 2003. *White-Washing Race: The Myth of a Color-Blind Society.* Berkeley: University of California Press.

Cohen, Cathy J. 1999. *The Boundaries of Blackness: AIDS and the Breakdown of Black Politics.* Chicago: University of Chicago Press.

Collier, Ruth Berins, and David Collier. 1979. "Inducements Versus Constraints: Disaggregating 'Corporatism.'" *American Political Science Review* 73(4): 967–86.

Dawson, Michael C. 2011. *Not in Our Lifetimes: The Future of Black Politics.* Chicago: University of Chicago Press.

Dawson, Michael C., and Cathy J. Cohen. 2002. "Problems in the Study of the Politics of Race." In *Political Science: The State of the Discipline,* edited by Ira Katznelson and Helen Milner. New York: W. W. Norton.

Draper, Alan. 1994. *Conflict of Interests: Organized Labor and the Civil Rights Movement in the South, 1954–1968.* Ithaca, N.Y.: Cornell University Press.

Dray, Philip. 2010. *There Is Power in a Union: The Epic Story of Labor in America.* New York: Anchor Books.

Du Bois, W. E. B. (1935) 1965. *Black Reconstruction: An Essay Toward a History of the Past Which Black Folk Played in the Attempt to Reconstruct Democracy in America, 1860–1880.* New York: Meridian Books.

———. 2003. *The Autobiography of W. E. B Du Bois: A Soliloquy on Viewing My Life from the Last Decade of Its First Century.* New York: International Publishers.

Farhang, Sean, and Ira Katznelson. 2005. "The Southern Imposition: Congress and Labor in the New Deal and Fair Deal." *Studies in American Political Development* 19(1): 1–30.

Fields, Barbara J. 1982. "Ideology and Race in American History." In *Region, Race, and Reconstruction: Essays in Honor of C. Vann Woodward,* edited by J. Morgan Kousser and James M. McPherson. New York: Oxford University Press.

——. 1990. "Slavery, Race, and Ideology in the United States of America." *New Left Review* 181(May–June): 95–118.

Frymer, Paul. 2008. *Black and Blue: African Americans, the Labor Movement, and the Decline of the Democratic Party.* Princeton, N.J.: Princeton University Press.

Goluboff, Risa L. 2007. *The Lost Promise of Civil Rights.* Cambridge, Mass.: Harvard University Press.

Gottschalk, Marie. 2000. *The Shadow Welfare State: Labor, Business, and the Politics of Health Care in the United States.* Ithaca, N.Y: Cornell University Press.

Gould, William B. 1977. *Black Workers in White Unions: Job Discrimination in the United States.* Ithaca, N.Y.: Cornell University Press.

Granovetter, Mark. 1985. "Economic Action and Social Structure: The Problem of Embeddedness." *American Journal of Sociology* 91(3): 481–510.

Hacker, Jacob S., and Paul Pierson. 2002. "Business Power and Social Policy: Employers and the Formation of the American Welfare State." *Politics and Society* 30(2): 277–326.

——. 2006. *Off Center: The Republican Revolution and the Erosion of American Democracy.* New Haven, Conn.: Yale University Press.

——. 2010. *Winner-Take-All Politics: How Washington Made the Rich Richer—and Turned Its Back on the Middle Class.* New York: Simon and Schuster.

Hall, Peter A., and David Soskice, eds. 2001. *Varieties of Capitalism: The Institutional Foundations of Comparative Advantage.* Oxford: Oxford University Press.

Hattam, Victoria C. 1993. *Labor Visions and State Power: The Origins of Business Unionism in the United States.* Princeton, N.J.: Princeton University Press.

Hill, Herbert. 1985. *Black Labor and the American Legal System: Race, Work, and the Law.* Madison: University of Wisconsin Press.

Holt, Thomas C. 2000. *The Problem of Race in the 21st Century.* Cambridge, Mass.: Harvard University Press.

Jacobs, Lawrence R., and Desmond S. King. 2010. "Varieties of Obamaism: Structure, Agency, and the Obama Presidency." *Perspectives on Politics* 8(3): 793–802.

Jacobs, Lawrence R., and Joe Soss. 2010. "The Politics of Inequality in America: A Political Economy Framework." *Annual Review of Political Science* 13: 341–64.

Johnston, Paul. 1994. *Success While Others Fail: Social Movement Unionism and the Public Workplace.* Ithaca, N.Y.: Cornell University Press.

Katznelson, Ira. 2005. *When Affirmative Action Was White: An Untold History of Racial Inequality in Twentieth-Century America.* New York: W. W. Norton.

King, Brayden G., and Nicholas A. Pearce. 2010. "The Contentiousness of Markets: Politics, Social Movements, and Institutional Change in Markets." *Annual Review of Sociology* 36: 249–67.

King, Desmond, and David Rueda. 2008. "Cheap Labor: The New Politics of

'Bread and Roses' in Industrial Democracies." *Perspectives on Politics* 6(2): 279–97.

King, Desmond, and Rogers M. Smith. 2005. "Racial Orders in American Political Development." *American Political Science Review* 99(1): 75–92.

———. 2011. *Still a House Divided: Race and Politics in Obama's America*. Princeton, N.J.: Princeton University Press.

Klinkner, Philip A., and Rogers M. Smith. 1999. *The Unsteady March: The Rise and Decline of Racial Equality in America*. Chicago: University of Chicago Press.

Krippner, Greta R., and Anthony S. Alvarez. 2007. "Embeddedness and the Intellectual Projects of Economic Sociology." *Annual Review of Sociology* 33: 219–40.

Lemann, Nicholas. 1992. *The Promised Land: The Great Black Migration and How It Changed America*. New York: Vintage Books.

Levi, Margaret. 2003. "Organizing Power: The Prospects for an American Labor Movement." *Perspectives on Politics* 1(1): 45–68.

Lichtenstein, Nelson. 2002. *State of the Union: A Century of American Labor*. Princeton, N.J.: Princeton University Press.

———. 2006. *Wal-Mart: The Face of Twenty-First Century Capitalism*. New York: The New Press.

———. 2009. *The Retail Revolution: How Wal-Mart Created a Brave New World of Business*. New York: Metropolitan Books.

Lieberman, Robert C. 1998. *Shifting the Color Line: Race and the American Welfare State*. Cambridge, Mass.: Harvard University Press.

———. 2008. "Legacies of Slavery? Race and Historical Causation in American Political Development." In *Race and American Political Development*, edited by Joseph Lowndes, Julie Novkov, and Dorian Warren. New York: Routledge.

Lowndes, Joe, Julie Novkov, and Dorian T. Warren. 2008. *Race and American Political Development*. New York: Routledge.

Marable, Manning. 2007. *Race, Reform, and Rebellion: The Second Reconstruction and Beyond in Black America, 1945–2006*, 3rd ed. Jackson: University of Mississippi Press.

Massey, Douglas S. 2007. *Categorically Unequal: The American Stratification System*. New York: Russell Sage Foundation.

McCall, Leslie. 2001. *Complex Inequality: Gender, Class and Race in the New Economy*. New York: Routledge.

McCarty, Nolan, Keith T. Poole, and Howard Rosenthal. 2006. *Polarized America: The Dance of Ideology and Unequal Riches*. Cambridge, Mass.: MIT Press.

McClain, Paula D., et al. 2009. "Group Membership, Group Identity and Group Consciousness: Evolving Racial Identity in American Politics." *Annual Review of Political Science* 12(June): 471–85.

Mettler, Suzanne. 1998. *Dividing Citizens: Gender and Federalism in New Deal Public Policy*. Ithaca, N.Y.: Cornell University Press.

Milkman, Ruth. 2006. *L.A. Story: Immigrant Workers and the Future of the U.S. Labor Movement*. New York: Russell Sage Foundation.

Nakano Glenn, Evelyn. 2002. *Unequal Freedom: How Race and Gender Shaped American Citizenship and Labor*. Cambridge, Mass.: Harvard University Press.

National Employment Law Project. 2011. "The Good Jobs Deficit: A Clower Look at Recent Job Loss and Job Growth Trends Using Occupationsl Data." Available at: http://www.nelp.org/goodjobsdeficit (accessed March 25, 2013).

O'Connor, Alice. 2000. "Poverty Research and Policy for the Post-Welfare Era." *Annual Review of Sociology* 26: 547–62.

Orren, Karen. 1991. *Belated Feudalism: Labor, the Law, and Liberal Development in the United States*. Cambridge: Cambridge University Press.

Pager, Devah, Bart Bonikowski, and Bruce Western. 2009. "Discrimination in a Low-Wage Labor Market." *American Sociological Review* 74(5): 777–99.

Parks, Virginia. 2010. "Revisiting Shibboleths of Race and Urban Economy: Black Employment in Manufacturing and the Public Sector Compared, Chicago 1950–2000." *International Journal of Urban and Regional Research* 35(1): 110–29.

Pierson, Paul, and Theda Skocpol, eds. 2007. *The Transformation of American Politics: Activist Government and the Rise of Conservatism*. Princeton, N.J.: Princeton University Press.

Pitts, Steven. 2007. "Bad Jobs: The Overlooked Crisis in the Black Community." *New Labor Forum* 16(1): 39–47.

Polanyi, Karl. 2001. *The Great Transformation: The Political and Economic Origins of Our Time*, 2nd ed. Boston, Mass.: Beacon.

Ranney, David. 2002. *Global Decisions, Local Collisions: Urban Life in the New World Order*. Philadelphia, Pa.: Temple University Press.

Rast, Joel. 1999. *Remaking Chicago: The Political Origins of Urban Industrial Change*. DeKalb: Northern Illinois University Press.

Reed, Adolph, Jr. 1999. *Stirrings in the Jug: Black Politics in the Post-Segregation Era*. Minneapolis: University of Minnesota Press.

———. 2002. "Unraveling the Relation of Race and Class in American Politics." *Political Power and Social Theory* 15: 265–74.

Roediger, David R. 1991. *The Wages of Whiteness: Race and the Making of the American Working Class*. London: Verso.

Sassen, Saskia. 1998. *Globalization and Its Discontents*. New York: The New Press.

Sides, Josh. 2004. *L.A. City Limits: African American Los Angeles from the Great Depression to the Present*. Berkeley: University of California Press.

Silver, Beverly J. 2003. *Forces of Labor: Workers' Movements and Globalization Since 1870*. Cambridge: Cambridge University Press.

Skocpol, Theda. 1995. *Protecting Soldiers and Mothers: The Political Origins of Social Policy in the United States*. Cambridge, Mass.: Harvard University Press.

Smith, Rogers M. 1997. *Civic Ideals: Conflicting Visions of Citizenship in U.S. History*. New Haven, Conn.: Yale University Press.

Squires, Gregory D., et al. 1987. *Chicago: Race, Class, and the Response to Urban Decline.* Philadelphia, Pa.: Temple University Press.

Stein, Judith. 1998. *Running Steel, Running America: Race, Economic Policy, and the Decline of Liberalism.* Chapel Hill: University of North Carolina Press.

Stone, Katherine V. W. 2004. *From Widgets to Digits: Employment Regulation for a Changing Workplace.* Cambridge: Cambridge University Press.

Thompson, J. Phillip III. 2006. *Double Trouble: Black Mayors, Black Communities, and the Call for a Deep Democracy.* New York: Oxford University Press.

Tilly, Charles. 1998. *Durable Inequality.* Berkeley: University of California Press.

Uchitelle, Louis. 2005 "Labor's Lost: For Blacks, a Dream in Decline." *New York Times,* October 23, 2005.

Wacquant, Loic. 2001. "Deadly Symbiosis: When Ghetto and Prison Meet and Mesh." *Punishment and Society* 3(1): 95–134.

Williams, Linda Faye. 2003. *The Constraint of Race: Legacies of White Skin Privilege in America.* University Park: Penn State University Press.

Wilson, William Julius. 1978. *The Declining Significance of Race.* Chicago: University of Chicago Press.

———. 1996. *When Work Disappears: The World of the New Urban Poor.* New York: Vintage Books.

———. 2009. *More Than Just Race: Being Black and Poor in the Inner City.* New York: W. W. Norton.

Wright, Erik Olin, and Rachel E. Dwyer. 2003. "The Patterns of Job Expansions in the USA: A Comparison of the 1960s and 1990s." *Socio-Economic Review* 1(3): 289–325.

Zeitlin, Maurice, and L. Frank Weyher. 2001. "'Black and White, Unite and Fight': Interracial Working-Class Solidarity and Racial Employment Equality." *American Journal of Sociology* 107(2): 430–67.

Zieger, Robert H. 2007. *For Jobs and Freedom: Race and Labor in America Since 1865.* Lexington: University of Kentucky Press.

Zukin, Sharon, and Paul DiMaggio, eds. 1990. *Structures of Capital: The Social Organization of the Economy.* Cambridge: Cambridge University Press.

PART II | Attitudes and Individual Behavior

Chapter 5 | A Measure of Justice: What Policing Racial Bias Research Reveals

Phillip Atiba Goff

How DOES ONE explain persistent racial inequality in the face of declining racial prejudice? This riddle, which I call the "attitude-inequality mismatch" question (or the AIM question, for short), is the fundamental problem facing contemporary scholars of race in the United States (as well as the rationale for this volume). A related and equally provocative question, however, is this: Why have we not answered this question yet? Racial attitudes have improved from the past half century (Devine and Elliott 1995; Dovidio 2001), but racial inequalities in law enforcement, health care, and education have not seen commensurate reductions during the same period (Gabbidon and Greene 2005; Jargowsky 1998; Massey and Denton 1993; Oliver and Shapiro 1995; Pager 2003; Sidanius and Pratto 1999; Wilson 1996). Why have we been left so long without answers to this foundational question?

This second question—Why is there such confusion when racial attitudes do not predict racial outcomes?—is the subject of the present chapter. Two related problems frustrate efforts to understand the AIM question. First, racism is hard to measure. Second, many assume that prejudice is the one and only cause of discrimination. For the purposes of this chapter, I refer to these two problems as the measurement problem and the attitude problem, respectively. Although these problems afflict multiple domains, they are peculiarly relevant to racial bias in policing.

157

DEFINING THE PROBLEMS

The *measurement problem* refers to the difficulty inherent in quantifying racism, racial discrimination, or any other violation of justice. This problem can be understood in terms of two separate components: causality and data. The *causality component* refers to the difficulty in distinguishing racial disparities from racial discrimination (Blank, Dabady, and Citro 2004; Goff et al. 2010; Ridgeway and MacDonald 2010). Whereas measuring racial disparities requires merely observing differences between groups, measuring racial discrimination requires the ability to relate those inequalities to some sinister causal factor. That is, measuring discrimination requires that one be able to determine what causes racial inequalities. If one can accomplish this feat of methodological gymnastics, and the cause is sinister, then it is safe to say that one has measured racial discrimination. As a point of illustration, in this chapter I offer the example of racial profiling.

Doubtless, there are profound racial disparities between African Americans, Latinos, whites, American Indians, and Asians with regard to criminal justice outcomes (Alpert and Dunham 2003; Baldus, Woodworth, and Pulaski 1990; Eberhardt et al. 2006; Muhammad 2010; Pager 2003; Sidanius and Pratto 1999; Tyler and Huo 2002). Yet as obvious as those disparities are, how should one go about demonstrating that they are also discriminatory? Noting that blacks, Latinos, and American Indians are disproportionately stopped, arrested, and incarcerated is not the same thing as saying that police discrimination is at least partially responsible for those disparities (Blank, Dabady, and Citro 2004; Fridell 2004; Goff et al. 2010; Ridgeway and MacDonald 2010). Similarly, it is possible to imagine that racial discrimination that occurs well before an individual has contact with an officer (for example, employment discrimination) might increase an individual's likelihood of being involved in illegal activities (for example, selling drugs or stealing food), which subsequently increases one's likelihood of being stopped and eventually becoming involved in the criminal justice system (Walker, Spohn, and Delone 2007).

Demonstrating discrimination on the part of officers or police departments, therefore, requires some way of determining that officer behaviors or departmental policies contribute to the racial disparities in stops and arrests. Scholars and practitioners have employed numerous metrics to assess racial profiling (Fridell 2004; Goff et al. 2010; Harris 2002; Ridgeway and MacDonald 2010), but it is not clear that there is a single best method. Consequently, if it is not clear what evidence would constitute proof that the behaviors of officers or policies of departments are responsible for racial disparities, then it is also not clear what would constitute an appropriate measure of racial discrimination in law enforcement. This is the first component of the measurement problem.

Should some intrepid researchers outwit the conceptual obstacles to measuring racism in police stops, they will quite likely confront the measurement problem's second and equally frustrating challenge: the *data component*. That is, the data that would be required often do not exist or are not made available. Again, in the context of law enforcement, agencies often choose not to record demographic information regarding the individuals they stop. If they do, this information often does not include individuals who were stopped but not cited or arrested. And where those data are collected, it is rare that an agency aggregates this information across the history of any given officer (which would allow one to detect which officers have relatively higher or lower rates of stopping people of various racial groups). Similarly, even if these data were collected, it is rare that multiple agencies store their data in a similar fashion, making it difficult to compare across departments and, consequently, to detect which agencies have relatively higher or lower rates of racial disparities in stops. Finally, in the highly unlikely event that significant numbers of agencies all kept racial data on all police contacts, aggregated those data across an officer's career, and kept the data in a similar fashion, each of these agencies would need to be willing to share these data with a single research team or to make them public—neither of which has historical precedent. And without these data, the cleverest of research designs may be little more than a provocative thought experiment.

Although these particular obstacles are unique to the problem of racial profiling, concerns with measuring causal relationships and gaining access to relevant data plague scholars in the realm of education, housing, employment, and health care, among others (Blank, Dabady, and Citro 2004; Massey and Denton 1993; Oliver and Shapiro 1995; Wilson 1996). For instance, a *New York Times* article about education reform recently reported Bill Gates, noting the inability to measure teacher performance, "Name a business where you have more than 100,000 employees and you have no idea who's more effective than others" (Nocera 2010). Gates's point, presumably, is that measuring effectiveness in education is both difficult and crucial. The same could be said about the issue of measuring teacher racial bias—or racial bias in judges, lawyers, loan officers, doctors, employers, and countless other domains. In other words, without good data, it becomes difficult to identify the precise mechanisms that produce racial inequalities. Consequently, as the saying goes, "If you can't measure it, you can't manage it." Any solution to the measurement problem will require rigorous methods of demonstrating causality as well as unfettered access to representative data.

In the absence of these methodological necessities, how do scholars and lay people make sense of racial inequalities? This brings me to the second key term of this chapter: the attitude problem. What I refer to as the *attitude problem* is the assumption that racial bigotry is the one and only cause of racial disparities. In the absence of clear causal data regarding racial disparities, it seems that many individuals resolve the measurement problem by assuming that individual racial biases (or an aggregation of them) are responsible. This tendency to attribute inequality to bias is understandable, given the bold-faced ugliness of chattel slavery and Jim Crow. Images of water hoses turned on college students, police dogs loosed on protesters, brutalized black and brown bodies, and segregated water fountains spring to mind when one thinks of the United States' history of racial conflict. Given the power of these images, it is easy to understand how racial injustice and racial bigotry become synonymous in the minds of many Americans.

The conflation of disparity with discrimination is most likely also facilitated by a tendency in humans to attribute behaviors to individuals rather than to situations. In the absence of convincing causal data, this "fundamental attribution error" is likely to direct attention to the behaviors of actors rather than to situations that facilitate them (Ross 1977). The tendency to attribute action to individuals' attitudes has limited scientific utility, as social psychologists have long known that attitudes are relatively poor harbingers of behaviors, predicting no more than 10 percent of behavior, at best (Dovidio 2001; LaPiere 1934; Wicker 1969). Yet lay people are not alone in making this mistake. Psychological research on racial inequality has focused disproportionately on racial attitudes and individual-level processes despite strong evidence that racial attitudes are poor predictors of racial discrimination (Dovidio 2001; Goff, Steele, and Davies 2008; Swim and Stangor 1998). The psychological science of racial bias, then, also most likely plays a role in creating the attitude problem.

In addition to these historical and scientific origins, the legal definition of discrimination may also play a role. Although academic and dictionary definitions of *discrimination* allow for multiple and diffuse causes of discrimination (that is, structural discrimination), the judicial system frequently requires evidence of discriminatory intent before ruling that a given set of facts constitutes discrimination. This is also known as the intent doctrine. Title VII of the 1964 Civil Rights Act does establish a provision to shelter individuals from protected classes against "disparate impact," but the overwhelming legal precedent in racial discrimination law follows the intent doctrine (Kang and Lane 2010). In other words, the court's ability to remedy racial discrimination suffers from the same attitude problem that afflicts psychological science and U.S. history. Consequently, in addition to whatever influence legal precedent and theory might have on the formations of one's implicit concepts of racism, there may also be strategic reasons to assume that prejudice is required for discrimination to occur.

This assumption of prejudice as the root cause of discrimination creates ambivalence about contemporary race relations—the AIM question. Being faced simultaneously with diminishing racial prejudice and persistent racial inequality creates a kind of cognitive dissonance, leaving one to ask, "How can inequality persist if the cause is retreating? How could prejudice be declining if inequality persists?" It also leaves one underprepared to defend against the claim that if an offending individual or group is not racist, then no remedy is needed for any observed inequalities.

Understanding the attitude problem aids in understanding the AIM question. The confusion results from an inability to imagine a world where racism does not require racist actors (Bonilla-Silva 2009; Goff, Steele, and Davies 2008). If one assumes that racial inequality and racist people are synonymous, then one should expect a decline in bigotry to be accompanied by a decline in inequality. And when racial inequality does not mirror racial attitudes, as is the case today, it is reasonable to be confused. As a result, a great deal of scholarship has been devoted to unearthing the hidden racial biases of individuals, in hopes of preserving this attitude-behavior paradigm. However, in addition to whatever amount of prejudice may have gone underground, there may also be objectionable causes of racial inequality that we ignore—that is, the 90 percent of behavior not predicted by attitudes—if we fixate on racial prejudice as the sole cause of racial inequality. Consequently, the attitude problem is both a source of confusion with regard to the current state of affairs and an obstacle to further innovation. Any solution to the attitude problem will need to test the relationship between prejudice and discrimination explicitly and also provide alternate testable mechanisms for the production of inequality.

SHAPING THE DISCOURSE

The study of policing is a relatively new tradition in the academy (Alpert and Dunham 2003; Bayley 1994). Although psychologists, sociologists, historians, and economists have long been interested in criminal justice, scholars have historically focused on criminal behavior, eyewitness testimony, and incarceration (Garland 1985; Ogloff 2000; Rafter 2008). The measurement problem, among other factors, may account for this discrepancy.

Although national aggregate databases on crime rates date back to 1880,[1] it is not possible to determine from these data what role racial biases might have played in the production of racial disparities. Similarly, though psychologists use scales that measure racial bias, law enforcement agencies have rarely made their officers available for research on racial attitudes until recently (Correll et al. 2007; Eberhardt et al. 2004; Goff et al. 2010). Additionally, because available data have mostly focused on arrests and convictions, it has not always been clear that the biases of officers played any role in these statistics at all. Why, for instance, should even the most biased officer be more likely to arrest a Latino murderer than a white murderer? These factors each encouraged most social scientists to ignore the study of law enforcement and racial discrimination, leaving the matter primarily to criminologists and historians.

Criminologists

The discipline of criminology arose out of an interest in predicting criminal behavior—particularly among the criminally insane (Garland 1985; Ogloff 2000; Rafter 2008). Although the bulk of early criminological research targeted psychopathology among criminal populations (with occasional racial analyses), scholars of criminal justice eventually developed a sizable body of research regarding the personality profiles prevalent in law enforcement as a complement to research on psychological profiles of criminals (Alpert and Dunham 2003; Weiss 2010). Consequently, when psychologists did approach the broad question of racial bias in law enforcement, they often did so by extending work on the police personality (Adlam 1982; Balch 1972; Bennett and Greenstein 1975; Evans, Coman, and Stanley 1992; Fenster and Locke 1973; Hanewicz 1978; Hogan and Kurtines 1975; Lester et al. 1980; McNamara 1967; Mills and Bohannon 1980; Niederhoffer 1967; Sherman 1980; Sidanius and Pratto 1999; Toby 2000; Walker 1992), supporting the hypothesis that police officers tended to have more conservative attitudes than community members.

When the issue of racial bias on the part of law enforcement garnered enough attention to interest criminology scholars, analyses tended either to be agnostic with regard to the causes of racial disparities or to point toward the personality profiles of law enforcement. For instance, criminologists frequently frame the issue of race and use of force in terms of "why, and how and when do police officers resort to force" (Waddington 2007, 370) rather than in terms of broader social and institutional factors.

Those critiques aside, criminologists have produced a myriad of approaches to racial bias in law enforcement—particularly with regard to the issue of racial bias in civilian stops. Across a broad range of techniques, quantitative scholars of policing have analyzed the relationship of police stops to populations—in benchmarking (Fridell 2004; Goff et al. 2010; Ridgeway and MacDonald 2010), arrest data (Harris 2002); observational and race-blind sampling methods (Engel and Calnon 2004; Walker, Spohn, and DeLone 2007); and consent search analyses (Dominitz and Knowles 2006; Knowles, Persico, and Todd 2001; Persico and Todd 2006; Sanga 2009; Smith and Petrocelli 2001)—to gauge the degree of disparity that officer biases and institutional policies produce.

Although matching stops or arrests to the residential or observed driving population cannot prove discrimination, it has helped establish the widespread existence of racial inequalities in police enforcement (Harris 2002). Similarly, attempts to use outcomes tests (for example, the percentage of discretionary searches that yield an arrest) have shown promise in identifying whether racial inequalities in police behaviors are justifiable. For instance, by comparing the rates of arrests that follow from discretionary searches of blacks to those same "hit rates" of whites, it is possible to determine whether individuals or departments conduct equally efficient searches of those two populations. If, for instance, searches of blacks yield arrests less frequently than searches of whites, then many would argue that it is reasonable to conclude that searches of blacks are at least less efficient than searches of whites.

However, claiming that a behavior or practice lacks efficiency is not the same as claiming that it constitutes discrimination. Additionally, economists bemoan the fact that outcomes data (such as discretionary searches) often neglect geographic variation (Sanga 2009) and can vary owing to statistical artifacts unrelated to bias or efficiency (Bjerk 2007). Still others suggest that there are racial differences in awareness that discretionary searches often require civilian consent (Sklansky 1998). This would lead whites to feel more comfortable refusing police search requests than blacks or Latinos, which would escalate the hit rates for nonwhites. Conversely, if officers believe that blacks and Latinos are less likely to refuse searches, they might be more likely to stop them, in the hopes of delivering an "easy bust." This practice, of course, would reduce the hit rate for nonwhites.

These problems of outcomes testing are often avoided by employing internal benchmarks within a department, which allows researchers to measure tendencies of an officer against other officers within an agency (Fridell 2004; Ridgeway and MacDonald 2010; Walker, Spohn, and DeLone 2007; Walker 2001, 2005; Wilson, Dunham, and Alpert 2004). Early warning systems (or, sometimes, early intervention systems) frequently work in this manner, attempting to predict negative officer behaviors based on how officers rank against their peers. However, by focusing on bench-marks within a department, it is difficult to detect department-wide pat-terns of behavior. These early warning systems also tend not to include predictors (such as racial attitudes or situational vulnerabilities to threats), making it difficult to determine why an officer is disproportionately en-gaged in negative behaviors.

Taken together, the criminology literature on policing bias (by far the largest disciplinary literature) still leaves many questions unanswered by virtue of the difficulty in demonstrating the causes of racial inequality. Although much is owed the field in terms of documenting racial dispari-ties, none of the current techniques is designed to provide quantitative evi-dence that objectionable factors cause racial inequality in policing outcomes.

Historians and Social Theorists

Although criminologists have dominated quantitative approaches to the study of police behavior, historians, without the need for data or causal mechanisms, also contribute much to the understanding of race and law enforcement. Historians and popular historical narratives have traced the role of law enforcement in the racial violence of Tulsa, Oklahoma; Detroit, Michigan; Newark, New Jersey; and Rosewood, Florida, among other lo-cations (Barker 1999; Blakeslee 2006; Websdale 2001). Similarly, scholars have unearthed numerous accounts that law enforcement had formally endorsed or participated in racial terrorism in the form of lynching, arbi-trary abductions, and physical intimidation (Gabbidon 2010; Gabbidon and Greene 2005; Glover 2009; Kappeler, Sluder, and Alpert 1998; Moody 2008; Provine 2007; Weitzer and Tuch 2006). These histories tell isolated stories that often include incidents of shockingly cruel racial violence. It is difficult to hear the stories of the Tulsa race riots or to read the accounts of the infamous Rosewood massacre and feel that the racist hearts of those responsible are not the principal evil.

The power of these narratives is increased by the fact that they extend beyond the context of black civilians and white officers. That is, historical narratives of police violence and harassment of many nonwhite groups implies that the common denominator is the bias of law enforcement of-ficers. For instance, law enforcement played a visible role in regulating symbolic racial threats during the Second World War, when municipal and state law enforcement were tasked with checking immigration documents, enforcing racially targeted curfews for Japanese Americans, and escorting Japanese "enemy aliens" to internment camps (Okihiro 2005; Weglyn

2000). Similarly, news reports of the Los Angeles Zoot Suit riots of the early 1940s featured prominent stories that depicted law enforcement engaging in discriminatory acts of violence against nonwhite civilians and promoting racial and ethnic segregation (Escobar 1999).

These cross-race commonalities have persuaded some theorists in philosophy and political science to posit that the very role of law enforcement is to keep nonwhites "in their place." And the notion that a principal function of police is to enforce this "out of place principle" has become a theoretical engine for scholarship on race and law enforcement (Anderson 1990; Escobar 1999; Fagan and Davies 2000; Gabbidon 2010; Gabbidon and Greene; 2005; Mills 1999; Muhammad 2010; Sidanius and Pratto 1999; Websdale 2001). Some historical evidence suggests that the desire to curtail the movement of nonwhites played a role in the expansion of early American law enforcement (Prassel 1972). Similarly, there is evidence that public financing of law enforcement has followed the symbolic threat of growing nonwhite populations rather than crime trends (Jackson 1989), further suggesting that law enforcement has historically been deployed to reduce racial threats rather than ensure public safety (chap. 8, this volume).

However, this analysis treats law enforcement behavior as a symptom of a larger racialized political conflict and often ignores the behaviors of law enforcement in the process. Few of these broader theories of racial disparity in law enforcement posit a specific causal mechanism (see Sidanius and Pratto 1999 for an exception), which often renders them peripheral to the study of police behavior. Consequently, the clinical diagnoses of criminologists and the vicious narratives of historians shaped this early research, and the emphasis each put on the prejudices of police informed later work in sociology, economics, and psychology. In other words, the initial measurement problem gave way to the attitude problem that one observes today.

PROFILING POLICING

In the past three decades, a broader collection of social scientists have begun studying policing in general, racial bias in law enforcement more specifically, and racial profiling in particular (Alpert and Dunham 2003; Bayley 1994). This is, in part, because data are becoming more available. With the advent of the Bureau of Justice Statistics and its efforts to promote the analysis of the FBI's Uniform Crime Report, it is now easier to gain access to and sort types of crime. Established in 1979, the bureau's goal is "to collect, analyze, publish, and disseminate information on crime, criminal offenders, victims of crime, and the operation of justice systems at all levels of government. These data are critical to federal, state, and local policy-makers in combating crime and ensuring that justice is both efficient and evenhanded" (Bureau of Justice Statistics, n.d.).

As a consequence of this mission, it is easier for a broader group of social scientists to access historical and contemporary data. Additionally, with the passage of the Hate Crime Statistics Act of 1990, the FBI also began tracking data on crimes for which race (or religion, ethnicity, sexual orientation, or other protected classes) is a factor. Federal consent decrees resulting from antidiscrimination litigation also produced significantly more attention and data on the topic of racial bias in law enforcement.[2] Aided by access to better data, research on racial bias in law enforcement gained critical momentum during the 1980s and 1990s owing to police misconduct that garnered public notoriety.

In the 1980s the so-called war on drugs resulted in an unprecedented increase in the incarceration of nonviolent offenders (Muhammad 2010; Gabbidon and Greene 2005; chap. 8, this volume). The increase in arrests and sentencing brought new attention to street life and the role that police played in the drug marketplace (Anderson 1990). This attention, in turn, cast light on nonwhite communities' historical mistrust of law enforcement and concerns of racial bias (Muhammad 2010; Tyler and Huo 2002).

Then, in 1991, Los Angeles police officers were videotaped severely beating motorist Rodney King. When the officers were acquitted a year later, black and Latino residents voiced their displeasure with what many perceived as sanctioned police racism through violent and destructive civil unrest. Not five years later, Los Angeles again became the center of national attention as the Rampart scandal revealed patterns of widespread police corruption in the Rampart Division of the Los Angeles Police Department. A series of litigations implicated seventy officers in police corruption, and as a result the department came under a federal consent decree designed to reduce corruption and racial bias.

The same year that the Rampart scandal first made headlines, the case of Abner Louima also attracted national attention. Louima was allegedly beaten and sodomized with the handle of a plunger while handcuffed and in New York Police Department custody. The resulting news coverage focused on racial bias in the city's law enforcement, often portraying it as epidemic (Muhammad 2010). A short two years later, New York police officers shot Amadou Diallo, an unarmed African American man, after mistaking his wallet for a weapon. Officers famously discharged their weapons forty-one times, killing Diallo. This collection of critical incidents inspired numerous media pieces on racial bias in law enforcement but, again, focused on the heinous acts of individuals rather than broader contextual explanations for racial inequality.

Because demonstrating a cause of racial inequality in policing is so difficult, and because both early scholarship and popular narratives frame racial profiling in terms of individual officer biases, the issue of racial profiling is peculiarly well positioned to offer conceptual aid to scholars interested in the AIM question. An interdisciplinary solution that isolates the causes of racial disparity in police behavior and clarifies the role of racial prejudice could serve as a model for scholars interested in other domains where the AIM question is central. In other words, the issue of racial profiling is well positioned to reduce both the measurement and the attitude problems.

So far, this opportunity has not been realized. The science has mirrored the media coverage in that it has largely focused on individual officer biases, assuming that the presence or absence of bigoted officers is tantamount to the presence or absence of racial profiling. This has resulted in a field that is still agnostic about the proper way to measure racial profiling and remains at odds with regard to where and when it still is a concern (Fridell 2004; Goff et al. 2010; Ridgeway and MacDonald 2010).

However, there is reason for optimism. Growing collaboration among researchers across disciplines and between researchers and groups of law enforcement executives has provided scholars and practitioners with a tentative roadmap for measuring—and therefore reducing—racial bias in law enforcement. Contemporary scholarship on racial profiling has tended to use one of four approaches to address the issue of racial profiling. These are benchmarking, instrumental variable analysis, outcomes testing, and community opinion research.

Benchmarking

By far the most popular approach in the media and in the minds of many casual observers is the method of population benchmarking (Fridell 2004; Goff et al. 2010; Ridgeway and MacDonald 2010). This method compares the racial distribution of stop rates (or some other police behavior) to the racial demographics of a region's population. Under this methodology, a police department whose vehicle stops were 50 percent African American while the population of the city they serviced was only 24 percent African American would be suspect. Frequently, when states or the federal Department of Justice require data collection regarding the issue of racial bias in law enforcement, these are the statistics they request. This is fairly weak evidence of racial bias on the part of law enforcement.

Part of the logic of this analysis is the attitude problem. In the case of news media and advocacy groups who track so-called racial profiling statistics, the assumption is that evidence of disparities is tantamount to evidence of sinister racial intent. A more refined form of benchmarking might account not only for a region's residential population but also for its population of commuters and other transient persons. Some careful sociological research has attempted to account for these patterns of movement as well as regional differences in police behavior within a given city (Meehan and Ponder 2002; Petrocelli, Piquero, and Smith 2003). Others have attempted to use the racial demographics of "not-at-fault" accidents to approximate commuter populations (Alpert, Smith, and Dunham 2008; Engel and Calnon 2004; Withrow 2004).

However, accident report data notwithstanding, the cost of estimating the temporal flow and racial demographics of urban populations is often prohibitive. Moreover, racial discrimination in employment, housing, wealth accruement opportunities, health care, and education may all occur independently of any bias on the part of law enforcement. Consequently, it is impossible to distinguish to what extent a disparity between population demographics and arrest demographics is a result of racially biased policing and how much owes to other forms of discrimination. This alone is reason enough to doubt population benchmarking as a methodology with which to measure racial bias in law enforcement generally and racial profiling specifically. Consequently, critics of studies using these methods can easily dismiss findings by arguing that a study is unable to account for actual racial disparities in the types of crimes that are committed or that crime is spatially distributed such that blacks or Latinos are overrepresented in the neighborhoods that are most heavily policed—perhaps even as a result of racial discrimination in housing.

This is the quintessential measurement problem in that the most common technique for measuring racial profiling (benchmarking) is not able to distinguish between discrimination that is exogenous to police contacts and discrimination that occurs between police and civilians. Worse, population benchmarking is not able to distinguish between disparities and discrimination. Still, states and federal agencies continue to mandate the collection of racial profiling data, which almost invariably means data that can only be analyzed in terms of population benchmarking (Fagan and Davies 2000). That a majority of agencies keep no data on racial profiling outside of racial benchmarks reveals how difficult it will be to gain a better picture of the role that race plays in police stops and interrogations.

Instrumental Variable Analysis

Economists' approaches to racial profiling have focused on instrumental variable analyses, which use incidental features of a context to establish causal relationships between variables when a controlled experiment is not possible. In the case of racial profiling, instrumental variable analysis has attempted to demonstrate that factors such as the ability to detect the race of a suspect (for instance, in daylight or evening light) may be related to the likelihood that an individual is stopped (Grogger and Ridgeway 2006). The vast majority of such analyses, however, attempt to isolate only the causal role of officer prejudices in producing racially disparate stop rates and tend to neglect broader structural analyses (Bjerk 2007; Engel, Calnon, and Bernard 2002; Harcourt 2007; Ridgeway and MacDonald 2010). Still, instrumental variable analysis serves as a significant improvement over coarse benchmarking in its ability to test causal mechanisms more directly.

Outcomes Testing

Researchers have begun to correct for the methodological limitations of population benchmarking and instrumental variable analysis by focusing on what happens after an individual has been stopped. This method has the benefit of sidestepping the question of an appropriate benchmark (though it, again, often assumes that officer bias is the mechanism responsible for producing racial disparities). In departments where civilian contact information is kept, for instance, it is possible to determine whether whites and nonwhites are equally likely to be searched or to be searched and then arrested, which might indicate officer bias (Fagan and Davies 2000).

Another common outcome test is consent search analysis, which measures the racial distribution of contraband obtained through consent searches. The logic behind these search analyses is that if officers secure similar contraband at equal rates from black, white, and Latino suspects, then officer bias is unlikely. Similarly, should officers secure contraband less frequently from black or Latino suspects than from white suspects, then this would imply that nonwhites are overrepresented among those who are stopped—suggesting a kind of racial profiling (Engel, Calnon, and Bernard 2002; Knowles, Persico, and Todd 2001; Zingraff et al. 2000).

This methodology, however, has its limitations. For instance, many arrest categories are excluded from the analysis. So-called Terry stops (stop, question, and frisk encounters) are not considered consent searches and are excluded, as are any stops or arrests that do not result in a search (for example, public intoxication, disorderly conduct, resisting arrest). Additionally, standard consent search analyses are unable to distinguish between departmental policies that may produce differential hit rates and individual biases that could do the same. That is, if a department adopts a targeted enforcement plan that encourages officers to search individuals in a given neighborhood or at a particular time, this may result in depressed hit rates over time, as both officer and citizens adjust to the policy. This does not necessarily reflect biases on the part of officers, however. Similarly, if a given neighborhood is better staffed than nearby areas, this could free officers to conduct more consent searches, which, in turn, might depress hit rates. Again, this would be the result of a policy, rather than an individual. Still, the advent of consent search analyses at least improves on the blunt instrument of population benchmarking in establishing a measure of objectionable bias rather than simply an indicator of disparities.

Community Opinion Research

Research that examines racial profiling from the perspective of community perceptions eschews the issue of benchmarks altogether (Sidanius and Pratto 1999; Tyler and Huo 2002; Weitzer and Tuch 2005). This research instead focuses on the harms to community trust, legitimacy, and ultimately public safety that result from perceptions that the police are racially biased. Community opinion research offers a valuable perspective in that the harms associated with racial profiling are merely assumed in research that attempts to measure whether profiling occurs. Unfortunately, though this research is reasonably unconcerned with the issue of benchmarks, it is often equally unconcerned with whether discrimination actually occurs. In fact, significant evidence suggests that individuals may fail to see racial discrimination in policing, even when it is clear, if they feel they themselves have been treated fairly (Sidanius and Pratto 1999; Tyler and Huo 2002). Moreover, public opinion tends to overestimate nonwhite representation in the criminal justice system (chap. 9, this volume), making it difficult to disambiguate perceptions that come from misinformation from those that come from officer behavior. Finally, public opinions tend to suffer from the attitude problem, such that most lay people imagine that racial bias in law enforcement is made manifest through the biases of individual officers. And it has been uncommon for public opinion researchers to challenge this implicit theory.

No Consensus

Each of the above methodologies suffers from both the measurement problem and the attitude problem, and none is recognized as a best practice in the field. The techniques are either modest in their ability to make strong causal statements about inequality or require access to hard-to-get data in order to do so. Moreover, they each tend to assume that racial prejudice is the culprit behind objectionable inequalities. This makes it difficult to explain the persistent outcry over racially disparate police stops in the face of ever-decreasing racial prejudices.

Some argue that policing is a peculiarly insular culture that has maintained racial biases even in the face of prejudice's declining social acceptance (Sidanius and Pratto 1999). However, this ignores the broader context of the AIM question. With growing evidence that police biases roughly mirror the biases of the broader population (Correll et al. 2007; Sidanius and Pratto 1999), it is unlikely that reductions of racial prejudice among officers will result in a reduction in racial disparities—just as the reduction in racial prejudice in the broader society has not been accompanied by broader reductions in racial inequality across many domains.

It is worth noting here that each of these analyses also has correlates in domains outside of law enforcement. Research in education has used benchmarking and outcomes testing for generations to gauge racial inequality in schools and has often struggled to identify causal mechanisms (Blank, Dabady, and Citro 2004). Similarly, researchers concerned with the acquisition of wealth have found it difficult to agree on a way to measure racial discrimination in the mechanisms that produce wealth inequality (Oliver and Shapiro 1995). There are no data readily available on the racial biases of loan officers, and scholars of racial segregation are left to engage in community surveys, benchmarking, instrumental variable analyses, and outcomes testing to triangulate the role of racial discrimination in housing inequality (Jargowsky 1998; Massey and Denton 1993; Wilson 1990, 1996).

Consequently, the best science on racial profiling appears plagued by the same measurement and attitude problems that plague broader AIM research. Promising new research initiatives, however, suggest that there is reason to be optimistic about the creation of better methods for solving both problems. Interdisciplinary collaborations among scholars and between researchers and police may offer a fresh perspective on these traditional obstacles.

A BETTER WAY TO MEASURE JUSTICE

In addition to these limitations, the established methodologies for the study of racial profiling also share a common limitation: none of them actually measure officer prejudice. In other words, none of the techniques explicitly test the underlying assumption that bias is at the root of racial inequality. Without data on racial prejudice, it is exceedingly difficult to determine what role bigotry does or does not play. The addition of social psychology to the study of policing, therefore, offers the ability to test the underlying assumptions of the attitude problem explicitly. When these methods are integrated with established approaches, it may be possible to develop a symptomology of biased policing that simultaneously reduces both measurement and attitude problems.

Implicit Bias

Although economists and sociologists began seriously studying bias in policing only during the past three decades, social psychologists are even newer to the field. Owing, at least in part, to psychologists' need to collect data from research participants—and law enforcement's corresponding wariness about being the subject of experimentation—social psychologists were slower than economists and sociologists to ply their discipline in the domain of race and policing. Unable to take advantage of the increased availability of secondary data sets, psychologists were forced to wait for individual law enforcement executives to decide that they wanted to learn more about the potential biases of their officers. Consequently, early research efforts in this domain were slow and inconsistent.

This began to change with the attention focused on the Diallo incident. The police shooting of Diallo was a touchstone for social psychologists not just because of the media attention to the case but because of two other features of the incident: the split-second decision of the officers to fire and their insistence that they actually saw a weapon and not the wallet that Diallo raised over his head before he was killed. These facets of the case overlapped with research that was already rising to prominence in implicit cognition and visual recognition (Eberhardt and Goff 2005).

This idea, that our hearts and minds may hold attitudes about which we are consciously unaware, continues to gather momentum as a way to explain the contemporary state of race relations (Greenwald, McGhee, and Schwartz 1998). In particular, the Implicit Association Test, which scholars argue can be used as a measure of one's automatic association between social identity groups and stereotypes, has become a popular measure of contemporary bias, replacing explicit measures as a so-called bonafide pipeline to assess individual racial attitudes.[3]

In the context of implicit bias research, and inspired by the Diallo incident, scholars have established a what they call a "shooter bias" effect. This effect reveals that most individuals tend to be faster to fire at dangerous black suspects than dangerous white suspects and more likely to fire at unarmed black than unarmed white suspects (Correll et al. 2002, 2007, forthcoming; Payne 2001; Payne, Lambert, and Jacoby 2002). Research in this paradigm tends to have participants play a computer simulation game where the goal is to shoot the armed but not the unarmed targets. In an effort to mimic the real world, participants are placed under strenuous time constraints. Researchers then vary the race of the armed and unarmed targets, and the participants again try to shoot the armed and but not the unarmed targets.

Despite the tendency for officers to demonstrate a similar shooter bias toward civilians, officers in research conducted by Joshua Correll and colleagues did not show the typical bias of shooting unarmed black suspects more often than unarmed white suspects. That is, though they were biased with regard to how quickly they shot black suspects, participants did not make a significant number of errors (that is, shooting more unarmed black targets). This suggests that police training may reduce the relationship between attitudes and behaviors, an important assumption of the attitude problem for psychologists to test (Correll et al., forthcoming).

The strong cognitive association between blackness and criminality has also led officers to incorrectly identify dark-skinned blacks as criminal suspects (Eberhardt et al. 2004) and can lead to greater endorsement of the death penalty for blacks who appear "most black" (Eberhardt et al. 2006). Similarly, the strong cognitive association between blackness and apes seems to be associated with increased endorsement of antiblack violence by police and with an increased use of the death penalty for blacks (Goff et al. 2008). Taken together, these deliberate tests of the link between prejudiced implicit attitudes and behavior suggest that implicit bias may be an important mechanism in producing racially disparate outcomes. It also suggests that the underlying assumption of the attitude problem is both testable and not without merit. However, with few exceptions (Eberhardt et al. 2006; Goff, Thomas, and Jackson 2008), this work has been largely confined to the laboratory and is only now being used to document real-world consequences.

Aversive Racism

Aversive racism attempts to explain subtle expressions of individual prejudice by assuming a conflict between one's genuinely egalitarian self-concept and one's implicit biases against certain racial groups (Dovidio and Gaertner 2004; Gaertner and Dovidio 1996). Because aversive racists are invested in their nonprejudiced self-concept, they will not engage in discriminatory behaviors in situations with strong social norms or when discrimination would be obvious to others or to themselves. However, when there is a way to rationalize their behavior as nonprejudiced, aversive racists will discriminate against target out-groups. Under these circumstances, aversive racists may discriminate against nonwhites without confronting a negative perception of themselves or members of their social group.

Rather than creating out-group hostility, aversive racism often creates prosocial behavior toward members of the in-group (Gaertner and Dovidio 1977). Outside of the laboratory, this theoretical perspective is echoed in the findings of the Kerner Commission (*Report of the National Advisory Commission on Civil Disorders* 1968), charged with investigating the causes of the 1967 race riots in the United States. The commission cited white America's failure to assist blacks in need, rather than actively trying to harm blacks, as a primary cause of racial disparities and, ultimately, civil unrest.

That aversive racism seems relatively common throughout the United States and stable across the past four decades suggests that the tension between egalitarian self-concepts and negative implicit attitudes is an important component in understanding racial inequality (Saucier, Miller, and Doucet 2005). It also suggests that people do not have to be overtly racist to perpetuate racism at a societal level. Although scant research has applied an aversive racism framework to the domain of racial profiling, the stability of aversive racism suggests that the concept would be a valuable addition to the racial profiling researcher's toolbox.

Identity Threat

Many social psychologists have engaged in efforts to redefine racial bias for the contemporary moment. But social psychology is also the study of how situations influence people. Chief among these in the domain of racial profiling are approaches that include identity threat (generally) and stereotype threat (specifically). Identity threats are those that trigger the concern that how one is seen in a particular context could have negative consequences (Steele, Spencer, and Aronson 2002). For instance, a bad dancer who finds that her new boyfriend's family values family dance night might feel concerned about the future of her relationship. It is important to note that there need not be a negative stereotype about one's group for an identity threat to have an effect.

Stereotype threat is the more specific concern that one has about conforming to or being evaluated in terms of a negative stereotype about one's group (Steele 1992, 1997). For instance, a woman who is taking a difficult math test may worry that, if she does poorly, an observer might attribute her performance to the fact that she is a woman. Since most women are aware that there are negative stereotypes about women in math, the concern that one will be evaluated in terms of those negative stereotypes constitutes stereotype threat (Steele 1992; Steele, Spencer, and Aronson 2002). This additional burden often leads to a weakening in performance that has the ironic feature of being stereotype-consistent behavior.

In the case of police officers, as with other dominant group members, the relevant stereotype is that they are racist (Frantz et al. 2004; Goff, Steele, and Davies 2008). Mounting evidence suggests that whites and other powerful group members are aware of the stereotype that they are biased against less powerful groups and that these biases lead to intergroup friction (Frantz et al. 2004; Goff, Steele, and Davies 2008; Shelton and Richeson 2006; Vorauer, Main, and O'Connell 1998). For example, my colleagues and I found that white participants experienced stereotype threat simply from anticipating a conversation with blacks on a sensitive topic such as racial profiling (Goff, Steele, and Davies 2008).

In our research, participants anticipating a conversation about racial profiling with a black partner reported that they experienced more stereotype threat than those who expected to discuss a less racially explosive topic: love and relationships. This experience of stereotype threat led participants to sit further away from black, but not white, conversation partners. Here, the experience of stereotype threat—and neither explicit nor implicit prejudice—produced aversive behavior that could be interpreted as discriminatory. In this way, well-intentioned blacks and whites respond to the threat of appearing racially prejudiced in undesirable ways—sometimes even before the interaction takes place.

It is also important to note that neither stereotype threat nor identity threats more broadly are attitudes per se. Rather, they are individual vulnerabilities to certain contexts. One could be a bad dancer without chronically worrying about one's relationships, and one could be an officer without habitually fretting over accusations of racism. However, when a situation arises in which the negative stereotype or characteristic becomes salient, then the threat becomes relevant and may affect behavior. Taken together, these two theoretical approaches offer a contextual lens through which to see individual behaviors.

Translating the Research to the Field

Each of these social psychological approaches adds to the toolbox for measuring racial profiling. Implicit bias and aversive racism frameworks allow researchers to test the role of prejudice in explicitly producing discrimination. Identity threat approaches, on the other hand, give researchers a way to measure the role of context in individual behavior—permitting an analysis of individuals that steers clear of the attitude problem. Each also offers the possibility of experimental methods that permit strong causal inferences. Taken together, they offer great advances in solving the measurement and attitude problems. But how useful are these approaches beyond the laboratory?

Some preliminary data are instructive on this point. Through the Consortium for Police Leadership in Equity (an organization that partners empirical social scientists with state and municipal law enforcement), my colleagues and I examined officers' racial attitudes and other psychological dimensions and then correlated individual officer psychological profiles with actual officer use of force histories. These preliminary data, collected with the Denver, Colorado, police department, stand as the first such research on record and provide an initial test of the utility of psychological tools to the study of racial profiling. The preliminary findings have been promising—and surprising.

My colleagues and I found that officer racial biases predicted the number of black and Latino citizens on which police used force. Specifically, as the racial bias of officers increased, so did the amount of force they used against blacks as compared with whites. Surprisingly, though, racial bias was not the most important factor in predicting use of force. Rather, officers' concern with appearing racist, or stereotype threat (Goff, Steele, and Davies 2008), and male officers' concern with demonstrating their manhood (Thompson and Pleck 1986) served as better predictors of differential use of force against nonwhite citizens than officer racial bias. Why might that be?

In the case of stereotype threat, the answer may be found in officer safety training, in which officers learn that they must remain in control of a situation to maintain a safe environment. Officers have two forms of authority at their disposal to effect that control. The first is moral authority, the authority that officers wield by dint of being law enforcement. Officer safety training in all the law enforcement agencies with which the Consortium for Police Leadership in Equity has partnered (and the majority of Major Cities Chiefs Association member cities) teaches officers that they should occupy the moral high ground in nearly all interactions and that citizens tend to respect both that perception and the authority inherent in the officer's position. When a citizen fails to respect that moral authority, police are empowered to use their second form of authority, physical means, to control a situation. Of course, when an officer is confronted with a group of black or Latino suspects who accuse him or her of being racist, moral authority is not an option. Consequently, interactions between officers and nonwhite suspects may become physical as a result of the officer's fear of having lost moral authority—an ironic consequence of an officer's egalitarian concerns in this policing context.

Why do concerns about perceived manhood produce racial bias in male law enforcement officers? Once again, the answer can be found in the police officer training program. Black and Latino suspects, particularly men, can represent a threat to moral authority as a result of the stereotype that black and Latino men are "hypermasculine" (Goff, Thomas, and Jackson 2008). Taken together, this research on perceived racist attitude and perceived diminished masculinity contributes to solving a long-standing measurement conundrum in the study of racial bias and introduces new theoretical language with which to approach the issue.

However encouraging these findings are, they contain several methodological limitations. The first is that attitude-behavior matching of this type is necessarily flawed chronologically—that is, attitudes are measured in the present, while behaviors took place in the past. It is not possible to argue in good conscience that officers' current attitudes caused their previous behaviors. In fact, because regression analyses are fundamentally correlations, it is not possible to say whether attitudes influence behavior more than past behaviors influence current attitudes. Additionally, though data collection efforts have already begun in several other cities, this is a brand new methodology, and it is not yet possible to determine how well these initial results generalize across departments. Finally, while this paradigm is able to sidestep issues of base rates and benchmarking, it is only able to deliver an analysis that identifies trends in officer behavior. This method provides no way to tell whether a department's policies are responsible for racially disparate stops or use of force, nor whether the department as a whole is disproportionately stopping specific racial groups.

To address this concern, law enforcement and an interdisciplinary collection of researchers have recently come together to establish an agenda for research that can compensate for the limitations of each of the established and emerging approaches to quantifying racial profiling. The resulting document, *The Contract for Policing Justice* (Goff et al. 2010), suggests that looking for a single metric of racial profiling is unlikely to produce an ideal result. In part, this is because racial profiling may not result simply from individual attitudes, meaning that researchers must account for multiple causes simultaneously. Rather than looking for a single measure of racial profiling, these scholars, chiefs, and sheriffs suggest treating the problem as a doctor might a complex disease. Racial profiling may have many symptoms that can be detected across several indicators.

This symptomological approach to racial profiling would require that researchers have access to benchmark data, outcomes tests, community opinions, and social psychological information, among other indicators. This information would be collected not in only one department but across a large number of comparable ones in order to examine the relationships between indicators. This analysis would permit both an assessment of the role of officer bias and an assessment of the relative role of a department in producing racially disparate law enforcement outcomes. With the support of progressive law enforcement executives, access to broad swaths of data is possible on an unprecedented scale. Similarly, a cross-disciplinary and multi-indicator instrument for assessing racial bias may provide a significantly improved test of racial discrimination in law enforcement.

By testing the relationships between predictors and particular outcome variables (that is, stops and use of force), researchers can produce evidence of a causal mechanism. Having secured the cooperation of a large portion of the law enforcement community, this agenda self-consciously addresses both components of the measurement problem. Similarly, by directly testing the assumption that prejudice is solely to blame for racial inequalities, the attitude problem is confronted and may be diffused. This, then, is the current best hope in the study of racial profiling: a collaborative effort between scholars and practitioners that takes seriously the measurement problem and the attitude problem.

CONCLUSIONS

This brief history suggests both how far the understanding of racial bias in law enforcement has come and how far it still has to go. Of note is the fact that the nature of racial bias in law enforcement is resistant to classical formulations of racial oppression. Specifically, measuring the prejudices of individual agents—even in the aggregate—is not sufficient for understanding the nature of racial disparities in stops, arrests, and police use of force. Similarly, noting racial disparities in these categories does not necessarily indicate the prejudices of officers or agencies but may reflect a complex interplay between broader sociopolitical factors (for example, education and housing disparities), state and local statutes (for example, Arizona's SB 1070), and officer and agency attitudes. The search for a way to measure biased law enforcement—particularly with regard to the issue of racial profiling—may prove an illustrative example beyond the limited domain of policing.

Of particular importance may be the role that directly confronting the measurement problem and the attitude problem has had in the formulation of racial profiling researcher's next steps. A similar approach in the domain of education, housing, health care, and employment disparities may yield a similar solution. Multiple indicators, used in concert, may yield a clearer picture than can any one indicator, as suggested by Devah Pager (chap. 9, this volume). In addition, the more directly the diagnostic approach confronts the concerns of establishing causality, securing the data, and problematizing the role of prejudice, the better chance it may stand to produce scholarly innovation. However, the lessons that racial profiling research has to teach those concerned with racial inequality may be far simpler. It seems that, if we cannot measure the problem, we cannot manage it. And if we assume that prejudice is the only cause, we may be lost should that assumption prove less than complete.

NOTES

1. The International Association of Chiefs of Police created the first such annual report, which eventually became the Uniform Crime Report in 1930.
2. A federal consent decree is a mechanism by which the U.S. Department of Justice can require certain behaviors from municipal law enforcement, such as data collection or racially representative hiring.
3. For details of the Implicit Association Test, see Project Implicit, Harvard University. Available at: https://implicit.harvard.edu/implicit/ (accessed January 15, 2011).

REFERENCES

Adlam, K. Robert C. 1982. "The Police Personality: Psychological Consequences of Being a Police Officer." *Journal of Police Science and Administration* 10(3): 344–49.

Alpert, Geoffrey P., and Roger G. Dunham. 2003. *Understanding Police Use of Force: Officers, Suspects, and Reciprocity.* Cambridge: Cambridge University Press.

Alpert, Geoffrey P., Michael R. Smith, and Roger G. Dunham. 2008. "Toward a Better Benchmark: Assessing the Utility of Not-at-Fault Traffic Crash Data in Racial Profiling Research." *Justice Research and Policy* 6(1): 43–70.

Anderson, Elijah. 1990. *Streetwise: Race, Class, and Change in an Urban Community.* Chicago: University of Chicago Press.

Balch, Robert W. 1972. "Police Personality: Fact or Fiction." *Journal of Criminal Law, Criminology, and Police Science* 63(1): 106–19.

Baldus, Davei C., George Woodworth, and Charles A. Pulaski. 1990. *Equal Justice and the Death Penalty.* Boston, Mass.: Northeastern University Press.

Barker, Joan C. 1999. *Danger, Duty, and Disillusion: The Worldview of Los Angeles Police Officers.* Long Grove, Ill.: Waveland Press.

Bayley, David H. 1994. *Police for the Future.* New York: Oxford University Press.

Bennett, Richard R., and Theodore Greenstein. 1975. "The Police Personality: A Test of the Predispositional Model." *Journal of Police Science and Administration* 3(4): 439–45.

Bjerk, David. 2007. "Racial Profiling, Statistical Discrimination, and the Effect of a Colorblind Policy on the Crime Rate." *Journal of Public Economic Theory* 9(3): 521–45.

Blakeslee, Nate. 2006. *Tulia: Race, Cocaine, and Corruption in a Small Texas Town.* New York: PublicAffairs.

Blank, Rebecca M., Marilyn Dabady, and Constance F. Citro. 2004. *Measuring Racial Discrimination.* Washington, D.C.: National Academies Press.

Bonilla-Silva, Eduardo. 2009. *Racism Without Racists: Color-Blind Racism and the Persistence of Racial Inequality in the United States.* Lanham, Md.: Rowman and Littlefield.

Bureau of Justice Statistics. n.d. "About the Bureau of Justice Statistics." Available at: http://bjs.ojp.usdoj.gov/index.cfm (accessed December 6, 2010).

Correll, Joshua, et al. 2002. "The Police Officer's Dilemma: Using Ethnicity to Disambiguate Potentially Threatening Individuals." *Journal of Personality and Social Psychology* 83(6): 1314–29.

Correll, Joshua, et al. 2007. "Across the Thin Blue Line: Police Officers and Racial Bias in the Decision to Shoot." *Journal of Personality and Social Psychology* 92(6): 1006–23.

Correll, Joshua, et al. 2010. "Measuring Prejudice, Stereotypes, and Discrimination." In *The SAGE Handbook of Prejudice, Stereotyping and Discrimination,* edited by John F. Dovidio, Miles Hewstone, Peter Glick, and Victoria M. Esses. Thousand Oaks, Calif.: SAGE Publications.

Devine, Patricia G., and Andrew J. Elliot. 1995. "Are Racial Stereotypes Really Fading? The Princeton Trilogy Revisited." *Personality and Social Psychology Bulletin* 21(11): 1139–50.

Dominitz, Jeffrey, and John Knowles. 2006. "Crime Minimization and Racial Bias: What Can We Learn from Police Search Data?" *Economic Journal* 116(515): F368–84.

Dovidio, John F. 2001. "On the Nature of Contemporary Prejudice: The Third Wave." *Journal of Social Issues* 57(4): 829–49.

Dovidio, John F., and Samuel L. Gaertner. 2004. "Aversive Racism." In *Advances in Experimental Social Psychology,* edited by Mark P. Zanna. San Diego, Calif.: Academic Press.

Eberhardt, Jennifer L., and Phillip Atiba Goff. 2005. "Seeing Race." In *Social Psychology of Prejudice: Historical and Contemporary Issues,* edited by C. S. Crandall and Mark Schaller. Seattle, Wash.: Lewinian Press.

Eberhardt, Jennifer L., et al. 2004. "Seeing Black: Race, Crime, and Visual Processing." *Journal of Personality and Social Psychology* 87(6): 876–93.

Eberhardt, Jennifer L., et al. 2006. "Looking Deathworthy: Perceived Stereotypicality of Black Defendants Predicts Capital Sentencing Outcomes." *Psychological Science* 17(5): 383–88.

Engel, Robin S., and Jennifer M. Calnon. 2004. "Examining the Influence of Drivers' Characteristics During Traffic Stops by Police." *Justice Quarterly* 21(1): 49–90.

Engel, Robin S., Jennifer M. Calnon, and Thomas J. Bernard. 2002. "Theory and Racial Profiling: Shortcomings and Future Directions in Research." *Justice Quarterly* 19(2): 249–73.

Escobar, Edward J. 1999. *Race, Police, and the Making of Political Identity: Mexican*

Americans and the Los Angeles Police Department, 1900–1945. Berkeley: University of California Press.

Evans, Barry J., Greg J. Coman, and Robb O. Stanley. 1992. "The Police Personality: Type A Behavior and Anxiety." *Journal of Criminal Justice* 20(5): 429–41.

Fagan, Jeffrey, and Garth Davies. 2000. "Street Stops and Broken Windows: Terry, Race, and Disorder in New York City." *Fordham Urban Law Journal* 28(2): 457–04.

Fenster, C. A., and Bernard Locke. 1973. "Neuroticism among Policemen: An Examination of Police Personality." *Journal of Applied Psychology* 57(3): 358–59.

Frantz, C. M., et al. 2004. "A Threat in the Computer: The Race Implicit Association Test as a Stereotype Threat Experience." *Personality and Social Psychology Bulletin* 30(12): 1611–24.

Fridell, Lorie A. 2004. *By the Numbers: A Guide to Analyzing Race Data from Vehicle Stops.* Washington, D.C.: Police Executive Research Forum.

Gabbidon, Shaun L. 2010. *Criminological Perspectives on Race and Crime.* New York: Routledge.

Gabbidon, Shaun L., and Helen Taylor Greene. 2005. *Race, Crime, and Justice: A Reader.* New York: Routledge.

Gaertner, Samuel L., and John F. Dovidio. 1977. "The Subtlety of White Racism, Arousal, and Helping Behavior." *Journal of Personality and Social Psychology* 35(10): 691–707.

———. 1996. "Affirmative Action, Unintentional Racial Biases, and Intergroup Relations." *Journal of Social Issues* 52(4): 51–75.

Garland, David. 1985. "The Criminal and His Science: A Critical Account of the Formation of Criminology at the End of the Nineteenth Century." *British Journal of Criminology* 25(2): 109–37.

Glover, Karen S. 2009. *Racial Profiling: Research, Racism, and Resistance.* London: Rowman and Littlefield.

Goff, Phillip Atiba, Claude M. Steele, and Paul G. Davies. 2008. "The Space Between Us: Stereotype Threat and Distance in Interracial Contexts." *Journal of Personality and Social Psychology* 94(1): 91–107.

Goff, Phillip Atiba, Margaret A. Thomas, and Matthew C. Jackson. 2008. "'Ain't I a Woman': Towards an Intersectional Approach to Person Perception and Group-Based Harms." *Sex Roles* 59:(5–6) 392–403.

Goff, Phillip Atiba, et al. 2008. "Not Yet Human: Implicit Knowledge, Historical Dehumanization, and Contemporary Consequences." *Journal of Personality and Social Psychology* 94(2): 292–306.

Goff, Phillip Atiba, et al. 2010. *The Contract for Policing Justice.* Los Angeles: Consortium for Police Leadership in Equity.

Greenwald, Anthony G., Debbie E. McGhee, and Jordan K. L. Schwartz. 1998. "Measuring Individual Differences in Implicit Cognition: The Implicit Association Test." *Journal of Personality and Social Psychology* 74(6): 1464–80.

Grogger, Jeffrey, and Greg Ridgeway. 2006. "Testing for Racial Profiling in Traffic

Stops from Behind a Veil of Darkness." *Journal of the American Statistical Association* 101(475): 878–87.

Hanewicz, Wayne B. 1978. "Police Personality: A Jungian Perspective." *Crime and Delinquency* 24(2): 152–72.

Harcourt, Bernard E. 2007. *Against Prediction: Profiling, Policing, and Punishing in an Actuarial Age.* Chicago: University of Chicago Press.

Harris, David A. 2002. *Profiles in Injustice: Why Racial Profiling Cannot Work.* New York: New Press.

Hogan, Robert, and William Kurtines. 1975. "Personological Correlates of Police Effectiveness." *Journal of Psychology* 91(2): 289–295.

Jackson, Pamela Irving 1989. *Minority Group Threat, Crime, and Policing: Social Context and Social Control.* New York: Praeger Press.

Jargowsky, Paul A. 1998. *Poverty and Place: Ghettos, Barrios, and the American City.* New York: Russell Sage Foundation.

Kang, Jerry, and Kristin A. Lane. 2010. "Seeing Through Colorblindness: Implicit Bias and the Law." *University of California (Los Angeles) Law Review* 58: 465–520.

Kappeler, Victor E., Richard D. Sluder, and Geoffrey P. Alpert. 1998. *Forces of Deviance: Understanding the Dark Side of Policing.* Prospect Heights, Ill.: Waveland.

Knowles, John, Nicola Persico, and Petra Todd. 2001. "Racial Bias in Motor Vehicle Searches: Theory and Evidence." *Journal of Political Economy* 109(1): 203–29.

LaPiere, Richard T. 1934. "Attitudes vs. Actions." *Social Forces* 13(2): 230–37.

Lester, David S., et al. 1980. "The Personalities of English and American Police." *Journal of Social Psychology* 111(1): 153–54.

Massey, Douglas S., and Nancy A. Denton. 1993. *American Apartheid: Segregation and the Making of the Underclass.* Cambridge, Mass.: Harvard University Press.

McNamara, John H. 1967. "Uncertainties in Police Work: The Relevance of Police Recruits' Backgrounds and Training." In *The Police: Six Sociological Essays,* edited by David J. Bordua. New York: John Wiley.

Meehan, Albert J., and Michael C. Ponder. 2002. "Race and Place: The Ecology of Profiling African-American Motorists." *Justice Quarterly* 9(3): 14–55.

Mills, Carol J., and Wayne E. Bohannon. 1980. "Personality Characteristics of Effective State Police Officers." *Journal of Applied Psychology* 65(6): 680–84.

Mills, Charles W. 1999. *The Racial Contract.* Ithaca, N.Y.: Cornell University Press.

Moody, Mia N. 2008. *Black and Mainstream Press' Framing of Racial Profiling: A Historical Perspective.* New York: University Press of America.

Muhammad, Khalil Gibran 2010. *The Condemnation of Blackness: Race, Crime, and the Making of Modern Urban America.* Cambridge, Mass.: Harvard University Press.

Neiderhoffer, Arthur. 1967. *Behind the Shield.* New York: Doubleday.

Nocera, Joe. 2010. "Lesson Plan from a Departing Schools Chief." *New York Times,* November 12. Available at: www.nytimes.com/2010/11/13/business/13nocera .html?pagewanted=2andref=education (accessed February 7, 2011).

Ogloff, James R. P. 2000. "Two Steps Forward and One Step Backward: The Law and Psychology Movement(s) in the 20th Century." *Law and Human Behavior* 24(4): 457–83.

Okihiro, Gary Y. 2005. *The Columbia Guide to Asian American History*. New York: Columbia University Press.

Oliver, Melvin L., and Thomas M. Shapiro. 1995. *Black Wealth / White Wealth: A New Perspective on Racial Inequality*. New York: Routledge.

Pager, Devah. 2003. "The Mark of a Criminal Record." *American Journal of Sociology* 108(5): 937–75.

Payne, B. Keith 2001. "Prejudice and Perception: The Role of Automatic and Controlled Processes in Misperceiving a Weapon." *Journal of Personality and Social Psychology* 81(2): 181–92.

Payne, B. Keith, Alan J. Lambert, and Larry L. Jacoby. 2002. "Best Laid Plans: Effects of Goals on Accessibility Bias and Cognitive Control in Race-Based Misperceptions of Weapons." *Journal of Experimental Social Psychology* 38(4): 384–96.

Persico, Nicola, and P. E. Todd. 2006. "Generalising the Hit Rates Test for Racial Bias in Law Enforcement, with an Application to Vehicle Searches in Wichita." *Economic Journal* 116(515): F351–67.

Petrocelli, Matthew, Alex R. Piquero, and Michael R. Smith. 2003. "Conflict Theory and Racial Profiling: An Empirical Analysis of Police Traffic Stop Data." *Journal of Criminal Justice* 31(1): 1–11.

Prassel, Frank R. 1972. *The Western Peace Officer: The Legacy of Law and Order*. Norman: University of Oklahoma Press.

Provine, Doris Marie 2007. *Unequal under Law: Race in the War on Drugs*. Chicago: University of Chicago Press.

Rafter, Nicole. 2008. *The Criminal Brain: Understanding Biological Theories of Crime*. New York: New York University Press.

Report of the National Advisory Commission on Civil Disorders. 1968. New York: Bantam Books.

Ridgeway, Greg, and John MacDonald. 2010. "Methods for Assessing Racially Biased Policing." In *Race, Ethnicity, and Policing*, edited by S. K. Rice and M. D. White. New York: New York University Press.

Ross, Lee. 1977. "The Intuitive Psychologist and His Shortcomings: Distortions in the Attitude Attribution Process." In *Advances in Experimental Social Psychology*, edited by Leonard Berkowitz. New York: Academic Press.

Sanga, Sarah. 2009. "Reconsidering Racial Bias in Motor Vehicle Searches: Theory and Evidence." *Journal of Political Economy* 117(6): 1155–59.

Saucier, Donald A., Carol T. Miller, and Nicole Doucet. 2005. "Differences in Helping Whites and Blacks: A Meta-Analysis." *Personality and Social Psychology Review* 9(1/2): 2–16.

Shelton, J. Nicole, and Jennifer A. Richeson. 2006. "Interracial Interactions: A Relational Approach." *Advances in Experimental Social Psychology* 38: 121–81.

Sherman, Lawrence W. 1980. "Causes of Police Behavior: The Current State of Quantitative Research." *Journal of Research in Crime and Delinquency* 17(1): 69–100.

Sidanius, Jim, and Felicia Pratto. 1999. *Social Dominance: An Intergroup Theory of Social Hierarchy and Oppression.* New York: Cambridge University Press.

Sklansky, David A. 1998. "Traffic Stops, Minority Motorists, and the Future of the Fourth Amendment." In *The Supreme Court Review,* edited by Dennis J. Hutchinson, David A. Strauss, and Geoffrey R. Stone. Chicago: University of Chicago Press.

Smith, Michael R., and Matthew Petrocelli. 2001. "Racial Profiling? A Multivariate Analysis of Police Traffic Stop Data." *Police Quarterly* 4(1): 4–27.

Steele, Claude Mason 1992. "Race and the Schooling of Black Americans." *Atlantic Monthly,* April, 68–78.

———. 1997. "A Threat in the Air: How Stereotypes Shape the Intellectual Identities and Performance of Women and African-Americans." *American Psychologist* 52(6): 613–29.

Steele, Claude M., Steven J. Spencer, and Joshua Aronson. 2002. "Contending with Group Image: The Psychology of Stereotype and Social Identity Threat." In *Advances in Experimental Social Psychology,* edited by Marl P. Zanna, 34: 379–440. San Diego, Calif.: Academic Press.

Swim, Janet K., and Charles Stangor, eds. 1998. *Prejudice: The Target's Perspective.* San Diego, Calif.: Academic Press.

Thompson, Edward H., and Joseph H. Pleck. 1986. "The Structure of Male Role Norms." *American Behavioral Scientist* 29(5): 531–43.

Toby, Jackson. 2000. "Are Police the Enemy?" *Society* 37(4): 38–42.

Tyler, Tom R., and Yuen J. Huo. 2002. *Trust in the Law: Encouraging Public Cooperation with the Police and Courts.* New York: Russell Sage Foundation.

Vorauer, Jacquie D., K. J. Main, and G. B. O'Connell. 1998. "How Do Individuals Expect to Be Viewed by Members of Lower Status Groups? Content and Implications of Meta-Stereotypes." *Journal of Personality and Social Psychology* 75(4): 917–37.

Waddington, David P. 2007. *Policing Public Disorder: Theory and Practice.* Portland, Ore.: Willan Publishing.

Walker, Samuel. 1992. *The Police in America.* 2nd ed. New York: McGraw-Hill.

———. 2001. "Searching for the Denominator: Problems with Police Traffic Stop Data and an Early Warning System Solution." *Justice Research and Policy* 3(1): 63–95.

———. 2005. *The New World of Police Accountability.* Thousand Oaks, Calif.: Sage Publications.

Walker, Samuel, Cassoa Spohn, and Miriam DeLone. 2007. *The Color of Justice: Race, Ethnicity, and Crime in America.* New York: Wadsworth Publishing.

Websdale, Neil. 2001. *Policing the Poor: From Slave Plantation to Public Housing.* Boston, Mass.: Northeastern University Press.

Weglyn, Michi N. 2000. *Years of Infamy.* Seattle: University of Washington Press.

Weiss, Peter A. 2010. *Personality Assessment in Police Psychology: A 21st Century Perspective.* Springfield, Ill.: Charles C Thomas.

Weitzer, Ronald, and Steven A. Tuch. 2005. "Racially Biased Policing: Determinants of Citizen Perceptions." *Social Forces* 83(3): 1009–30.

———. 2006. *Race and Policing in America: Conflict and Reform.* New York: Cambridge University Press.

Wicker, Allan W. 1969. "Attitudes Versus Actions: The Relationship of Verbal and Overt Behavioral Responses to Attitude Objects." *Journal of Social Issues* 25(4): 41–78.

Wilson, G., Roger Dunham, and Geoffrey Alpert. 2004. "Prejudice in Policing: Assessing an Overlooked Aspect in Prior Research." *American Behavioral Scientist* 47(7): 896–910.

Wilson, William J. 1990. *The Truly Disadvantaged: The Inner City, the Underclass, and Public Policy.* Chicago: University of Chicago Press.

———. 1996. *When Work Disappears: The World of the New Urban Poor.* New York: Alfred Knopf.

Withrow, Brian L. 2004. "A Comparative Analysis of Commonly Used Benchmarks in Racial Profiling: A Research Note." *Justice Research and Policy* 6(1): 71–92.

Zingraff, M. T., et al. 2000. *Evaluating North Carolina State Highway Patrol Data: Citations, Warnings, and Searches in 1998.* Available at: www.nccrimecontrol.org/shp/ncshpreport.htm (accessed February 17, 2011).

Chapter 6 | The Social Psychology of Symbolic Firsts: Effects of Barack Obama's Presidency on Student Achievement and Perceptions of Racial Progress in America

Valerie Purdie-Vaughns and
Richard P. Eibach

First indications, whether observed in the silent, mysterious phenomena of physical nature, or in the moral or intellectual developments of human society, are always interesting in thoughtful men. . . . John Brown used to say he had looked over our people as over a dark sea, in the hope of seeing a head rise up with a mind to plan and a head to deliver. Any movement of the water arrested his attention. In all directions, we desire to catch the first sign. . . . There is a calm and quiet satisfaction in the contemplation of present attainments; but the great future, and the yet unattained, awaken in the soul the deepest springs of enthusiasm and poetry.

—Frederick Douglass, 1865

As FREDERICK DOUGLASS noted when he observed some of the first political achievements of emancipated black Americans, the human imagination is captivated by pioneers. Indeed, popular history is often a chronicle of pioneers: the first explorer to circumnavigate the globe, the first woman appointed to the United States Supreme Court, the first man to walk on the moon, the first successful heart transplant on a human patient. These and other pioneers capture the public's imagination because they challenge people's prior beliefs about the limits of human nature or

186

the constraints on what is achievable in human societies. It is this power of symbolic firsts to change people's perceptions of their own limitations and those of other members of their social group that is the focus of our analysis.

In particular, we wish to highlight how symbolic firsts can alter people's perceptions of the constraints and opportunities afforded to them as a function of their social group memberships, what psychologists have termed a person's identity contingencies (Purdie-Vaughns et al. 2008; Steele 2010). Our analysis focuses on the influence of the first black president of the United States as a symbolic first that may potentially influence identity contingencies in two relevant domains of American life: race and education achievement, on one hand, and perceptions of racial progress in society, on the other.

Symbolic firsts are transformative public figures, historic characters, and pioneers who are symbols of special achievement widely expected to inspire others. John F. Kennedy was a symbolic first. Before Kennedy was elected president, many people wondered whether the American presidency was a realistic aspiration for Catholics. For many years anti-Catholic bigotry was prevalent in the United States, and many American voters feared that a Catholic president would put the interests of the Vatican over the interests of the American people (White 1962). Such anti-Catholic bigotry appears to have played a role in Al Smith's defeat in the 1928 presidential election.

Kennedy's election in 1960, however, demonstrated that anti-Catholic prejudice was no longer an insurmountable barrier to the nation's highest elected office. Being elected president could no longer be said to be contingent on one's being a Protestant Christian. Moreover, as Americans observed Kennedy's behavior in office and it became clear to them that he was not deferring to the Vatican, the attitudes of many Americans quite likely became more open to voting for Catholic candidates for high office in the future, further altering the constraints and opportunities of American Catholics. Indeed, willingness to vote for a Catholic candidate dramatically increased after Kennedy's election and continued to rise in the years that followed (Servin-Gonzalez and Torres-Reyna 1999). In short, the symbolic significance of Kennedy's election may have helped to change the identity contingencies of all American Catholics.

Barack Obama is also a symbolic first. No one can miss the historic significance of the election of the first black American president and the first person of color worldwide to govern a country with a white majority. Before Obama was elected people wondered whether it was possible for a black American to be elected to the nation's highest office. Indeed, nationally representative surveys show dramatic changes in white and black respondents' attitudes toward a black president between 2006, when Obama was an unlikely contender, and 2008, when he was elected. In 2006, when asked "Do you think America is ready for a black president or not?" 31 percent of white and 42 percent of black respondents said no. By April 2008, negative responses dropped to 20 percent of white and 29 percent of black respondents. That question is no longer relevant: a majority of voters in the 2008 presidential election cast ballots that indicated their readiness to elect a black president. Although being elected to high office undoubtedly still presents particular challenges for racial minority candidates, it can no longer be said that being elected president is contingent on race.

Obama's political success has stimulated much interest in questions about the power of racial symbolic firsts to alter people's perceptions of the constraints and opportunities afforded to them and to others who share their social identities. Symbolic firsts stimulate reflection about progress, progress that has been made and progress left to be achieved in the future. Symbolic firsts also stimulate reflection about one's self and one's family and how one's life space may be transformed by society-altering events. Such reflections often center on people's current attitudes and behaviors and the future possibilities for their children. Thus it is perhaps unsurprising that pundits and laypeople alike conjecture about how Obama's presidency might inspire student achievement, particularly among racial minority students, and potentially alter people's perceptions of racial progress.

IDENTITY CONTINGENCIES AND SYMBOLIC FIRSTS

A complete assessment of whether people expect to be successful in a particular situation—finishing a marathon, doing well on a test, becoming an attorney general or even president—depends on their view of what is possible for them given the particulars of their social identity. Social identities create contingencies that influence people's actual and perceived opportunities for success in particular domains of everyday life. The social psychologist Claude Steele (2010, 3) defines *identity contingencies* as "the things you have to deal with in a situation because you have a given social identity, because you are old, young, gay, a white male, a woman, a black, Latino, political conservative or liberal, diagnosed with bipolar disorder, a cancer patient, and so on. Generally speaking, contingencies are circumstances you have to deal with in order to get what you want or need in a situation."

Identity contingencies can be actual (for example, a police department that stops more black than white drivers in a small town) or perceived (the perception that police officers profile blacks). Contingencies of identity are not merely figments of imagination: they stem from the historical and present-day circumstances, structural barriers, access to resources, laws, policies, and everyday practices that are transmitted through and held in place by individuals and institutions. Most relevant to our analysis of symbolic firsts is the notion that important features of everyday life can serve as cues about a person's identity contingencies in any particular setting (Purdie-Vaughns et al. 2008).

These identity contingency cues can be any person, place, symbol, or object that implicitly or explicitly conveys information about how one's group identity may affect one's opportunities in that setting (Purdie-Vaughns et al. 2008). Because of the interpretive dimension of these cues, what serves as a cue for one group in a particular situation may not do so for another group in the same situation.

The same cue can be interpreted in radically different ways depending on the identity of the interpreter. For instance, as a symbolic first, Obama's racial identity may serve as a cue for liberals and conservatives alike. For many liberals, his racial identity may be viewed as an important milestone in an ongoing endeavor to expand racial opportunity in American society. By contrast, for some white conservatives, Obama's racial identity may convey a threat to their perceived control over their country.

Finally, contingency cues can powerfully affect one's immediate social experience. Herein lay the strengths and limitations of symbolic firsts. Because symbolic firsts achieve greatness, they are unusually high-profile representatives of their social group, and thus their successes and failures can have an outsize effect on people's attitudes. The success of a symbolic first can inspire and motivate individuals who share that person's social identity. However, when a symbolic first suffers setbacks, morale and motivation can be undermined for those who share that person's social identity. Assuredly, any symbolic first will experience both accomplishments and setbacks, and, for better or worse, other people's ups and downs can be inextricably tethered to those of the symbolic first.

For those assessing their probability of success in a particular domain, group identity (for example, racial and gender identity) has been shown to serve as a powerful cue that affects feelings of comfort and belonging, particularly in settings where one's group has experienced discrimination. For instance, for black professionals (Purdie-Vaughns et al. 2008) and female scientists (Murphy, Steele, and Gross 2007), merely receiving information that a corporate setting or science laboratory employs substantial numbers of other blacks or women dramatically increases motivation, aspirations, and institutional trust among black business school students and female undergraduate science majors. In these experiments, whites and men respectively were unaffected because minority representation and gender representation were not cues that conveyed information about their identity contingencies in this particular context.

As a symbolic first, Obama's racial identity serves as an identity contingency cue, an important feature of daily life in America that conveys information about the constraints and opportunities afforded to other racial minorities, or to others with nontraditional backgrounds, based on their group identity. If members of underrepresented groups attend to group representation as a cue about their identity contingencies, then racial minority students may attend to Obama's identity as a cue that conveys what is possible for them and members of their group in school. Moreover, any American who perceives Obama as a symbolic first may perceive his identity as a cue conveying information about the state of racial progress more broadly in America. It is this reasoning that lends us to use the identity contingency framework to outline research on Obama's possible effect on school achievement, his potential effect on some white conservative parents, and the influence of his presidency on popular impressions that we are moving toward a postracial America.

SYMBOLIC FIRSTS AND THE PSYCHOLOGY OF ACADEMIC ACHIEVEMENT

As the sociologist Thomas Cottle (1974, 85) has noted, "The teachings of [black children's] parents and their very own histories and perceptions reveal for them the forces that play upon them and keep them where they are. . . . Children are not only little people, they are shadow people whose needs and personalities are only indirectly faced up to. For their barest outlines to be visible, one needs the light of institutions and government to beat down on their bodies." Children do not vote. They are not political constituents. They do not understand complex legal and political terminology. Yet their perceptions of the constraints and opportunities they face based on one or more of their group identities—their contingencies of identity—are barometers for racial progress in two important ways.

First, as Cottle suggests, their views about their everyday experiences in school reflect broader societal forces such as economic resources (Is my school clean?) and policies (Am I bused across town?) that aim to either lessen or maintain racial inequality in American education. Second, their views about what is possible for them or members of their group may reflect actual changes in the environment in how members of their group are perceived. For instance, if Obama's racial identity serves as a cue conveying that stereotypes are less likely to constrain their own opportunities in school, then students' perceptions may reflect the broader idea that his achievements—as least temporarily—stand as a society-wide disconfirmation of negative racial stereotypes. Accordingly, research on how the political achievements of Obama affect young children in school provides a unique window into the broader theme in this volume: how racial inequalities can be mitigated or perpetuated by factors that go beyond behavior openly justified in racist terms.

The idea that children's political attitudes and views of themselves are important barometers for racial progress is not new. In the 1972 presidential election, when the incumbent Republican president Richard Nixon was challenged by Senator George McGovern, Cottle interviewed black children from Roxbury, Massachusetts, before and after the election (Cottle 1974). The stark contrast between their ability to alter their views of themselves based on their race compared with that of children after the 2008 presidential election dramatically illustrates the power of symbolic firsts.

He paused for a moment and looking at me, through me perhaps. "I ain't voting for no one. No one here I'd vote for." [William D. Williams, eleven-year-old black boy, fifth grade]

"Why not?" [Cottle]

"Nobody out there running who speaks for me. President has to represent you, right?"

"Supposedly." [Cottle]

"Well, neither 'Govern or Nixon can do that for me. No way they can do it. They ain't black, neither of 'em, and they don't have no black friends with 'em. Whenever you see 'em they're always with white people. They ain't even got women with them, except their wives once in a while, but that don't mean anything. That's just to make sure that everybody knows they're married and have a family and stuff like that. If Nixon really wanted to do something he'd make sure we all had money." (Cottle 1974, 28)

Compare these observations of an eleven-year-old in 1972 with those of eleven-year-old children in 2008, commenting on the election a week after Obama's victory:

"[Barack Obama's election is] important to me because Barack Obama's won ment [sic] that we can do anything no matter what race we are." [Black sixth-grade student]

"Yes, [Barack Obama's election is important] because it will show racist stereotypers that blacks aren't dumb but smart." [Black sixth-grade student]

Our common sense suggests that, at least compared with the significance of the 1972 election, Obama's achievements positively affected minority children. Common sense also suggests that the children's responses
after the 2008 election reflect a shift in broader perceptions of societal opportunities and racial progress compared with those of children after the
1972 election. But the critical question is whether, as a symbolic first,
Obama alters students' perceived contingencies in their own school environment and the effect this has, if any, on academic performance.

Symbolic Firsts and the Academic Achievement Gap

The academic achievement gap between academically at-risk racial minority students and their white peers has long concerned the education
community and social policy makers. At every level of family income and
school preparation, black and Latino students earn relatively lower standardized tests scores and school grades (Bowen and Bok 1998). A 2007
National Assessment of Education Progress report finds that the difference in average reading and math scores of black and white eighth-graders
was virtually unchanged between 2007 and the early 1990s. Moreover, between the years 2004 and 2007, 10 out of every 100 African Americans and
22 out of every 100 Latino students had not received a high school diploma or its equivalent; for white students, this number dropped to 6 out
of every 100 (Planty et al. 2009).

Systemic structural changes informed by education policies yield the
most consistent long-term effects on student motivation and achievement.
Obama's intense interest and involvement in education reform throughout his first term is notable. He delivered more than twelve speeches on
education during his presidential campaign and transition and has called
for a radical transformation of urban schools (Obama 2006). Throughout
his first term, no candidate has made such consistent rhetorical and financial commitments to education since Lyndon Johnson, who had been a
former high school teacher before he entered politics (Darling-Hammond
2009).

Although Obama rarely explicitly engages the relevance of his identity
as a role model, he undeniably believes in his potency as a symbolic first.
In 2006, for instance, when pressed by his wife in a strategy session to ar-
ticulate what would distinguish an Obama presidency from a Hillary Clinton or John Edwards presidency, Obama responded, "When I take that
oath of office, there will be kids all over this country who don't really think
that all paths are open to them, who will believe that they can be anything

they want to be. And I think the world will look at America a little differently" (Obama, quoted in Kantor 2009). In spite of educators' and Obama's own enthusiasm about his potential to inspire students, the impact of his achievements on them is unclear; empirical research has great potential to clarify the effect of Obama's success on minority student achievement.

The Effect of Symbolic Firsts on Children's Views of Themselves

If a symbolic first has the power to alter the perceived contingencies one may face in a given social setting, then the significance of Obama's achievements may have an impact on students' perceived experience of the racial climate in their schools, expectations of their own performance, and perhaps even actual academic performance. The assumption underlying this posited Obama effect is that reflecting on Obama leads to positive outcomes for racial minorities in domains, such as education, where they often contend with negative racial stereotypes (Marx, Ko, and Friedman 2009; Aronson et al. 2009; Purdie-Vaughns et al. 2010).

The explanation for this effect rests on the much-studied premise that racial minorities experience elevated stress in school. This extra stress arises from their fear that they could be seen in light of a negative stereotype about the intellectual ability of their racial or ethnic group (Steele, Spencer, and Aronson 2002; Steele 2010). In situations where the stereotype applies, such as test-taking situations, the fear that they may confirm the stereotype in the minds of others causes minority students to experience added stress. It is now well established that such stereotype threat causes stress and cognitive impairment (Blascovich et al. 2001; Schmader and Johns 2003; Steele and Aronson 1995) and undermines academic performance. Symbolic firsts such as Obama are proposed to buffer students against the detrimental effects of this psychological threat.

The lived experience of stereotype threat is palpable in a letter written by Audrey Delgado, a Latina fifth-grade student, who implores President Obama to change testing in her school. "As a kid and student I know that taking a test isn't very fun. For instance, when you're in a room and it's quiet, you're focusing on your test; you studied for hours the night before but you still feel uncomfortable. I always think I know I can do this, but why am I not confident? I know that personally for me it's because I know I'm doing well in school that I feel pressured to do well on a test. It may not be the same for other kids" (Delgado 2009, 226). Although Audrey never explicitly mentions race as a source of test anxiety (people experiencing stereotype threat rarely do), she describes an added pressure to perform on tests, a pressure not faced by other students. This is the nature of stereotype threat: an enigmatic, insidious source of stress that racial minority students contend with unbeknownst to others.

The possibility that Obama's highly publicized achievements could alleviate psychological threat and boost performance is suggested by social psychology studies showing the positive effects of same-race role models on test performance. Laboratory studies of role models show that they can positively affect motivation (Lockwood and Kunda 1999), and students contending with negative stereotypes perform better on challenging tests in the presence of mock role models who share their group identity (Marx and Roman 2002; McIntyre, Paulson, and Lord 2003; McGlone, Aronson, and Kobrynowicz 2006). Two conditions facilitate such role model effects: the role model must be perceived as highly competent in the specific domain (Marx and Roman 2002), and the role model's achievements must be perceived as personally relevant and attainable in the future (Lockwood and Kunda 1997).

An Experimental Test of the Obama Effect in Schools

One week after the 2008 presidential election, our research team set out to test this "Obama effect" directly (Seabrook 2008). In particular, we examined whether experimentally manipulating the salience of the first black American president mitigates threat in middle school students and affects academic achievement. Our sample consisted of students from families of middle to lower socioeconomic status in a suburban northeastern middle school whose student body is approximately half black and half white. We focused on a sample of sixth-grade students as they entered middle school because this is an important and vulnerable developmental period in which focusing on a valued role model might have particular impact.

We exploited well-documented social-psychological processes that have demonstrated that simply making salient a personally relevant target person or mental construct can affect people's behavior or performance (or both). Accordingly, students were randomly assigned (by a flip of a coin) to reflect on either the recent presidential election and Obama's achievements (Obama salience condition) or on their own health habits (control condition) approximately one week after the 2008 presidential election. These reflections took the form of a short survey in which participants answered open- and closed-ended questions about the importance of the Obama election (or health habits, in the control condition). Immediately following this experimental manipulation, all students completed measures of psychological threat (asked to rate how much they agreed or disagreed with statements such as "In school, I worry that people will think I am dumb if I do badly" and "In school, I worry that people will judge me because of what they think about my racial group"). These measures were repeated with the same students at the end of sixth grade and the beginning of seventh grade. We also collected school records over the course of this experiment to assess the effect, if any, of a brief Obama salience prime on academic achievement over the same time period. Both students and experimenters were unaware of the experimental conditions, and students were unaware that the experiment was about Obama's potential effect on school performance.

Given past research on role model effects, we predicted that the impact of Obama's achievements would diminish threat and boost achievement among racial minority students but leave whites unaffected. The symbolic significance of Obama's achievements should serve as a society-level disconfirmation of stereotypes about minorities' ability to succeed in mainstream institutions, thereby altering their perceived contingencies about what school holds in store for them.

In addition, we suspected that the significance of Obama may positively affect both black and white students' academic performance, an issue that other research on role models had not addressed. It has been found that reflecting on a person one admires leads to "elevation," an inspirational emotional state associated with learning (Haidt 2003; Haidt and Keltner 2004). Obama's life story could be perceived as an example of someone's succeeding in spite of adversity and thus could be inspirational to all students regardless of their race. If both racial minorities and whites admire Obama, this should confer benefits to both black and white students' academic performance.

We first tested whether there were differences in threat by student race (black or white) and condition (reflecting about Obama or reflecting about daily health habits) in November 2008, one week after the presidential election and immediately after our Obama salience manipulation. If students worry that they might confirm negative intellectual stereotypes applied to their racial group, having them reflect on the recent election of Barack Obama should mitigate this worry, suggesting that success is attainable and that stereotypes might be changing. Consequently, we expected a reduction in threat only for black students in the Obama salience condition. This is precisely what we found: black students in the Obama salience condition reported significantly less threat than black students in the daily habits control condition. White students were unaffected by the Obama salience manipulation.

Next, we examined how long the effect persisted. Social identity threat was tracked through the fall of seventh grade, a full calendar year after the election. Remarkably, black students in the Obama salient condition reported experiencing less threat for the entire academic year of sixth grade, though the effect faded by the fall of seventh grade. Again, no such effects were found among black students in the control condition or white students in either condition.

Finally, we examined grades (as assessed by official school records in all required courses). To examine whether the Obama salience manipulation affected academic performance in the quarter following the intervention, we ran a statistical model on students' second-quarter grade point average (GPA) to test whether students in the Obama prime condition would perform better than students in the control condition (controlling for first-quarter GPA). Results revealed a significant effect of condition but no effect of race or gender. That is, for any given level of preintervention first-quarter GPA, black and white students in the Obama salience condition had significantly higher second-quarter grades than those in the control condition. This effect was large enough that, if a student was on the border between two grades, reflecting on Barack Obama would have boosted grades to the higher of the two. Given the brevity of the prime and the length of time between the intervention exercise and the end of the second quarter (approximately seven weeks), this finding, while modest, is quite remarkable. Follow-up analysis on measures assessing how students felt about Obama help explain this effect. In this sample of students, all students, regardless of race, reported that they identified with Obama and reported tremendous respect and admiration for him.

What explanation do we offer for these two distinct yet important findings? Other school interventions studied in our laboratory produce similar nonintuitively large and long-term effects for groups contending with psychological threat (for example, racial minorities, women in science) (Cohen et al. 2009; Cook et al. 2012; Purdie-Vaughns et al. 2009). Insights from this research help explain how and why the Obama salient manipulation worked. With respect to findings specific to black students, Obama's election and inauguration very likely altered the actual social environment at that period of time. The election thus served as an identity contingency cue that signaled that stereotypes based on one's race were less likely to constrain opportunities in one's proximal environment.

Given that expressive writing crystallizes and makes what one is thinking about concrete, our brief writing exercise designed to increase the salience of Obama was the catalyst that allowed black students to benefit from racially meaningful changes that took place in school, which, in turn, altered minority students' perceptions of how threatening their immediate environment was and how much threat was tied to their racial identity. Because threat operates through recursive feedback loops, early reductions in threat, triggered by these micro shifts in how minority students were perceived, altered black students' construal of threat in their immediate school environment, perpetuating positive effects over time (Cohen et al. 2009; Cook et al. 2012).

With respect to performance among all children regardless or race, we found that students tended to look on Obama's achievements with awe and admiration. People can experience awe in response to charismatic leaders, and these emotion responses motivate self-improvement and personal change (Haidt and Keltner 2004). Because adolescence is a time when identities and values are formed, awe-inspiring experiences are most common among adolescents. Indeed, adolescents are particularly likely to be influenced by role models in their environment (Erikson 1968), especially models that they perceive to be similar to them or to who they would like to be (Bandura 1968; Mussweiler 2003). Two days before the election and one week before this study was conducted, Obama was described in the local paper as follows: "Obama offers that 'something'—call it charm, charisma, a positive vision for the future, a voice of empowerment, a role model for youth—Obama has 'it'" ("Election '08: Obama Choice for the Future," *Clarion Ledger* [Jackson, Miss.], November 2, 2008). Our findings are most consistent with the interpretation that racial minority and white students in this experiment perceived Obama as a role model and a charismatic leader and that written exercises prompting them to reflect about his achievements intensified positive responses and led to an increase in grades eight weeks after the election.

These findings are important because they begin to clarify whether and how symbols of achievement such as Obama can affect student achievement. Yet just as being a symbolic first can have positive consequences in the domain of education, this very symbolism can lead to negative consequences as well. The underlying premise for both positive and negative consequences is the same. Symbolic firsts serve as cues that convey contingencies attached to a particular identity. But when an identity is externally contingent, it has the power to change for the better or for the worse, depending on changes in external cues. If Obama's presidency comes to be widely seen as a failed presidency, he may transform from a high-profile symbol of black success to a symbol of black failure. This sort of contamination of a previously positive role model was seen recently in the case of Tiger Woods, whose reputation as an inspiring role model for children in general and racial minority children in particular was damaged, perhaps beyond repair, by sensationalist media stories about his sexual affairs and the breakdown of his marriage.

Symbolic Firsts and the Persistence of Racial Inequality in Schools

The potential positive consequences that a symbolic first, such as President Obama, can have on educational achievement may be limited in size, scope, and population. Educators, policy makers, and parents are likely to be unaware of how and when the Obama effect influences students, thus leading them to overestimate how much his symbolic significance contributes to directly reducing the achievement gap. To the extent that a symbolic first such as Obama does alter students' imagination of their potential in school, his influence may be limited to particular age groups and populations.

For instance, it may be that the Obama effect bolsters student achievement only for those who are young enough to imagine that Obama's achievements might be attainable for them. Psychologists have shown that role models facilitate performance for those who perceive the role models' achievements as attainable for themselves and for members of their group (Lockwood and Kunda 1997). Our study involved students at the age of eleven, an age at which psychological threat can undermine aspirations (McKown and Strambler 2009) but reflecting on an inspiring role model can strengthen them. Other studies using older students in college failed to show an Obama effect. One such study assessed performance on the Medical College Admissions Test by students enrolled in a summer program to help facilitate medical school acceptance (Aronson et al. 2009). Although the results were highly speculative, given that Obama attained extraordinary success at a relatively young age, college students may have found comparisons to Obama threatening and aspirations comparable to his beyond their reach (Buunk and Mussweiler 2001; Lockwood and Kunda 1997). Although older students may find Obama's message more comprehensible and his symbolic significance inspiring, reflecting on his achievements may fail to confer benefits on test performance because they no longer find his achievements to be personally attainable. Thus rather than looking at Obama as a model of their own potential future success, older students may view Obama as a social comparison figure, whose remarkable achievements dwarf their own.

Moreover, even among young students, symbolic firsts may not have the power to consistently bolster performance. Students' own difficulties in school may influence their perceptions of the personal relevance of a symbolic first's achievements. Throughout middle school and high school, student performance tends to decline, with steeper declines found among racial minority students than among whites (Eccles, Lord, and Midgley 1991). As students begin to struggle in school they may perceive Obama's achievements as beyond their grasp, diminishing his effectiveness as an inspirational figure for them.

Finally, it is important to test Obama effect interventions in less privileged environments, for instance, urban and economically impoverished schools. Obama's campaign, which continues to resonate in schools as of 2012, used hope as a core principle around which Obama laid his vision for reclaiming America. Although schools may often borrow this theme along with his campaign slogan—"Yes, we can!"—offering hope without substantive resources is disingenuous in many poor, urban, inner-city schools. Hope has been an overused, underactualized theme in the lives of urban poor youth (Duncan-Andrade 2009). The sociologist Jeffrey Duncan-Andrade uses the term "hokey hope" to expose how the theme of hope can target students' individual responsibility to achieve in the absence of even minimal resources to thrive in school: "Individualistic up-by-your-bootstraps hyperbole [suggests that] if urban youth work hard and play by the rules, then they will go to college and live the 'American Dream'" (Duncan-Andrade 2009, 182). Hokey hope ignores real inequalities that impact the lives of urban youth. This kind of hope ultimately projects a middle-class multicultural opportunity structure that is inaccessible to the overwhelming majority of working-class, urban youth of color (Duncan-Andrade 2009). Furthermore, when hokey hope is articulated in schools it has the potential to shift educators' attention to individual-focused solutions and away from addressing the structural inequities in urban schools.

Following the election of Obama, there was much public discussion about expectations that the academic performance of black students would dramatically improve. Indeed, in our study of the Obama effect, many of the black sixth-grade students openly discussed Obama's significance as the first black president. For instance, in response to the question "Is it important to you who won the United States presidential election? If so, why?" one student wrote, "Yes because we finally got a black man whose [sic] president." Another student wrote about herself reflecting on the event in the future: "Yes because if I have children I could say 'He is the first black president.'" These students explicitly referenced Obama's racial identity, but notably they mentioned his racial identity as important to them; we, as the experimenters, did not.

This leads to yet another way that Obama's symbolic significance for racial minority achievement must be qualified. Specifically, it may be important to employ subtle methods to induce students to view a symbolic figure as a role model. The present study increased the salience of Obama by asking students questions about Obama and their attitudes toward the election. Other research shows that subtly making characteristics of a person's identity more salient can help performance (Shih, Pittinsky, and Ambady 1999), but making those same characteristics more overt can undermine performance because the perceiver then feels excessive pressure to meet positive expectations (Cheryan and Bodenhausen 2000).

WHEN SYMBOLIC FIRSTS THREATEN PEOPLE'S WORLDVIEWS

On September 8, 2009, President Obama delivered his first Back to School presidential address. Schools nationwide televised the address, and the White House made supplemental resources available to schools (that is, back-to-school goal-setting materials). Obama's address challenged students to take personal responsibility for their education, set goals, and work hard throughout the upcoming year. What was intended to be a nonpartisan motivational address quickly polarized the nation, with supporters adamantly in favor of the speech and adversaries clamoring to protect their children from it (Chandler and Shear 2009).

Supporters found Obama's remarks inspiring. Obama's well-publicized modest beginnings and fast rise had clear implications for the upward mobility component of the American Dream (that is, smart students who work hard can rise to the top) (Hochschild 1996). As the first black president, Obama is also seen as inspirational to students from nontraditional backgrounds, particularly black youth. Furthermore, his address was skillfully crafted to connect with young people (for example, he referenced X-Box, YouTube, Twitter, and his personal troubles in school). From this vantage point, Obama's symbolic significance, his oratory skills, and his affirming messages about education (for example, every student is good at something) were intended to produce an uplifting, motivating boost to the school year.

Yet from another vantage point, Obama's remarks were deeply threatening. For some families, Obama symbolizes a threat to their core values (Silverleib 2009). Rather than perceiving his address as carrying a universal message, adversaries feared that Obama's Back to School address was a thinly disguised indoctrination of their children to a socialist agenda. His oratory skills were also threatening. Conservative activists alleged that the speech would further a cult of personality and that Obama was a seductive pied piper threatening to lure their children away from their families' political views (Silverleib 2009). Many parents were particularly troubled that a federal office could distribute uncensored school materials locally without parental permission and ultimately kept their children from school to prevent them from watching the address (Silverleib 2009).

It is perhaps not surprising that one of the first dramatic episodes of backlash against Obama played itself out in a school setting. Schools have often been the front line of the culture war between progressives and conservatives (Hunter 1991), with many emotional battles over such issues as the use of busing to integrate schools, restrictions on the expression of religion in public schools, and the sexual education curriculum. For quite some time, conservative parents have feared that they are losing control over their children's education, and Obama's election seems to have amplified many of those concerns.

Conservative opinion leaders have often suggested that white parents have good reason to be afraid of how Obama's presidency will influence their children. On his website the Drudge Report, conservative blogger Matt Drudge occasionally posts links to stories implying that Obama's image is being used to indoctrinate students in opposition to their parents' values. These stories are accompanied by alarming headlines like: "SHOCK VIDEO: School Kids Taught to Praise Obama" (Nobles 2004) and "Obama to High School Students: I Tried Drugs as a Teen" (Shapiro 2010). One site that Drudge linked to compared videos of school children singing songs about President Obama to a scene of the zombie children in the horror movie *Village of the Damned* (quoted in "Disgusting Pro-Obama Ad Exploits Kids," *The Rush Limbaugh Show*, WABC-AM, October 29, 2012).

These fears of Obama's negative effects on children sometimes emphasize racial threats. The influential conservative talk radio host Rush Limbaugh (2009) expressed the idea that white students might be disadvantaged by Obama's presidency with characteristic directness when he commented on an incident in which white students were beaten up by some of their black peers:

> It's Obama's America, is it not? Obama's America—white kids getting beat up on school buses now. You put your kids on a school bus you expect safety but in Obama's America the white kids now get beat up with the black kids cheering "yeah, right on, right on, right on, right on." And of course everybody said the white kid deserved it. He was born a racist, he's white. . . . We can redistribute students while we redistribute their parents' wealth. I mean we can just redistribute everything. Just return the white students to their rightful place—their own bus with bars on the windows and armed guards.

Limbaugh's suggestion that Obama is somehow responsible for creating a school climate that encourages racially motivated violence against white students may be absurd, but it is also an exaggerated version of a common tendency among racially conservative white Americans to see the gains of black Americans as entailing losses for whites (Eibach and Keegan 2006; Eibach and Purdie-Vaughns 2009). In a recent interview Obama himself speculated that a sense that progress for black Americans somehow disadvantages whites has contributed to the conservative backlash against his election:

> America evolves, and sometimes those evolutions are painful. People don't progress in a straight line. Countries don't progress in a straight line. So there's enormous excitement and interest around the election of an African-American President. It's inevitable that there's going to be some backlash, potentially, to what that means—not in a crudely racist way, necessarily. But it signifies change, in the same way that immigration signifies change, in the same way that a shift from a manufacturing-based economy to a service-based economy signifies change, in the same way that the Internet signifies change and terrorism signifies change. . . . [Progress] requires each of us, every day, to try to expand our sense of understanding. And there are going to be folks who don't want to promote that understanding because they're afraid of the future. They don't like that evolution. They think, in some fashion, that it will disadvantage them or, in some sense, diminishes the past. I tend to be fairly forgiving about the anxiety that people feel about change because I think, if you're human, you recognize that in yourself. (Quoted in Remnick 2010, 584–85)

If the controversy over Obama's address to students on the importance of education seems extreme, the issue at stake was not that Obama would inculcate a certain attitude toward school in America's children but rather that he would implant alien values that extended beyond learning to ideology and racial beliefs. Indeed, the zombie imagery and sensationalist headlines paint a picture of a generation of youngsters as vessels for "Obama's America," where traditional values are replaced with radical ones. In the most extreme articulation of this fear, Obama's elevated status is linked to negative attitudes toward whites. In this way, then, Obama's position to influence America's youth suggests another kind of Obama effect, by which his unique influence as a symbolic first is seen as a threat to white Americans.

In previous research we have found that white Americans, particularly those who value group dominance, tend to believe that the progress racial minorities have made toward equality entails losses for whites (Eibach and Keegan 2006). This idea that the gains of black Americans and other racial minorities symbolized by Obama's election to the presidency entail losses of status and resources for white Americans may be reflected in Obama opponents' rallying cry to "take back America" and allegations by conservative opinion leaders such as Glenn Beck and Rush Limbaugh that white people are victims of "reverse racism" perpetrated by the Obama administration. The idiom of white backlash can also be detected in the rhetoric and imagery that is sometimes found at Tea Party rallies, antigovernment websites, and other forums that express grievances against the Obama administration. To illustrate, Rush Limbaugh characterized Obama's economic policy as slavery reparations, and Glenn Beck accused Obama of having a "deep-seated hatred for white people." Although most of Obama's more mainstream opponents are probably motivated by principled political objections to his policy agenda rather than backlash against perceived threats to white dominance, it seems clear that racial anxieties play some role in shaping reactions to Obama's election and policies.

Taken together, the research and commentary described here suggest that just as Obama's status as a symbolic first can alter contingencies of identity for racial minorities, it also alters perceived contingencies for some racially conservative white Americans. To them, Obama symbolizes a threat to their core values and their ability to control the environment their children grow up in. Moreover, as recent events show, conservative whites' fears that policies benefiting racial minorities will harm whites can have a significant effect on our social and political climate. Thus a full assessment of Obama's election will need to take into account how his status as a symbolic first has the potential to provoke a conservative backlash and increase racial polarization.

SYMBOLIC FIRSTS AND PERCEPTIONS OF AMERICA AS A POSTRACIAL SOCIETY

In addition to their inspirational function as role models, symbolic firsts are also salient examples of historical change that can change people's attitudes about present-day social conditions and their perceptions of the necessity for further government attention to problems of racial equality. Indeed, Obama's election to the presidency was viewed by many as a dramatic symbol of America's progress in overcoming the racial inequalities of its past. Some commentators explicitly cited Obama's election as evidence that America had entered a new, "postracial" era in which racism could no longer be considered an impediment to achievement.

For example, on the evening of Obama's election, the former New York City mayor Rudolph Giuliani said, "We've achieved history tonight and we've moved beyond . . . the whole idea of race and racial separation and unfairness" (quoted in Wise 2008). On November 5, 2008, the morning after Obama's election victory, the *Wall Street Journal*'s editorial board commented, "A man of mixed race has now reached the pinnacle of U.S. power only two generations since the end of Jim Crow. This is a tribute to American opportunity. . . . One promise of his victory is that perhaps we can put to rest the myth of racism as a barrier to achievement in this splendid country. Mr. Obama has a special obligation to help do so." And in an election-day opinion piece in the *Washington Post*, Richard Cohen made a similar point: "Just as John F. Kennedy was only incidentally a Catholic, so is Obama only incidentally a black man. It is not just that he is post-racial; so is the nation he is generationally primed to lead. . . . My fellow Americans, we have overcome."

All of this celebratory discussion of a postracial America has understandably led some to worry that Obama's election may distract the public's attention from America's persisting racial inequalities, leading many to become less supportive of social policies to ameliorate these inequalities (Wise 2008). Psychological research on racial attitudes suggests that these worries may be justified. White Americans are often eager to emphasize that racial inequality is a problem of the past. For example, compared with black Americans, white Americans are more likely to focus on how much more racial equality there is today than in the past, and they are less likely to take into account persisting inequalities (Eibach and Ehrlinger 2006). This leads white Americans to have an overall more favorable opinion of the nation's progress toward equality (Eibach and Ehrlinger 2006), which in turn causes whites to be less supportive of egalitarian policies such as affirmative action (Brodish, Brazy, and Devine 2008). So to the extent that white Americans view Obama's election as further evidence of the nation's progress toward racial equality, they may become less committed to social policies aimed at addressing persisting inequalities.

Recent evidence supports this concern. A longitudinal study found that Obama's election significantly increased participants' perceptions of racial progress and decreased their support for egalitarian policies such as affirmative action and school desegregation (Kaiser et al. 2009). Other research shows that when white Americans have recently been given an opportunity to express their approval of Obama they are subsequently more likely to discriminate against black people, presumably because expressing approval of Obama affirms their image as nonracist and thereby excuses subsequent unfavorable behavior toward black Americans (Effron, Cameron, and Monin 2009).

However, other research suggests that, though reduced public support for policies promoting racial equality may be a predictable consequence of egalitarian achievements like Obama's election, it is not an inevitable consequence. Awareness of goal achievements can have either a motivating effect or a demotivating effect on a person's persistence toward a goal, depending on how the person interprets his or her goal achievements (Fishbach and Dhar 2005). A person who interprets his or her goal achievements as symbolizing progress toward that goal will tend to psychologically disengage from the goal and prioritize other competing goals. However, a person who interprets his or her goal achievements as symbolizing commitment to that goal will tend to become more psychologically invested in that goal and continue to prioritize it over other competing goals. For example, in a study by Fishbach and Dhar (2005) participants were asked to think about a goal-consistent behavior (for example, studying in pursuit of the goal of academic success). Then participants in the progress-frame condition were asked to rate their progress toward the goal (for example, academic success) while participants in the commitment-frame condition were asked to rate their commitment to the goal. Finally, after rating either their progress or commitment, participants reported how likely they would be to behave in ways that prioritized a competing goal (for example, socializing at night). As the researchers predicted, participants in the progress-frame condition reported that they would be more likely to prioritize a competing goal, while participants in the commitment-frame condition reported that they would be less likely to prioritize a competing goal.

We recently applied this goal representation model to study Americans' reactions to evidence of increasing racial equality (Eibach and Purdie-Vaughns 2011). In one study participants read a passage describing a number of ways that racial conditions in the United States have improved over time. Immediately after reading this passage a group of participants who were assigned to the progress-frame condition were asked to rate how much progress Americans had made toward racial equality. A second group of participants who were assigned to the commitment-frame condition were asked to rate how committed Americans are to racial equality. Finally, after making the specified rating, participants then rated their own support for prioritizing racial equality policies. As predicted, participants in the commitment-frame condition were more supportive of prioritizing racial equality than participants in the progress-frame condition.

An important implication of this finding is that we may need to be more mindful of the motivational implications of the different ways that we might talk about historic achievements such as Obama's election to the presidency. If we are careful to frame these achievements in terms of our collective commitment to social justice, then these achievements can inspire us to work even harder to fulfill our egalitarian goals.

CONCLUSION: ON HERO WORSHIP

Charles Horton Cooley (1902, 312) commented, at the beginning of the past century, "[The worship of heroes] has a great place in all active, aspiring lives, especially in the plastic period of youth. We feed our characters, while they are forming, upon the vision of admired models." Now, however, we live in a cynical era in which heroes and role models are viewed with great skepticism. The modern media culture has undermined many of the mechanisms by which heroic myths were formerly created and propagated. And holding leaders accountable, which is a principal function of modern democratic government, is often incompatible with hero worship. Furthermore, it is now recognized that heroic myths often serve a system-justifying function. Indeed, the personal success of heroic exemplars is often cited by defenders of the status quo to refute social justice advocates' claims that there are systemic inequalities in society. This is particularly the case when heroes are members of historically disadvantaged groups. Indeed, we reviewed evidence that Obama's rise to the presidency has been used to support the claim that racism is a problem of the past as we enter a new postracial era in which policies to promote racial justice are no longer needed. Given all this, skepticism of heroes and heroic narratives, in general, and the heroic framing of Obama's achievements, in particular, is well justified.

However, though it is important to question the use of heroic myths to whitewash social injustices, it is also important to acknowledge the potential beneficial functions heroes can play in individuals' lives. Cooley's (1902) quotation implies that if we were to give up heroes altogether, we might lose a crucial social mechanism for character formation and personal aspiration. Indeed, research suggests that heroes may function to help people define the meaning and purpose of their lives. Research on the psychology of heroes shows that individuals who reflect often on the meaning of their lives are more likely to report having heroes (Porpora 1996). Individuals incorporate representations of these heroes into their own self-concepts (Sullivan and Venter 2005). Furthermore, when individuals are exposed to heroic models of moral virtue or outstanding achievement they experience distinct positive emotions and physiological changes, which motivate them to behave in ways that follow the example of these heroes (Algoe and Haidt 2009; Silvers and Haidt 2008). Finally, individuals indicate that their personal heroes provide them with a sense of purpose and moral direction (Porpora 2001). Cumulatively, these findings support Arthur Schlesinger's admonition, "Let us not be complacent about our supposed capacity to get along without great men. If our society has lost its wish for heroes and its ability to produce them, it may well turn out to have lost everything else as well" (quoted in Porpora 2001, 170).

As the first black American president, Obama has great potential to alter the perceived contingencies for achievement for racial minorities in American society, and thus he may serve as an inspirational role model for many students, particularly racial minority students. However, Obama's high profile as a symbolic first quite likely means that both his successes and his failures could have an outsize influence on people's perceptions of black Americans. Furthermore, Obama's presidency has been accompanied by an apparent intensification of political polarization, perhaps in part owing to a conservative backlash against what has been perceived to be the irresponsible hero worship of Obama by many on the left. Finally, as a symbolic figure of racial progress, Obama has the potential to reinforce a popular impression that racial inequality is a problem of the past and that we are now living in a postracial society.

Thus we conclude with a complicated view of Obama's status as a symbolic figure. Following Cooley, we would reject the overly cynical view that there is no room for heroes in modern society. Clearly, heroes play an important role in social development, and a figure like Obama, who represents a symbolic first, has the potential to be an inspiring role model for many. However, the research we have reviewed suggests that we must be careful in how we use Obama's symbolism and what lessons about the opportunities and limitations of our society we take away from the historic event of electing the first black American president.

The Obama presidency's capacity to symbolize both how far the nation has come and how far it has yet to go in addressing problems of racial injustice was dramatically illustrated by Obama's public remarks on a Florida case in which Trayvon Martin, an unarmed black teenager who was minding his own business, was tracked and fatally shot by a neighborhood safety volunteer. Commenting on this tragic event, Obama empathized with the pain of his family and local community, saying, "My main message is to the parents of Trayvon Martin. You know, if I had a son, he'd look like Trayvon." Obama's comment marks the first time in our history that a U.S. president could address suffering within the black community in a direct, personal way, speaking as a member of that community. The cultural significance of this type of recognition from the nation's top political leader should not be underestimated. However, that a black man who had achieved the highest elected office in the land could still so readily imagine his own child dying a premature death in a racially charged incident shows just how far the nation still needs to go to achieve racial justice.

REFERENCES

Algoe, Sara B., and Jonathan Haidt. 2009. "Witnessing Excellence in Action: The Other-Praising Emotions of Elevation, Admiration, and Gratitude." *Journal of Positive Psychology* 4(2): 105–27.

Aronson, Joshua, et al. 2009. "The Obama Effect: An Experimental Test." *Journal of Experimental Social Psychology* 45(4): 957–60.

Bandura, Albert. 1968. "Imitation," *International Encyclopedia of the Social Sciences*, vol. 7, edited by D. L. Sills. Pp. 191–215. New York: Macmillan.

Blascovich, Jim, et al. 2001. "African-Americans and High Blood Pressure: The Role of Stereotype Threat." *Psychological Science* 12(3): 225–29.

Bowen, William G., and Derek Bok. 1998. *The Shape of the River*. Princeton, N.J.: Princeton University Press.

Brodish, Amanda B., Paige C. Brazy, and Patricia G. Devine. 2008. "More Eyes on the Prize: Variability in White Americans' Perceptions of Progress Toward Racial Equality." *Personality and Social Psychology Bulletin* 34(4): 513–27.

Buunk, Bram P., and Thomas Mussweiler. 2001. "New Directions in Social Comparison Research." *European Journal of Social Psychology* 31(5): 467–75.

Chandler, Michael A., and Michael D. Shear. 2009. "Some Schools Will Block or Delay Obama's Pep Talk for Students. *Washington Post*, September 4, 2009. Available at: www.washingtonpost.com/wp-dyn/content/article/2009/09/03/AR2009090300965.html (accessed April 8, 2013).

Cheryan, Sapna, and Galen V. Bodenhausen. 2000. "When Positive Stereotypes Threaten Intellectual Performance: The Psychological Hazards of "Model Minority" Status." *Psychological Science* 11(5): 399–402.

Cohen, Geoffrey L., et al. 2009. "Recursive Processes in Self-Affirmation: Intervening to Close the Minority Achievement Gap." *Science* 324(5925): 400–03.

Cook, Jonathan E., et al. 2012. "Chronic Threat and Contingent Belonging: Protective Benefits of Values Affirmation on Identity Development." *Journal of Personality and Social Psychology* 102(3): 479–96.

Cooley, Charles Horton. 1902. *Human Nature and the Social Order*. New York: Scribners.

Cottle, Thomas J. 1974. *Black Children, White Dreams*. Boston, Mass.: Houghton Mifflin.

Darling-Hammond, Linda. 2009. "President Obama and Education: The Possibility for Dramatic Improvements in Teaching and Learning." *Harvard Educational Review* 79(2): 210–23.

Delgado, A. 2009. "Barack Obama for My Education." *Harvard Educational Review* 79(2): 225–26.

Duncan-Andrade, Jeffrey M. R. 2009. "Note to Educators: Hope Required When Growing Roses in Concrete. *Harvard Educational Review* 79(2): 181–94.

Eccles, Jacquelynne S., Sarah Lord, and Carol Midgley. 1991. "What Are We Doing to Early Adolescents? The Impact of Educational Contexts on Early Adolescents." *American Journal of Education* 99(4): 521.

Effron, Daniel A., Jessica S. Cameron, and Benoît Monin. 2009. "Voting for Obama Licenses Favoring Whites." *Journal of Experimental Social Psychology* 45(3): 590–93.

Eibach, Richard P., and Joyce Ehrlinger. 2006. "'Keep Your Eyes on the Prize': Ref-

erence Points and Group Differences in Assessing Progress Towards Equality."
Personality and Social Psychology Bulletin 32(1): 66–77.

Eibach, Richard P., and Thomas Keegan. 2006. "Free at Last? Social Dominance,
Loss Aversion, and White and Black Americans' Differing Assessments of Progress Towards Racial Equality." *Journal of Personality and Social Psychology* 90(3):
453–67.

Eibach, Richard, and Valerie Purdie-Vaughns. 2009. "Change We Can Believe In?
Barack Obama's Framing Strategies for Bridging Racial Divisions. *Du Bois Review* 6(1): 137–52.

———. 2011. "How to Keep on Keeping On: Framing Civil Rights Accomplishments to Bolster Support for Egalitarian Policies." *Journal of Experimental Social
Psychology* 47(1): 274–77.

Erikson, Erik H. 1968. *Identity: Youth and Crisis.* New York: W. W. Norton.

Fishbach, Ayelet, and Ravi Dhar. 2005. "Goals as Excuses or Guides: The Liberat-
ing Effect of Perceived Goal Progress on Choice." *Journal of Consumer Research*
32(3): 370–77.

Haidt, Jonathan. 2003. "The Moral Emotions." In *Handbook of Affective Sciences,* edited by R. J. Davidson, K. R. Scherer, and H. H. Goldsmith. Pp. 852–70. Oxford:
Oxford University Press.

Haidt, Jonathan, and Dacher Keltner. 2004. "Appreciation of Beauty and Excel-
lence." In *Character Strengths and Virtues,* edited by Christopher Peterson and
Martin E. P. Seligman. Washington, D.C.: American Psychological Association
Press.

Hochschild, Jennifer L. 1996. *Facing Up to the American Dream: Race, Class, and the
Soul of the Nation.* Princeton, N.J.: Princeton University Press.

Hunter, James D. 1991. *Culture Wars: The Struggle to Define America.* New York:
Basic Books.

Kaiser, Cheryl R., et al. 2009. "The Ironic Consequences of Obama's Election: Decreased Support for Social Justice." *Journal of Experimental Social Psychology*
45(3): 556–69.

Kantor, Jodi. 2009. "The Obamas' Marriage." *New York Times Magazine*, October
2009.

Limbaugh, Rush. 2009. "From Kids on Bus to Kanye West: Race Rules All in
Obama's America." *The Rush Limbaugh Show*, WABC-AM. Transcript. September 15. Available at: www.rushlimbaugh.com/home/daily/site_091509/con
tent/01125106.guest.html (accessed April 8, 2013).

Lockwood, Penelope, and Ziva Kunda. 1997. "Superstars and Me: Predicting the
Impact of Role Models on the Self. *Journal of Personality and Social Psychology*
73(1): 91–103.

———. 1999. "Salience of Best Selves Undermines Inspiration by Outstanding Role
Models." *Journal of Personality and Social Psychology* 76(2): 214–28.

Marx, David M., Sei Jin Ko, and Ray A. Friedman. 2009. "The "Obama Effect": How a Salient Role Model Reduces Race-Based Performance Differences. *Journal of Experimental Social Psychology* 45(4): 953–56.

Marx, David, and Jasmin Roman. 2002. "Female Role Models: Protecting Women's Math Test Performance. *Personality and Social Psychology Bulletin* 28(9): 1183–93.

McGlone, Mathew S., Joshua Aronson, and Diane Kobrynowicz. 2006. "Stereotype Threat and the Gender Gap in Political Knowledge." *Psychology of Women Quarterly* 30(4): 392–98.

McIntyre, Rusty B., René Paulson, and Charles Lord. 2003. "Alleviating Women's Mathematics Stereotype Threat Through Salience of Group Achievements." *Journal of Experimental Social Psychology* 39(1): 83–90.

McKown, Clark, and Michael J. Strambler. 2009. "Developmental Antecedents and Social and Academic Consequences of Stereotype-Consciousness in Middle Childhood." *Child Development* 80(6): 1643–59.

Murphy, Mary C., Claude. M. Steele, and James J. Gross. 2007. "Signaling Threat: How Situational Cues Affect Women in Math, Science and Engineering Studies." *Psychological Science* 18(10): 879–85.

Mussweiler, Thomas. 2003. "Comparison Processes in Social Judgment: Mechanisms and Consequences. *Psychological Review* 110(3): 472–89.

Obama, Barack. 2006. *The Audacity of Hope: Thoughts on Reclaiming the American Dream.* New York: Three Rivers Press.

Planty, Michael et al. 2009. "The Condition of Education." U.S. Department of Education, National Center on Education Statistics 2009081. Available at: http://nces.ed.gov/pubs2009/2009081.pdf

Porpora, Douglas V. 1996. "Personal Heroes, Religion, and Transcendental Metanarratives." *Sociological Forum* 11(2): 209–29.

———. 2001. *Landscapes of the Soul: The Loss of Moral Meaning in American Life.* New York: Oxford University Press.

Purdie-Vaughns, Valerie, Claude M. Steele, Paul G. Davies, and Ruth Ditlmann. 2008. "Social Identity Contingencies: How Diversity Cues Signal Threat or Safety for African-Americans in Mainstream Institutions." *Journal of Personality and Social Psychology* 94(4): 615–30.

Purdie-Vaughns, Valerie, Geoffrey L. Cohen, Julio Garcia, Rachel Sumner, Jonathan C. Cook, and Nancy Apfel. 2009. "Improving Minority Academic Performance: How a Values-Affirmation Intervention Works. *Teachers College Record,* September 23.

Purdie-Vaughns, Valerie, Rachel Sumner, and Geoffrey L. Cohen. 2010. "Malia and Sasha: Re-envisioning Black Youth." In *Obama and a Post-racial America?,* edited by G. S. Parks. New York: Oxford University Press.

Remnick, David. 2010. *The Bridge: The Life and Rise of Barack Obama.* New York: Alfred A. Knopf.

Schmader, Toni, and Michael Johns. 2003. "Converging Evidence That Stereotype

Threat Reduces Working Memory Capacity." *Journal of Personality and Social Psychology* 85(3): 440–52.

Seabrook, Andrea. 2008. "Students React to Obama's Historic Nomination." *All Things Considered*. NPR, June 7, 2008.

Servin-Gonzalez, Mariana, and Oscar Torres-Reyna. 1999. "Trends: Religion and Politics. *Public Opinion Quarterly* 63(4): 592–621.

Shih, Margret, Todd L. Pittinsky, and Nalni Ambady. 1999. "Stereotype Susceptibility: Identity Salience and Shifts in Quantitative Performance. *Psychological Science* 10(1): 80–83.

Silvers, Jennifer, and Jonathan Haidt. 2008. "Moral Elevation Can Induce Nursing." *Emotion* 8(2): 291–95.

Silverleib, Alan. 2009. "Many Conservatives Enraged over Obama School Speech." *CNN.com.*, September 5. Available at: www.cnn.com/2009/POLITICS/09/04/obama.schools/index.html (accessed May 18, 2010).

Steele, Claude M. 2010. *Whistling Vivaldi.* New York: W. W. Norton.

Steele, Claude M., and J. Aronson. 1995. "Stereotype Threat and the Intellectual Test Performance of African Americans." *Journal of Personality and Social Psychology* 69(5): 797–811.

Steele, Claude M., S. J. Spencer, and J. Aronson. 2002. "Contending with Group Image: The Psychology of Stereotype and Social Identity Threat. In *Advances in Experimental Social Psychology*, edited by M. P. Zanna, vol. 34. San Diego, Calif.: Academic Press.

Sullivan, Michael P., and A. Venter. 2005. "The Hero Within: Inclusion of Heroes into the Self. *Self and Identity* 4(2): 101–11.

White, Theodore H. 1962. *The Making of the President 1960.* New York: Atheneum.

Wise, Tim 2008. "Between Barack and a Hard Place: Racism and White Denial in the Age of Obama." *Washington Post*, March 29. Available at: www.washingtonpost.com/wp-srv/style/longterm/books/chap1/barackandahardplace.htm (accessed April 8, 2013).

PART III | Politics and the State

Chapter 7 | Unhappy Harmony: Accounting for Black Mass Incarceration in a "Postracial" America

Vesla M. Weaver

As AMERICANS ALTERED history in sending the first black man to the White House, another less celebrated record was charted: one-third of young black men witnessed Barack Obama's milestone under the jurisdiction of the criminal justice system. In addition, 13 percent of black men could not cast a vote, as they were disenfranchised owing to a past or current criminal record (The Sentencing Project 2009).

Why, during an era of formal equality, do large disparities in imprisonment persist? Why did disparities grow from a more equal criminal justice system? Why, in the aftermath of one of the largest rights expansions, did black mass incarceration begin?

Racial inequality in criminal justice has grown and persisted over time, so much that it now dwarfs egregious disparities in poverty, homeownership, and unemployment. In this chapter, I offer a broad view of a tight link between the institutional development of criminal justice and racial inequality. To understand racial inequality in criminal justice outcomes, I argue, we must understand the timing and interaction of major punitive policy changes from above and structural economic transformations on the ground.

There are two stories to be told. First, several significant policy choices that increased the likelihood of incarceration and sentence length took hold at a pivotal moment in our nation's racial history. Second, these policy innovations interacted with racialized concentrated poverty and joblessness and the residual effects of decades of discrimination, segregation, and urban blight. Neither of these factors alone required black mass incarceration to develop. Together, however, they nearly ensured a racialized punishment regime.

Part I traces the growth of the racial incarceration gap since the mid-century. Racially disparate imprisonment is not simply the residue of past discrimination during the nation's inglorious racial history. Rather, it is a new form of inequality, constructed in an era of more "equality," occurring immediately after one of the most impressive interventions into the condition of black Americans. The scale of black punishment has no historical analog.

Part II takes a historical journey through the policy changes that have taken place since the mid-1960s that revolutionized criminal justice. Many of these policy decisions were motivated by race, or what I've called frontlash, in which strategic political elites made an end run around civil rights gains by deploying the racialized "law and order" strategy. This strategy was not based just on rhetorical appeals that faded with time; instead, it produced a series of policy changes that brought the federal government more deeply into crime control and sent billions of dollars to states to invest in criminal justice. Racial considerations thus helped motivate punitive legislation and criminal justice expansion.

Part III disembarks on a parallel historical survey, namely a broad understanding of the black urban experience, largely borrowing from sociologists and economists. The second story to be told deals with an array of community-level inequalities that at first seem distinct from concerns over racial incarceration. Punitive policy development collided with several transformations in the urban economy, creating a perfect recipe of factors for black mass incarceration. The portrait of the black urban experience holds the elements for a potent synthesis with the newfound institutional will to incarcerate offenders.

But though the contemporaneous institutional development and devastation of black communities in the 1970s provides an explanation for how black mass incarceration began, another process explains its persistence in contemporary society. The final section discusses several mechanisms of "feedback" that reinforced black mass incarceration, even absent its original cause.

To ameliorate racial disparity in criminal justice, undoing punitive policies is necessary, but that alone is not sufficient, since those policies have spurred feedbacks separate from the initial policy choice—racialized media coverage and popular stereotypes of crime, negative economic consequences of custodial involvement, and the community-level consequences of concentrated incarceration—that cannot simply be undone with policy retrenchment. Thus a hybrid approach to both the racialized poverty pro-

duced by contact with the criminal justice system and to criminal punishment is necessary.

RACIAL DISPARITIES ACROSS THE TWENTIETH CENTURY

On any given day, 11 percent of black men aged twenty to thirty-four (Pew
Center on the States 2007) are incarcerated in America's prisons and jails.
If we look at the prevalence of imprisonment—those people who ever experienced confinement—17 percent of American black men have been behind bars by 2001 (Mauer 2010). If we broaden our view to those under
correctional control, 33 percent of young adult black men (aged twenty to
twenty-nine) were under some type of correctional supervision in 2005
(Tonry and Melewski 2008).

These staggering numbers are even worse among the most disadvantaged; experts estimate that nearly one-fourth of young black men aged
sixteen to twenty-four who did not finish high school have been confined
in juvenile detention, jail, or prison (compared with only 6 percent of
whites) ("Study Finds That About 10 Percent of Young Male Dropouts Are
in Jail or Detention," *New York Times*, October 9, 2009).

Not only are blacks more likely than their white counterparts to encounter the criminal justice system, the racial disparity enlarges with the degree
of contact. For instance, though blacks constitute 12 percent of the general
population, they make up about one-third of those arrested, 38 percent of
those convicted, and 40 percent of those incarcerated. Among inmates,
blacks make up 38 percent of the general prison population but almost half
of those sentenced to life terms and 56 percent of those confined for life
without parole in 2008 (Nellis and King 2009).

These contemporary inequalities in criminal justice exposure are well
known by now, and many studies have examined the predictors of disparity at one point in time. But rarely is attention paid to that disparity over
time (but see Muller 2012). We know even less about why blacks have
become so much more likely to experience incarceration now than in prior
years. By focusing on a snapshot in time, we obscure the tremendous expansion of racially disproportionate carceral involvement since the 1970s.

Racial disparities are certainly not new. Blacks have always been more
likely than whites to be punished in the United States. They were more
likely to toil on repressive prison farms in the aftermath of Reconstruction.
After slavery, they were bought and sold as convict labor. They were 95
percent of those sent to the gas chamber by all-white juries for the crime of
rape. However, that disparity has grown to breathtaking levels in the decades since the civil rights era. Four decades back, blacks were incarcerated at one-eighth of their current level; indeed, for most of our nation's

Figure 7.1   Prison Admissions, by Race, 1926 to 1996 (percentage)

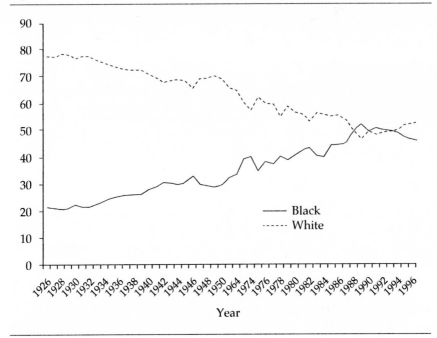

Source: Author's compilation based on Eckberg (2006, table Ec309–27).
Note: For prison admissions from 1970 to 1985, "blacks" is actually nonwhites.

history, blacks made up only one-third of prisoners (Stuntz 2008). Since then, racial disparities have mushroomed. Incarceration of all citizens has seen alarming expansion in the past few decades, but black incarceration has exploded. Incarceration has increased by a factor of six since the early 1970s, and blacks make up more than half of this overall growth (Gottschalk 22006).

Data from the *Historical Statistics of the United States* on state and federal prison admissions present racial distributions in prison admissions. Figure 7.1 depicts the racial composition of people admitted to prison each year since 1926, the earliest year for which the data exist. For most of the nation's history, whites made up the vast majority of prisoners and the percentage of blacks was only slightly higher than their share of the general population. The trend lines steadily converge until 1988, when, during the height of the war on drugs, blacks made up a larger share of those admitted to prison (even while their share of the general population increased only slightly). The racial composition of people admitted to prison has inverted over time. This magnitude of racial disparity in the criminal jus-

Figure 7.2   Sentenced Prisoners in State and Federal Prisons, by Race, 1960 to 2008

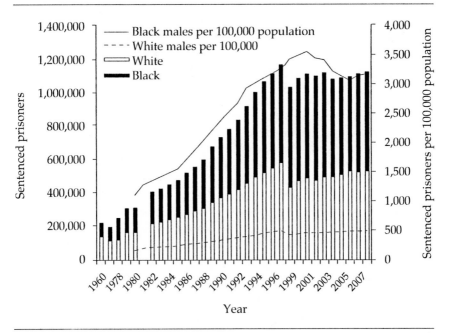

Sources: Author's compilation based on U.S. Bureau of Justice Statistics (various years); Cahalan (1986).

Note: Sentenced prisoners are those sentenced to a year or more. Data for the years 1981 and 1998 are not available. The reason for the drop in incarceration for whites and blacks from 1997 to 1999 is that before 1999, the Bureau of Justice Statistics did not distinguish Hispanics by race; in 1999 and forward, Hispanics are enumerated separately and so are not counted as black or white in the figure after that date.

tice system is a relatively recent phenomenon. Mass incarceration was driven in large part by blacks.

Figure 7.2 depicts the increase in imprisonment (that is, the number of prisoners sentenced to at least a year behind bars) separately by race since 1960, using data from the Census Bureau and from the Bureau of Justice Statistics. Consistent with the trend in prison admissions, blacks also constitute a greater share of the daily population in state and federal prisons. The overall increase in prisoners regardless of race is substantial, but the black male incarceration rate (as a share of the total black male population) has increased tremendously since 1980 and is nearly seven times the rate of incarceration for white men. Among men in state and federal prisons and local jails in 1997, 6,838 black men per 100,000 (6.8 percent of black men) were behind bars, compared with 990 white men per 100,000 in the population (1 percent) (Correctional Populations in the United States 1997). The black rate of incarceration increased at a much faster pace—almost four times the increase in the white rate (the black rate increased by 1,834 per 100,000, the white rate increased by only 483) (Tonry and Melewski 2008). If incarceration of blacks had remained at 1980 levels, fewer than one-third of blacks in jail or prison today would be there (Tonry and Melewski 2008). The percentage of blacks under correctional supervision—which includes jail, probation, and parole—increased from 5 percent in 1985 to 9 percent in 1997 (Pastore and Maguire 2000).

One could also consider not just blacks in prison or admitted to prison at one moment in time (as in figures 7.1 and 7.2) but also the portion of the black male population that has ever been imprisoned or convicted of a felony. Using data from the sociologists Christopher Uggen, Jeffrey Manza, and Melissa Thompson (2006), figure 7.3 demonstrates that in 1968, just five decades ago, 15 percent of black adult males had ever been convicted of a felony and 7 percent had ever been to prison; by 2004, this proportion had swelled considerably, such that more than one-third of adult black men had ever had a felony and 17 percent had ever been incarcerated. Black men were more than twice as likely to experience incarceration or have a felon record in 2004 as in 1968.

What is particularly troubling is that, unlike most other forms of racial disparities, which have diminished with distance from the Jim Crow era, the experience of greater criminal justice contact has actually gone in the opposite direction. Incarceration became a more common experience for those blacks who came of age during the civil rights battles and is magnified even further for the most recent birth cohort, those coming of age now. Black men in the birth cohort of 1965 to 1969 were two times as likely as those born two decades earlier to experience imprisonment during their lives; among those who did not complete high school, 60 percent have been behind bars (Western 2006). Thus in contrast to improvements in educational attainment, occupational mobility, and income, and despite gains in the number of black elected officials, blacks were much more likely relative to whites to be behind bars, and this gap increased for later generations.

Although it is clear that blacks were more likely than whites to be incarcerated over time, that does not say much about whether blacks were given disproportionately long sentences. The available data offer less systematic information on the type of sentences given to blacks and whites over time. However, data on the median length in months of time served behind bars for various offenses is available. Figure 7.4 depicts the time served for blacks and whites separately, by offense category and for two comparison years. In 1964 racial disparities in the length of time served in prison were relatively small or nonexistent; for several crimes, including robbery, assault, and mo-

Figure 7.3   Current or Former Felons and Prisoners among the Adult
Population (percentage)

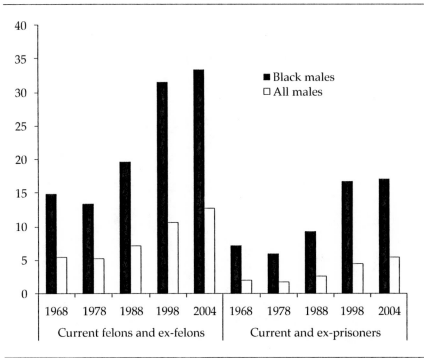

Source: Author's compilation based on Uggen, Manza, and Thompson (2006, tables 1 and 2).

tor vehicle theft, whites actually served longer sentences behind bars than
blacks. The right-hand side of the figure shows what happened by 2005.
Blacks served more time behind bars than whites across all offense categories, and for certain crimes, the disparity is glaring.

What can explain the rapid rise of black incarceration and the divergence between the races in a period of ostensibly greater racial equality?
Two factors are widely assumed to explain disproportionate black imprisonment: criminality and bias and discrimination within the justice system.
But on close examination, both of these fall short.

Such disparities and their increase over time cannot be explained by
criminality. The Federal Bureau of Investigation's Uniform Crime Reports
(on which are based the *Historical Statistics of the United States* 2006; *Statistical Abstracts of the United States*; and *Sourcebook of Criminal Justice Statistics*)
present data on the racial distribution of arrests collected over time. Arrests are an imperfect proxy for crime and contain an unknowable amount

Figure 7.4   Median Time Served, by Race and Offense, 1964 and 2005
(months)

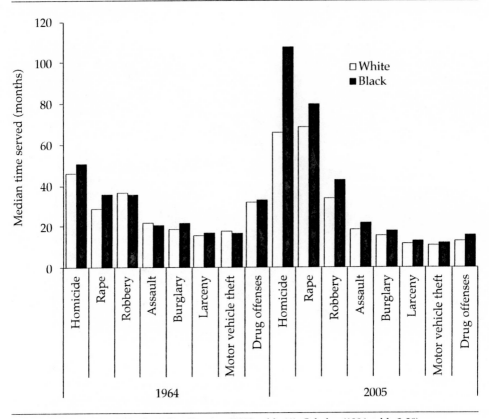

Source: Author's compilation based on Bonczar (2003, table 11); Cahalan (1986, table 3-28).

of racial bias themselves. However, they are the only measure collected
over time that can show whether blacks were committing a greater share
of offenses (or getting picked up for a greater share) each year, which may
explain their greater likelihood of going to prison.

To measure black incarceration over time, I rely on data collected by the
National Prison Statistics since 1926 on the race of people admitted to prison
by year. Figure 7.5 overlays the portion of all people admitted to prison who
were black with blacks as a percentage of all arrests. First, arrest rates do not
explain the level of black incarceration. More important, greater black incarceration was not the result of changes in the distribution of criminal offending: blacks did not make up a greater portion of offenders in 2006 than they

Figure 7.5   Blacks' Share of Arrests and Prison Admissions, 1926 to 2006 (percentage)

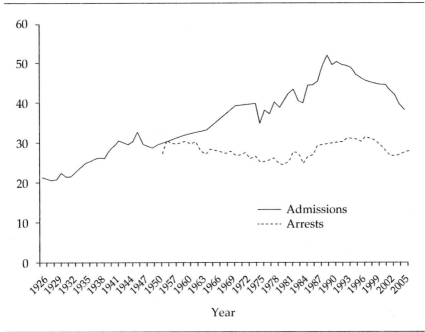

Year

Sources: Author's compilation based on Eckberg (2006, table Ec309-327); Bonzcar (2011); U.S Census Bureau (various years); Maguire (n.d.).
Note: For prison admissions from 1970 to 1985, "blacks" is actually "nonwhites." For prison admissions after 1997, includes both new court commitments and parole revocations but does not include federal prison admissions. Arrests by race are the number of individuals, not the number of arrests. The results do not depend on which of these units of measurement is used.

did in the past. In 1960 blacks represented 30 percent of all arrests and 32 percent of admissions to prison. In the years that followed, a wide gap opened up between arrests and prison admission, with blacks' share of admission to prison exceeding their share of arrests; by 1992 blacks still constituted one-third of arrests but were half of prison admissions. Second, large racial disparities in the criminal justice system are relatively recent. Contact with criminal justice was not always a "routine life event" for black men (Western and Wildeman 2009, 231). Although blacks were always more likely to be incarcerated, as late as 1960 blacks constituted a share of the prison population commensurate with the racial distribution of offenses. In short, blacks were more likely to be confined on this side of history, even though they were no more likely to be in the group of offenders (arrestees). Thus even with the biased indicator of arrests, differential offending cannot explain the changing makeup of prison admissions.

Comparing arrest data with prison admissions data presents a surprising finding. Staggering disparities in punishment continued to rise despite the fact that the black proportion of arrests remained relatively flat. But perhaps the mismatch of the two trend lines can be explained by blacks committing a greater share of violent crime. A common explanation for the higher rate of black incarceration at a point in time is that blacks commit more crime and are more likely to commit imprisonable offenses (Tonry 1995). Although this is true, for it to explain rising disparities blacks would have had to constitute a greater share of offenders committing imprisonable offenses over time. The data suggest the exact opposite: blacks' share of violent offenses actually declined. For example, in 1964 blacks represented 51 percent of arrests for violent offenses; this portion steadily declined, and by 1997 only 40 percent of those arrested for violent offenses were black. What did change is what constituted an imprisonable offense and the penalties for it. Arrests were more likely to result in imprisonment over time, particularly for the offenses that blacks had a greater chance of being arrested for (that is, drugs). Thus the higher incidence of black arrests may explain some of the disparity in imprisonment at a point in time but cannot explain the widening inequalities in punishment over the decades. Disproportionate black incarceration grew over time as black arrests remained flat and as the black share of violent crime decreased. Otherwise stated, declining black commission of violent crime as a share of all violent crime had little effect on racial disparities.

Another way of examining racial disparity in incarceration is to analyze the amount of incarceration that would be explained by differentials in arrest rates, with the important caveat that arrests themselves contain a residual racial disparity not explained by delinquency. Alfred Blumstein's (1983) seminal analysis of racial disproportionality in the 1980s found that a large portion of imprisonment in 1979 was explained by black arrests. In other words, after accounting for different arrest profiles (an admittedly imperfect proxy for criminality), Blumstein found only a small residual of unexplained variation in incarceration and concluded that black incarceration was largely a function of black offending. Recently, another criminal justice expert, Michael Tonry, reestimated the impact of black arrests on incarceration disparities using Blumstein's method, and by 2004 "a much smaller part of the racial disparities in imprisonment can be explained by arrest patterns in 2004 than Blumstein found for 1979" (Tonry and Melewski 2008, 17). For some categories of crime, the unexplained variation was substantial; for example, after accounting for differences in arrests by race, the unexplained variation in assault and drugs incarceration was almost 60 percent and more than one-third for almost all offenses except homicide and auto theft. So, though black arrests can explain some of the black disparity in imprisonment, they cannot explain the tremendous expansion in that disparity over time or why the racial distribution of arrests explained less and less of imprisonment variation over time.

The second prevailing explanation of racial inequality in criminal justice understands disparities as arising from bias and discrimination in criminal justice operations and practice. Studies have found ample evidence of discrimination in almost every crevice of the criminal justice system, from street stops to the decision to arrest to the conviction, plea bargaining, and sentencing stage. Other studies counter that once prior criminal record and other factors are taken into account, race is not an important predictor of outcomes. I largely avoid that debate here. Although discrimination and bias may be important for understanding contact with criminal justice at a point in time, it does not explain why disparities grew over time. Discrimination works as an explanation of the growth in disparities only if it grew over time or if it accompanied other developments that gave discrimination in the criminal justice system a greater impact. Conscious intent by the agents and institutions of criminal justice does not help us understand why blacks became more likely to experience incarceration on this side of the civil rights struggle.

The focus on bias in sentencing by individual judges has obscured the fact that the unbridled expansion in the punishment of blacks would have occurred even without conscious bias of the agents of criminal justice. Because existing explanations have focused solely on bias and discrimination in the inner workings of the criminal justice system, they have largely missed the important political development of punitive crime policies. Race was important not just in relation to bias against suspects and offenders and the decisions by individuals about stopping, convicting, and sentencing them but also in how crimes were defined and penalties expanded. Racial considerations helped motivate policies that changed the likelihood of incarceration, changes that were more likely to affect blacks. Thus though blacks are overwhelmingly targeted by police and receive harsher penalties, there is a larger political and economic context for understanding why those outcomes increased in importance over time.

A similar argument locates the so-called war on drugs as central in fostering racial disparities, largely because of the massive sentencing differences and because blacks were greater targets of drug enforcement (Alexander 2010). Although the war on drugs was important, racial disparities were already enlarging at least a decade earlier. Through their preoccupation with crime campaigns of recent vintage, such as Three Strikes Laws and the war on drugs—policy changes that occurred at least a decade after the long rise in incarceration had commenced—criminal justice scholars missed the key episode of change in crime policy and the political dynamics in which they were located, a crime war that predated Ronald Reagan's presidency. If one tugs at the historical cord of criminal justice, one finds that it leads back to policy changes in the 1960s that overcame significant impediments to federal intervention in crime control. By the time of the drug war, mandatory minimums, determinate sentencing, and habitual offender laws were flourishing, and the weight of two decades of explosive growth in manpower, technology, and new prisons secured the institutional supports for mass incarceration.

This leaves us with a striking paradox: as the nation collectively hailed the election of the first black president, more blacks were incarcerated than in the more repressive racial order. Criminal justice disparities did not lessen with the overwhelming decline in overt discrimination. Blacks are more likely to experience the punitive arm of the state during the seemingly postracial era than in the era of Jim Crow racism. Thus the question becomes not just why do these disparities exist but also why did they become more severe at the very moment of legislatively driven racial progress, uplift, and advance? Why are massive racial disparities relatively recent as other gaps have begun to close?

EXPLAINING THE GROWTH OF BLACK MASS INCARCERATION IN TWO PARTS

My earlier research lays the groundwork for the case that the modern criminal justice system had its roots in the battle over racial equality in the 1960s (Weaver 2007). A brief tour of that argument follows. Through a process I term *frontlash*, elites mobilized around crime and violence after suffering serious defeats in civil rights, resulting in several policy departures that invested in criminal justice.

Criminal Justice Policy Shifts in the Aftermath of Civil Rights

Once the clutch of Jim Crow had loosened, the same actors who had fought a losing battle against civil rights legislation shifted the "locus of attack" (Weaver 2007, 230) by injecting crime onto the national agenda. Recycling an old argument used in attacks against civil rights—that integration breeds crime—to be consistent with new racially egalitarian norms, they publicly linked racial disorder to ordinary crime. Aided by two prominent focusing events—crime and riots—strategic entrepreneurs enmeshed the problem of racial unrest and crime in proposals for tougher crime legislation. Rivals of civil rights progress defined racial discord as criminal and argued that crime legislation would be a panacea to racial unrest. This strategy imbued crime with race and depoliticized racial struggle, a formula that foreclosed earlier alternatives to solve the "root causes" of crime. Crime was fused to anxiety about ghetto revolts, and racial disorder—initially defined as a problem of minority disenfranchisement—was redefined as a crime problem, which helped shift debate from social reform to punishment. Rather than a genuine response to mounting crime, then, the series of unprecedented punitive federal crime bills were located in the struggle over the civil rights agenda. More than merely symbols of a rhetorical strategy to electrify white voters' resentment, the set of policy changes that resulted sped the development of the carceral state.

That campaign was a major turning point in crime policy and understandings about crime. The progress that had been made in addressing social ills through Lyndon Johnson's War on Poverty was halted midstream and replaced with crime control. More of the Kerner Report's recommendations on law enforcement were implemented than its vast program for reducing deprivation in the cities. Crime became a reason for not expanding civil rights and social justice; as action on civil rights withered, the criminal justice system was expanded. In addition, the originally popular idea that crime would be best attacked by solving its root causes in poverty and disadvantage suffered a crippling blow, replaced with a punitive consensus of cracking down on crime through tougher punishments.

If this moment were just a rhetorical strategy that faded as riots and crime no longer occupied the agenda, the story would be less important. But it resulted in the most important (and punitive) pieces of crime legislation in the nation's history, which would construct the modern criminal justice system. Among them, the Organized Crime Control Act of 1970 gave mandatory thirty-year sentences for offenders who had two prior convictions or who were deemed to be "dangerous special offender[s]"; the District of Columbia Court Reorganization and Criminal Procedure Act of 1970 allowed no-knock police entry and preventive detention, allowed life sentences for a third felony, eliminated jury trials, and allowed juveniles to be tried as adults; the Omnibus Safe Streets and Crime Control Act of 1968 overturned three Supreme Court decisions on the rights of the accused, issued strong riot penalties, relaxed prohibitions on wiretapping and electronic surveillance, and moved the administration of federal crime programs from the Department of Health, Education, and Welfare to the Department of Justice.

Safe Streets began the first major anticrime program by the federal government, producing a sustained investment in crime control and law enforcement that would utterly transform the criminal justice landscape. The act established a large federal and state crime control bureaucracy, led to unparalleled growth in police and correctional financing and manpower, prompted a flurry of state policy changes in penalties, and innovated primordial and fragmented state and local law enforcement and criminal justice. Title I of the law authorized a major program of federal aid to assist state and local law enforcement and created a national agency in the Department of Justice, the Law Enforcement Assistance Administration (LEAA), to administer the grants. During the 1970s, the LEAA became the fastest-growing agency of the federal government, with twice the budget of the Federal Bureau of Investigation and half the entire budget of the Department of Justice. By the time the LEAA was abolished in 1982, it had doled out millions of dollars in grants.

The LEAA had two immediate effects important for understanding how incarceration expanded and why minorities became its chief constituents. First, it quickly transformed the capacity and infrastructure of the criminal justice system. After its inception and throughout its fourteen-year tenure, the LEAA distributed more than 155,000 grants to states, cities, and criminal justice agencies for 80,000 projects. Most of the money went directly to bolstering the financial and manpower resources of the police and corrections and not to nonprofits or groups representing citizens and community members. The result was that a previously fragmented and weak local patchwork system of law enforcement and prisons became in a matter of years a professionalized, united, and powerful coalition with a strong incentive to maintain funds for criminal justice. It also meant that groups that may have favored rehabilitative or preventative approaches were cut out of the windfall of new resources.

The institutional landscape of criminal justice witnessed an explosion in manpower and new technologies to confront crime, and it immediately grew a muscular criminal justice bureaucracy as depicted in figures 7.6 and 7.7. In the first five years of the LEAA's operation, criminal justice spending doubled; by 1985 it had tripled. Growth in the size and capacity of criminal justice naturally followed. Nationally, police forces doubled in size, and the number of correctional employees tripled from 1960 to 1980. Spending on police increased by a factor of eight from 1964 to 1974. Over the decade of 1970 to 1980, 6,350 new criminal justice agencies were fashioned.

In contrast to historical precedent, when crime was largely left up to the states, the federal government became a much more important financier of state and local criminal justice; in just five years in the 1970s the proportion of state and local spending on criminal justice funded by the federal government increased from 3 percent to 12 percent. The provisions of the

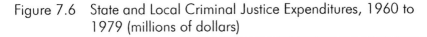

Figure 7.6   State and Local Criminal Justice Expenditures, 1960 to 1979 (millions of dollars)

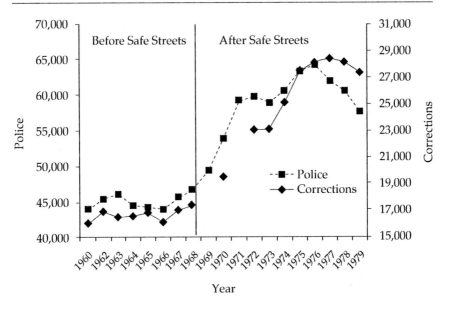

Source: Statistical Abstract (U.S. Census Bureau, various years). Compiled by author and converted into 2005 constant dollars using the GDP.

grants made sure states would follow the federal government in increasing their commitment to criminal justice, putting criminal justice on a path with a strong logic of growth.[1]

The LEAA windfall had an immediate impact that has not been appreciated: it made punishment much cheaper for states. Safe Streets was responsible for awakening sleepy state systems of criminal justice to an interest in reform. Safe Streets increased the importance of criminal justice on state agendas and stimulated state expansion in criminal justice, resulting in bursts of change in state criminal codes and waves of technological innovation and vitally increasing their capacity to arrest, monitor, and punish.

The LEAA generated momentum at the state level for dramatic investments in punishment. As states received hundreds of thousands of grants to update their criminal justice systems, there was an unprecedented level of reform, and the content of reform bent in a punitive direction. Before Safe Streets, states rarely amended their criminal codes and sentencing

Figure 7.7   State and Local Criminal Justice Employees, 1960 to
            1979

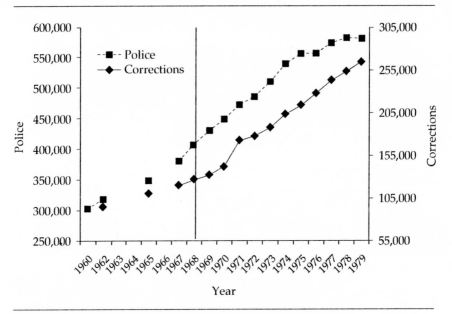

Source: Author's compilation of U.S. Census Bureau (various years).

policies. In the decade after the start of the LEAA, every single state altered its sentencing policy in some fashion. The LEAA-inspired State Planning Agencies (SPAs), developed in every state as a condition of the grants, were charged with planning for criminal justice reform within the state's borders. More than 80 percent of SPAs designed and drafted legislative proposals; many were given the explicit responsibility of drafting bills and revamping the state's penalty structure. New money from the LEAA, federal requirements, and aggressive state planning agencies led to a wave of change across the states in sentencing policies and penalty structures. An analysis of state changes in nine states found that the frequency of sentencing laws increased, its content became more punitive, and the scope of behaviors defined as crimes expanded (Jacob 1985).

According to summary of the state changes from 1971 to 1981 by the National Institute of Justice, penalties were increased in a majority of states and decreased in none: the majority of states passed habitual offender laws or increased their severity; all but two states enacted mandatory minimum sentences; half of the states restricted parole eligibility, and parole was completely eliminated in eight states; and "good time" provisions for early

Figure 7.8   Sentencing Reforms in the States, by Type

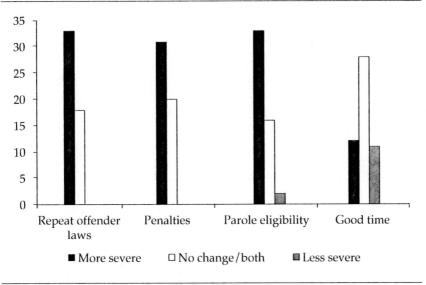

■ More severe   □ No change/both   ▨ Less severe

Source: Author's compilation based on Shane-DuBow, Brown, and Olsen (1985).

release were decreased in twelve states. Figure 7.8 depicts these changes in sentencing policy. By 1981 fifteen states had abandoned indeterminate sentencing for determinate, fixed sentences, and seven had initiated sentencing guidelines. Many others enacted time-served requirements, sentence enhancements for crimes involving drugs and weapons, and victim restitution, and thirty-five passed capital punishment laws. By the end of the decade, early release was largely abolished, mandatory minimum penalties were attached to most offenses, and juvenile waivers meant that kids were tried and incarcerated as adults. These state policy changes resulted in rises in sentence length, time served, and risk of imprisonment. More people were incarcerated and for longer spans.

Soon after these reforms were enacted and began to take shape, custodial populations swelled. After declining for eight years, the population in the nation's prisons and jails rose. From the beginning of the LEAA to its demise, the U.S. prison population grew from 196,429 to 487,593. The parole population grew from 155,100 in 1974 to 225,827 in 1980. Every single state in the union increased its prison population from 1970 to 1980; in some states, including North Carolina, Texas, and Florida, the prison population doubled. Crime predicted only a small portion of the increase; instead, the flurry of policy changes expanding penalties were responsible

(Blumstein and Beck 1999). For example, California's sentencing changes, many of which derived from the state planning agency in that state, altered sentence appeals, eliminated parole, increased penalties, cut judicial discretion, and imposed mandatory sentences and severe habitual offender laws. The changes were applied retroactively to existing as well as new prisoners. California's prison population rose by 12 percent in the first year of implementation. After the passage of the notorious Rockefeller drug law in New York in 1973, that state's prison population rose by 500 percent, despite falling crime (Drucker 2002).

Predictably, because the reforms increased sentences, prison populations ballooned. Prison time lengthened for all categories of offender. The addition of several thousand prisoners meant that more space was required to house and oversee them, and by the mid-1970s states were facing severe overcrowding in their correctional facilities. The LEAA offered to pay for 75 percent of the cost of prison construction after a 1973 amendment to Safe Streets, encouraging states to build more prison facilities to keep up with prison population increases. From 1969 to 1977, the LEAA gave $170 million for corrections; required to "buy in," states contributed millions more to prison construction during the decade. Based on Census Bureau estimates, the number of state correctional facilities more than tripled, from 578 prisons in 1970 to 2,090 by 1980 (Cahalan 1986). The modern criminal justice system had taken shape.

It is generally understood that these punitive sentencing policies not only increased incarceration in the aggregate but also disproportionately affected blacks. Because they are contextually linked to race, many sentence enhancements and mandatory terms have a greater effect; blacks are more likely to be in situations that trigger an enhancement, including living in public housing, being near a school zone, having a prior record, and having a firearm (Schlesinger 2008).

For instance, drug sentence enhancements (that increase the sentence for drug distribution within a certain distance of a school zone) affect blacks much more because they are more likely to live in urban areas where distribution will always be in school zone proximity. In addition to these indirect mechanisms, it is also well established that in practice judges decide to apply these enhancements and mandatory terms to blacks more than whites. Blacks receive 80 percent of mandatory sentences (Mauer 2010). For example, they represent 45 percent of inmates incarcerated under the Three Strikes Law in California (compared with 29 percent of the prison population generally) (The Sentencing Project, n.d.). Blacks constituted more than 60 percent of those sentenced under Florida's harsh 10-20-Life law (though just 15 percent of the prison population in that state) and received longer sentences on average (Kunselman, Johnson, and Rayboun 2003).[2] Under the

Rockefeller drug laws—the harshest drug laws in the nation—black males were forty times as likely as white males to receive mandatory sentences (94 percent of Rockefeller inmates are black and Latino) (Drucker 2002). The implementation of these policies, then, would widen racial disparities in addition to greater aggregate incarceration.

However, the disparate application of these policies is not solely to blame. In a concurrent development, the policies that supported a major transformation in criminal justice took hold at an important moment in racial history. The centuries-long investment in Jim Crow and black oppression was being lifted, a small black middle class had begun to grow, and blacks began to have political and economic power. But the track to addressing social ills and poverty during the Great Society and the War on Poverty was halted midstream as the blending of race and crime in public discourse shifted attention away from poverty efforts and toward crime control and "law and order." This moment remade the carceral state, though dramatic policy changes were only part of the story of criminal justice expansion and racial disproportionality.

This political development intersected with another. As the nation embraced punitive policies, another transformation was about to occur. The large-scale investment in punishment and political development occurred alongside rapid shifts in the urban economy, themselves policy driven, which resulted in widespread devastation in black neighborhoods in the inner city. The institutional development in punishment almost seemed to anticipate the dislocation of urban economies and the resulting devastation it had on black communities. Thus though many of the policy changes had race in the foreground (frontlash), racialized consequences easily arose through their potent synthesis with the birth of the black "underclass." A race-laden crime campaign motivated policy changes that interacted with growing racial inequalities on the ground to have an unsurprising effect: prisons swelled, and minorities constituted most of their new clientele.

Urban Decline and the Rise of Black Mass Incarceration

The investment in police and corrections coincided with an epidemic of joblessness, concentrated poverty, and decaying neighborhoods wrought by industrial decline and segregation. "The newly punitive system of criminal sentencing would have had largely symbolic significance, but for the ready supply of chronically idle young men that came to swell the nation's prisons and jails" (Western and Wildeman 2009, 224). The tremendous shifts in the urban economy, suburbanization, deunionization, segregation, and the spiral of central city deterioration are a familiar story from work by

William Julius Wilson, Robert Sampson, John Kasarda, Douglas Massey, and Richard Freeman. However, they have been largely forgotten in our narrative and causal explanations of black mass incarceration (but see Western 2006). Criminal justice policies were only part of the story of the stunning expansion in incarceration and surveillance; for the increase in incarceration and racially disparate effects, another process was important.

The cities had barely cooled from the civil disorders that rocked the nation when the labor market in the central city went into decline. Around the early 1970s, cities saw a precipitous decrease in manufacturing and jobs that had supported low-skilled, low-wage workers in the previous decades. Particularly in the central cities, jobs that employed blacks on the lower rungs of the skills ladder, and had been one of the main attractions of northern-bound blacks in the Great Migration, made an exodus to the suburbs. As goods-producing jobs vanished, the demand for low-skilled, uneducated workers plummeted. Cities recorded enormous growth in jobs favoring college graduates and professionals but simultaneously saw thousands of jobs in the low-skilled sector disappear; in the 1970s manufacturing employment declined by 30, 41, and 47 percent in New York, Detroit, and Chicago, respectively (Kasarda 1993). The shift in industry opened up a gap between the availability of people with meager education and skills and the supply of low-skilled jobs.

These shifts hit urban blacks hardest. As the opportunities available to poorly educated blacks declined, the employment of blacks who had not finished high school decreased by 30 percent, and for those with a high school diploma, 20 percent. In cities including Baltimore, New York, Philadelphia, St. Louis, and Washington, the jobless rate among black men with low levels of education nearly doubled (Kasarda 1993). Whites did not lose jobs close to these rates, largely because it was black men who were concentrated in the jobs and sectors that saw the most devastation. Moreover, the earnings of all low-skilled men fell sharply as the real wage for low-skilled laborers decreased after 1974 and through the 1980s, opening up a wider gulf between rich and poor (Freeman 1996). However, wages and employment declined more for blacks than for whites, resulting in the growth of earnings inequality and disparities in employment between young black and white men through the 1980s (Bound and Freeman 1992). Young black men faced a weaker attachment to the labor force as their time worked and earnings fell. Young urban blacks' prospects for economic advance, though accompanied by a widening of legal rights through civil rights expansions, stagnated.

The deteriorating economic condition for low-skilled and low-educated black men was compounded by several additional factors. First, the federal government largely withdrew its investment in cities (Jones-Correa

2001). The dismantling of the social safety net exacerbated these trends, as community action, rent supplement, and Model Cities programs were replaced with a steady infusion of criminal justice resources into cities (including the Impact Cities initiative, which channeled funds to crime control). Second, attracted by new opportunities in the suburbs, wealthier and more-educated whites and blacks left the city, pulling out an important tax base, thriving institutions, and businesses and intensifying the concentration of poverty left behind in the urban areas (Wilson 1987; Jargowsky 1997). In New York, the population of whites shrank by 1.4 million, while the black population increased substantially (180,000); the same was true for several other cities (Kasarda 1993). Not all blacks could leave, and the blacks trapped in the urban core were those who were the least educated and poorly situated, giving rise to the term *spatial mismatch,* used by economists and sociologists to describe the lack of fit between the population of black men with few skills in urban centers and the supply of skilled jobs that remained in urban environments after deindustrialization.

The decrease both in blue-collar jobs and union density along with the out-migration of middle-class whites and blacks to the suburbs meant that young low-skilled black men were left in a vacuum of economic opportunities. In the aggregate, blacks posted gains in education and income; for inner-city blacks, however, these gains were lost. The decline in black economic opportunity among the least educated lasted until at least the 1990s.

Third, the deepening of residential segregation during the 1970s gave rise to spatial inequality and further devastated the prospects of urban blacks. Blacks left in the city faced a racially discriminatory housing market. Discriminatory lending practices and redlining, urban renewal and slum clearance, and highway construction all contributed to the concentration of poor blacks in racially isolated areas. From 1970 to 1980, racial segregation increased substantially in all large northern cities (Massey and Denton 1998). Meanwhile, deindustrialization and the recession of the 1970s caused a collapse in urban housing prices and, in relative terms, a large increase in suburban housing prices (Jargowsky 1997). Impoverished families began to concentrate in the cheaper housing found in urban areas. Meanwhile, fair housing and other civil rights laws were defanged, given little enforcement power. Poor blacks were largely trapped in central-city housing, and housing stock precipitously declined. Bleak housing prospects and low residential mobility combined with the spatial mismatch to give rise to severe spatial inequality.

In this situation, spatial inequality, concentrated poverty, and segregation grew, giving rise to the "urban underclass." From 1970 to 1990, black unemployment became increasingly spatially focused in parts of urban communities (Wagmiller 2007). Low-skilled minorities were concentrated in areas where no low-skilled jobs remained (Stoll, Holzer, and Ihlanfeldt 2000). Because more-mobile blacks had moved to the suburbs, disadvantaged minorities in the inner city were largely isolated from the middle class.

The decline in black fortunes was absorbed by a small number of areas, altering the whole neighborhood environment and setting off a spiral of decline in decaying neighborhoods, including the increase in chronic joblessness and the formation of small villages of concentrated poverty, blight, and crime. This left behind large sections of the city where unemployment and poverty festered and neighborhoods where job prospects were nonexistent. The labor market for this demographic group went from viable to bleak within a matter of years. The effects for urban blacks were disastrous. Consider some indicators. Blacks in the core of the city were now living in areas where the vast majority of their neighbors were deeply poor and underemployed. In 1970 one in five poor black children lived in ghetto areas characterized by extreme poverty, but by 1980 it was two out of five (Wilson 1987). In New York, 70 percent of blacks lived in poor areas, whereas that exact proportion of whites lived in nonpoor areas (Sullivan 1989). The chances of living around other impoverished, unemployed people went up.

The proportion living in poverty areas rose by more than 20 percent from the beginning of the 1970s to the next decade; in five cities, those living in extreme poverty areas, where more than 40 percent were in poverty, rose 161 percent (Wilson 1987). Just 7 percent of poor whites lived in such areas in 1980, compared with 39 percent of poor blacks. Areas of high unemployment similarly grew. Black unemployment was 60 percent in some areas of the central city. As one sociologist notes, "We have witnessed the formation of an immobilized subgroup of spatially isolated, persistently poor ghetto dwellers characterized by substandard education and high rates of joblessness, mother-only households, welfare dependency, out-of-wedlock births, and crime" (Wilson 1987, 44). Most blacks in cities were in situations of extreme disadvantage; Sampson and Wilson (1995, 43) find that the worst neighborhoods for whites were better than the neighborhood where the average black resided: "Even given the same objective socioeconomic status, blacks and whites face vastly different environments in which to live, work, and raise their children."

The concentration of disadvantage had unsurprising effects for urban black neighborhoods. Despite gains in formal civil rights and aggregate improvement in education, and the growth of an economically mobile black middle class, a group of disadvantaged, vulnerable men were now segregated in blighted neighborhoods with a gaping hole of employment and a quickly declining social safety net ready to meet the new risks of poverty and unemployment. By the end of the 1970s, black families were much more likely to live in distressed neighborhoods. Black children grew up in neighborhoods of serious economic disadvantage and a host of social ills. Rife with chronic joblessness, poverty, and dilapidated housing, these neighborhoods were criminogenic environments. Blacks were much more likely by the end of the 1970s than before to experience neighborhoods with multiple disadvantages that were petri dishes for crime. The neighborhood ecology of blacks in the central city exposed them to multiple aspects of economic hardship and resulting neighborhood disorganization not replicated in white neighborhoods—low access to jobs, weak labor force attachment, high drop-out rates, and segregation and isolation. These factors have all been shown to be important predictors of central-city crime and homicide. The urban sociologists Robert Sampson and William Julius Wilson (1995, 179–80) demonstrate that by the end of the 1970s, blacks were "differentially exposed to criminogenic structural conditions."

The confluence of these factors created a ready supply of young, disadvantaged men for the punitive sentencing policies, aggressive policing practices, and burgeoning prison capacity. Concentrated poverty, joblessness, and decaying neighborhood quality accomplished two things—it increased the returns from criminal activity, and it drew increasing police presence to these areas. Poverty tightly correlates with unemployment and crime. However, even more than individual socioeconomic status, high levels of concentrated poverty and unemployment in the environment may act as a "social multiplier," amplifying the effects that lowered real wages and employment opportunities have on crime rates among uneducated males (Glaeser, Sacerdote, and Scheinkman 2002). Indeed, numerous studies have found evidence of "concentration effects": racial segregation, urbanization, and population density are strongly predictive of crime (Land, McCall, and Cohen 1991; Massey 1994); joblessness and inequality are strongly associated with higher crime rates (Chiricos 1987; Freeman 1996); increased black isolation correlates with higher rates of crime committed by blacks (Shihadeh and Flynn 1996); and the poverty of a spatially concentrated area within a city is a better predictor of homicide rates for blacks and whites than an individual's class (Lee 2000).

Given the concentration of poor and unemployed, black neighborhoods became magnets for police attention. The neighborhood contexts of most blacks made police more willing to make arrests (Lauritsen and Sampson 1998).

At the same time, some economists suggest that the rewards from crime may have increased owing to the collapse of the labor market and new illegal economic opportunities created by the drug trade, which increased the "supply of men to crime" (Freeman 1996, 30). As real wages and job prospects from legitimate sources contracted and as the returns to crime increased, criminal activity among less-skilled men grew, and the drug trade burgeoned. Thus the rewards from crime increased greatly at precisely the same time that legal economic opportunities were evaporating (Freeman 1996).

And this is exactly what happened. Cities that experienced the greatest economic deprivation of their black populations saw the greatest rise in the black murder rate (Shihadeh and Ousey 1996). Black violence was sensitive to the availability of low-skilled jobs and the level of economic hardship in city centers (Shihadeh and Ousey 1996). Scholars have found a strong association between rates of crime and violence in American cities and changes in the availability of low-skilled jobs between 1970 and 1990, which increased economic deprivation. For example, a study of Baltimore during the 1970s found that areas where poverty became entrenched and the "underclass" grew experienced the biggest increases in violence (Taylor and Covington 1988). Moreover, suburbanization, associated with a myriad of disadvantages, strongly predicted serious black crime in the city (Taylor and Covington 1988). The decline in earnings of poorly educated males explained a 23 percent increase in offenses by young males from about 1975 to the late 1980s (Grogger 1998). Cities with the biggest "flight to the suburbs" also saw drastic increases in crime rates (Shihadeh and Ousey 1996). Poor urban areas saw their arrest rates triple (Freeman 1996). Those states with the highest proportion of blacks living in urban centers saw the highest disproportion of black arrests (Bridges and Crutchfield 1988).

As the concentration of poverty and joblessness and blight left blacks more likely to grow up in criminogenic neighborhoods and more likely to commit crime, the tremendous expansion in police manpower and sentencing changes that expanded punishments meant that both violent and low-level black offenders were more likely to be arrested, incarcerated after arrest, serve longer sentences, and be readmitted after parole. Blacks arrested in the 1970s faced mandatory terms, provisions that added "enhancements" to their sentences for having a prior record or for an offense that was accompanied by a gun or drugs or near a school, and they were less likely to be paroled before their sentence was complete. The incarceration rate of these men grew tremendously. Bruce Western, Meredith Kleykamp, and Jake Rosenfeld (2004) found that if the earnings and availability of jobs had remained stable in these years, the rate of prison admissions would be 25 percent lower by 2001. The cohort of blacks growing up in the central city during the 1970s were more likely to experience violence, heavy police surveillance in their neighborhoods, and the punitive arm of the state.

We cannot see in what areas incarceration happened over time—those data do not exist. But it seems a straightforward assumption that greater crime in the inner city and in areas of structural disadvantage, which has been demonstrated, would lead to greater incarceration. Although the poor have always been more likely than the nonpoor to be involved in the criminal justice system, an analysis by two sociologists shows that the proportion of inmates who were below the poverty level before being incarcerated jumped from 40 percent to 60 percent from just 1974 to 1986 (Wheelock and Uggen 2008). The proportion of inmates with a full-time job has similarly decreased since the mid-1970s. Sampson and John Laub (1993) found that places with more-concentrated poverty and income inequality between the races experienced higher degrees of juvenile incarceration, especially black juveniles.

Policies that we know were responsible for increasing incarceration were moving in one stream; in the other stream, urban dislocations were constructing a black "underclass" living in criminogenic neighborhoods, who were more likely to face arrest at the end of the decade. Combine these streams, and young black men were now more likely to face incarceration.

A lack of data prevents a full testing of this argument, but it is clear that policy changes affected blacks the most. By 1980 the black share of the prison population in state and federal prisons had increased to 44 percent, from 37 percent in 1960. By 1993, Richard Freeman (1996) estimates, one-third of black men aged twenty-five to thirty-four who dropped out of high school were incarcerated, and many more were on probation or on parole. This accords with Bruce Western's (2006) finding that the black men coming of age in the 1970s had rates of incarceration that were double those of black men coming of age in the 1950s.

The development of black mass incarceration was the predictable effect of two factors: cumulated disadvantage and devastation of central-city blacks and major policy change. Add economic decline and vulnerable, poor, idle black youth to new sentencing laws, and the product is black mass incarceration. Policy change explains why these dislocations and the crime they bred led to a quick, radical expansion in the prison population. Increasing urban arrests helped supply disadvantaged, jobless men, and punitive developments meant that they would be increasingly likely to face incarceration after arrest.

THE PERPETUATION OF BLACK MASS INCARCERATION

The rise of black mass incarceration created an important feedback effect. Incarceration itself, particularly high levels in communities, has reproduced the mechanisms for further racially extreme levels of incarceration. Incarceration and racialized poverty have become mutually reinforcing.

Sentencing policy changes and the expansion of criminal justice capacity may have set the process in motion, but incarceration leads to several dynamics that virtually ensure its continued expansion. In particular, current black incarceration can invite greater future incarceration through intergenerational transmission and through alterations in the social, economic, and cultural conditions of the neighborhoods to which offenders return.

Black children now are much more likely to grow up in households where one or both parents have been removed at some point to prison. The sociologist Christopher Wildeman (2009) finds that by the age of fourteen, white children born in 1978 had a 2.4 percent risk of having a parent incarcerated; for those born in 1990, the risk was 4.2 percent. Black children's risk of having a parent incarcerated by the age of fourteen grew from 15.2 percent for children born in 1978 to 28.4 percent for those born in 1990 (Wildeman 2009). In fact, blacks were as likely to have a mother incarcerated as white children were to have their father incarcerated. The concentration of parental incarceration is even higher among children of high school dropouts, more than half of whom had been behind bars by the year 2000 (Western and Wildeman 2009). With high proportions of black adults—men and women—behind bars, black children today are much more likely to grow up with at least one parent incarcerated. Indeed, one of the primary reasons so many black children grow up in foster homes or in single-parent households is that their parents are likely to be incarcerated.

The reason this matters for the persistence of incarceration is that parental incarceration substantially increases the likelihood of future contact with criminal justice of their children, both directly and indirectly through the effects of incarceration on family life and stability. One study that followed male children to adulthood found that having a brother or a male neighbor incarcerated resulted in a greater likelihood that a child would be incarcerated as an adult (Johnson 2009). Another analysis has found that, controlling for delinquency, black preteens were more likely to have police intervention by eighth grade and twice as likely as whites by the tenth grade (Crutchfield et al. 2009). Less than 10 percent of white teenagers had been arrested by their second year in high school, but among blacks, one-fourth had. One of the largest predictors of teenage arrest was having a parent with a history of arrest (Crutchfield et al. 2009). The direct effect of parental imprisonment occurs because children of inmates are more likely to exhibit aggressive and antisocial behaviors that lead to delinquency (Wildeman 2010b).

Controlling for other things, children of inmates are more likely to be involved in crime and violence themselves. The indirect effect occurs because incarceration leaves children at greater risk of being homeless or impoverished or of growing up in single-parent households—all of which lead to a greater propensity for crime and criminal justice contact (Wildeman 2010a). Joseph Murray and David Farrington (2005) found that separation from a parent before the age of ten because of parental imprisonment predicted antisocial or delinquent behavior, as well as other risk factors contributing to delinquency (low family income, poor supervision, and so on) better than other forms of parental separation (hospitalization, death, divorce). Susan Philips et al. (2006), in a longitudinal study of rural North Carolina youth, found that parental involvement in the criminal justice system was itself associated with children's exposure to two types of family risks: economic strain and instability. Children who experience economic strain and instability are at higher risk for behavioral problems such as delinquency later in life. Thus greater incarceration of blacks, many of whom are parents, alters the risk of incarceration of their offspring; as Western and Wildeman (2009, 241) note, "Under these circumstances, the inequalities of mass incarceration will be sustained not just over a lifetime, but from one generation to the next."

That reality is already being borne out. Experts estimate that if current trends continue, one-third of black babies born at the millennium will at some point in their lives be imprisoned (not including those who will be confined in jails or juvenile facilities) (Tonry and Melewski 2008). Consider the situation of black children today. Although black youth were only 16 percent of the population aged ten to seventeen and 28 percent of juvenile arrests, they represented nearly 60 percent of those under the age of eighteen admitted to adult jails (American Sociological Association 2007). Black youngsters were 56 percent of the population of teenagers receiving the most draconian sentence available: life without the possibility of parole (Nellis and King 2009).

By adulthood, it is exceptional for a young black male from an urban area not to have been under the purview of the criminal justice system at least once; it has become an "experience of the expected" (Hagan, Shedd, and Payne 2005). A recent survey of black youth between the ages of fifteen and twenty-four found that nearly two-thirds had been stopped and questioned by the police, a quarter had been arrested, 10 percent had been convicted, and 3 percent had a felony on their records by early adulthood (Cohen 2005). Black teens attend schools with greater police presence (Crutchfield et al. 2009). In fact, schools in Baltimore now have a regular probation officer on staff to deal with the large portion of school kids undergoing supervision, and not a single Chicago city school is without police officers, metal detectors, and routine searches of school lockers for drugs. Indeed, prison and police contact has become a normal stop in the transition to adulthood; as Senator Jim Webb has observed, "The principal nexus between young African-American men and our society is increasingly the criminal justice system" (Senate Joint Economic Committee 2007, 21).

For many black Americans, incarceration has replaced more traditional life events as a defining political experience. Research by Bruce Western shows that black men are now more likely to come into contact with the criminal justice system than they are to receive welfare, serve in the military, belong to a union, or receive a college education; black men in this cohort who did not complete high school are more likely to be in the carceral system than in the labor market (Western 2006). In one survey, more than half of young black men reported being unfairly stopped by police, and three-quarters reported that they or a close friend had been to prison (*Washington Post*, Kaiser Family Foundation, and Harvard University 2006). More black men reported having been arrested or stopped than having voted.[3]

In a large panel study of five thousand mostly poor families, more men received criminal justice interventions than social programs. Figure 7.9 charts the percentage of male respondents who had contact with institutions of criminal justice compared with receipt of various antipoverty program benefits in the fourth wave of the study. The results are striking; they underscore the prevalence of the punitive arm of the state in the lives of America's poor. Indeed, if we remove the earned income tax credit, fathers were more likely to have had contact with the punitive than the redistributive side of the state.

Incarceration critically alters the social, economic, and cultural conditions of many blacks and their neighborhood environments. Blacks are released back into their communities with fewer skills, more antisocial and criminogenic norms from prison life, and a record that acts as another barrier to employment. By lessening wages, and the likelihood of employment and marriage and increasing the likelihood of family poverty, child homelessness, and risk of diseases including AIDS and tuberculosis, higher rates of incarceration actually perpetuated these factors, some of which were themselves important predictors of involvement in crime and the criminal justice system.

A bevy of studies by economists, sociologists, and public health scholars has found that incarceration reduces lifetime earnings by $86,000 (Western 2006), increases the risk of unemployment, increases the risk of contracting the AIDS virus, and explains a nontrivial portion of black poverty. High rates of black incarceration could "explain one-third to one-half of the relative decline in black male employment rates" (Raphael 2004, abstract). Given these effects, incarceration actually serves to project onto and en-

Figure 7.9   Fathers' Contact with Welfare State and Criminal Justice System (percentage), 2003 to 2006

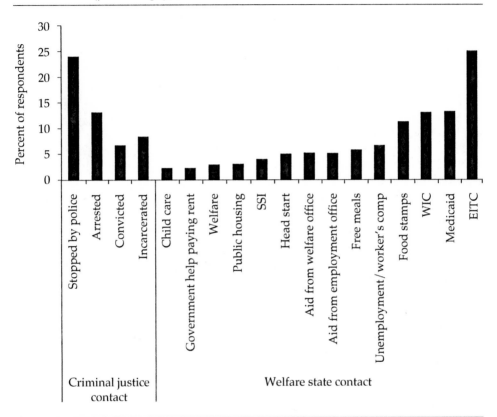

Source: Author's analysis of the Fragile Families and Child Wellbeing Study (2003–2006).

large other forms of inequality: the substantial black-white disparity in marriage would be cut in half without incarceration (Western, Lopoo, and McLanahan 2004); the black-white gap in infant mortality would be decreased by 23 percent if incarceration had stayed at its 1973 level (Wildeman 2012); and incarceration explains approximately 70 percent of racial health disparities such as AIDS (Massoglia 2008).[4] There is also evidence that the large number of black unwed mothers is a function of the incarceration of black males. One such study finds that in certain areas of Washington, D.C., where incarceration is concentrated, for every 100 women there are only 62 men (Braman 2004). All of these effects—more poverty,

244 Beyond Discrimination

more jobless males, more single-parent households—are strongly correlated with more crime and more violence.

As the sociologist Devah Pager aptly notes in chapter 9 in this volume, "Steeply rising incarceration rates among blacks cast a shadow of criminality across the black population." Pager's field experiments show how the widespread belief in black criminality made employers wary of hiring blacks, even those without a conviction; indeed, one of the first things some employers asked when confronted with a black applicant was not about his education and other credentials but about whether he had a rap sheet. And the real or perceived belief by employers and other gatekeepers that black men have criminal records can "be used to regulate access and opportunity across numerous social, economic, and political domains."

This is not simply a matter of individual outcomes; incarceration of black men increasingly changes neighborhood dynamics and furthers spatially concentrated disadvantage. In some communities, contact with criminal justice authorities is ubiquitous; consider, for example, the nation's capital, where experts estimate that one-half of young black men are wards of the state (Beckett and Sasson 2004). Ten percent of young black men in the inner city in 2004 were incarcerated on any given day, and one-third would be at some point in their lifetime (American Sociological Association 2007). Prisoners are largely concentrated in several cities, certain communities within those cities, and even neighborhood blocks. Consider for instance, where prison inmates call home. One-third of prisoners return to just one county in Michigan, 80 percent of whom are residents of Detroit, and 41 percent reside in just eight zip codes.[5] In Texas, seven neighborhoods in Houston receive more returning prisoners than several entire counties in the state of Texas. Almost three-quarters of the entire population of prisoners in New York state came from just seven community board districts (of more than fifty board districts in the city) (Fagan, West, and Holland 2003). These areas are deep reservoirs of criminal justice involvement, where law enforcement and discipline are part of the architecture of community life.

In several cities, there are neighborhood blocks where the government is spending more than a million dollars a year to incarcerate ("Million Dollar Blocks," *Village Voice*, November 9, 2004). Because inmates return with fewer job prospects and are at greater risk of poverty, and because these people are being absorbed by only a few areas, incarceration further embeds poverty, segregation, and high levels of joblessness and economic deprivation and entrenches them in small areas. Places that already are undergoing high levels of joblessness, poverty, single-headed households, segregation, and crime become even more likely to have these features as a direct result of greater incarceration and surveillance.

Research also suggests that incarceration negatively affects community norms, diminishing the informal social controls that prevent crime. The reason is that in neighborhoods where incarceration is high, because so many people experience prison, the social stigma and fear of going to prison has disappeared (Fagan and Meares 2008). As one scholar notes, "An individual growing up in a neighborhood that suffers from high unemployment and a high concentration of incarceration, where as many as 10% of all males age 25 to 29 may be behind bars, is more likely to view incarceration as inevitable, as a right of passage, or as normal. More to the point, that individual is more likely to see criminality as acceptable, or even desirable" (Capers 2008, 28).

High levels of incarceration also lead to more crime and further increases in incarceration. Todd Clear, Dina Rose, and Judith Ryder (2001) examine the effects of removal and reentry of offenders in the same community (in this case, high-incarceration neighborhoods in Tallahassee, Florida). They find that high rates of admission to prison are positively correlated to an increase in crime in the following year. Whereas low levels of incarceration result in diminishments in crime, high levels lead to more crime because they can weaken personal identity with a community and community relationships that would otherwise create informal social control (Clear et al. 2003). Incarceration also leads to more aggressive police and parole surveillance, leading, in turn, to more incarceration and parole revocation (Fagan, West, and Holland 2003).

Thus increases in incarceration actually fostered the conditions for more and more incarceration and for its further identification with certain small neighborhoods. So when the labor market rebounded, these communities had already begun to experience extreme rates of removal and return owing to the prison intervention; the experience of imprisonment brought with it more poverty, more blight, more segregation and joblessness, and new criminogenic norms in a tight feedback loop. These feedbacks reinforced the carceral expansion and made racial disparities more likely even as crime and black crime declined.

UNDERSTANDING RACIAL INEQUALITY IN A POSTRACIAL AMERICA

What does the development of black mass incarceration say about a postracial America? The two stories elaborated on in this chapter illustrate why, when, and how a major aspect of contemporary racial inequality grew, persisted, and created feedbacks that further reinforced it in the midst of large declines in overt racism and, in fact, on the heels of one of the largest interventions to undo institutional commitments to racial hierarchy.

I want to suggest another feedback, namely, that black mass incarceration and the daily depictions of black predators in the news media have helped construct ideas about black mass incarceration that shield it from opposition on racial grounds. The development described here has helped construct a link between blacks and criminality in the public's mind, and as long as criminality and not bias is at the root, America's black mass incarceration of its previously enslaved population stands legitimated and inoculated from potential challenge. A powerful narrative has emerged to ascribe black mass incarceration in a postracial era to race-neutral factors: blacks are more targeted by police and more incarcerated because they are more criminal. The majority of people think that the reason more blacks are locked up is that more blacks commit crime and violence.

Consider two recent polls. One asked a nationally representative sample of Americans why "Blacks are more often arrested and sent to prison than Whites" and found that 80 percent of whites gave the unqualified response that "many younger Blacks don't respect authority" (Peffley and Hurwitz 2010, 89). Greater black offending, then, confirms the racial fairness of a disproportionately racial prison system and justifies black mass incarceration. As long as blacks commit more crimes, confining large swaths of their communities is justifiable. As Pager (chap. 8, 267) notes in this volume, "Invoking this formal category [criminal], then, may legitimate forms of social exclusion that, based on ascriptive characteristics alone, would be more difficult to justify," providing a "new rationale" for why deep disparities exist in a formally equal polity. At the same time, decoupled from this narrative is one that emphasizes the criminogenic conditions in which many blacks live and the predictable effects of segregation, joblessness, and concentrated poverty for criminal offense patterns. Thus black mass incarceration becomes normal, a natural outgrowth of black criminality.

This widespread acceptance of one of the biggest racial disparities since Jim Crow is what Ian Lopez (2010, 51) has termed "commonsense racism": "For most Americans . . . even extreme racial disparities evoke not a sense of moral outrage but something closer to its opposite, a belief in the basic fairness of the world as currently organized. . . . Shocking disparities in incarceration rates prove for most not the racial injustice of the current situation but the primal fact of minority depravity." The construction of enormous racial disparities in criminal justice involvement become "commonsense." In a perverse way, this narrative (black crime is the cause of higher black incarceration) strengthens with distance from overt forms of discrimination that characterized the pre–civil rights era.

In other words, as our inglorious racial history is distanced with time, our punitive expansion becomes more separated from its racial motivations, and so too does the black crime narrative become ever more logical, assuming a factual, taken-for-granted quality in popular public opinion, media, and even academic narratives.

The powerful black criminality narrative narrowed the range of ideas in the post–civil rights era. Because racially disparate offense rates created a seemingly legitimate justification for the hyperincarceration of blacks, only the explicit and visible presence of overt discrimination could contend with it. In other words, if we could find disparate application of the law toward blacks and differential treatment by the justice system, then the criminal justice system would be shown to violate norms of equality. Not surprisingly, a number of academic studies and news accounts focused on ferreting out egregious bias. Studies too numerous to cite have addressed the question of overt discrimination in criminal justice. Similarly, encyclopedic volumes have been dedicated to the racial impact of the war on drugs, another easy case because overt bias was written into the law through the infamous 100-to-1 disparity between criminal sentences for crack and cocaine users. Academics designed studies that could measure disparate sentencing, controlling for prior record and socioeconomic status. This method unselfconsciously assumes that offending is curiously nonracial. Undoing discrimination in criminal justice is the politically easy case, and locating bias is a fail-safe way of challenging the black criminality narrative. But prevailing accounts, with their almost obsessive focus on locating individual discrimination of police and courts, have missed the bigger picture. The focus on the cases in which black offense rates are not the explanation or on unexplained variation in sentences that are not based on prior record or current offense disguises the role of race and racial history.

As the psychologist Philip Atiba Goff notes in chapter 6, page 161, of this volume, it is difficult to measure racial bias in criminal justice when "faced simultaneously with diminishing racial prejudice and persistent racial inequality." It is this gap that has prevented scholars from understanding massively high rates of arrest and incarceration in black communities in the post–civil rights era. Journalists, academics, and lay people alike do not yet have a language and conceptual tools for describing stunning racial disparities in the absence of racial bias in attitudes—or "racism without racists" (Bonilla-Silva 2006). In this situation, the discrimination narrative and the black criminality narrative have been presented as the only alternatives, collapsing a more historically informed set of mechanisms by which racial disparities in criminal justice involvement and contact can occur in the absence of measurable racial bias and easily visible intent. Goff argues that to truly understand contemporary racial inequalities, we need to move beyond both the attitude problem—the notion that "racial bigotry is the one and only cause of racial disparities," and the measurement problem—the difficulty of "quantifying racism."

This chapter has attempted to move beyond these two problems, showing how huge racial disparities developed absent overt racial bias. At the same time, this does not mean that race does not matter. Much to the contrary, the nation's historical racial hierarchy is just in the background. But contemporary racial attitude bias is not sufficient to explain contemporary black incarceration rates. Even with perfect equality in police treatment and court processing, black disparities in incarceration would still have increased at a quick clip. Even without discrimination, blacks were worse off—more likely to commit crime and more likely to get lengthy prison sentences under new penal regimes. To be clear, racial discrimination did not disappear from criminal justice, but the tremendous expansion in black incarceration relied on the dynamic interaction of two mechanisms—massive policy change and the creation of criminogenic conditions in black communities—mechanisms that are overlooked by focusing instead on individual bias. If we search only for overt discrimination in policing, adjudication, and sentencing of offenders, we will miss this interaction of racially tinged policy responses to crime at the very moment the black "underclass" was being steadily constructed. Moreover, understanding black mass incarceration does not require complex stories about social control; it was the largely predictable effect of the adoption of major punitive policies and diminishing black opportunities in the city.

CARCERAL INEQUALITY IN A "POSTRACIAL" NATION

In a strange twist of racial progress, the generation of blacks who will grow up with the nation's first black president will also grow up more likely than any before it to experience prison either themselves or vicariously.

The analysis presented here juxtaposes two relatively familiar descriptive stories to resituate an understanding of our current racial situation. Fifty years after the civil rights movement, indeed, even after the election of our first black president, many are wont to conclude that America has achieved a racial milestone, if not racial enlightenment. Although certain recent improvements cannot be discounted, we have reason to question the scope of racial progress.

Racial progress today remains partial and incomplete, owing to a relatively recent and enduring gap that has opened up between the experiences of blacks and whites: criminal justice contact. The rise of black mass incarceration constitutes a major setback of progress for blacks in a "post-racial" era, one that has a distinctive trajectory from other racial disparities. First, the development of racialized incarceration stands apart in that it occurred in the aftermath of civil rights expansions as other inequalities were lessening and overt legal discrimination was at least formally eradicated by laws.

In earlier work (Weaver 2007), I have sought to explain a moment in American political development that accounts for the incredible size and strength of the carceral state. Here I have extended that account. Something more serious has happened: the development of racial economic depression beginning in the 1970s—right after my account of frontlash begins—is now properly understood as providing the bodies for the carceral system. Thus, second, the story of the truly disadvantaged is a story of those structurally situated to encounter a system that had been designed with race in the immediate background.

One of the most problematic observations for the postracial thesis, if my account is taken where it stands, is that though the experience of incarceration and police contact is much greater for black high school dropouts and inner-city youth, one of the striking aspects of the expansion of punishment is that it has occurred across lines as well. Thus what began as an unhappy harmony between a racial carceral state and the black poor has now reached beyond those bounds—fifty years past civil rights. The black middle class, despite its greater fortunes, is now more likely to come into contact with criminal justice, probably more so than poor whites. Consider the example from Larry Bobo's survey on race and crime, which asked respondents whether they had a close friend or relative who was currently in prison. Fewer than 5 percent of high-income whites with a college degree but almost one-third of the equivalent group of black respondents had intimate exposure to incarceration. Moreover, "the rate of such exposure for the very highest status African Americans exceeds that of the very lowest status whites" (Bobo and Thompson 2010, 350).

Hundreds of studies have addressed the inner workings of criminal justice policy and practice. Although important in establishing differential treatment in the criminal justice system, they are only part of the story. Here, I take a broader view of the links between institutions and the economy of the black poor. This research locates important policy changes colliding with transformations in the deteriorating condition of urban blacks that fostered racially disproportionate incarceration. At the very moment that economic deprivation led to criminogenic neighborhoods, we embraced punitive policies that would increasingly use punishment and incarceration to deal with crime and violence. Developments in the political economy of the inner city corresponded to investments in punishment, and the result should not have come as a surprise. More blacks were incarcerated.

When the carceral state is studied in isolation, the common prescriptive wisdom is that turning back the dial on punitive measures or eradicating systemic discrimination would greatly alleviate the racial composition of our carceral system. But owing to the interaction between a racially motivated crime policy and racially grounded socioeconomic depression, removing discrimination or undoing punitive policies will not be enough because the interaction has led to self-sustaining feedbacks that now create both poverty and the conditions for more spatially concentrated incarceration—hence, the unhappy harmony. Retracting punishment policies alone will not soften disparities or reverse incarceration's deleterious effects on black community. In any case, we should not easily accept the assertion that America is postracial—it distracts from the real work left to be done.

NOTES

1. These stipulations included a mandatory buy-in provision that required states to match the federal funds. States were also required to expand their criminal justice budget by 5 percent a year in order to receive grants. States also had to demonstrate that they were willing to assume the costs of the project once the grant ended. Finally, states had to allocate a portion of the funds according to "level of effort," which meant that the localities spending the most would get the most in funding.

2. Under this law, people convicted of a felony with a weapon receive a mandatory ten-year sentence; if the weapon is discharged during the commission of a crime, the mandatory sentence is twenty years; and if the fired weapon results in death, they must receive a life sentence.

3. In a recent survey of Latinos, 23 percent had been stopped and questioned by the police, 15 percent had been arrested, 13 percent had been convicted, and 12 percent had been incarcerated (Lopez and Livingston 2009).

4. It is also the case that racial disparities in criminal justice have helped rosy the picture of inequality. Studies by Bruce Western demonstrate that swollen prison populations actually obscure the true extent of inequality, primarily because the large population of prisoners is completely absent from statistics on economic performance like unemployment and wages. Readjusting for this reveals a stark finding: the investment in punishment is the reason for our low unemployment relative to European countries and the reason for the appearance of swiftly decreasing unemployment rates in the 1990s. The often celebrated closing of the black-white wage gap was similarly an artifact of rapidly expanding confinement of the black population. Furthermore, Western and

Becky Pettit (2000) estimate that standard labor force data "understate black-white inequality in employment among young dropouts by about 45%" because they fail to take into account the disproportionately large number of young blacks incarcerated.

5. Statistics on the concentration of prisoners are from various Urban Institute reports available at: www.urban.org/projects/reentry-portfolio/publications .cfm.

REFERENCES

Alexander, Michelle. 2010. *The New Jim Crow: Mass Incarceration in the Age of Color-blindness*. New York: The New Press.

American Sociological Association. 2007. "Race, Ethnicity, and the Criminal Justice System." ASA Series on How Race and Ethnicity Matter. Available at: http://www.asanet.org/images/press/docs/pdf/ASARaceCrim.pdf (accessed April 1, 2013).

Beckett, Katherine, and Theodore Sasson. 2004. *The Politics of Injustice: Crime and Punishment in America*. 2nd ed. Thousand Oaks, Calif.: Sage Publication.

Blumstein, Alfred. 1983. "On the Racial Disproportionality of United States' Prison Populations." *Journal of Criminal Law and Criminology* 73(3): 1259.

Blumstein, Alfred, and Allen J. Beck. 1999. "Population Growth in U.S. Prisons, 1980–1996." *Crime and Justice* 26(17): 17–61.

Bobo, Lawrence D., and Victor Thompson. 2010. "Racialized Mass Incarceration: Poverty, Prejudice, and Punishment." In *Doing Race: 21 Essays for the 21st Century*, edited by Hazel Rose Markus and Paula Moya. New York: W. W. Norton.

Bonczar, Thomas P. 2003. *Prevalence of Imprisonment in the U.S. Population, 1974–2001*. Special report. U.S. Department of Justice, Bureau of Justice Statistics.

———. 2011. "National Corrections Reporting Program: Most Serious Offense of State Prisoners, by Offense, Admission Type, Age, Sex, Race, and Hispanic Origin. U.S. Department of Justice, Bureau of Justice Statistics. May 5. Available at: http://bjs.ojp.usdoj.gov/index.cfm?ty=pbdetail&iid=2065 (accessed April 1, 2013).

Bonilla-Silva, Eduardo. 2006. *Racism Without Racists: Color-Blind Racism and the Persistence of Racial Inequality in the United States*. Lanham, Md: Rowman & Littlefield.

Bound, John, and Richard B. Freeman. 1992. "What Went Wrong? The Erosion of Relative Earnings and Employment Among Young Black Men in the 1980s." *Quarterly Journal of Economics* 107(1): 201–32.

Braman, Donald. 2004. *Doing Time on the Outside: Incarceration and Family Life in Urban America*. Ann Arbor: University of Michigan Press.

Bridges, George S., and Robert D. Crutchfield. 1988. "Law, Social Standing, and Racial Disparities in Imprisonment." *Social Forces* 66(3): 699–724.

Cahalan, Margaret Werner. 1986. *Historical Corrections Statistics in the United States, 1850–1984.* U.S. Department of Justice, Bureau of Justice Statistics, Washington, D.C.

Capers, I. Bennett. 2008. "Policing, Race, and Place." *Harvard Civil Rights-Civil Liberties Law Review* 44(1): 43–78.

Chiricos, Theodore. 1987. "Rates of Crime and Unemployment: An Analysis of Aggregate Research Evidence." *Social Problems* 34(2): 187–212.

Clear, Todd R., Dina R. Rose, and Judith A. Ryder. 2001. "Incarceration and the Community: The Problem of Removing and Returning Offenders." *Crime and Delinquency* 47(3): 335–51.

Clear, Todd R., et al. 2003. "Coercive Mobility and Crime: A Preliminary Examination of Concentrated Incarceration and Social Disorganization." *Justice Quarterly* 20(1): 33–64.

Cohen, Cathy J. 2005. "Black Youth Culture Survey." Chicago: Black Youth Project. Available at: www.blackyouthproject.com (accessed April 1, 2013).

Correctional Populations in the United States, 1997. November 2000. U.S. Department of Justice, Bureau of Justice Statistics, Washington, D.C.

Crutchfield, Robert D., et al. 2009. "Racial Disparities in Early Criminal Justice Involvement." *Race and Social Problems* 1(4): 218–30.

Drucker, Ernest. 2002. "Population Impact of Mass Incarceration under New York's Rockefeller Drug Laws: An Analysis of Years of Life Lost." *Journal of Urban Health: Bulletin of the New York Academy of Medicine* 79(3): 1–10.

Eckberg, Douglas. 2006. "Sentenced Prisoners Admitted to State and Federal Institutions, by Race: 1926–1996" table Ec309-327. In *Historical Statistics of the United States, Earliest Times to the Present: Millennial Edition,* edited by Susan B. Carter, Scott Sigmund Gartner, Michael R. Haines, Alan L. Olmstead, Richard Sutch, and Gavin Wright. New York: Cambridge University Press.

Fagan, Jeffrey, and Tracey Meares. 2008. "Punishment, Deterrence, and Social Control: The Paradox of Punishment in Minority Communities." *Ohio State Journal of Criminal Law* 6(173): 173–229.

Fagan, Jeffrey, Valerie West, and Jan Holland. 2003. "Reciprocal Effects of Crime and Incarceration in New York City." *Fordham Urban Law Journal* 30(5): 1551–602.

Fragile Families and Child Wellbeing Study, 2003–2006. Available at: http://www.fragilefamilies.princeton.edu (accessed April 1, 2013).

Freeman, Richard B. 1996. "Why Do So Many Young American Men Commit Crimes and What Might We Do About It?" *Journal of Economic Perspectives* 10(1): 25–42.

Glaeser, Edward L., Bruce I. Sacerdote, and Jose A. Scheinkman. 2002. "The Social Multiplier." Working Paper ISSU 9153. Cambridge, Mass.: National Bureau of Economic Research.

Gottschalk, Marie. 2006. *The Prison Gallows: The Politics of Mass Incarceration in America.* Cambridge: Cambridge University Press.

Grogger, Jeff. 1998. "Market Wages and Youth Crime." *Journal of Labor Economics* 16(4): 756–91.

Hagan, John, Carla Shedd, and Monique R. Payne. 2005. "Race, Ethnicity, and Youth Perceptions of Criminal Injustice." *American Sociological Review* 70(3): 381–407.

Jacob, Herbert. 1985. "Governmental Responses to Crime in the United States, 1948–78." Computer file. Research conducted by Herbert Jacob, Northwestern University. 2nd ICPSR ed. Ann Arbor, Mich.: Inter-university Consortium for Political and Social Research, producer and distributor.

Jargowsky, Paul A. 1997. *Poverty and Place: Ghettos, Barrios, and the American City.* New York: Russell Sage Foundation.

Johnson, Rucker. 2009. "Ever-Increasing Levels of Parental Incarceration and the Consequences for Children." In *Do Prisons Make Us Safer? The Benefits and Costs of the Prison Boom,* edited by Steven Raphael and Michael Stoll. New York: Russell Sage Foundation.

Jones-Correa, Michael. 2001. "Structural Shifts and Institutional Capacity: Possibilities for Ethnic Cooperation and Conflict in Urban Settings." In *Governing American Cities: Interethnic Coalitions, Competition, and Conflict,* edited by Michael Jones-Correa. New York: Russell Sage Foundation.

Kasarda, John D. 1993. "Urban Industrial Transition and the Underclass." In *The Ghetto Underclass: Social Science Perspectives* (updated edition), edited by William Julius Wilson. Newbury Park, Calif.: Sage Publications.

Kunselman, Julie C., Kathrine A. Johnson, and Michael C. Rayboun. 2003. "Profiling Sentence Enhancement Offenders: A Case Study of Florida's 10-20-Lifers." *Criminal Justice Policy Review* 14(2): 229–48.

Land, Kenneth C., Patricia L. McCall, and Lawrence E. Cohen. 1991. "Characteristics of U.S. Cities with Extreme (High or Low) Crime Rates: Results of Discriminant Analyses of 1960, 1970, and 1980 Data." *Social Indicators Research* 24(3): 209–31.

Lauritsen, Janet L., and Robert J. Sampson. 1998. "Minorities, Crime, and Criminal Justice." In *The Handbook of Crime and Punishment,* edited by Michael Tonry. New York: Oxford University Press.

Lee, M. R. 2000. "Concentrated Poverty, Race, and Homicide." *Sociological Quarterly* 41(2): 189–206.

Lopez, Ian F. Haney. 2010. "Post-Racial Racism: Crime Control and Racial Stratification in the Age of Obama." *California Law Review* 98(3): 1023–2129.

Lopez, Mark Hugo, and Gretchen Livingston. 2009. "Hispanics and the Criminal Justice System: Low Confidence, High Exposure." Washington: Pew Hispanic Center. April 7.

Maguire, Kathleen, ed. n.d. *Sourcebook of Criminal Justice Statistics.* University at Albany, Hindelang Criminal Justice Research Center. Available at: http://www.albany.edu/sourcebook (accessed April 17, 2013).

Massey, Douglas. 1994. "Getting Away with Murder: Segregation and Violent Crime in Urban America." *University of Pennsylvania Law Review* 143(5): 1203–232.

Massey, Douglas, and Nancy Denton. 1998. *American Apartheid: Segregation and the Making of the Underclass.* Cambridge, Mass.: Harvard University Press.

Massoglia, Michael. 2008. "Incarceration, Health, and Racial Disparities in Health." *Law and Society Review* 42(2): 275–306.

Mauer, Marc. 2010. "Two-Tiered Justice: Race, Class, and Crime Policy." In *The Integration Debate: Competing Futures for American Cities*, edited by Chester Hartman and Gregory Squires. New York: Routledge.

Muller, Christopher. 2012. "Northward Migration and the Rise of Racial Disparity in American Incarceration, 1880–1950." *American Journal of Socoiology* 118(2): 281–326.

Murray, Joseph, and David P. Farrington. 2005. "Parental Imprisonment: Effects on Boys' Antisocial Behaviour and Delinquency through the Life-course." *Journal of Child Psychology and Psychiatry* 46(12): 1269–98.

Nellis, Ashley, and Ryan S. King. 2009. *No Exit: The Expanding Use of Life Sentences in America.* Washington, D.C.: The Sentencing Project.

Pastore, Ann L. and Kathleen Maguire, eds. 2000. *Sourcebook of Criminal Justice Statistics, 1999.* U.S. Department of Justice, Bureau of Justice Statistics. Washington, DC: USGPO.

Peffley, Mark, and Jon Hurwitz. 2010. *Justice in America: The Separate Realities of Blacks and Whites.* New York: Cambridge University Press.

Pew Center on the States. 2007. "One in 100: Behind Bars in America in 2008." Online report available at: http://www.pewstates.org/uploadedFiles/PCS_Assets/2008/one%20in%20100.pdf (accessed April 1, 2013).

Philips, Susan D., et al. 2006. "Disentangling the Risks: Parent Criminal Justice Involvement and Children's Exposure to Family Risks." *Criminology & Public Policy* 5(4): 677–702.

Raphael, Steven. 2004. "The Socioeconomic Status of Black Males: The Increasing Importance of Incarceration." Available at: http://urbanpolicy.berkeley.edu/pdf/Ch8Raphael0304.pdf (accessed April 1, 2013).

Sampson, Robert J., and John H. Laub. 1993. "Structural Variations in Juvenile Court Processing: Inequality, the Underclass, and Social Control." *Law and Society Review* 27(2): 285–311.

Sampson, Robert J., and William Julius Wilson. 1995. "Toward a Theory of Race, Crime, and Urban Inequality." In *Crime and Inequality*, edited by J. Hagan and R. D. Peterson. Stanford, Calif.: Stanford University Press.

Schlesinger, Traci. 2008. "The Failure of Race Neutral Policies: How Mandatory Terms and Sentencing Enhancements Contribute to Mass Racialized Incarceration." *Crime and Delinquency* 57(1): 56–81.

Senate Joint Economic Committee. 2007. *Mass Incarceration in the United States: At*

What Cost? Opening Statement of Senator Jim Webb. October 4. 110th Congress, 1st sess.

The Sentencing Project. 2009. "Criminal Justice Primer: Policy Priorities for the 111th Congress." Available at: http://www.sentencingproject.org/doc/publications/cjprimer2009.pdf (accessed April 1, 2013).

———. n.d. "Schools and Prisons: Fifty Years after Brown v. Board of Education." Available at: www.sentencingproject.org/doc/publications/rd_brownvboard.pdf.

Shane-DuBow, Sandra, Alice P. Brown, and Erik Olsen. 1985. *Sentencing Reform in the United States: History, Content, and Effect.* U.S. Department of Justice, National Institute of Justice, Office of Development, Testing, and Dissemination, Washington, D.C.

Shihadeh, Edward S., and Nicole Flynn. 1996. "Segregation and Crime: The Effect of Black Social Isolation on the Rates of Black Urban Violence." *Social Forces* 74(4): 1325–52.

Shihadeh, Edward S., and Graham C. Ousey. 1996. "Metropolitan Expansion and Black Social Dislocation: The Link Between Suburbanization and Center-City Crime." *Social Forces* 75(2): 649–66.

Stoll, Michael A., Harry J. Holzer, and Keith R. Ihlanfeldt. 2000. "Within Cities and Suburbs: Racial Residential Concentration and the Spatial Distribution of Employment Opportunities across Sub-Metropolitan Areas." *Journal of Policy Analysis and Management* 19(2): 207–31.

Stuntz, William J. 2008. "Unequal Justice." *Harvard Law Review* 121(8): 1969–2040.

Sullivan, M. 1989. *Getting Paid: Youth Crime and Work in the Inner City.* Ithaca, N.Y.: Cornell University Press.

Taylor, Ralph B., and Jeanette Covington. 1988. "Neighborhood Changes in Ecology and Violence." *Criminology* 26(4): 553–89.

Tonry, Michael. 1995. *Malign Neglect: Race, Crime, and Punishment in America.* New York: Oxford University Press.

Tonry, Michael, and Matthew Melewski. 2008. "The Malign Effects of Drug and Crime Control Policies on Black Americans." *Crime and Justice* 31(1): 1–44.

Uggen, Christopher, Jeff Manza, and Melissa Thompson. 2006. "Citizenship, Democracy, and the Civic Reintegration of Criminal Offenders." *Annals of the American Academy of Political and Social Science* 605(1): 281–310.

U.S. Bureau of Justice Statistics. Various years. "Publication and Products: Prisoners." Available at: http://bjs.gov/index.cfm?ty=pbse&sid=40 (accessed April 12, 2012).

U.S. Census Bureau. Various years. *Statistical Abstracts of the United States.* Washington, D.C.

Wagmiller, Robert L. 2007. "Race and the Spatial Segregation of Jobless Men in Urban America." *Demography* 44(3): 539–62.

Washington Post, Kaiser Family Foundation, and Harvard University. 2006. *African American Men Survey.* Menlo Park, Calif.: Henry J. Kaiser Family Foundation.

Weaver, Vesla M. 2007. "Frontlash: Race and the Development of Punitive Crime Policy." *Studies in American Political Development* 21(2): 230–65.

Western, Bruce. 2006. *Punishment and Inequality in America.* New York: Russell Sage Foundation.

Western, Bruce, Meredith Kleykamp, and Jake Rosenfeld. 2004. "Crime, Punishment, and American Inequality." In *Social Inequality,* edited by Katherine Neckerman. New York: Russell Sage Foundation.

Western, Bruce, Leonard M. Lopoo, and Sarah McLanahan. 2004. "Incarceration and the Bonds Between Parents in Fragile Families." In *Imprisoning America: The Social Effects of Mass Incarceration,* edited by Mary Pattillo, David Weiman, and Bruce Western. New York: Russell Sage Foundation.

Western, Bruce, and Becky Pettit. 2000. "Incarceration and Racial Inequality in Men's Employment." *Industrial and Labor Relations Review* 54(1): 3–16.

Western, Bruce, and Christopher Wildeman. 2009. "The Black Family and Mass Incarceration." *Annals of the American Academy of Political and Social Science* 621(1): 221–42.

Wheelock, Darren, and Christopher Uggen. 2008. "Punishment, Crime, and Poverty." In *The Colors of Poverty: Why Racial and Ethnic Disparities Persist,* edited by Ann Chih Lin and David R. Harris. New York: Russell Sage Foundation.

Wildeman, Christopher. 2009. "Parental Imprisonment, the Prison Boom, and the Concentration of Childhood Disadvantage." *Demography* 46(2): 265–80.

———. 2010a. "Parental Incarceration, Child Homelessness, and the Invisible Consequences of Mass Imprisonment." Fragile Families Working Paper WP09-19-FF.

———. 2010b. "Paternal Incarceration and Children's Physically Aggressive Behaviors: Evidence from the Fragile Families and Child Wellbeing Study." *Social Forces* 89(1): 285–309.

———. 2012. "Imprisonment and Infant Mortality." *Social Problems* 59(2): 228–57.

Wilson, William Julius. 1987. *The Truly Disadvantaged: The Inner-City, the Underclass, and Public Policy.* Chicago: University of Chicago Press.

Chapter 8 | The "Stickiness" of Race in an Era of Mass Incarceration

Devah Pager

IN THE SUMMER of 2009, the Harvard professor Henry Louis Gates Jr. was unceremoniously arrested at his home in Cambridge, Massachusetts, when police mistook him for a burglar. The flurry of media attention, culminating with a "beer summit" hosted by President Obama, revived long-standing debates about the prevalence of racial profiling and the degree to which deeply entrenched associations between blackness and criminality continue to shape the opportunities and experiences of African Americans today.

In many ways, the Gates incident tapped into one of the most "sticky" features of race in contemporary America. Blacks in this country have long been regarded with suspicion and fear; but unlike progressive trends in other racial attitudes, associations between race and crime have changed little in recent years. Survey respondents consistently rate blacks as more prone to violence than any other American racial or ethnic group, and the stereotype of aggressiveness and violence is most frequently endorsed in ratings of African Americans (Chiricos, Welch, and Gertz 2004; Sniderman and Piazza 1993, 45; Smith 1991).[1] The stereotype of blacks as criminals is deeply embedded in the collective consciousness of white Americans, irrespective of the perceiver's level of prejudice or personal beliefs (Devine and Elliot 1995; Eberhardt et al. 2004; Graham and Lowery 2004).

Whereas long-standing associations between race and crime appear to have changed little over time, the social realities underlying these associations surely have. Despite falling crime rates since the early 1990s, rates of incarceration have steadily increased, and racial disparities in incarceration have remained persistently large. Indeed, the massive expansion of the criminal justice system over the past three decades has fundamentally

257

altered the institutional context in which ideas about crime and criminals are shaped. By marking large numbers of young men with an official record of criminality, the criminal justice system may inadvertently reinforce and legitimate long-standing assumptions about blackness and crime.

This chapter considers the direct and indirect pathways through which race and criminal background affect patterns of racial disparities in employment. Black men who have had prior contact with the criminal justice system pay an especially steep penalty in their search for work relative to white men with comparable criminal histories. Even blacks without criminal records are significantly disadvantaged, with the penalty for blackness comparable to having a felony conviction. Moreover, interviews with employers suggest that perceptions of criminality and violence ascribed to young black men continue to represent a salient dimension of contemporary racial attitudes. These findings suggest one possible far-reaching consequence of recent crime policies: steeply rising incarceration rates among blacks cast a shadow of criminality across the black population. Within this context, blacks with or without criminal records are likely to be viewed by employers with suspicion.

THE STICKINESS OF RACIAL INEQUALITY IN EMPLOYMENT

Despite legal bans on discrimination and the liberalization of racial attitudes since the 1960s, important forms of social and economic inequality continue to differentiate the experiences of black and white Americans. Particularly among those at the bottom half of the distribution, rapid gains beginning in the 1960s slowed, and in some cases reversed, during the 1980s and 1990s. Even at the high point of economic expansion in the late 1990s, when unemployment rates were dropping steadily for all groups, black men were still more than twice as likely to be unemployed as their white counterparts. Over time, blacks, and young black men in particular, have become increasingly likely to drop out of the labor market altogether when faced with the prospect of long-term unemployment or marginal employment opportunities (Holzer, Offner, and Sorensen 2005).[2] Even before the current economic crisis, nearly one-third of young black men were out of work, and if those who were incarcerated at the time are included, the jobless rate for young black male dropouts was a staggering 65 percent (Western 2006, 92).

What explains these persistent racial disparities? The truth of the matter is, the employment problems of blacks are vastly overdetermined. Far more factors contribute to black employment problems than would be necessary to produce the observed trends: the manufacturing sector declined

(Wilson 1978); jobs moved from the central city (Freeman and Holzer 1986); black students' test scores have lagged behind those of whites as the returns to cognitive skills have increased (Murnane, Willett, and Levy 1995); blacks have access to less effective social networks for finding work (Royster 2003); and blacks face increasing job competition from women and immigrants (Waldinger 1999). Each of these factors has surely contributed to persistent racial inequality in employment, and each has received extensive attention in the research literature.

But one major institutional change has received less attention in research on labor-market outcomes: the growth of the criminal justice system. Although it operates outside the formal labor market, the criminal justice system can be thought of as a labor-market institution because of its role in segregating and marking large numbers of economically marginalized men (Western and Beckett 1999; Pager 2007).

RACIAL DISPARITIES IN CRIME AND PUNISHMENT

The past four decades have seen an unprecedented expansion of the criminal justice system, with rates of incarceration increasing more than fivefold from 1970 to 2010. The United States holds the dubious distinction of having the highest rate of incarceration in the world, with more than 2 million individuals currently behind bars. But the expansive reach of the criminal justice system has not affected all groups equally. As Vesla Weaver describes in chapter 8 in this volume, African Americans have felt the impact of the prison boom most acutely. Blacks make up more than 40 percent of the current prison population but represent just 12 percent of the U.S. population (Bureau of Justice Statistics 2006). At any given time, more than 10 percent of all black men between the ages of twenty-five and twenty-nine are behind bars; roughly a third are under criminal justice supervision. Over the course of a lifetime, nearly one in three young black men—and well over half of young black males without a high school degree—will spend some time in prison. According to these estimates, young black men are more likely to go to prison than to attend college, serve in the military, or, in the case of high school dropouts, to be in the labor market (Bureau of Justice Statistics 1997; Pettit and Western 2004). Prison is no longer a rare or extreme event among our nation's disadvantaged. Rather, it has become a normal and anticipated marker in the transition to adulthood.

To be sure, to some degree these disparities reflect differences in the level of criminal activity between groups. Particularly for violent crimes such as homicide, for example, blacks are represented in roughly equal proportion among those arrested and those imprisoned (Garland, Spohn, and Wodahl 2008; Sampson and Lauritsen 1997; Blumstein 1993). In the case of drug crimes, by contrast, which have been a major source of prison growth since 1980, there is evidence to suggest that whites outnumber blacks in both consumption and distribution, despite enforcement trends in the opposite direction (Gfroerer and Brodsky 1992; Caulkins and McCaffrey 1993; Blumstein 1993). Overall, then, even taking into account racial disparities in rates of offending for certain crimes, significant disparities in criminal justice interventions remain.

The major changes in the pathways to prison in recent decades have not been driven by changes in criminal behavior. Rates of criminal offending for almost all crime types (and especially violent crime) declined substantially through the 1990s as incarceration rates continued to soar.[3] Rather, sharp changes in sentencing laws have led to higher rates and longer terms of imprisonment for any given offense. Alfred Blumstein and Allen Beck (1999) estimate that during the steepest rise in incarceration, in the 1980s and 1990s, only 12 percent of the increase in incarceration can be accounted for by increases in crime (nearly all of which represent increasing arrests for drug crimes). By far the greater part (88 percent) of rising incarceration rates can be attributed to changes in crime control policies, including a 51 percent increase in the likelihood of incarceration following arrest and a 37 percent increase in the average length of sentences. Thus changes in the handling of criminal offenders, more than increases in crime, have been primarily responsible for the growth in incarceration since 1980.[4]

The massive increase in the scale of imprisonment has had important consequences for the salience of the criminal justice system in the lives of African Americans. When a tiny fraction of the population was involved in the criminal justice system, racial disparities were less visible; today, by contrast, a similar degree of racial disparity is magnified by the scale of incarceration. For example, 12 percent of young black men, though less than 2 percent of young white men, are incarcerated at any given time (Bureau of Justice Statistics 2006, table 1.29). The salience of the prison among today's disadvantaged young men is a unique feature of the late twentieth and early twenty-first centuries.

RACE AND CRIME ON TELEVISION

High levels of criminal justice contact among blacks contributes to widespread associations between race and crime. These associations are further fueled by media coverage of crime, which tends to depict criminal episodes in a heavily racialized context. A study of local television news in Chicago, for example, has found that the largest share of news stories featuring blacks (on any topic) portrayed blacks as the perpetrators of violent crimes (Entman and Rojecki 2000). More often than news about Oprah, or Michael Jordan, or Barak Obama (all one-time Chicago residents), and more often than news about the thousands of black corporate leaders and community organizers in the city, stories about blacks become newsworthy when they have broken the law (see also Gilliam and Iyengar 2000; Chiricos and Eschholz 2002).

The frequency of coverage focusing on black criminals does have some basis in reality. Higher arrest rates for blacks will logically translate into greater news coverage of black criminals. But direct comparisons of local crime reports with corresponding arrest rates do not support a straightforward explanation. Travis Dixon and Daniel Linz (2000), for example, compared news reports about crime in the Los Angeles metro area with arrest rate data from the California Department of Corrections. Their findings indicate that blacks were 75 percent more likely to be represented as perpetrators in crime reports than their actual arrest rate would have predicted. White offenders, by contrast, were shown on television about 25 percent less often than their arrest rate would have predicted.[5] Existing racial disparities in criminal justice involvement are often exaggerated in the news, with blacks more often—and whites less often—shown in custody than actual crime statistics reveal to be representative.

Other studies of race and crime in the news have found media coverage of black criminals to be skewed not only in frequency but also in kind. A study by Robert Entman and Andrew Rojecki (2000) found that news coverage of blacks in custody was more likely to present mug shots (as opposed to live images or images taken before arrest) or images of blacks in handcuffs and under the physical restraints of a white police officer than coverage of whites in custody. In coverage of individuals accused of violent crimes, local news broadcasts were nearly twice as likely to provide an on-screen name for whites (47 percent) as for blacks (26 percent) (Entman 1990). According to Entman (1990, 82), "The presence of the accused's name provides a sense of his or her individual identity. Its absence may suggest that individual identity does not matter, that the accused is part of a single undifferentiated group of violent offenders: just another Black criminal." The more menacing and less individualized images of black suspects provide vivid "evidence" in support of racial stereotypes, depicting blacks as dangerous, violent, and criminal.

With the majority of Americans identifying television as the source of "most of your news about national and international issues" (Pew Research Center 2011), media distortions of the frequency and severity of offending among blacks can have important consequences for how Americans think about race and how they think about crime. The vast overrepresentation of black criminals in the news is linked to distorted images of the connection between race and crime. For example, following nearly two decades of prison expansion in the United States, one survey asked, "Of all the people arrested for violent crimes in the United States last year, what percent do you think were black?" The modal response to this question was 60 percent, an exaggeration by roughly 35 percent of the actual proportion at that time.[6] Similarly, an experiment in which individuals were shown a short news clip describing a murder—in which the race of the alleged perpetrator was not identified—found that more than 40 percent of subjects falsely recalled having seen a black perpetrator (Gilliam and Iyengar 2000, table 2).[7] When the most common image of blacks on TV shows blacks as criminal offenders, the associations between race and crime become increasingly automatic.

These associations remain deeply embedded in the unconscious and can affect the cognitive processing and behavior of even those individuals who consciously repudiate racial stereotypes or discrimination (Eberhardt et al. 2004; Devine, 1989; Sagar and Schofield 1980; Payne, 2001; Correll, Wittenbrink, and Judd 2002). Social psychological experiments have found that subjects are more likely to interpret ambiguous actions as threatening when the actor is portrayed as African American.[8] Subjects instructed to shoot potentially armed targets (presented in a videogame) are more quick to do so when the target is African American (Correll, Wittenbrink, and Judd 2002). Reinforced by some combination of higher crime rates, media distortions, and cultural biases, race persists as a powerful heuristic with which to assess danger. Particularly in interactions that contain some ambiguity, or in decisions made under pressure, evaluations are easily colored by these pervasive (and often unconscious) stereotypes about black aggressiveness or threat.

RACE, CRIME, AND GETTING A JOB

The pervasiveness of images of blacks in custody and behind bars presumably plays a role in perpetuating deeply entrenched associations between race and crime. To what extent do these dynamics shape the attitudes and expectations of employers? And in what ways might these lingering associations affect employment opportunities?

A number of studies have used in-depth interviews to explore the attitudes and experiences of employers (Pager and Karafin 2009; Kirschenman and Neckerman 1991; Wilson 1996; Waldinger and Lichter 2003; Moss and Tilly 2001). A surprising finding in these studies is the extent to which employers appear willing to speak candidly about race, even when this entails expressing strong negative attitudes about racial minorities. Among a range of concerns echoed in these studies, the issue of criminality and violence emerges frequently in discussions of young black men. In a recent study I conducted with Diana Karafin, about a third of the fifty-five employers we spoke with raised concerns that black men might have a threatening or criminal demeanor. One employer reported, "I think a lot of white people are scared of black people. . . . I think they are scared of them, intimidated by them, they don't feel comfortable around them." Another explained simply, "Half of them are in jail" (Pager and Karafin 2009, 82).

Other studies report similar findings. According to an employer interviewed by William J. Wilson (1996, 125), "People are afraid of black men. . . . I would say, well, maybe he's got a criminal record, but, he's—or I would just be a little bit more apprehensive." A manager for an employment agency interviewed by Philip Moss and Chris Tilly (2001, 107) explained, "You have people right now who are afraid to hire black males, because they think there is a certain level of violence associated with black males." These employers make clear the strong associations of black men with danger, crime, and the criminal justice system, factors that appear incompatible with legitimate work.

In discussing their concerns, some employers appeared apologetic or embarrassed for acknowledging their reservations about black men; some pointed to broader structural forces that have played a role in producing the current situation (for example, Pager and Karafin 2009, 76). And virtually all employers, even after expressing strong negative views about black men as a group, insisted that their own hiring decisions were based exclusively on the merits and qualifications of an individual applicant, whether "white, black, yellow or green" (employer at a retail clothing store, cited in Pager and Karafin 2009, 80). When asked what his sense was of how African American men are doing in terms of employment compared with other groups, the manager of a supply company simply said, "Skip that question because that has nothing to do with me. I just hire people based on their abilities." Another employer for a retail sales company expressed a common sentiment of universality: "Number one, they are all the same to me. When I look, I don't look at religion, I don't look at what color you are because we are all human beings." These employers appear committed to an evaluation process that is blind to race or color.

It is difficult to know to what degree employers are concealing the extent of their own racialized decision making. But even taking the employers' claims at face value, a growing body of research suggests that racialized associations operate more powerfully at an unconscious level, subtly shaping evaluations and decision making in ways that are invisible even to the actors themselves (for example, Dovidio and Gaertner 2000; see also the excellent discussion in chapter 6 in this volume). Furthermore, both race and criminal background are sensitive topics, which can lead to strained or uneasy interactions even among the most well-meaning individuals. Indeed, mere discomfort in interactions can produce some of the same consequences as intentional discrimination.

As an example, an experimental study in which subjects were asked to interview job applicants in a simulated hiring situation found that in their interviews with black applicants subjects showed a greater number of pauses and speech errors, and terminated the interviews more quickly than in their interviews with white applicants. Job candidates (of any race) subjected to interviews characterized by these nonverbal disruptions were, in turn, evaluated as less qualified by external observers (Word, Zanna, and Cooper 1974). Anxiety or discomfort in interracial interactions or with former offenders can thus produce outcomes that look very similar to outright discrimination (see Crocker, Major, and Steele 1998). Based on interviews with employers, then, it appears that there may be a strong link between criminalized images of black men and the stickiness of race in employment contexts. Whether or not these are based on conscious decision making, the powerful negative associations attached to young black men are likely to play a role in shaping their interactions, opportunities, and experiences.

FROM EMPLOYER ATTITUDES TO HIRING OUTCOMES

The candid remarks made by employers concerning their negative views about African Americans—and, in particular, their associations of black males with violence and crime—imply that black applicants may not fare well in these settings. At the same time, employer attitudes are not necessarily the primary factor driving hiring decisions. Indeed, a long literature studying the relationship between attitudes and behavior questions this link (LaPiere 1934). A 2005 study that directly compared attitudes and behaviors in this domain finds little relationship between employer attitudes about hiring black and white former offenders and behavioral measures of actual hiring outcomes (Pager and Quillian 2005). Similarly, Moss and Tilly (2001, 151) report the puzzling finding that "businesses where a plurality of managers complained about black motivation [and other negative characteristics] are more likely to hire black men."[9] Hiring decisions are influenced by a complex range of factors, racial attitudes being only one. The stated preferences of employers, then, leave uncertain the degree to which negative attitudes about blacks translate into active forms of discrimination.

Moving beyond the study of employer attitudes, research on employer decision making can shed some light on the employment consequences of race and criminal background. I took up this question in a recent series of field experiments investigating the impact of race and criminal background on employment in low-wage labor markets. In these studies (conducted in Milwaukee and New York City), I hired groups of young men to pose as job applicants (also called testers). The testers were college students or college graduates who were carefully selected and matched on the basis of age, race, physical appearance, and general style of self-presentation. The testers were assigned fictitious resumes that reflected equivalent levels of education and work experience (reporting only a high school degree and limited work experience). In addition, on some teams, one tester was randomly assigned a criminal record.[10] The testers were sent to apply for hundreds of real job openings for entry-level positions (those jobs requiring no previous experience and no education beyond high school), randomly selected from the classified advertisements in the major city newspapers. Job categories included restaurant workers, retail sales positions, warehouse workers, couriers, drivers, and laborers, among others. We then measured the percentage of applicants who received either a job offer or a callback, by race and criminal background.

The findings suggest a strong effect of both race and criminal background. White applicants with a criminal record were half as likely to receive a callback as equally qualified white applicants with no record (34 percent versus 17 percent). Among blacks the effect was even larger: black applicants with a prior felony conviction were only a third as likely to receive a callback as equally qualified black nonoffenders (14 percent versus 5 percent) (Pager 2003).

A follow-up study in New York City revealed a largely similar story (see Pager, Western, and Sugie 2009). Although the effect of a criminal record for whites was not as large in New York as in Milwaukee (roughly a 30 percent penalty), the racial differential was much larger (roughly a 60 percent penalty for blacks). Overall, then, the results of two field experiments support the conclusions that a felony conviction represents a serious barrier to employment and that this barrier tends to be significantly larger for blacks than for whites. According to these results, black former offenders appear doubly disadvantaged: not only are blacks more likely to be incarcerated than whites, but they also appear to be more strongly affected by the stigma of a criminal record.

But blacks were not penalized by their criminal record alone. Indeed, these results suggest that even blacks with clean backgrounds fare far worse than their white counterparts. In both cities, black applicants with no criminal record received only half the rate of callbacks as equally qualified whites and, in fact, fared no better than white felons. That employers viewed black applicants as essentially equivalent to whites just released from prison is strong evidence of the stickiness of race in this context.

This research cannot identify the precise source of employers' reluctance to hire blacks. Indeed, it is difficult if not impossible to "get inside an employer's head" to determine what combination of conscious or unconscious considerations may have led to the racial preferences we observed. Based on the evidence reviewed here, however, it is not unreasonable to expect employers' concerns about blacks to be shaped by their associations with crime. A number of interactions between testers and employers support this theory. On several occasions, for example, black testers were asked in person (before submitting their applications) whether they had a prior criminal history. For these employers, a young black man immediately aroused concern about criminal involvement, and this issue took center stage before getting to matters of education, work experience, or qualifications. None of the white testers, by contrast, were asked about their criminal histories up front. These experiences are consistent with Elijah Anderson's (1990) account of the suspicion with which young black men are often viewed. According to Anderson (1990, 190), "The anonymous black male is usually an ambiguous figure who arouses the utmost caution and is generally considered dangerous until he proves he is not." Overcoming this initial stereotype becomes one of the first challenges facing the young black male job applicant, particularly in low-wage labor markets where fewer objective indicators (college attendance, related work history, and so forth) are available for, or relevant to, the evaluation.

THE CREDENTIALING OF STIGMA

Real and representational trends in crime and punishment over the past three decades have contributed to a charged image of young black men. In this context, part of the stickiness of race stems from the particular institutional contexts in which race is made salient. In previous work I discuss how the criminal justice system has positioned itself as a major institution of racial stratification, with criminal records serving as a principle mechanism for the sorting and stratifying of opportunities (Pager 2007). Most states make criminal records publicly available, often through online repositories, and accessible to employers, landlords, creditors, and other interested parties.[11] With increasing numbers of occupations, public services, and other social goods becoming off-limits to former offenders, these records can be used as the official basis for eligibility determination or exclusion.

The state, in this way, serves as a credentialing institution, providing official and public certification of those among us who have been convicted of a crime. The "credential" of a criminal record, like education or professional credentials, constitutes a formal and enduring classification of social status, which can be used to regulate access and opportunity across numerous social, economic, and political domains. Within the employment domain, the criminal credential has indeed become a salient marker for employers, and increasing numbers make use of background checks to screen out undesirable applicants. The majority of employers claim that they would not knowingly hire an applicant with a criminal background (Holzer 1996); and the results reported here suggest that behavioral measures are consistent with these expressed attitudes.

But the power of the criminal credential does not stop with those bearing its official mark. Particularly in cases where the certification of a particular status is largely overlapping with other status markers (for example, race, gender), public assumptions about who is and who is not a credential holder can become generalized or exaggerated. Because blacks are so strongly associated with the population under correctional supervision, it becomes easy to assume that any given young black man is likely to have—or to be on his way to acquiring—a criminal record. As expressed by David Cole (1995, 2561), "When the results of the criminal justice system are as racially disproportionate as they are today, the criminal stigma extends beyond the particular behaviors and individuals involved to reach all young black men, and to a lesser extent all black people. The criminal justice system contributes to a stereotyped and stigmatic view of African-Americans as potential criminals." Invoking this formal category, then, may legitimate forms of social exclusion that, based on ascriptive characteristics alone, would be more difficult to justify.[12] In this way, negative credentials make possible a new rationale for exclusion in ways that reinforce and legitimate existing social cleavages.

The consequences of mass incarceration may, then, extend far beyond the costs to the individual bodies behind bars and to the families that are disrupted or the communities whose residents cycle in and out. The criminal justice system may itself legitimate and reinforce deeply embedded racial stereotypes, contributing to the persistent chasm in this society between black and white.

This chapter was prepared for the conference, "Racial Inequality in a Post-Racial World?" sponsored by the Center on African-American Politics and Society (CAAPS) and the School of International and Public Affairs at Columbia University, held May 21 and 22, 2010, at the Russell Sage Foundation. Support for this research comes from the National Institute of Child

Health and Human Development, the National Science Foundation, and the W. T. Grant Foundation. Direct all correspondence to Devah Pager, Department of Sociology, Princeton University, pager@princeton.edu.

NOTES

1. General Social Survey data show that 54 percent of whites rated blacks at five or higher on a violence scale of one to seven in 1990; ten years later, the percentage had dropped only slightly, to 48 percent of whites (author's calculations).
2. Current Population Survey data show that in the early 1980s, only 14 percent of young white men (aged twenty to thirty-five) with a high school diploma were not working compared with 25 percent of their black counterparts. By 2000 the jobless rate for young high school–educated white men had dropped below 10 percent, but joblessness among black men of the same age and education cohort was around 22 percent. Racial inequality in joblessness had thus increased, and at the height of the economic boom in 2000, employment rates for young noncollege blacks were little better than during the recession of the early 1980s.
3. During the 1990s, official crime rates fell by 30 percent, while incarceration rates rose by 60 percent (Bureau of Justice Statistics 2003, tables 3.106.2004 and 6.28.2004).
4. More recently, rising imprisonment rates have also been influenced by the growing number of individuals sent back to prison for violations of parole. Between 1990 and 1998, the number of new court commitments to prison increased by only 7 percent, while the number of return parole violators increased by 54 percent. Between 1999 and 2009, the percentage of prison admissions from parole violations remained steady at roughly 35 percent (Bureau of Justice Statistics 2010). Of parole violators sent back to prison, roughly half had been convicted of new crimes; the remainder were returned to prison for technical violations of the conditions of parole (Bureau of Justice Statistics 2002).
5. When attention is limited to serious crimes (felonies), results are identical. See also Daniel Romer, Kathleen Jamieson, and Nicole deCouteau (1998), who find a similar overrepresentation of blacks as violent perpetrators (and whites as victims) relative to official crime statistics in Philadelphia; Mary Beth Oliver (1994) does not find this overrepresentation in her analysis of "reality-based" police shows (for example, *Cops*). A recent review by Diana Mutz and Seth Goldman (2010) finds mixed results, depending on the measure of overrepresentation and the context of the study.
6. This survey item comes from the 1991 National Race and Politics Survey. Available at: http://sda.berkeley.edu/cgi-bin/hsda?harcsda+natlrace (ac-

cessed April 3, 2013), and the Federal Bureau of Investigation's Uniform Crime Reports, 1990.

7. When the race of the perpetrator was not identified, 44 percent of respondents falsely recalled seeing a black perpetrator; 19 percent falsely recalled seeing a white perpetrator. In conditions in which the race of the suspect was identified, subjects were better able to recall the suspect's race when he was presented as black (70 percent) than when he was presented as white (64 percent). See also Quillian and Pager (2001).

8. Two classic social psychological studies touch on these issues: Birt Duncan (1976) finds that mildly aggressive behavior is perceived as more threatening when the actor is African American than when the actor that is white; and when H. A. Sagar and J. W. Schofield (1980) presented subjects with verbal accounts of ambiguous interactions, they found that actors depicted as African American were viewed as more threatening than otherwise identical white actors. Sagar and Schofield (1980) find that this effect holds for both black and white subjects, suggesting that the underlying mechanism is most likely a more generalized cultural stereotype rather than personal prejudice or racial animosity.

9. Across a series of analyses controlling for firm size, starting wage, the percentage black in the relevant portion of the metropolitan area, and the business's average distance from black residents in the area, the authors find that employers who overtly criticize the hard skills or interaction skills of black workers are between two and four times as likely to hire a black worker (Moss and Tilly 2001, 151–52).

10. *Criminal record* is defined in this study as having been convicted of a drug felony (possession, intent to distribute) and having served eighteen months in prison. Testers rotated which member of a team presented himself as the former offender so that any unobserved differences across test partners would be effectively controlled.

11. More than 71 million criminal history records were maintained in state criminal history repositories by the end of 2003 (Bureau of Justice Statistics 2006b). As of 2005, thirty-eight states provided public access to their criminal record repositories, and twenty-eight made some or all of this information available online (Legal Action Center 2004).

12. See also Glenn Loury's (2002, 67) discussion of "spoiled identity" and Michelle Alexander's (2010) discussion of the "new Jim Crow." More generally, John Dovidio (2001, 835) argues that because most Americans today "consciously endorse egalitarian values, they will not discriminate directly and openly in ways that can be attributed to racism; however, because of their negative feelings they will discriminate, often unintentionally, when their behavior can be justified on the basis of some factor other than race."

REFERENCES

Alexander, Michelle. 2010. *The New Jim Crow: Mass Incarceration in the Age of Color-blindness*. New York: The New Press.

Anderson, Elijah. 1990. *Streetwise: Race, Class, and Change in an Urban Community*. Chicago: University of Chicago Press.

Blumstein, Alfred. 1993. "Racial Disproportionality Revisited." *University of Colorado Law Review* 64(3): 743–60.

Blumstein, Alfred, and Allen J. Beck. 1999. "Population Growth in U.S. Prisons, 1980–1996." In *Prisons*, edited by Michael Tonry and Joan Petersilia. Chicago: University of Chicago Press.

Bureau of Justice Statistics. 1997. "Lifetime Likelihood of Going to State or Federal Prison." Washington: U.S. Department of Justice.

———. 2002. *Recidivism of Prisoners Released in 1994*. Edited by Patrick Langan and David Levin. Washington: U.S. Department of Justice.

———. 2003. *Sourcebook of Criminal Justice Statistics*. Washington: U.S. Department of Justice.

———. 2006. "Prison and Jail Inmates at Midyear 2005." Washington: U.S. Department of Justice.

———. 2006b. "Survey of State Criminal History Systems." Washington: U.S. Department of Justice, NCJ 210297.

———. 2010. "Prisoners in 2009." Washington: U.S. Department of Justice.

Caulkins, Jonathan P., and Daniel McCaffrey. 1993. *Drug Sellers in the Household Population*. Santa Monica, Calif.: Rand, 1993.

Chiricos, Ted, and Sarah Eschholz. 2002. "The Racial and Ethnic Typification of Crime and the Criminal Typification of Race and Ethnicity in Local Television News." *Journal of Research in Crime and Delinquency* 39(November): 400–20.

Chiricos, Ted, Kelly Welch, and Marc Gertz. 2004. "The Racial Typification of Crime and Support for Punitive Measures." *Criminology* 42(2): 358–90.

Cole, David. 1995. "The Paradox of Race and Crime: A Comment on Randall Kennedy's 'Politics of Distinction.'" *Georgetown Law Journal* 83(Sept.): 2547–71.

Correll, Joshua, Bernd Wittenbrink, and Charles M. Judd. 2002. "The Police Officer's Dilemma: Using Ethnicity to Disambiguate Potentially Threatening Individuals." *Journal of Personality and Social Psychology* 83(6): 1314–29.

Crocker, Jennifer, Brenda Major, and Claude Steele. 1998. "Social Stigma." In *Handbook of Social Psychology*, edited by D. Gilbert, Susan Fiske, and G. Lindzey. Boston, Mass.: McGraw Hill.

Devine, Patricia. 1989. "Stereotypes and Prejudice: Their Automatic and Controlled Components." *Journal of Personality and Social Psychology* 56(1): 5–18.

Devine, Patricia, and Scott Elliot. 1995. "Are Racial Stereotypes Really Fading? The Princeton Trilogy Revisited." *Personality and Social Psychology Bulletin* 21(11): 1139–50.

Dixon, Travis L., and Daniel Linz. 2000. "Overrepresentation and Underrepresentation of African Americans and Latinos as Lawbreakers on Television News." *Journal of Communication* 50(2): 131–54.

Dovidio, John F. 2001. "On the Nature of Contemporary Prejudice: The Third Wave." *Journal of Social Issues* 57(4): 829–49.

Dovidio, John F., and Samuel L. Gaertner. 2000. "Aversive Racism and Selection Decisions." *Psychological Science* 11(4): 315–19.

Duncan, Birt L. 1976. "Differential Social Perception and Attribution of Intergroup Violence: Testing the Lower Limits of Stereotyping of Blacks." *Journal of Personality and Social Psychology* 34(4): 590–98.

Eberhardt, Jennifer L., et al. 2004. "Seeing Black: Race, Crime, and Visual Processing." *Journal of Personality and Social Psychology* 87(6): 876–93.

Entman, Robert M. 1990. "Modern Racism and the Images of Blacks in Local Television News." *Critical Studies in Mass Communication* 7(4): 332–45.

Entman, Robert M., and Andrew Rojecki. 2000. *The Black Image in the White Mind: Media and Race in America*. Chicago: University of Chicago Press.

Freeman, Richard B., and Harry J. Holzer, eds. 1986. *The Black Youth Employment Crisis*. Chicago: University of Chicago Press, for National Bureau of Economic Research.

Garland, Brett E., Cassia Spohn, and Eric J. Wodahl. 2008. "Racial Disproportionality in the American Prison Population: Using the Blumstein Method to Address the Critical Race and Justice Issue of the 21st Century." *Justice Policy Journal* 5(2): 1–42.

Gfroerer, Joseph, and Marc Brodsky. 1992. "The Incidence of Illicit Drug Use in the United States, 1962–1989." *British Journal of Addiction* 87(9): 1345–51.

Gilliam, Franklin D., and Shanto Iyengar. 2000. "Prime Suspects: The Influence of Local Television News on the Viewing Public." *American Journal of Political Science* 44(3): 560–73.

Graham, Sandra, and Brian S. Lowery. 2004. "Priming Unconscious Racial Stereotypes About Adolescent Offenders." *Law and Human Behavior* 28(5): 483–504.

Holzer, Harry J. 1996. *What Employers Want: Job Prospects for Less-Educated Workers*. New York: Russell Sage Foundation.

Holzer, Harry J., Paul Offner, and Elaine Sorensen. 2005. "What Explains the Continuing Decline in Labor Force Activity among Young Black Men?" *Labor History* 46(1): 37–55.

Kirschenman, Joleen, and Katherine Neckerman. 1991. "We'd love to hire them, but . . . : The Meaning of Race for Employers." In *The Urban Underclass*, edited by Christopher Jencks and P. E. Peterson. Washington, D.C.: Brookings Institution.

LaPiere, Richard T. 1934. "Attitudes vs. Actions." *Social Forces* 13(2): 230–37.

Legal Action Center. 2004. *After Prison: Roadblocks to Reentry*. A Report on State

Legal Barriers Facing People with Criminal Records. Edited by Paul Samuels and Debbie Mukamal. New York: Legal Action Center.

Loury, Glenn C. 2002. *The Anatomy of Racial Inequality*. Cambridge, Mass.: Harvard University Press.

Moss, Philip, and Chris Tilly, 2001. *Stories Employers Tell: Race, Skill, and Hiring in America*. New York: Russell Sage Foundation.

Murnane, Richard, John Willett, and Frank Levy. 1995. "The Growing Importance of Cognitive Skills in Wage Determination." *Review of Economics and Statistics* 77(2): 251–66.

Mutz, Diana, and Seth Goldman. 2010. "Mass Media." In *The Sage Handbook of Prejudice, Stereotyping, and Discrimination*, edited by John Dovidio et al. London: Sage Publications.

Oliver, Mary Beth. 1994. "Portrayals of Crime, Race, and Aggression in 'Reality-Based' Police Shows: A Content Analysis." *Journal of Broadcasting and Electronic Media* 38(2): 179–92.

Pager, Devah. 2003. "The Mark of a Criminal Record." *American Journal of Sociology* 108(5): 937–75.

———. 2007. *Marked: Race, Crime, and Finding Work in an Era of Mass Incarceration*. Chicago: University of Chicago Press.

Pager, Devah, and Diana Karafin. 2009. "Bayesian Bigot?: Statistical Discrimination, Stereotypes, and Employer Decision-Making." *Annals of the American Academy of Political and Social Sciences* 621(January): 70–93.

Pager, Devah, and Lincoln Quillian. 2005. "Walking the Talk: What Employers Say Versus What They Do." *American Sociological Review* 70(3): 355–80.

Pager, Devah, Bruce Western, and Naomi Sugie. 2009. "Sequencing Disadvantage: Barriers to Employment Facing Young Black and White Men with Criminal Records." *Annals of the American Academy of Political and Social Science* 623(May): 195–213.

Payne, B. Keith. 2001. "Prejudice and Perception: The Role of Automatic and Controlled Processes in Misperceiving a Weapon." *Journal of Personality and Social Psychology* 81(2): 181–92.

Pettit, Becky, and Bruce Western. 2004. "Mass Imprisonment and the Life Course: Race and Class Inequality in U.S. Incarceration." *American Sociological Review* 69(2): 151–69.

Pew Research Center for the People and the Press. 2011. "Internet Gains on Television as Public's Main News Source." Available at: http://www.people-press.org/2011/01/04/internet-gains-on-television-as-publics-main-news-source/ (accessed April 3, 2013).

Quillian, Lincoln, and Devah Pager. 2001. "Black Neighbors, Higher Crime? The Role of Racial Stereotypes in Evaluations of Neighborhood Crime." *American Journal of Sociology* 107(3): 717–67.

Royster, Deidre A. 2003. *Race and the Invisible Hand: How White Networks Exclude Black Men from Blue-Collar Jobs.* Berkeley: University of California Press.

Romer, Daniel, Kathleen H. Jamieson, and Nicole J. deCouteau. 1998. "The Treatment of Persons of Color in Local Television News: Ethnic Blame Discourse or Realistic Group Conflict?" *Communication Research* 25(3): 286–305.

Sagar, H. Andrew, and Janet W. Schofield. 1980. "Racial and Behavioral Cues in Black and White Children's Perceptions of Ambiguously Aggressive Acts." *Journal of Personality and Social Psychology* 39(4): 590–98.

Sampson, Robert J., and Janet L. Lauritsen. 1997. "Racial and Ethnic Disparities in Crime and Criminal Justice in the United States." *Crime and Justice: Ethnicity, Crime, and Immigration; Comparative and Cross-National Perspectives* 21: 311–74.

Sniderman, Paul M., and Thomas Piazza. 1993. *The Scar of Race.* Cambridge, Mass.: Belknap Press of Harvard University Press.

Waldinger, Roger. 1999. *Still the Promised City? African-Americans and New Immigrants in Postindustrial New York.* Cambridge, Mass.: Harvard University Press.

Waldinger, Roger, and Michael Lichter. 2003. *How the Other Half Works: Immigration and the Social Organization of Labor.* Berkeley: University of California Press.

Western, Bruce. 2006. *Punishment and Inequality in America.* New York: Russell Sage Foundation.

Western, Bruce, and Katherine Beckett. 1999. "How Unregulated Is the U.S. Labor Market? The Penal System as a Labor Market Institution." *American Journal of Sociology* 104(4): 1030–60.

Wilson, William Julius. 1978. *The Declining Significance of Race: Blacks and Changing American Institutions.* Chicago: University of Chicago Press.

———. 1996. *When Work Disappears: The World of the New Urban Poor.* New York: Vintage Books.

Word, Carl O., Mark P. Zanna, and Joel Cooper. 1974. "The Nonverbal Mediation of Self-Fulfilling Prophecies in Interracial Interactions." *Journal of Experimental Social Psychology* 10(2): 109–20.

PART IV | Economics and Markets

Chapter 9 | The Ghetto Tax: Auto Insurance, Postal Code Profiling, and the Hidden History of Wealth Transfer

Devin Fergus

> ZIP-code profiling in insurance has been one of the most tenacious forms of discrimination. For decades good drivers in Black residential neighborhoods have been charged more. Basic economic fairness should mean that my driving record, not my ZIP code, would shape [my] premium. This history of economic discrimination must end, and the new regulation [Proposition 103] is a long-overdue step in that direction.
>
> —James Lawson, SCLC of Greater Los Angeles

IN THE RECENT health care debate, President Obama and his conservative critics such as George Will found rare common ground by appropriating auto insurance as the model for health insurance, whose reform the president called "key to turning around the economy" (Associated Press 2009). For African American and Latino consumers, however, holding up auto insurance as a triumph is a deeply troubling rewriting of history, one that buries from public memory the hidden consumer tax inner-city and inner-ring city motorists—disproportionately female, African American, and Latino—have paid since the 1970s, when auto insurance became mandatory in most states. This hidden consumer tax totals as much as $20,000 over the driving span of a typical urban motorist.[1]

A part of a larger "ghetto tax," auto insurance rates are primarily based on one's postal or ZIP code rather than one's driving record.[2] In California, for example, millions of urban motorists pay higher premiums to insurers than nonurban motorists with the same driving record. Collecting reve-

277

nues from urban drivers, auto insurers such as California's largest, State
Farm, effectively passed these savings on, in the form of lower rates, to
suburban and exurban drivers. This form of redlining (a term appearing
regularly in the trade publication *National Underwriter*) costs urban drivers
millions each year.

Although insurers insisted their postal code calculus was color blind,
no one denied the disparate racial impact of these policies. As a result,
California motorists living in mostly black or Latino neighborhoods are
typically charged substantially more for the same amount of auto insurance provided to drivers from white communities. Car insurance in black
neighborhoods, for example, costs 37.5 to 83.5 percent more than in communities populated primarily by non-Latino whites. In real dollars, the
biggest auto insurers charge a good driver an additional $537 to $974 per
year for moving from a mostly white to a black neighborhood. Similar
subsidies exist in the more populous Northeast, where drivers with inner-
city ZIP codes typically pay as much as $400 more each year than similar
suburban drivers. As insurers profiled drivers by postal code, in what I
term PC profiling, they effectively contributed to the redistribution of
wealth in California and nationally. In California alone, in 2006, urban motorists living in middle- and lower-income communities paid the state's
largest auto insurer, State Farm, approximately $204 million more in auto
premiums—a subsidy then passed on in the form of reduced insurance
rates to individual motorists living in wealthier neighborhoods with equal
or worse driving records (Consumers Union 2006b). This chapter examines
how auto insurance serves as one example of the hidden, taxes-in-kind
that have driven racial wealth disparity in recent decades.[3] Required by
law but provided exclusively by the private sector on a for-profit basis,
auto insurance is often a forgotten piece in the financial puzzle of the
wealth gap.

My analysis of Proposition 103, an effort in California to control rising
insurance costs, interweaves key themes introduced in this volume, including the limits of individualism, postracialism, and the ongoing explanatory power of racial discrimination as a causal factor in the persistence of the racial wealth gap. As is shown in chapter 5 in this volume by
Dorian Warren, who excavates the chronic underemployment and unemployment experienced by Latinos and African Americans, labor markets
serve as an important driver of racial inequality. By focusing on expenses
or consumption, rather than employment and income, my chapter, similar
to Oyo Kwate's, also in this volume (chap. 11), balances the political economic ledger. It does this by providing an inside view of the color-blind
mechanisms that perpetuate discrimination in auto insurance pricing, un-
covering how even race-neutral policies in consumer pricing extracts financial resources from communities of color and thus exacerbates the ra-

cial wealth gap. This stands in distinction from employment, in which the primary discernable pattern, according to Warren, is racial exclusion that persists in "limiting employment opportunities for African Americans and Latinos regardless of education." On the consumption side of the ledger, captive racial consumer markets are often about inclusion, though in high-cost terms—a practice often termed "reverse redlining"—rather than exclusion.

Several of the key themes emerging in this chapter—most notably, interest convergence of suburbia and central cities along with hidden racial tensions cloaked by explicit money and policy arguments—builds on the new suburban history. As a subfield of urban history, the new suburban literature has sought to complicate earlier narratives, which tended to highlight the crushing class conformity, racial homogeneity, and intractable conflicts with central cities. In particular, recent scholarship has pointed toward the dialogue that often existed inside metropolitan America, while at the same time capturing the racial, ethnic, and class complexity often overlooked by previous scholars. Scholars have also sought to bring the state back in—through explorations of the role money and policy play in exacerbating racial and class inequality. To quote Kevin Kruse and Thomas Sugrue, the editors of *New Suburban History*, "In postwar metropolitan America, where you lived has determined your access to goods and services and how much they cost in the form of taxes" (Kruse and Sugrue 2006, 6).

My work expands this construction of formal taxation, as articulated by Kruse and Sugrue, limning the mechanisms that perpetuate and protect the network of informal shadowy subsidies, described herein as a ghetto tax, that central-city residents pay for goods and services, which are often used to offset the costs of wealthier and less deserving residents outside the inner city. Although they have been effective at putting the state back in, historians have still been slow, relative to other social scientists, in considering how race, deregulation, and consumer financial issues beyond housing entwine in a post–civil rights period to have an outsized impact on the lived experience of African Americans since the 1970s. With deregulation as its backdrop, this chapter exposes the hidden and subtle ways urban America and inner-ring suburbia pay more and how color-blind mechanisms (for example, the use of postal codes in auto insurance pricing) serve to expose the stickiness of race.[4]

THE POLITICS OF POSTAL CODE PROFILING

On the eve of the post–Cold War era in 1988, America found itself embroiled in a crisis of national identity later known as the culture wars. That year Colorado, Arizona, and Florida placed on their ballots immigration and English-only initiatives. In Michigan and Arkansas, abortion dominated election conversation. For Maryland, the issue was gun control, the National Rifle Association, and a ban on cheap hand guns; in South Dakota, voters debated whether to accept gambling. Yet of all the hot-button social issues that have dominated domestic discourse since the late 1980s, none was more costly and hotly contested, according to the national television news networks, than the so-called insurance wars (*ABC Evening News* 1988). With drivers required by law to purchase auto insurance, in almost no other realm did government touch so many pocketbooks (*ABC Evening News* 1988).

With the world's eighth largest economy and a population 50 percent greater than any other state, California was where the future happened first. That was certainly the case with Proposition 103, a package of auto insurance reform initiatives passed in 1988 with the popular intention of pegging pricing to a driver's record while disentangling pricing from factors unrelated to driving, such as ZIP code and marital status.[5] Civil rights and consumer groups, national media, and policy makers anticipated that Proposition 103 would provide a model for the nation. Believing as California went so would go the nation, more money poured into the state to defeat Proposition 103 than either of the presidential candidates, George Dukakis or George H. W. Bush, spent on their campaigns for the California vote that year. Yet despite 103's passage, for the next generation the insurer status quo prevailed, in California and throughout the country, and with it the continued redistribution of wealth. But Proposition 103, what the *Wall Street Journal* once anticipated to be "the next populist revolt," did not produce the results expected.[6]

Since 1986, California motorists had watched their insurance rates go up 58 percent, giving them the third highest rates in the country by 1988. In an effort to stave off escalating insurance costs, consumer activists launched Proposition 103.[7] Proposition 103's main provisions stipulated, among others, a rate cut for policyholders, an independent regulatory agency to oversee the industry, and an elected insurance commissioner. But no feature of Proposition 103 proved more popular among consumers or more troubling to insurers than its stipulation that insurance be based primarily on one's driving record, not territorial factors.

Insurers contended that Proposition 103 was seeking to remove the free market from pricing. As insurers' logic went, the ballot's stated initiative— "to encourage competition in the insurance marketplace"—was based on the false premise that high rates were the consequence of an insurance monopoly that ignored related costs like hospital expenses, auto repairs, and litigation. More generally, insurers argued that they were a private business, which needed to safeguard industrial trade secrets like how rates were calculated. The architects of Proposition 103, in insurers' view, signaled yet another example of socialism and the desire to have the state further encroach on the sanctity of the free enterprise system, empowering government to set rates, not just review them (National Underwriter 1992–93). "What [103 proponents] actually want is a state takeover of the insurance business." On the particularly controversial issue of postal code profiling, insurers argued there was "wide agreement among actuaries that territory should have a greater weight than is allowed by Proposition 103."[8] Arguing that it had the objectivity of science on its side, the industry contended its statistics-driven analysis stood in stark contrast to the rights-based appeals of 103's civil rights and consumer advocates, for whom emotions ostensibly outweighed evidence. Backers of 103 believed, as the industry adviser and Berkeley law professor Stephen Sugarman explained, "It simply isn't right for individual motorists to be ruled by the impersonal tyranny of actuarial science."[9]

While Proposition 103 would not have abolished territorial rating, requiring only that insurers put greater weight on merit-based driving, insurers interpreted any concession to diminishing postal codes in formulating rates as a difference without much distinction.[10] An insurance industry spokesperson charged that Prop 103, by overturning ZIP code profiling, was bent on "seeking to redistribute wealth" in California and, potentially, throughout the nation.[11] The insurance industry, envisioning California as the firewall state in which to stop any potential national consumer backlash, outspent 103 proponents $65 million to $2.3 million.[12]

In the campaign's final stretch, insurance companies waged a fierce financial battle. Up to 70 percent of its October campaign budget went to negative advertising. These ads targeted Proposition 103, claiming its passage would lead to wealth redistribution to Los Angeles–area drivers by unhinging auto insurance from postal codes. Insurers put much of their money behind a series of spots that attacked 103 with the tag line, "Why should we pay more so Los Angeles can pay less?"[13] The ad contended that a rate hike for a majority of California's drivers would result if Proposition 103 succeeded in "eliminating rate-setting based on claims within ZIP codes." Such television attack ads ran statewide except in the heavily minority media markets of San Diego and Los Angeles.[14]

Nationally, what made the 1988 insurance wars the most contested issue in California and the costliest nonpresidential campaign in U.S. history was not merely the fear of uncoupling postal codes from rate pricing; it was also the fear of the ripple effect should the proposition pass. Californians had watched their rates jump in the 1980s, and other states experienced similar hikes at the hands of insurers, making the rate increases an issue in more than a dozen states at the time, which offered either ballot initiatives or legislative reform. As it spread, the most popular provision of 103 among consumers was reform of postal code profiling. Territorial rating as a political issue would, in the aftermath of the election, take hold in Ohio, Florida, Maryland, and Pennsylvania; drivers in Cleveland, Miami, Baltimore, and Philadelphia paid more than their statewide averages.[15] New York was also fairly typical. There, 79 percent of drivers living in the Bronx's urban core were assigned to the high-cost risk pool versus 41 percent of the rest of Bronx motorists and 16 percent of the rest of the state.[16]

It was anticipated that if the reform measure passed in California, similar if not more aggressive rate-cut initiatives might sweep through other states. Fearing a national ripple effect, in which insurers risked losing billions of dollars, the $60 million or so insurers spent in its California campaign, from January through the November 8 election, was considered a smart, preemptive investment. Given the national implications, nearly three times as much was spent on trying to defeat 103 than on any single campaign in California history, and the biggest financier came from outside the state, the Illinois-based State Farm, which gave $3.6 million.[17] Despite unprecedented contributions (in both financial and in-kind spending as insurance workers allocated more than $2 million in man hours) and eroding popular support for Prop 103, insurers failed to completely close the gap, remaining behind in three major statewide polls.

On November 8, voters narrowly approved Proposition 103, by 51.1 to 48.9 percent. Despite the razor-thin margin, the election was not as close as the final numbers might suggest. The electorate clearly favored 103 above the other insurance options on the ballot that year. No other initiative received more than 42 percent of the yes vote. For example, the major insurer no-fault initiative, Proposition 104—requiring motorists to collect from their own insurance companies, regardless of who caused an accident, limiting contingency fees for plaintiffs' attorneys, and preventing more-stringent state regulation of the insurance industry—was rejected 3-to-1 by voters.[18] In this way, Proposition 103's victory signaled perhaps an unparalleled historic moment in modern proposition movements: a progressive proposition cause that was backed by civil rights, consumer, and immigrant groups and met with democratic approval.

So who voted yes for Proposition 103? And where was Proposition 103 most and least popular? Los Angeles County voters provided Proposition 103 the margin of victory with a 600,000 vote margin. The proposition faired worse outside the Bay area in Northern California.[19] As expected, urban and inner-city motorists in Los Angeles, San Diego, and San Francisco intensely supported Proposition 103. But the crucial swing vote tended to be a suburban couple, often married with children, and white.

They backed the measure believing doing so would result in having their own insurance rates cut. The promise of Proposition 103 stemmed from its unifying consumer appeal. The proposition galvanized the average California consumer against moneyed interests in ways that previous initiatives, which often pitted whites and suburbia against racial minorities and the inner city, had failed to do. Nor did those arrayed against it fit neatly into preconceived patterns. Dianne Feinstein offers one example. Feinstein, the former mayor of arguably America's most liberal city, San Francisco, not only backed the insurance bill of Proposition 104; she cowrote it. Generally regarded as more anti-consumer than most ballot choices, Proposition 104 capped noneconomic damages and restricted future regulations on the industry.[20]

Nationally, the competing reactions of Wall Street and Main Street captured the clash of interests distinguishing finance capitalists from consumers. On Wall Street, markets reacted with a stock sell-off of publicly traded auto insurance companies as insurers saw their prices drop. Meanwhile, in the afterglow of the 103 victory, consumer groups from thirty states contacted proposition architect Harvey Rosenfield's office to inquire how to launch a voter revolt of their own.[21] As the *Wall Street Journal* editors braced its readers, Proposition 103 augured America's next great populist revolt on the coattails of auto insurance.[22] But insurers had more fight left than either the *Wall Street Journal* or many Proposition 103 supporters anticipated.

Within twenty-four hours, the auto insurance industry struck back. The very next day, Wednesday, November 9, the nation's sixth and ninth largest insurers, Travelers and the Fireman Fund, respectively, announced they would stop writing insurance in California and pull out of the state altogether.[23] Meanwhile others, including Safeco, GEICO, and the market leader State Farm, stopped writing good-driver policies for new customers; instead, regardless of record, they shunted them off to subprime subsidiaries, where new policyholders were charged rates as high as 60 percent more than premiums paid by existing holders.[24] By November 15, eighteen of the fifty-seven largest insurers had rejected all new applications or stopped accepting auto insurance at all.[25]

Insurer stonewalling contributed to rising apathy and disaffection, especially among voters of color. According to one study of the next major election season after 103's passage, the June 1990 primaries, three out of four eligible adults did not vote. Usually reliable older voters signaled the loss of confidence.[26] "I just got fed up," said one retired man, sixty-eight, from San Pablo. "We passed Proposition 103, and then they're fooling around with it" (Robert Reinhold, "Apathy and Disaffection on the Rise among California Voters." *New York Times,* June 12, 1990, p. A14). Given that seniors, the most reliable voting segment, increasingly found themselves disaffected from the political process, the stalled implementation of 103 could only help further depress turnout among minorities (Asian, African American, and Latino), who represented 30 percent of the state's adult population but, on average, only 15 percent of voters. Conversely, white voters over the age of sixty typically made up 30 percent of actual voters while representing only 21 percent of voting-age Californians.[27] If noncompliance characterized insurer response to Proposition 103 before 1995, the industry was only emboldened by the upset election victory and tenure of Charles Quackenbush, a Silicon Valley Republican assemblyman, as state commissioner of insurance.

THE STICKINESS OF RACE IN POSTAL CODE PROFILING

Insurers consistently claimed the intent of their policies was color blind, but the stickiness of race remained an inescapable if submerged theme. By *stickiness of race*, I mean that though language, culture, and citizenship, as well conceptions of the undeservedness, often function as discrete categories of discrimination in their own right, they may also serve as proxies for race (Espinoza and Harris 1997). The intertwining of race with these proxies appeared pivotal in 1994, when insurers seized the political-cultural moment to help elect Charles Quackenbush as the state's first-ever elected insurance commissioner, tipping the scales away from the favored Latino candidate, East Los Angeles Democrat state senator Art Torres, to the long-shot Quackenbush, who would ultimately be captured by the very businesses he was charged with regulating.

How much Torres's late-campaign collapse is tied to that year's highly controversial ballot battle, Proposition 187, may never be fully known. Still, it would be naïve not to take Prop 187 into consideration. Prop 187 made it illegal, among other things, to offer undocumented immigrants such public services as education and nonemergency medical care. Whether intended or not, many read a racialized subtext encoded in this initiative, seeing the proposition as intended to rescue white Californians not so much from the undocumented immigrant, which this proposition officially targeted, as from the sense of siege many whites felt amid a rising presence generally of immigrants of color, especially Latinos—be they legal or not. That the highest-profile Latino running for office in 1994, a time of heightened racial tensions between non-Latinos and Latinos in California, was bidding to become the state's next insurance regulator did not help Torres's bid for commissioner. Equally important was an October infusion of insurer financing, totaling nearly 75 percent of all money spent.

Insurance dollars underwrote a series of anti-Torres television ads, which branded the Latino from Los Angeles as too sympathetic to criminals and the "king of special interests."[28] Such attack ads paid huge dividends, according to Field Poll reports. Before the ads, Torres had maintained a double-digit advantage since the primaries; after their airing, he fell permanently behind Quackenbush (Lipsitz 1998, 47–55).

In addition, as a microcosm of Democratic losses nationally, Torres was swept up in the on-rushing Republican electoral tide, which in 1994 lifted the GOP to newfound control at the federal and state levels. In Congress, Republicans ruled for the first time since 1952. In the states, Republicans possessed a majority of governorships for the first time in three decades while taking control of a majority of state legislatures for the first time in fifty years. The national Republican tide helped to end California Democrats' twenty-five-year majority in the state assembly. Business-friendly GOP candidates running for statewide office rode this electoral tidal wave as well—despite the fact that registered Democrats outnumbered Republicans 2-to-1 in California (Thomas 2006). All this boded well for the insurance companies.[29] Not surprisingly, the industry exhibited less will to abolish postal code profiling under Chuck Quackenbush, whose victory was, in the editorializing words of the *Sacramento Bee*, "bankrolled" by insurers.[30]

Quackenbush took office in January 1995, and his first thirty days confirmed civil rights and consumer advocates' worst fears. He enacted a series of new emergency regulatory measures that gave insurance companies even greater authority to base rates on criteria primarily unrelated to driving safety records; rolled back consumer-friendly settlement arrangements; and deployed the stalling tactic of calling for further hearings on auto insurance rather than implementing the exhaustive report of his predecessor, John Garamendi, whose study of 10 million policyholders was generally regarded as the most thorough of its kind in California's history.[31]

From this point, the new regulatory commissioner spent much of his remaining tenure shifting premium burdens and costs away from corporations onto consumers. While the growth in overall rates, adjusted for inflation, slowed down from 1994 to 1996, rates increased twice in three years during the mid-1990s, Quackenbush's time in office. But nothing remained more guarded under a Quackenbush regulatory regime than ZIP code–based profiling. California's new insurance head actually tightened the tethering of rates to where one lived rather than how one drove. He did so by allowing geographical factors, such as an area's average wage and income level, to be used in computing rates.

In response, three of California's largest cities successfully filed suit against redlining policies in March 1998. Los Angeles, Oakland, and San Francisco filed suit "to force Quackenbush to put an end to that subterfuge," which, in the litigants' words, freed insurers to actually deepen its "regulations" (Consumers Union 1998; Spanish Speaking Citizens' Foundation, Inc. et al. v. Quackenbush 1998). These cities represented more than 8 million Californians. City attorneys were joined by Consumers Union, Southern Christian Leadership Conference, and the Spanish Speaking Citizens Foundation.[32] Latino and black civil rights organizations saw ZIP-code redlining in the historic vein of centuries-long discriminatory practices and charged Quackenbush with colluding with insurers in perpetuating economic hardships and disfranchisement of minorities. "California needs leadership from the insurance commissioner in ending unfair ZIP code rating," proclaimed Genethia Hayes, the executive director of the SCLC of Greater Los Angeles.[33] The veteran civil rights activist James Lawson would add years later, when the case was still tied up in courts because of insurance interposition, "This history of economic discrimination must end" (U.S. Newswire 2006).

At the heart of the lawsuit against Quackenbush was the charge that the commissioner continued the discriminatory practice known as redlining by allowing insurers to give too much weight to ZIP codes. So how did such "voodoo mathematics" ("Auto Insurance: 3 Cities Sue Over ZIPCode Redlining." Los Angeles Sentinel, April 15, 199, p. A1), as plaintiffs dismissed it, work? The 103 law required that rates be based primarily on three mandatory factors within a motorist's control, in decreasing order of importance: driving safety record, annual mileage driven, and years of driving experience. Insurers were then permitted to use up to sixteen optional factors if they "had a substantial relationship to risk of loss" (Cal. Ins. Code sec. 1861.02). These optional factors could not have a greater impact on rates than the mandatory factors approved by the electorate.

Under Quackenbush, however, regulations allowed insurers to take an average of all optional factors, rather than awarding individual numerical weights for each optional factor. In this way, the public and consumer advocacy groups never could determine how much weight was given to neighborhood factors. By using this averaging method, insurers were able to give a high weight to nondriving factors such as ZIP code, gender, marital status, and school grades, thereby masking the actual value these specific factors were assessed. Exactly how much numerical weight was given to ZIP code was unknown, because it, along with gender, then combined with other factors given extremely low weights. Thus when averaged the mean weight for all optional factors could be less than any of the three mandatory factors of driving record, miles driven, and experience—allowing ZIP codes to still have an inordinate impact. Such statistical sleight of hand by the industry under Quackenbush kept the public in the dark, as consumers never quite knew how much postal codes factored into a company's decision.

It was estimated that Quackenbush's ZIP-code rate calculus exacted a financial cost well into the millions for urban and working-class motorists—among a segment of Californians assumed to be least likely to possess either savings or investments. For example, a twenty-two-year-old male driver in South Los Angeles (formerly South Central) paid quadruple ($7,844) what a San Luis Obispo citizen did ($1,706) over his lifetime, despite identical driving profiles. Oakland experienced a similar disparity, between upscale Montclair ($3,398) and Fruitvale ($4,417). Quackenbush's unwillingness to challenge postal code profiling, which allowed these disparities to exist in contravention to 103, compelled city attorneys from these respective cities to act. As James Hahn, Los Angeles's city attorney who turned mayoral hopeful, said, "What Quackenbush has done is undermine the will of the people, who overwhelmingly voted to enact Proposition 103, by letting insurance companies hide the ball on redlining practices."[34]

Allowing the industry's silence on trade secrets to prevent full disclosure signaled another significant way in which Quackenbush protected auto insurance redlining. At issue were voter will and the public's right to know versus the corporate right to privacy. These matters had a direct bearing on postal code profiling. Data was considered essential to track redlining, for without it, it was unclear how much race, gender, and geography inequitably affected rates. One intent of Proposition 103 was to remedy insurer secrecy: it required insurance commissioners to collect insurance pricing and other underwriting information and to then make this data available to the public, thereby bringing greater transparency to redlining and its weight in rate-setting practices. But Quackenbush's lack of vigor in enforcing the full-disclosure provision allowed insurers to continue PC profiling.[35]

CAMPAIGN FINANCE REFORM, 1998–2000

The reality was that PC profiling was inseparable from campaign finance. With Quackenbush up for reelection in 1998, insurance dollars drowned out his opponent with a flood of television and radio campaign ads. At least a dozen insurance companies with direct interest in his office's decisions donated to Quackenbush's coffers. Outspent by approximately 4-to-1 and down by double digits, Diane Martinez, a three-term Democratic assemblywoman, had no plans to run any television ads to catch her opponent in the final days, as Quackenbush had done to beat Torres four years earlier.[36] Heavily indebted to insurers, Quackenbush began his second term by repaying his benefactors, making it easier for insurers to drop drivers for minor violations. In a state where insurance is mandated by law, this new "driver cancellation" policy had the net effect of rerouting hundreds of thousands of motorists into the highly lucrative subprime (predatory or high-risk) auto insurance market.

By the time Quackenbush resigned from office in 2000 to avoid impeachment, he faced a surfeit of scandals charging him with waiving up to $3 billion of industry fines in exchange for campaign contributions.[37] Even the insurance industry had accused him of extortion. "He's the most egregious example we have currently with respect to elected officials raising campaign contributions from those they regulate or have an impact on with respect to legislation," Tony Miller, California's former secretary of state turned campaign reform advocate, told reporters.[38]

The problems transcended Quackenbush. They were systemic. Moneyed interests transformed Quackenbush, a Notre Dame graduate, Air Force veteran, and Silicon Valley entrepreneur into a corporate vassal whom campaign finance reformers named Exhibit A. His detractors claimed that Quackenbush provided the best public case of money's influence shaping policies and tainting politicians. Yet before taking office as commissioner, Quackenbush spent a decade as a state elected official without a hint of financial scandal. As a primary candidate, Quackenbush was one of the few Republicans running on a platform of rejecting industry money, telling the *San Diego Union Tribune* in 1994 that taking company money is "like handing a loaded gun to the Democratic strategists. . . . They'll just accuse you of being bought and paid for by the industry."[39] That Quackenbush—a likable moderate Republican regulator, once thought to have a bright political future—morphed into California's "most egregious example" of an elected official taking campaign contributions from an industry he is supposed to be regulating illustrates how special interest money in the political system distorts social policy and democratic will. Even the free market–friendly *The Economist* summed up the relationship as too corrupted by conflicts of interest: "Surely it is a little absurd to allow insurance commissioners to raise money from" those they regulate (*The Economist* 2000, 28).

A state audit in the fall of 2000 seemed to corroborate this view. To summarize the fifty-seven-page report, lax enforcement under Quackenbush was the result not of independent policy considerations but of political and personal financial payoffs. Under Quackenbush, obfuscation replaced transparency—preventing "policyholders and consumers from obtaining critical information about the business practices of insurers," concluded the auditors (Howard 2000). By refusing to enforce full disclosure, Quackenbush enabled insurers to continue profiling motorists based on ZIP code. Despite an eighteen-month investigation of and guilty plea by his deputy commissioner, federal, state, and county prosecutors believed they lacked sufficient evidence to indict Quackenbush.[40] Voters themselves shouldered blame. Preoccupied in the 1990s with more hot-button cultural issues like Propositions 187 (immigration) and 209 (affirmative action), abortion, and flag burning, voters paid little attention to the erosion of oversight, though the insurance issue directly affected more than 20 million Californians—a far greater number than immigrants, African Americans, pregnant women, or those burning flags in the state.

REDISTRIBUTION AND RISKY BUSINESS

Throughout the 1990s, the insurance industry resisted the implementation of Proposition 103. A frequent claim advanced by insurers was that attempts to end PC profiling was little more than a socially engineered effort to redistribute wealth to the least deserving driver. Under Proposition 103, the state's leading insurance lobby wing, by claiming that the majority would subsidize the minority of bad and uninsured drivers, allowed it to seize rhetorically on contemporary cultural critiques about rewarding society's undeserved. The fact remained, however, that insurers' bottom line hinged on defending values that conservatives, moderates, and a growing number of liberals at the time found most objectionable: namely, the privileging of social factors and identity politics over individual merit.

First, from the view of the state's leading insurance trade group, the Association of California Insurance Companies, rescinding the territorial rating system was tantamount to wealth redistribution. "Examples abound as to what happens when government arbitrarily tries to control the price of products and services," said Jim Snyder, the president of the Personal Insurance Federation of California (PIFC), a trade association whose members included California's largest insurers. Government intervention would result in a "mass subsidization" program, according to three of the nation's largest insurance trade associations. From insurance consortiums like PIF, the Association of California Insurance Companies, and the National Association of Independent Insurers, merit-based initiatives like Proposition 103 "would result in discriminatory pricing by, in effect, forcing subsidies for high-risk drivers at the expense of others" (National Underwriter 1995, 7).

Second, the high-risk driver was the least deserving, insurers contended. Under any alteration, the drivers ostensibly behaving badly—including the motorists without insurance, with a higher incidence of traffic accidents and citations, sometimes with subprime credit, or with a personal history of making bad life choices that often resulted in her or his living in a poor neighborhood—stood to be the primary beneficiaries of any insurance reform.

Third, insurers were concerned with more than redistributing wealth and rewarding risky behavior. As they saw it, good drivers stood to be victimized by such social engineering. Adhering to Proposition 103 would result in "a giant subsidy program that would force good drivers . . . to pay more for their auto insurance so bad drivers could pay less," wrote Barry Carmody, the president of the Association of California Insurance Companies, in a 1995 op-ed column.[41] Appropriating the contemporary language of victimization, Carmody expanded his analysis in a second op-ed one month later, saying that 103 punished merit to reward the unworthy. Citing a study of one of California's largest insurers, Carmody claimed that insurers stonewalled Prop 103 not to protect their profit margin but to protect the deserving driver: "66 percent of California's bad drivers would get rate decreases while 53 percent of the good drivers would see their premiums increase."[42] If rates were too high, Carmody concluded, it was because so many Californians remained uninsured, as high as 14 percent by some estimates. The "uninsured motorist problem in the state . . . penalizes people who buy insurance with an additional financial burden." For Carmody, "It all boils down to fairness . . . pure and simple."[43]

Proposition 103, according to industry insiders, sacrificed fairness at the liberal altar of equality. Insurers impressed on suburban and exurban motorists that they were the victims of a liberal regulatory elite that rewarded the bad behavior of mostly urban drivers. Proposition 103, then, fit part of a larger pattern, in which the worthy majority of society ended up paying the social costs for the personal failures of society's most undeserving—in this example, uninsured motorists and insured motorists unable or unwilling to move out of impoverished neighborhoods.

INDIVIDUAL MERIT VERSUS IDENTITY POLITICS

In fact, throughout the history of PC profiling, auto insurers had highlighted the importance of social factors and identity over individual motorists' merit. This was the case in 1962, when George Joseph, the founder of Mercury General Corporation, helped pioneer the use of neighborhoods and ZIP codes in calculating rates. By the 1970s, privileging social forces had become a state and national mainstay in auto insurance pricing (Wallace 2006). Environmental factors outside an individual driver's control—traffic congestion, local litigation rates, auto thefts, accidents, higher medical and car repair costs, and the like—explained rate differentials among neighborhoods. But for the insured with clean driving records, such as Brendan Mulholland, a forty-year-old Oakland geologist debating whether to move two blocks away, where his new ZIP code would save him 20 percent every year on his auto insurance, the issue was how territorial rating resulted in the unintended consequence of undermining the ethos of individual merit: "The whole premise of basing auto insurance premiums on locality as opposed to individuality is wrong."[44] For insurers, however, arguments about individual merit were, in the view of one industry consultant and expert, "strange" (Wallace 2006).

Not that the insurance industry did not endorse a version of merit. Rather, insurers and their lobbyists offered consumers a fundamentally competing notion of merit; one where "merit" considered forces beyond a motorist's control. "The problem," as Carmody explained, was that consumers devalued social forces. "For instance, should rural drivers pay more for insurance even though they cost far less to insure than drivers who live in congested cities where accidents and lawsuits are far more frequent? . . . And should older people pay more so young people can pay less?" (Barry Carmody, "Redistributing Car Insurance Rates." *Sacramento Bee*, April 19, 1995). The identity politics of postal codes more than individualism ultimately informed the industry's governing philosophy. Such typecasting resulted in the ghettoizing of policyholders. The ghettoization of policyholders was most likely an unintended consequence of insurers' desire for what the industry considered a less expensive, more cost-effective system of determining insurance policy rates, which would yield higher profits and larger dividends for their stockholders.

Ghettoizing motorists in this way conformed to a wider contemporary trend, increasingly taking hold after the mid-1970s, to openly appeal to and profit from cultural segmentation among American consumers. This trend was characterized by a move away from mass marketing, and a two-decade color-blind approach, to isolating markets. Key, according to the social and economic historian Lizabeth Cohen (2003), was psychographics—a new technique introduced by marketers and social scientists who, building on earlier demographic variables of age, education, race, and gender, began applying newer profiles around the values, lifestyles, behavioral traits, and attitudes of targeted consumers. Psychographics worked from the assumption that it was sound science and business to charge consumers more because of the risks they posed and choices they made, such as "choosing" to live in unsafe neighborhoods (read *lifestyles*), cultures, or communities. In these new isolated markets, neighborhood profiles or behavioral traits, as opposed to race, for example, took on greater explanatory power. Narrowcasting incorporated (or reincorporated) disaffected groups into the commercial marketplace. But these new isolated markets did not mature under the watchful eye of the federal government; instead, this newfangled practice of targeting publics came of age amid the greatest period of lax regulation in the twentieth century (Cohen 2003, 292–328). This was particularly acute in the financial services industry, where women and blacks, having equal legal access to auto insurance and equity lenders for the first time, nonetheless found themselves marketed and steered to high-cost loans and insurance.

Creating a cultural taxonomy enabled lobbyists to tap another dominant motif of the 1980s and 1990s: the ostensible moral failing of society's undeserving who, through poor personal decisions, perpetuated a collective culture of poverty. The system was already "unfair," wrote Carmody, in that it rewarded bad behavior. "It is bad enough that we have a major uninsured motorist problem in this state, which penalizes people who buy insurance with an additional financial burden. Now, Rosenfield [Prop 103's creator] is asking many of those same insured drivers to shoulder an even greater insurance cost so that bad drivers and others can pay less" (Barry Carmody, "Redistributing Car Insurance Rates." *Sacramento Bee*, April 19, 1995). "This is a matter of fairness. . . . Those who cost the system more should pay higher premiums. Those who cost the system less should pay lower rates" (Carmody 1995). Yet the solution the industry habitually turned to was more based more on sociology than on individual drivers; the insurers' common refrain was that miles driven, years of experience, and driving record were inadequate factors to accurately judge insurance risk.[45] Bias was built into insurance, Carmody acknowledged elsewhere: "Some subjectivity—business judgment—must be allowed in the business of insurance so long as that subjectivity is fairly applied by individual insurers" (Howard 1997)

As insurers saw it, the motorists who were least deserving were those who made bad life choices, such as living in poorer neighborhoods. The general counsel for the Association of California Insurance Companies, Jeff Fuller, echoing its president, told reporters, "We do not discriminate on the basis of race, wealth, national origin." On the contrary, Fuller admonished media, it was risky personal behavior that explained the rate gap. "Insurance is all about discrimination. It's all about discriminating between different risks."[46]

Beyond disputes of the likely victims and beneficiaries of Proposition 103, insurers' focus on "fairness" may have also delayed solving what the association president regarded as the major problem for motorists: uninsured drivers. By 2004, with 25 percent of the state's motorists lacking insurance, California had the second highest rate of uninsured motorists in the United States and well above the national average rate of 14.6 percent.[47] Insured drivers generally stood to benefit from lowering the premium bar-

rier for poorer motorists in poorer communities, many of whom could not
afford the higher auto insurance premiums, because lowering premiums
would have translated into insuring more drivers. This, in turn, would
have had the broader effect of spreading risk by increasing the pool of the
insured and thereby reducing premiums for all drivers—young and old,
women and men, rural and urban. For policyholders at least, it is cheaper
to cover 50 percent more drivers than none of the uninsured at all. "This
issue . . . has serious economic implications," insisted Oakland's city attorney, Jayne W. Williams. Heightening the bar to entry, she added, "will
push many residents of lower income neighborhoods in Oakland out of
the automobile insurance market."[48]

GENDER AND GEOGRAPHY

Nowhere was insurers' willingness to subsume individualism arguments
under social factors and identity politics more apparent than in relation to
gender. Insurers had regularly insisted that ameliorating postal code profiling would result in women drivers paying more.[49]

Since the 1980s, the insurance business lobbied hard to uphold gender
as a factor in rating in the United States and Canada, charging that its
elimination would unfairly hike rates for women drivers.[50] In 1983, when
Congress debated antidiscrimination legislation to prohibit sex categoriza-
tions in insurance, the American Council of Life Insurance chimed in,
strongly objecting to the presentations of politicians and the press. It was
not only harmful to the industry, according to the council's president, but
it would most likely have "a severe economic impact" on women, who
"pose very different risks."[51] "Women will suffer," another East Coast lob-
byist predicted three years later, when Pennsylvania looked at ending sex-
based classification in auto insurance.[52] Yet groups such as the National
Organization for Women and the League of Women Voters saw the continuation of gender-based pricing to be an insurance shell game—a hidden
tax in which women, under the current system, had their rates lowered in
one category of insurance only to pay a much steeper rate in another. Ultimately, women actually paid more.

Consider auto insurance pricing. Women paid proportionally higher
costs than they would have in a system based, for example, on miles
driven each year, because they drove less than men. "The insurance industry's refusal to use mileage as a rating factor continues discrimination
against all low-mileage drivers and costs women in Pennsylvania over
$100 million per year in overcharges," the National Organization for
Women's state chapter president asserted. Perhaps more significantly,
gender-neutral laws would most likely be applied not just in auto rating

but throughout the entire insurance pricing process, where classifications based on sex continued, including for pensions, annuities, and health care. Insurers cared less about women-protectionist policies in these three areas of insurance practice, in which women generally paid more than men. In overcharging women as low-mileage drivers and penalizing them as women, the National Organization for Women and the League of Women Voters concluded, insurers preferred identity over merit because they deemed identity-based rating more profitable.[53] Consequently, billions might be lost if the insurance business ended gender categorization in insurance.

What also eluded industry experts was the correlation between gender and poverty. Because more women than men tend to live in poverty, particularly single mothers, more women stood to disproportionately benefit from ending postal code profiling. Consider ZIP code 93234 in the Central California community of Huron, where the median household income was reported to be $25,521. There, three out of four households in poverty were headed by women. Similarly, in 93701, Fresno, where more than 90 percent of households earned $50,000 or less (and the median household income was $14,213), female householders with children under the age of eighteen accounted for 70 percent of families living below the poverty level. Poverty figures were consistently bleaker for females with young children, as was the case in 93615, another Central California town, where the median household income was just $26,694. Although less than one-half of female-headed households with children under eighteen lived below the poverty level, almost two out of three female households caring for children aged five or under lived in poverty.

In contrast, wealthy neighborhoods, such as America's most famous ZIP code, Beverly Hills's 90210—where 36 percent of households in the 1990s made $200,000 or more and the median household income was $112,572, placing it in the top 1 percent in the state—had only 18.1 percent of households headed by females with children under eighteen living below the poverty level. In the wealthier 92067 San Diego suburb of Rancho Santa Fe, where median household income was $196,298 and nearly one-half of its population made $200,000 or more, not a single female-headed household, with or without children, lived below the poverty level, according to the 2000 U.S. Census (U.S. Bureau of the Census 2003).[54] Even in poor neighborhoods with sizable white populations, women suffered. In Van Nuys, for instance, whose population was approximately one-half white and female, full coverage for a woman with twenty-two years of driving experience cost $943 more per year than full coverage for a similar woman driver in Pasadena (Consumers Union 2006a, 5). Nationally, women, who possessed less wealth and earned roughly eighty cents to the dollar paid to a man, were also far less likely to live in better neighborhoods with lower territorially rated insurance premiums. This, combined with women's general lack of access to credit, limited women's residential opportunities. More significantly, the language of Prop 103 never struck down the use of gender in the rate formula, allowing insurers to use gender while minimizing territorial ratings.

The industry's gender argument belied the lived reality of motorists in black or Latino communities as well. For example, a twenty-two-year-old female driver with a perfect driving record—that is, no accidents, no tickets—who drove her 1996 Acura primarily to go to work paid, on average, 12.9 percent ($152) higher premiums to California's three largest insurers (State Farm, Farmers, and Allstate) if she lived in a predominantly Latino ZIP code and 59.7 percent ($704) more in a black ZIP code than a female with the same driving profile living in Huntington Beach.[55]

BEVERLY HILLS 90210 VERSUS INGLEWOOD 90301

Although insurers typically regarded any reform in ZIP code profiling as "artificial," few disputed the disparate racial impact of perpetuating postal code profiling.[56] Black and Latino poor motorists paid more. But fearful of being accused of taking race into account in calculating premiums, the insurance industry insisted its process was color blind. "Insurance companies don't use race as part of their rating criteria," said Carmody's successor, Sam Sorich, the president of the Association of California Insurance Companies, in 2005, though he noted that "territory is a significant factor."[57]

Those who wished to undo postal code profiling were, according to one former George H. W. Bush administration official turned independent insurance broker in San Antonio, Texas, nothing but social engineers. Agents are knowledgeable and practical field underwriters, he said, not "liberal social engineers who crafted 103 and who are now planning to implement a similar socialist medicine in Texas," using the regulatory environment to overturn insurance's natural order.[58]

Of course ZIP codes, the most contentious tool used by insurance practitioners in determining rates, were anything but "natural." Rather, the modern American ZIP (zone improvement plan) code system was a European import: it was invented in Germany in 1941 to expedite wartime communication and adopted domestically in the United States in the early 1960s, by a federal regulator with the U.S. Postal Service—the very metonym of the built environment, socially conceived by state planners to reduce mixed-use spaces.[59] Once the coding was insourced by the government, direct-marketing theoreticians adapted it for the private purposes of market segmentation, as marketers, vendors, and salespersons "narrow-

casted" specific commercial products, from music to auto insurance to consumers.[60] In this way, ZIP codes stood as the very instantiations of artificial
man-made creations, the socially conceived designs of town planners, such
as regulators and professors, and what suburban scholars such as Robert
Fishman (1989, ix, 206) have dubbed the "built environment."[61]

Although others agreed with the insurance industry that location
should matter in setting premium rates, they contended that ZIP codes
were an ineffectual predictor. Instead, the exhaustive findings of one expert risk-assessment firm, based on 15 million policyholders and 2 million
claims, discovered that the best indicator of risk to carriers involved landmarks. Landmark theory contended that the most accurate determinant
for insurers was what publics were served in a particular communal space.
"While ZIP codes may be convenient and necessary for speedy mail deliv-
ery, they are not a particularly good predictor of property/casualty insurance losses," the study concluded (PR Newswire 2005, 1). Rather, car theft,
vandalism, and auto accidents were a far more likely occurrence around
landmarks like restaurants or bars. Conversely, the greater number of
houses of worship—mosques, synagogues, freestanding and storefront
churches—in a neighborhood, the lower the likelihood of auto accidents
(and thefts) in the area (Liedtke 2005; PR Newswire 2005).

Certainly urban black America is rife with cheap restaurants and bars,
and the prevalence of these establishments helps to partially explain the
inflated premiums. Few would deny this. That said, the black (and Latino)
urban landscape is equally dotted with mosques, churches, and day care
facilities that, based on place-based socioeconomic characteristics, should
have some deflationary influence on pricing premiums. But it apparently
does not. As Michael Stoll and Paul Ong demonstrate in their study "Why
Do Inner City Residents Pay Higher Premiums?" race and income remain
major determinants in what people pay. Even after neighborhood-based
primary (claim and loss rates) and secondary (accident and crime location
statistics) risk factors, both typically used by insurers, were taken into account, simulations conducted by Stoll and Ong (2008, 7), looking at independent contributions of both risk and redlining factors, reveal that traditional redlining (not place-based risk factors such as the presence of bars
or churches) "explain more of the gap in auto insurance premiums between black (and Latino) and white neighborhoods and between poor and
nonpoor neighborhoods." In sum, legitimate place-based factors may have
played a role in pricing discrepancies, but apparently so did race.

Years later the California Department of Insurance revealed that insurers misled the public by actually altering its evidence: "Insurers had ma-
nipulated their own data calculations to make the claim" that some drivers
would see massive rate hikes if postal code policies were abolished (U.S.

Newswire 2006). Yet this truth could be concealed, especially under Quackenbush, who opposed public disclosure of pricing and other underwriting
data—information thought essential in tracking auto insurance redlining.
For without this evidence, it was virtually impossible to ascertain whether
or how large a role ZIP codes and other nonindividual factors played. In
not pressing for full disclosure from the insurance industry, then, Quackenbush failed to enforce another key provision of 103, which required that
all information submitted by insurers to the commissioner be available for
public inspection. Only after Quackenbush left office in 2000 would his
successor press insurers to follow the law by releasing pricing and other
data.[62] The industry's foiling of 103 was, in no small measure, tied to industry representatives' talents in branding 103 with the hot-button cultural issues of the mid-1990s, particularly affirmative action and the ostensibly undeserving minority who reaped benefits from the majority.

The stakes were so high because it was anticipated that other states
would follow California's model. California was not the only state where
the insurance industry waged a struggle over this issue by appropriating
language of individual merit, personal responsibility, and social redistribution. In Texas, an equally fierce battle over rate pricing was emerging. Industry insiders feared 103-like measures might migrate to the Lone Star
State. One state insurance board member, responding to 103-like proposals
in Texas, declared that under the proposed system, careful drivers would
see premiums rise, and that "the majority, in effect, would be forced to
subsidize the minority." Insurance, he opined, is "not a social distribution
system."[63] Yet the reality, as one midwestern underwriter admitted, was
that "all insurance is a game of subsidies." "The question," he added, "is
who is going to subsidize who?"[64] In state after state since the 1990s, the
uniform answer to the subsidy question rested largely on where one lived,
not how one drove. In other states, the merit issue hinged not just on identity and social factors but on factors equally unrelated to driving merit,
such as whether the motorist had a college degree or a prime credit score.

The industry embedded the insurance debate in a larger context of a
minority critique—corresponding with the cultural contemporary moment when affirmative action, immigration, and welfare dominated the
political rhetoric, a moment in which critics charged that personal responsibility and merit were subsumed under the principle of equality and that
policies such as Proposition 103 stemmed from social engineering goals of
regulators. Thus though zip codes were not as socially charged as race,
insurers and their supporters invoked familiar narratives of the 1980s and
1990s. Ironically, their argument for personal responsibility and merit—essential traits of individualism—was belied by an insistence on PC profiling
and identity politics.

What motivated insurers to adamantly support the continued use of social factors in determining insurance rates may never be completely known. Three reasons seem most plausible. First, insurers feared that altering the calculus—by favoring individual motorists merit over broader social and environmental forces—would result in lowering profits. Second, it is likely that insurers were motivated by the rhetoric and debates of the time. Whether by accident or design, insurers saw their struggle through the lens of the cultural-political debates of the 1980s and 1990s and the fight against "social engineering" and subsidizing the "undeserving poor," even though the territorial rating system itself was predicated on PC profiling, which relied heavily on a different set of social engineers.

Last, the dim prospects for cross-selling partly explain why insurers maintained the use of social factors, fearing 103 might take a bite out of their business's bottom line. Like other consumer financial services, the insurance industry targeted motorists who would most likely renew policies or buy additional consumer financial products and services. On cross-sells, insurance agents were willing to "eat" or amortize front-end expenses over a longer period for the existing customer, since by cultivating such loyalty they might persuade the client to buy a range of other products (for example, home insurance, annuities, life insurance), which promised to yield lucrative, long-term financial rewards. For insurers, the industry-wide perception was that such future cross-sells were far less likely to be made to urban, working-class, or minority insurance shoppers. Viewing these as transient transactions, insurers charged higher expenses for PC-profiled consumers, out of a belief that the company would be unable to recoup their initial transaction and service costs with additional sales over time.[65]

Cross-sells grew exponentially more lucrative after 1999, when the landmark Gramm-Leach-Bliley Act freed insurers and other financial institutions to merge or create subsidiaries across the financial service sectors. For the first time since the Great Depression, banking and insurance companies could merge. This change permitted financial conglomerates to make cross-sells for a variety of financial products to their customers. An insurance agent could now sell an existing customer a mortgage or home equity loan on top of his or her car insurance. But for the PC-profiled driver, it certainly did not provide greater consumer financial product information, as was expected. In fact, the one-stop shopping allowed by financial deregulation would only further diminish the incentive for insurers to offer lower rates to postal code–profiled drivers (Wells and Jackson 1999, 2, 5, 8).

HYPERDEREGULATION, FRAMING, AND REGULATORY CAPTURE

A set of causal mechanisms has helped to sustain postal code profiling. They include hyperderegulation, cognitive and ideological framing, and relational mechanisms, also called regulatory capture, exemplified by the changing relationship between vested interests and political candidates (Tilly 2001). These mechanisms may not have been responsible for creating the disparity in rate pricing, but they have been critical in perpetuating it.

Take, for instance, the impact of hyperderegulation. A broader climate of a laissez-faire approach toward regulatory enforcement and unfettered capitalism made it nearly impossible to rein in the abuses of the free market even after consumers had overwhelmingly voted for regulators to do so. Indeed, no branch of government assumed itself accountable to see that vote realized. The state's lawmakers stood silent while the interpreters of law actually rolled back some of the provisions of California's Proposition 103. The chief enforcer of the state's law, Governor George Deukmejian, widely considered to be hostile to regulatory policy, stood idly by, refusing to throw the weight of his office behind the new commissioner through either his enforcement powers or the bully pulpit. The courts lacked the enforcement powers to compel insurers or regulators to act. Disillusioned and overwhelmed, some consumers gave up on reforming the rating system altogether, and weariness set in relatively early. According to a 1989 poll by Mervin Field, though a substantial majority of the 1,007 Californians polled liked 103 (62 percent, versus 20 percent who thought the law a bad idea), only 29 percent believed they would ever see rate rollbacks under the new law.

Nationally, the lack of implementation of 103 most likely dampened optimism in other states that postal code–based pricing could be easily abolished. Whereas thirty states initially expressed interest in reforming the territorial rating system in November 1988, that number dwindled to a fraction of this figure once implementation of 103 stalled. Instead, consumer organizing gave way to individuals accommodating themselves to the rating system. In Pennsylvania, for example, one Pittsburgh neighborhood banded together and petitioned to be rezoned rather than demand that the rating system be changed. Meanwhile, better-off Coloradans, concerned about the possibility of price hikes in auto and possibly health insurance, fought against having their ZIP code folded into a neighboring ZIP code, thought to be in a less desirable part of northwestern Denver.[66]

The epicenter of opposition to the territorial rating system, though, may well have been America's Motor City, where Detroit residents paid an average of $1,200 more each year for car insurance. "[Unaffordable insurance rates] is the most common complaint that I hear from my constituents," according to Morris Hood III, the ranking member of Michigan's House Insurance Committee (No Author Given, "Plan to Lower Insurance Rates Gains Momentum." *Michigan Chronicle*, August 17–23, 2005, p. A1). Rather than attempt to reform the rating system, however, half of Detroit drivers engaged in individual acts of personal resistance, operating cars with no insurance, as compared with roughly one in ten Michiganders. Individual resisters included the press secretary of Detroit's embattled mayor Kwame Kilpatrick, who was caught illegally registering his vehicle under a false suburban address.[67] "There is absolutely no benefit at this point for people [in Detroit] to purchase insurance," said Detroit state house member Nelson Saunders.[68] These and other actions kept in place the disparate pricing without changing or challenging structural inequality.

For opponents of 103, a climate of hyperderegulation also made the job of ideological framing much easier. Corporate interests, in particular, couched their opposition to 103 as part of a wider struggle about the fundamental role of government in society. Specifically, insurers claimed that 103 signaled the latest example of "creeping socialism," in which the state actively sought to redistribute wealth from the deserving to the undeserving. (Such postulates ignore the initiative process, which gave consumers a direct say in the actions taken by government.) Before such fears of creeping socialism and wealth redistribution could fully resonate with motorists, insurers needed to satisfy their immediate concern over increasing costs. Thus insurers gave in on one-time rate rollbacks and refunds. By granting drivers a one-time rollback or refund, insurers could then have greater support (or, at a minimum, less opposition) to keeping intact their system of postal code–based pricing.

Immediate rate relief enabled more industry-friendly ideological frames to come to the fore. Insurers, for example, capitalized on the imagined geographic space of California's inner cities, which was often described as populated by society's least deserving citizens. Trade groups played on the unfounded perception that California's suburban and farm families were being forced to foot the bill for the undeserving inner-city motorist. The Association of California Insurance Companies and other industry reps touted public opinion polls that showed "almost 7 out of 10 persons feel it is unfair to make suburban and rural residents pay higher auto insurance premiums to subsidize those living in urban areas" as proof of yet another example of the drain urban America was on the rest of society (Personal Insurance Federation of California, American Insurance Association, and Association of California Insurance Companies 2003). Such framing aimed to undo (or at least neuter) Proposition 103 by exploiting the perception of a predominantly white, suburban majority being made to subsidize an undeserving urban minority.[69]

Relational forces are a third mechanism at play in the story of Proposition 103. By *relational factors* I mean factors that alter the connections between groups (for example, regulators and insurers). What experts underestimated was the increasing importance in the mid-1990s of corporate funding of political campaigns (Fields et al. 1990). Charles Quackenbush's campaign and tenure as insurance commissioner personified "regulatory capture." A long-shot candidate to win the general election in 1994, Quackenbush was catapulted ahead of his rival by the infusion of insurance money. Indebted, Quackenbush spent his time in office defending insurance interests over those of the consumers. Even in the rare instance when he did collect regulatory settlements, Quackenbush often applied the funds to public relations efforts, including paying for political polls and advertisements to further prop up his political career.[70] Ironically, experts had predicted in 1990 that changing the office of insurance commissioner to an elected post, rather than one appointed by the governor as it had been, would lessen the possibility of regulatory capture. In fact, it probably made candidates more beholden to the industry. As the story of Quackenbush showed, a financial service sector driven by a high-stake interest in the outcome of social policy and possessing the means to capture a state regulator could easily overwhelm weak campaign finance laws.

Stymieing 103 in California effectively shut down similar ballot initiatives elsewhere. Insurers nimbly elided implementation of Proposition 103 by offering token discounts and one-time rebates to consumers. Rates dropped further for consumers in California than in any other state. For corporations, acceding to a one-time rate rebate and modest price reduction enabled them to keep intact a far more lucrative scheme: the territorial rating system. Today, auto insurance continues to be pegged primarily to where one lives rather than how one drives. Postal code profiling has continued to perpetuate one of the most surreptitious policies of wealth redistribution in our society, helping us understand why, even in moments when income gaps among whites, women, and minorities have closed or remained the same, the wealth differential has widened in the United States over the past quarter century.

AUTO INSURANCE AND THE RACIAL WEALTH GAP

Auto insurance offers a window into the persistence of racial wealth disparity in America. According to a U.S. Census report, by 2002 the wage gap between blacks and whites had actually shrunk by 3 percent since 1979 (DeNavas-Walt, Cleveland, and Webster 2003, 22–23). Yet despite closing income gaps between minorities and whites and between women and men, racial and gender wealth disparities between these same groups have widened over the same time.

If income does not explain the wealth gap, what mechanisms do? Sundry nonincome mechanisms affect wealth accumulation: family inheritance, stocks and long-term investments, mortgage and home equity markets, and pensions and other savings vehicles.[71] These factors are often overlapping, complementary, and mutually reinforcing. Each has exacerbated the racial wealth gap. Perhaps the most familiar example of interlocking causality is family inheritance and housing. Scholars, notably sociologists such as Thomas Shapiro and Melvin Oliver and economic historians such as Robert Margo and William Collins, have pointed out that family inheritance has made a significant difference in housing, the single most important way families accumulate wealth. Unearned inherited wealth has the capacity to lift individuals and families beyond their own achievements. It also can shed light on the racial wealth gap. White families are four times more likely than African Americans to receive an inheritance, and the median inheritance is ten times greater for white families (Fessler 2011).

Given that an inheritance is most commonly used for a down payment on a house, the economic advantage of inheritance for homeownership goes a long way in explaining blacks' inability to close the racial homeownership gap, which shrank by only 1 percent between 1910 and 2007—a disparity that persisted despite the narrowing of racial gaps in income and schooling. Family inheritance also makes a measurable difference in the racial asset gap, as most family assets come by way of generational transfer. Despite the boom years of 1990s, blacks in 1999 were still twice as likely as whites (54 and 25 percent, respectively) to live below the asset poverty line (Shapiro 2004, 2–4; see also Collins and Margo 2011).

The legacy of white racial advantage also suggests that housing parity has been resistant to antiracist federal action since the Fair Housing Act of 1968. Although blacks are far less likely to own homes, black wealth is, nonetheless, principally tied up in home equity. Consequently, the plummeting home values since 2007 have disproportionately affected them and Latinos. Figures from before and after the recession of 2008 to 2011 paint a grim picture of the disappearance of three decades of gains since the civil rights era in the span of little more than three years: in early 2008, before the recession, the average minority family owned ten cents for every dollar owned by the average white family. Today that ten cents has been reduced to a nickel. Beyond blacks' heavy asset concentration in homeownership at a time of plummeting home values, there are other interlocking causes, notably, asset allocation. Not nearly as leveraged in housing as racial minorities, whites' assets included long-term pensions, mutual funds, and the stock market. Most of these investments have largely rebounded from the nadir of 2008 (Kochhar, Fry, and Taylor 2011). By contrast, the housing market has not. Whites' diversified portfolios, along with higher unemployment among blacks and Latinos, have exacerbated the racial wealth gap (Keister 2000).

The interlocking causes of inequality in insurance and other financial vehicles are aptly illustrated by the largest publicly held insurer in the country, MetLife. By actively soliciting blacks more than any of its competitors, MetLife was also the nation's leading carrier of black policyholders throughout much of the twentieth century. But it sold blacks different, more costly products. By the 1960s, MetLife's disparate pricing policies touched every aspect of finance in which it interacted with black policyholders, including stock options, pensions, and health, life, and, of course, auto insurance. Race-based practices of the company resulted in blacks receiving higher premiums and lower stock options. Nonwhites were frequently subjected to more complicated application processes that yielded smaller, more expensive policies that carried fewer benefits. Insurers justified charging more to blacks as a hedge against their not keeping up with their payments—a problem for companies that feared losing money if policies lapsed, because sales commissions were paid up front. Understandably, MetLife feared this would affect its bottom line. Racial distinctions then were regarded as a catch-all that automatically took all such factors into account in a simple, inexpensive way.

By 1966, a decade before the 1976 federal law barred race from being taken into account when setting the terms of contracts, the industry's leader had already begun the shift; it simply replaced race with what MetLife internal memos began to call "area underwriting." "Area underwriting can be put into practice before the introduction of the revised application forms which will not have a question on race," one MetLife actuary stated at the time. Thus area underwriting became the preferred race-neutral language adopted in every sector of its business, including car insurance. The net result was the same as it had been during the race-negative language days: a disparate impact on blacks in the more than ninety cities in which area underwriting was used. (High residential segregation in MetLife strongholds like Newark, New York, Washington, Baltimore, Detroit, and Chicago made this strategy easier to carry out.) Millions of these older policies remain in force well into the twenty-first century. Insurers may have had nonprejudicial reasons for initiating and continuing its disparate treatment, but the effects persist.[72]

Auto insurance is only one part of the broader crisis of a growing wealth gap. But it can also be reimagined as a contributing solution to the problem. One such potential solution might be to apply savings taken from reform of the territorial rating system and to individual development accounts (IDAs). For a typical urban motorist living in South Los Angeles, California, this could mean that as much as $974 each year (the differential amount insured drivers pay in predominantly African American and Latino ZIP Codes, according to the Consumers Union (2005) would be placed each year in an account for a specific investment purpose—for example, a down payment for college or a house, a retirement account that would remain invested until at least the age of sixty-five. Government or insurers might even consider providing matching funds as is typically done with IDAs. It might also consider making the program tax exempt to offset the fact that middle- and low-income wage earners—the target population of TRS reform—pay a much larger share of state and local taxes than wealthier families, according to a 2013 distributional analysis of the tax systems in all 50 states conducted by the Institute on Taxation and Economic Policy (Davis et al. 2013). (This would apply only in the forty-nine states in which auto insurance is mandated by law. Insurers would be legally protected, as they have been in California, with the right to earn a minimum nonconfiscatory return.) Individual development accounts were designed to promote savings for the purchase of assets like buying a home, pursuing a postsecondary education, or investment retirement among low-income persons. (Pilot programs have shown remarkable promise in their limited application, substantially increasing homeownership rates from 21.2 percent to 52.2 percent.) Because setup of these accounts is usually accompanied by a host of financial literacy classes and counseling, as well as screenings of suitable mortgage products, IDAs have also been credited with making more economically responsible citizens. Rates of foreclosure and default for IDA homeowners have be much lower than the national average.

Asset-building proponents are now considering ways to expand IDA programs. As just one tool in the IDA tool kit, auto insurance and other hidden taxes more generally might create another important savings opportunity for low-income families with fewer resources. What makes IDAs more attractive than direct cash transfer or redistributive policies such as revenue acts is that they reinforce a Western tradition older than capitalism itself: reward for individual merit.

Bringing a more merit-based system to auto insurance would not only help Americans save via IDAs, but it could also pay a second dividend:

higher savings rates have been linked to improving access to postsecond-ary education, family stability, and economic mobility. The idea that sav-ings from territorial rating system reform could be placed in IDAs under-scores the larger point that hidden taxes such as auto insurance differentials are best understood in context—as just one new yet largely forgotten tool in the wealth-building tool kit that is available to state and federal policy makers.

Finally, ZIP codes matter beyond auto insurance as they are factored into housing, working, shopping, and primary and secondary schooling. "The biggest influence on our financial health isn't how much we save. . . . Nor is it the funds we choose in our 401(k) plans," writes Scott Burns, a syndicated columnist specializing in personal finance and investment. "It is our ZIP code—where we buy and own a house. Pick the right area, and your future is golden. Pick the wrong area, and you'll always be behind the folks who happened to buy in the right place."[73] One's ZIP code is often a determinant of employment and consumption, in and even beyond the United States. "I throw away resumes of people who are from . . . Arab or black [neighborhoods]," acknowledged Claude Bebear of the world's larg-est insurer, AXA. Postal codes often help determine the prices consumers pay at grocery stores, fast food franchises, and retail clothing shops (Graddy and Robertson 1999). Postal codes continue to be a factor in the inequity of funding in primary and secondary education, because, in many states, school district budgets are traditionally derived from local property taxes, whose revenue stream is often attributed to the neighborhood ZIP code.[74]

CONCLUSION

The story of Proposition 103 lies at the confluence of financial deregula-tion and postracial politics. When first principles of the free market and individualism conflicted, it was markets that appeared primus inter pares (first among equals). Having long pronounced merit the basic building block of Western culture and advancement, most prominently over the use of environmental and identity-based remedies such as affirmative ac-tion to right social wrongs, conservatives and many liberals often abetted or fell silent when faced with the erosion of individual merit at the visible hands of the free market. The primacy afforded the free market system not only pierced the myth surrounding individual merit, it also served as the mechanism that exacerbated already existing racial inequality.

Claims of race neutrality by insurers and defenders collapsed under the disparate racial reality. Nothing gave greater credence to the power of race than the failure of arguments predicated on merit, which had been propagated since the early 1970s to oppose affirmative action and other racial remedies, to end the territorial rating system as a primary factor in determining insurance rates. The system was tantamount to a ghetto tax in auto insurance, which enabled the quarantining of consumers of color through postal code–based profiling without ever mentioning race. As a result of this racial subsidy, the premiums of rural and suburban motorists were underwritten by central and inner-city motorists. Over the driving span of the typical motorist, this subsidy costs urban motorists more than tens of thousands of dollars.

In a putatively postracial age, race has had surprising staying power. The stickiness of race was evident in the PC profiling that operated in the consumer finance world of auto insurance. Put simply, it remained "politically correct" to profile based on postal or ZIP code. Although over the past three generations or so, governments, the private sector, and civil society have taken public stances to root out racial, ethnic, sex, age, and religious discrimination and its vestiges from contemporary life, ZIP code discrimination remains both persistent and illustrative of a last refuge of acceptable prejudice in multicultural, free market liberal democracies such as the United States. In America, one's ZIP code may be used by local governments to apportion tax dollars (for example, for public education, rather than according to a parent's income); and despite the outlawing of racial redlining, banks and other members of the financial services industry still deny or charge extra for loans, credit, and insurance premiums to households in low-income or working-class neighborhoods as delineated by their ZIP codes. Postal code profiling assumed greater currency in a post–civil rights world as governments, corporations, and civil society all shied away from making explicit racial arguments for discriminatory policies.

Tax policy sends cultural messages about what sorts of behavior a society values, the economic historian Sheldon Garon (2011, 375) has recently written. America's de facto ghetto tax functions similarly. As the history of Proposition 103 shows, the de facto ghetto tax may well suggest something beyond how wealth is perpetuated in contemporary America. It may well be that the primacy of social factors and policies of identity over the ethos of individual merit is the nation's transcendent value, more interwoven into the fabric of American society than heretofore imagined.

I wish to thank the Russell Sage Post Racial workshop participants and volume editors for their assistance. In addition, I also wish to thank the insights of Rajeev Date, Brian Balogh, Dorothy Brown, Sheryll Cashin, Reid Cramer,

Joe Crespino, William Darity, Kathleen Frydl, Brett Gadsden, Sheldon Garon, Gary Gerstle, Jacob Hacker, Darrick Hamilton, Lynn Itagaki, John L. Jackson, Jerome Karabel, George Lipsitz, Vincent Lloyd, Manning Marable, Waldo Martin, Kimberly McKee, Ajay Mehrotra, Tamara Nopper, Gail O'Brien, Karsten Paerregaard, Shana Redmond, Carolina Reid, Thomas Schwartz, Patricia Sullivan, and the Closing the Racial Wealth Gap Initiative.

NOTES

1. The $20,000 amount is based on a 2006 Brookings Institution Report of twelve sampled metro areas (Fellowes 2006, 5, 37). Urban drivers in low- to moderate-income neighborhoods paid, on average, $400 more for twelve months of auto insurance to insure the same car and driver risk as those in higher income neighborhoods. The $400 figure has been extrapolated over a period of fifty years, which is a typical driving span of a motorist.

2. By *ghetto tax* I mean a cryptic collection of fees and charges paid by quarantined consumers who are typically cordoned off by race, age, gender, and geography and, increasingly, by the middle class.

3. Other examples in consumer finance include subprime mortgages, unsubsidized student loans, and shadow retail bank loans by the payday loan and car title industries. There is also a formal tax process of wealth removal and redistribution, which has been widely discussed in the growing body of literature around critical tax theory, led by Dorothy Brown, Beverly Moran, and Katherine Newman, among others.

4. For the distinctive role of history in "setting the record straight" on policy and inequality, see Katznelson (2005, xi).

5. A coalition of community and low-income organizations had actually unsuccessfully challenged California's mandatory auto insurance law, claiming it was unconstitutional to require the purchase of auto insurance without also protecting consumers from territorial rating, which was unaffordable to many poor consumers. Although it was sympathetic to plaintiffs' claim, the court, conscious not to legislate from the bench, stated that it was a matter for the California State Assembly. See King v. Meese, 43 Cal.3d 1217 (1987).

6. David Shribman, "State Legislatures Move to Bring Big Increases in Auto Insurance Rates to a Screeching Halt," *Wall Street Journal*, July 10, 1989, A12.

7. The populists are "gang[ing] up on big interest groups who own state legislatures," commented the initiative expert Thomas Cronin, a Colorado College political scientist and the author of a book on the modern proposition movement. Robert Reinhold, "The Nation: California Has 29 on the Ballot: With Proliferation of Ballot Initiatives, Suddenly Everyone's Interest Is Special," *New York Times*, November 6, 1988, E4.

8. Benjamin Zycher, "Insurance Fraud," *Wall Street Journal*, October 9, 1989, A12.

9. Stephen Sugarman, "Why Prop 103 Will Fail," *San Diego (Calif.) Union*, May 14, 1989.

10. D. C. Carson, "Insurers Smash Their Own Record on Spending in Proposition War," *San Diego (Calif.) Union*, October 8, 1988.

11. Michael Smolens, "Insurance Industry Fears 103 More than Any Other," *San Diego (Calif.) Union*, October 20, 1988.

12. James V. Grimaldi and Jeff Weir, "Car Insurance Sparks 'Initiative Warfare,' 5 Measures on November Ballot Threaten California's 77-Year Old Petition Process," *Orange County (Calif.) Register*, September 18, 1988.

13. Carson, "Insurers Smash Their Own Record."

14. Smolens, "Insurance Industry Fears 103."

15. Sonja Steptoe, "Policy Dispute: Auto Insurers Face Drive by Consumers for Rate Reductions—Rollback Voted in California Spurs Activists Elsewhere; Some Firms Drop Lines," *Wall Street Journal*, November 22, 1988, A1; LaBarbara Bowman, "Group Pushes Insurance Reform in 14 States," *USA Today*, January 11, 1989, 3A; Nora Lockwood Tooher, "California Leads Charge in Auto Insurance Rate Revolt," *Providence (R.I.) Journal*, January 22, 1989; Erik Ingram, "Insurers Buying National Ads to Stem Revolt," *San Francisco (Calif.) Chronicle*, February 20, 1989.

16. Mark Green, New York City commissioner of consumer affairs, "How Minorities Are Sold Short," op-ed, *New York Times*, June 18, 1990, A21; even between predominantly black communities a discrepancy often existed, as was the case in Maryland, where Landover drivers paid $570 compared with the more affluent Mitchellville drivers, who paid $390. See David Montgomery, "For Some, It's All in the Numbers," *Washington Post*, October 4, 1993, D1.

17. Carson, "Insurers Smash Their Own Record."

18. Richard B. Schmitt and Sonja Steptoe, "California's Voters Shake Up Insurers," *Wall Street Journal*, November 10, 1988, 1.

19. Vlae Kershner and Sabin Russell, "Prop. 103 Wins/Insurers Halt New Policies—State Turmoil," *San Francisco (Calif.) Chronicle*, November 10, 1988; Sabin Russell, "Insurers Panic over Prop. 103," *San Francisco Chronicle*, November 10, 1988.

20. Vlae Kershner, "Insurance Industry Accused of False TV Ads about Prop 103," *San Francisco (Calif.) Chronicle*, September 30, 1988.

21. Schmitt and Steptoe, "California's Voters Shake Up Insurers"; see also Historical Data for New York Stock Exchange Composite Index. Available at: http://www.nyse.com/about/listed/nya_resources.shtml (accessed November 2012). From this link you can access the Excel spreadsheet of the Historical Data.

22. Shribman, "State Legislatures Move to Bring Big Increases in Auto Insurance to a Screeching Halt."

23. Kershner and Russell, "Prop. 103 Wins"; Russell, "Insurers Panic over Prop. 103"; Ron Roach, "Voters Revolt, Pass 103," *San Diego (Calif.) Tribune*, November 9, 1988.

24. Jeff Weir, "State Farm Ordered to Hearing on Rate Discrimination," *Orange County (Calif.) Register*, January 27, 1989.

25. Vlae Kershner and William Carlsen, "New Moves in Battle over Prop 103," *San Francisco (Calif.) Chronicle*, November 15, 1988.

26. Carriers' campaign of nullification and interposition was successful in part because of an apparent loss of motorist will. . . . Yet five years later, most insurers remained in noncompliance with the court-ordered rebate. Among the most recalcitrant were California's two largest insurers, State Farm Insurance Group and Farmers Insurance Group. Combined, they controlled 40 percent of the California market, and others followed their lead. Many individuals responded like Vincenza Scarpaci, a typical policyholder. Recounting his failed attempts with his insurer, State Farm, Scarpaci told his local newspaper editor that it was fruitless to hold out hope that insurers would comply. Not even the state supreme court's decision to uphold the refund made a difference, for auto carriers "refuse[d] to accept the ruling." The Petaluma, California, resident went on: "I wrote to State Farm to protest its behavior [withholding the rebate]. I received no reply. Instead, this same company that has no profits to refund to policyholders spent another untold amount of money to lobby against Prop 186 this fall. My conclusion: Neither the welfare of the policyholder nor their legitimate concerns are as important to this company as its control over the insurance market and unrestricted profits." Disillusioned, Scarpaci gave up and switched carriers. But having individual consumers switch carriers because insurers selected which laws it opted to obey was no . . . solution to auto insurance in California. . . . [S]uch selective adherence to the courts, by . . . State Farm, was an assault on the principle of law and order.

Edmund Sanders, "Quackenbush: Rebates May Be Small; Insurance Commissioner Backs Away from Pledge to Give Prop. 103 Rollbacks Early." *Daily News* (Los Angeles), March 17, 1995.

27. Robert Reinhold, "Apathy and Disaffection on the Rise among California Voters," *New York Times*, June 12, 1990, A14.

28. Quackenbush political ads, 1994. "Chuck Quackenbush." ID# 60441-60444 in Julian P. Kanter Political Commercial Archive Television Ads, University of Oklahoma, Norman, Oklahoma.

29. Jack Skinner, a Texas insurance broker and former G. H. W. Bush official, celebrated the loss of House leadership by Democrats in Washington. Skinner expected the turnover of Democratic-controlled chairmanships—such as

Henry Gonzalez, chair of banking; Jack Brooks, state supreme court justice, and Daniel Rostenkowski, member of ways and means—to "have a dramatic impact on the way insurance is conducted in the state of Texas." Jim Skinner, "Election Results May Help Texas Insurance Market," *San Antonio (Tex.) Express*, November 20, 1994.

30. "Martinez for Insurance Commissioner, Incumbent Commissioner Bankrolled by Industry," editorial, *Sacramento (Calif.) Bee*, October 17, 1998.

31. Quackenbush claimed that $46 million was owed in refunds to insurers but reserved the right to seek an additional refund of $32 million, depending on 20th Century's losses from the recent Northridge earthquake—an issue that had nothing to do with Proposition 103 and auto insurance. See also Haggerty (1995).

32. Quackenbush's evasion of 103 gave consumer groups and other plaintiffs no choice: "If he won't implement the will of the people, the courts should force him to," a 103 Enforcement Project spokesperson told the press. Rick Orlov, "City Joins Call to End Insurance Redlining," *Los Angeles (Calif.) Daily News*, March 27, 1998, n.p.

33. "Auto Insurance," *Los Angeles (Calif.) Sentinel,* April 15, 1998, A1; Proposition 103 Enforcement Project v. Quackenbush (1998) 64 Cal. App. 4th 1473 [76 Cal. Rptr. 2d 342]; Spanish Speaking Citizens' Foundation v. Quackenbush.

34. Orlov, "City Joins Call to End Insurance Redlining."

35. Quackenbush essentially shared State Farm's and the industry's view that pricing and other underwriting data were trade secrets. Both Quackenbush's replacement and the courts fundamentally disagreed, however. State Farm sued Quackenbush's successor, John Garamendi, to block him from releasing the data. State Farm lost at the lower, appellate, and highest state courts. It brought the California Supreme Court a straightforward suit, which the court later dispatched by unanimously affirming voters and prior judges: insurers "may not invoke the trade secret privilege to prevent disclosure." "Court Upholds Insurance Redlining Lawsuit," *Los Angeles (Calif.) Sentinel*, April 29–May 5, 2004, A5.

36. Eric Young, "Insurance Contest," *Sacramento (Calif.) Bee*, October 19, 1998.

37. "Candidates Accept Insurance Donations," *Monterey County (Calif.) Herald*, October 17, 2002, n.p.

38. Scott Lindlaw, "Campaign-Finance Reform," *San Diego (Calif.) Union Tribune*, April 21, 2000.

39. James P. Sweeney, "Candidates Fight over Insurance Industry Aid," *San Diego (Calif.) Union Tribune*, September 20, 1994.

40. Steve Lawrence, "State Decides Not to Indict Quackenbush," *San Diego (Calif.) Union Tribune*, February 6, 2002.

41. Barry Carmody, "Sacramento—Proposition 103," *San Francisco (Calif.) Chronicle*, September 8, 1995.

42. Barry Carmody, "Fairness Drives Current Insurance System," *San Jose (Calif.) Mercury News,* September 13, 1995, 6B.

43. Barry Carmody, "Change in Auto Rates Could Hurt," *Fresno (Calif.) Bee,* May 1, 1995.

44. Jessica Guynn, "Advocates Seek Reforms on Insurance," *Contra Costa (Calif.) Times,* December 5, 2003, A01.

45. Barry Carmody, "Proposed Rate Changes Hit Good Drivers with Bad News," *Sacramento (Calif.) Bee,* May 21, 1995.

46. Guynn, "Advocates Seek Reforms on Insurance."

47. The Insurance Research Council calculates the uninsured driver proportion using the ratio of claims made by individuals who were injured by uninsured drivers (uninsured motorists coverage) to claims made by individuals injured by insured drivers (bodily injury liability coverage). Colorado's estimate is inflated because bodily injury claims are subject to a $2,500 threshold and uninsured motorists claims are not. In other states, the thresholds are the same. Insurance Research Council (2006).

48. "Suits Filed Against ZIP Coded Auto Insurance Rates," *Oakland (Calif.) Post,* April 8, 1998.

49. "Should young female drivers, who tend to have fewer accidents, pay more even though young males tend to have the greater number of tickets and accidents?" Carmody asked frequently, particularly in op-eds. Barry Carmody, "Redistributing Car Insurance Rates," *Sacramento (Calif.) Bee,* April 19, 1995.

50. Similarly, during the late 1980s in Canada, where auto insurance rates jumped 40 percent in only two years, a public outcry prompted Premier David Peterson to set up an Ontario provincial insurance board, hoping to keep insurance out of the hands of government and primarily a free market enterprise. The board banned insurance companies from considering age, sex, marital status, and physical disability in calculating rates. Women were "losers," according to the board's chair, as they bore the major cost of any readjustment in order to subsidize young male drivers. The Canadian system still allowed non-driving-related factors such as conviction rate and region to be used. Robert Brehl, "Young Women to Pay Higher Car Insurance," *Toronto Star* (Canada), September 2, 1988, A3.

51. Richard Schweiker, "Defective New Insurance Legislation," *New York Times,* November 16, 1983, A30.

52. Stephen Drachler, "Gender-Based Auto Insurance Rates Vetoed by Thornburgh," *Morning Call (Pa.),* February 22, 1986.

53. "Insure Against Sex Discrimination," editorial, *New York Times,* November 2, 198, A30.

54. Unfortunately, similar characteristics are not available for earlier censuses.

55. Where the ghetto tax appeared the highest was in black communities. One major insurer, for example, hiked up rates 83 percent, an average of $794, more

in some majority black communities. See Press Release, December 20, 2005. "California insurers charge as much as $794 per year more to good drivers living in predominantly Black, Latino Zip Codes." Available at: http://www.consumersunion.org/pub/core_financial_services/002991.html (accessed March 25, 2013).

56. John Howard, "Rules Would Bar Address as Factor in Car Insurance," *Los Angeles (Calif.) Daily News*, May 24, 1996.

57. Sorich replaced Carmody in 2002. Liedtke (2005).

58. Skinner, "Election Results May Help Texas Insurance Market."

59. In 1944 Robert Moon proposed using a three-digit code, which described generally a sectional facility of a region for mail sorting and distributing (for example, 554 for part of Minnesota); two later digits, for larger cities, were added to the three-digit code (for example, 55416 for Minneapolis, Minnesota). Douglas Martin, "Robert Moon, an Inventor of the ZIP Code, Dies at 83," *New York Times*, April 14, 2001, C6.

60. The direct-marketing theoretician Martin Baier, whose name grew to be synonymous with segmentation, published the first article in 1967 on market segmentation using ZIP codes, in the *Harvard Business Review* (Baier 1967), and wrote a college textbook on direct marketing. He then founded the nation's first direct marketing center at the University of Missouri, Kansas City, where he built the discipline by refining the segmentation techniques of sampling, customer valuation, and multivariate and regression analyses. Williams (1988); Baier (1967).

61. For an overview of theories exploring the nexus between race, the built environment, and suburbia, see Pritchett (2005).

62. "Court Upholds Insurance Redlining Lawsuit."

63. Skinner, "Election Results May Help Texas Insurance Market."

64. Jack Norman, "Where You Live Is What You Pay," *Milwaukee (Wisc.) Journal*, May 28, 1995.

65. For a slightly different interpretive view of cross-sells and racial discrimination in the realm of auto insurance, see Harrington and Niehaus (1998, 449, 467).

66. George Lane, "Denver ZIP Code Plan Stirs Concerns," *Denver (Colo.) Post*, Rockies ed., March 11, 2002, B-02.

67. The insurance industry actually put the overall number of uninsured Michigan motorists during this period (1999–2004) slightly higher at 17 percent. See http://www.insurancejournal.com/news/national/2006/06/28/69919.htm (accessed March 31, 2013); Shareef Wright, "Redlining: Detroit Pays More," *Michigan Citizen*, July 5, 2003, p. A1; David Josar, "Police Detain Detroit Mayor's Press Secretary," *Detroit News*, November 3, 2007 [no page number listed or provided].

68. Associated Press, "Insurance law changes are sent to governor, the measure

would permit insurers to charge based on neighborhood criteria and not the broader regional data," *Grand Rapids Press*, February 7, 1996, p. B3; [No Author], "Plan to lower insurance rates gains momentum," *Michigan Chronicle*, August 17–23, 2005, p. A1.

69. Cognitive and psychological mechanisms often operate at the individual level, unlike environmental and relational mechanisms.

70. Douglas Heller, "The 'Quack Quake' Is Over," op-ed, *Santa Monica Mirror*, July 23, 2000. Available at: http://cwd.grassroots.com/insurance/nw/?postId=13 71&pageTitle=The+%22QuackQuake%22+is+Over%2C+Now+the+Clean -Up+Must+Begin.

71. For the definitive work on savings historically and transnationally, see Garon (2011, 317–64).

72. Scott Paltrow, "Old Memos Lay Bare MetLife's Use of Race to Screen Customers," *Wall Street Journal*, July 24, 2001, A1; Scott Paltrow, "Uncovered Losses: Life Insurers' Race Bias in Decades Past Affects Policyholders Even Now," *Wall Street Journal*, December 26, 2000.

73. Scott Burns, "ZIP, Not 401(K), Is What Makes Your Cash Grow," *Chicago Daily Herald*, May 8, 2005.

74. Though ZIP codes are often referred to in such policy debates as public school funding, it is as a misleading shorthand for neighborhood city boundaries that determine local property taxes. Dan Hardy, Amy Worden, and Nick Pipitone, "Study: PA Schools Need Cash," *Philadelphia Inquirer*, November 15, 2007, p. A1; Ellen Mitchell, "Path to Status: Coveted ZIP Codes," *New York Times*, October 4, 1992, Section 13LI, p. 1; C. T. Bowen, "School Budget Shortfall Faces a New Foe: Apathy," *Pasco Times (Florida)*, May 23, 2012, p. 2.

REFERENCES

ABC Evening News. 1988. Video. Television News Archive, Vanderbilt University, Nashville Tennessee. October 13.

Associated Press. 2009. "Obama Said Open to Taxing Health Benefits." June 2.

Baier, Martin. 1967. "ZIP Code—New Tool for Marketers." *Harvard Business Review*, January–February 45(1): 136–40.

Cohen, Lizabeth. 2003. *A Consumers' Republic: The Politics of Mass Consumption in Postwar America*. New York: Knopf.

Collins, William J., and Robert A. Margo. 2011. "Race and Home Ownership from the End of the Civil War to the Present." *American Economic Review* 101(3): 355–59.

Consumers Union. 1998, March 26. "Cities of Los Angeles, Oakland, and San Francisco Join Civil Rights and Consumer Groups in Lawsuits over Zip Code-Based Auto Insurance Rates." Press Release. Available at: http://www.consumersunion.org/pub/core_newmoney/001962.html (accessed November 2012).

———. 2005. "California Insurers Charge As Much As $974 per Year More to Good Drivers Living in Predominantly Black, Latino ZIP Codes." Press release. December 20. Available at: http://www.consumersunion.org/pub/core_financial _services/002991.html (accessed February 2, 2013).

———. 2006a. "Where You Live Determines What You Pay." In *Auto Insurance Premiums Vary Widely by Zip Code for Good Drivers in California.* Insurance Commissioner John Garamendi's Public Hearing on Automobile Insurance Premiums. San Francisco, California. February 24.

———. 2006b. "State Farm Announces It Will Follow New California 'Good Driver' Rregulations and Drop Rates by 8% or $204 Million Statewide." Press release. August 17.

Davis, Carl, et al. 2013. *Who Pays? A Distributional Analysis of the Tax Systems in All 50 States,* 4th ed. Washington, D.C.: Institute on Taxation and Economic Policy. Available at: http://www.itep.org/whopays (accessed February 5, 2013).

DeNavas-Walt, Carmen, Robert W. Cleveland, and Bruce H. Webster Jr. 2003. "Current Population Reports: Consumer Income." U.S. Bureau of the Census. September. Available at: www.census.gov/prod/2003pubs/p60-221.pdf (accessed November 2012).

The Economist. 2000. "United States: Quacking in His Boots." June 10.

Espinoza, Leslie, and Angela P. Harris. 1997. "Embracing the Tar-Baby: LatCrit Theory and the Sticky Mess of Race." *California Law Review* 85(5): 1585–645.

Fellowes, Matt. 2006. "From Poverty, Opportunity: Putting the Market to Lower Income Families." Brookings Institution Report. Available at: http://www .brookings.edu/research/reports/2006/07/poverty-fellowes (accessed March 30, 2013).

Fessler, Pam. 2011. "Making It in the U.S.: More Than Just Hard Work." *Morning Edition.* NPR, September 15. Available at: http://www.npr.org/2011/09/15/ 140428359/making-it-in-the-us-more-than-just-hard-work (accessed February 2, 2013).

Fields, Joseph A., et al. 1990. "Wealth Effects of Regulatory Reform: The Reaction of California's Proposition 103." *Journal of Financial Economics* 28(1–2): 233–50.

Fishman, Robert. 1989. *Bourgeois Utopias: The Rise and Fall of Suburbia.* New York: Basic Books.

Garon, Sheldon. 2011. *Beyond Our Means: Why America Spends While the World Saves.* Princeton, N.J.: Princeton University Press.

Graddy, Kathryn, and Diana C. Robertson. 1999. "Fairness of Pricing Decisions." *Business Ethics Quarterly* 9(2): 225–43.

Haggerty, Alfred G. 1995. "Quackenbush Cuts a Deal on Prop 103." *National Underwriter,* February 6.

Harrington, Scott, and Gregory Niehaus. 1998. "Race, Redlining, and Automobile Insurance Pricing." *Journal of Business* 71(3): 439–69.

Howard, J. C. 1997. "Calif. Regulations Decried as 'Jim Crow.'" *National Under-writer*, October 22.

———. 2000. "California State Auditor Hammers Quackenbush." *National Under-writer*, October 30.

Insurance Research Council. 2006. "Uninsured Drivers Increasing; Vary by State; Miss. Highest, Maine Lowest." *Insurance Journal*, June 28, 2006. Available at: http://www.insurancejournal.com/news/national/2006/06/28/69919.htm (accessed February 3, 2013).

Jackson, Kenneth. 1985. *Crabgrass Frontier: The Suburbanization of the United States.* New York: Oxford University Press.

Katznelson, Ira. 2005. *When Affirmative Action Was White.* New York: Oxford University Press.

Keister, Lisa A. 2000. "Race and Wealth Inequality: The Impact of Racial Differences in Portfolio Behavior on the Distribution of Household Wealth." *Social Science Research* 29(4): 477–502.

Kochhar, Rakesh, Richard Fry, and Paul Taylor. 2011. *Wealth Gaps Rise to Record Highs Between Whites, Blacks, Hispanics.* Washington, D.C.: Pew Research Center. July 26.

Kruse, Kevin M., and Thomas J. Sugrue. 2006. *The New Suburban History.* Chicago: University of Chicago Press.

Liedtke, Michael. 2005. "Car Insurance Costs Higher in Hispanic, Black Neighbor-hoods." *The Daily Journal*, San Mateo, Calif. Available at: http://archives.sm dailyjournal.com/article_preview.php?id=52461 (accessed March 19, 2013).

Lipman, Pauline. 2009. "The Cultural Politics of Mixed-Income Schools and Housing: A Racialized Discourse of Displacement, Exclusion, and Control." *Anthropology and Education Quarterly* 40(3): 215–16.

Lipsitz, George. 1998. *Possessive Investment in Whiteness.* Philadelphia, Pa.: Temple University Press.

National Underwriter. 1992–93. "Insurers Battle Garamendi over Calif. Prop. 103 Rebates." December 28, 1992–January 4, 1993.

———. 1995. "California Insurers Blast Anti-Redlining Proposal." December 11.

Ó' Tuathail, Gearoid. 1996. *Critical Geopolitics: The Writing of Global Space.* Minneapolis: University of Minnesota Press.

Personal Insurance Federation of California, American Insurance Association, and Association of California Insurance Companies. 2003. Joint press release, December 4. Available at: www.pifc.org/media/pdfiles/2003/pr120403.pdf (accessed November 2012).

"Plan to lower insurance rates gains momentum." 2005. *Michigan Chronicle*, August 17–23, p. A1.

PR Newswire. 2005. "Why People Who Live Close to Restaurants Are More Likely to Have an Accident and Pay More for Auto Insurance." December 6.

Pritchett, Wendell. 2005."From Theory to Practice: Race, Property Values, and Suburban America in the Post-War Years." Proceedings of Reconceptualizing the History of the Built Environment in North America, The Charles Warren Center, Cambridge, Mass. Available at: http://warrencenter.fas.harvard.edu/builtenv/Paper%20PDFs/Pritchett.pdf (accessed March 19, 2013).

Proposition 103 Enforcement Project v. Quackenbush, 64 Cal. App. 4th 1473 [76 Cal. Rptr 2d 342] (1998).

Shapiro, Thomas M. 2004. *The Hidden Cost of Being African American: How Wealth Perpetuates Inequality.* New York: Oxford University Press.

Stoll, Michael, and Paul Ong. 2008. "Why Do Inner City Residents Pay Higher Premiums? The Determinants of Automobile Insurance Premiums." Working Paper 1467276. Berkeley: University of California Transportation Center (January).

Thomas, Evan. 2006. "Decline and Fall (United States Congress, Newt Gingrich's 'common sense revolution,' and the Republican Party) (Cover story)." *Newsweek. HighBeam Research.* Available at: http://www.highbeam.com/doc/1G1-154352517.html (accessed April 17, 2013).

Tilly, Charles. 2001. "Mechanisms in Political Processes." *Annual Review of Political Science* 4(1): 21–41.

U.S. Newswire. 2006, July 14. "Consumers Union Applauds California Rules Barring Zip Code-Based Auto Insurance; CU Urges Other States to Give Drivers Similar Relief." Available at: http://www.insuranceusa.com/general/consumers-union-applauds-calif-rules-barring-zip-code-based-auto-insurance-cu-urges-other-states-to-give-drivers-similar-relief/ (accessed March 30, 2013).

Wallace, George. 2006. "Dangling Propositions." *Declarations and Exclusions,* February 6.

Wells, F. Jean, and William D. Jackson. 1999. *Major Financial Services Legislation, Gramm-Leach-Bliley Act: An Overview.* Congressional Research Service Report for Congress. December 16.

Williams, Terry C. 1988. "Practitioners: Dogs That Climb Trees." *Direct Marketing,* May.

Chapter 10 | Racial Segregation and the Marketing of Health Inequality

Naa Oyo A. Kwate

They drink it thinkin' it's good, but they don't sell that shit in the White neighborhood.

—Public Enemy, "1 Million Bottlebags," 1991

Why is it that there is a gun shop on almost every corner in this community? . . . For the same reason that there is a liquor store on almost every corner in the Black community. Why? They want us to kill ourselves.

—Furious Styles, *Boyz N The Hood*, 1991

THE DISMANTLING OF state-sanctioned discrimination substantiates in the American imagination the notion of a postracial world, particularly with the election of President Barack Obama. But anyone walking through a black neighborhood knows that the United States is not "postracial." The persistence of de facto segregation in most U.S. cities reminds us that we have not moved beyond the strictures of race. African Americans stand alone in the level of segregation they have faced for several decades in many U.S. cities (Massey and Denton 1993), and though there have been declines in U.S. segregation over time, they are relatively small (Iceland, Sharpe, and Steinmetz 2005) and unequally distributed across race and income groups (Fischer 2003). Moreover, relatively recent policies such as exclusionary density zoning have further contributed to segregation (Rothwell and Massey 2009).

If the modest declines in post–civil rights black-white segregation repudiate the notion of a postracial United States, so too do the sequelae of segregation. Racial residential segregation has been described as the cornerstone on which black-white health disparities rest, because segregation blocks access to socioeconomic resources that promote health and increases exposure to environmental insults that damage health (Williams and Collins 2001). For example, residential segregation constrains access to high-quality schooling, and education (and thereafter, occupation and income) is strongly and positively associated with health. Empirical studies showing negative associations between segregation and health (Chang 2006; Cooper et al. 2007; Subramanian, Acevedo-Garcia, and Osypuk 2005; White and Borrell 2006) give weight to theoretical elaborations about why segregation should be harmful to health. Compared with whites, black people in the United States experience disproportionate morbidity and mortality for many diseases and chronic conditions (for example, cardiovascular disease, obesity, diabetes, and cancer).

Other aspects of the social geography of black neighborhoods that might appear to be much more trivial—for example, how many fast food restaurants and alcohol ads are around—also play a fundamental role in understanding the persistence of racial inequality and the perpetuation of health disparities. Fast food and advertising are both as American as apple pie and seemingly prosaic in day-to-day living. Nonetheless, racialized marketing for these products has a profound influence directly and indirectly on how racial inequalities—in this case, health disparities—are sustained. A central theme throughout this volume is the notion that practices, processes, and institutions that appear to be racially neutral often have racially disparate consequences. This is certainly true for consumer marketing, a process typically constructed as merely a function of consumer demand and other objective market forces. It is true that marketers identify and target a variety of demographic segments, not all of which center on race; over-the-counter medicines may be marketed to seniors via television programs known to have older audiences. But when race is the demographic axis along which marketing is deployed, it necessarily relies on the marginalized position of black people in the United States; race is never neutral (Bonilla-Silva 1996).

Marketing's purpose is to create perceptions of nonmaterial value among consumers in order to prompt purchases (Grier and Kumanyika 2008), to effect top-of-mind preferences that often operate outside of awareness. In so doing, marketing is pernicious in shaping health-related behaviors. Clearly, marketing is just one of many factors that converge to shape what people consume; among others are individual taste preferences, cognitive factors including knowledge about how to shop for and cook healthy foods (Resnicow et al. 2000), social factors such as using food to project social position (Inness 2001; Mintz 2002), and contextual factors such as the economic condition of the country (Neuhaus 1999). But herein lies the import of marketing: it exudes a subtle and pervasive influence on all of these factors. For example, Americans' knowledge about and preferences for certain foods, shopping, and meal preparation are shaped in part by marketing. African Americans and members of other distinctive and socially disadvantaged groups respond more favorably to targeted advertising (Grier and Kumanyika 2008), most likely owing in part to the scarcity of self-images in the media. For that reason, it is troublesome that, as shown elsewhere in this volume, black consumers are connected to dysfunctional markets. In relation to fast food and alcoholic beverages, the dysfunction inheres not only in the products being marketed, which are themselves deleterious to health, but also in the methods used to promote them.

Two aspects of marketing are the promotion of products through advertising and other persuasive communication and the placement of products, their distribution, and their accessibility to target consumers (Grier and Kumanyika 2008). Fast food restaurants and alcohol ads appear in both black and white neighborhoods, but dissimilarities in their prevalence, content, and marketing strategies reinforce racial hierarchy and create starkly different outcomes related to health. The literature shows that fast food and alcohol are disproportionately and intensively marketed in black neighborhoods; the opening quotations in this chapter show that these processes have not gone unnoticed and are not viewed by the black "counterpublic" (Dawson 2001, 29) as the logical product of rational market forces.

Fast food and alcohol consumption are associated with many of the health conditions (for example, obesity, cardiovascular disease, diabetes) for which black-white health disparities are marked. In racially segregated localities, marketing for fast food and alcohol encourages indiscriminate consumption of products known to contribute directly to chronic disease, thereby perpetuating inequality for black health. In this regard, racialized marketing is clearly a focal point for understanding disparities in health chances. But more broadly, racially disparate marketing of these products harms health because by relegating undesirable commodities to black spaces and reifying negative connotations of blackness, it embodies and reproduces racism.

The arrangement of resources along racial lines is racist (Brooks 2009); in the United States, life and death are organized along racial lines, a profound statement of racism in this country. But as critical race theorists assert, racism does not comprise only those acts motivated by invidious antipathy. Hegemonic processes and narratives embedded in the structure of society operate to subordinate black people, rendering them of lesser im-

Figure 10.1   Structural Factors Underlying Vice Product Marketing, Inequality, and Health

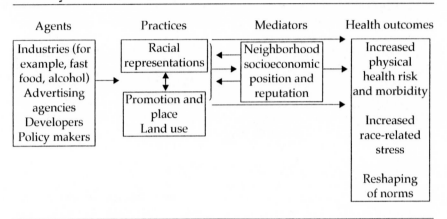

Source: Author's compilation.

portance and sustaining disparate resources and cultural discourses (Delgado and Stefancic 2001; Brooks 2009). This kind of racism is ordinary, encoded in the day-to-day life transactions (Delgado and Stefancic 2001). For that reason, it is useful to study neighborhood retailers and advertising precisely because they are routine aspects of daily living.

Figure 10.1 shows some of the interrelationships among agents, practices related to marketing, and socioeconomic mediators that interact and ultimately compromise communal physical and mental health. The figure is not meant to depict a linear trajectory of individual consumption patterns, though some of the health outcomes are, in part, a reflection of health behaviors (for example, dietary and alcohol intake). I also do not mean to suggest that health outcomes are the inexorable result of structural conditions that remove any decision-making capability from individuals. The focus here is on the interrelationships between structural factors that work in concert to produce and reproduce social inequalities—which shape both the density of vice products and disparities in health outcomes.

Agents, in this case, create marketing strategies directed at black audiences and create and support conditions that foster these strategies. Like other media domains, they also create representations—depictions and framing of black people in the dominant society. Representations are crucial in defining access to political and social power (hooks 1992) and act as deeply embedded frames in our psyche that make it difficult to use or maintain images or narratives that are contrary to the dominant ones (Hall 1998). Marketing strategies and representations are mutually reinforcing: representations of black people in the United States lead agents to employ particular marketing strategies (for example, connecting certain alcoholic beverages to hip-hop and other black cultural productions); these strategies, in turn, inform ideas and frames about blackness. Taking these together, racialized marketing harms health directly by increasing risk of morbidity and race-related stress and indirectly by worsening the socioeconomic position and reputation of black neighborhoods.

FAST FOOD MARKETING IN BLACK NEIGHBORHOODS

In metropolitan areas, fast food outlets are frequently located in commercial and central business districts, in tourist areas, near transportation hubs, and in suburban shopping centers and strip malls. In the residential areas of central cities, fast food is more prevalent in black neighborhoods, and that association is not attributable to differences in socioeconomic position (Block, Scribner, and DeSalvo 2004; Hurwitz et al. 2009; Kwate et al. 2009; L. V. Moore et al. 2009). Fast food outlets also make up a greater proportion of total restaurants in these communities. Of all the restaurants in Latino and black South Los Angeles, 73 percent were limited service and 27 percent full service, compared with 42 percent and 58 percent, respectively, in predominantly white West Los Angeles (Lewis et al. 2005). In New York City, the opening of an Applebee's in Brooklyn's Bedford-Stuyvesant in recent years made it the first national full-service restaurant to open in the neighborhood since the 1960s (Chamberlain 2004).

What have garnered less empirical study are the factors that have led to the greater observed densities of fast food. Devin Fergus (chap. 10, this volume) describes the ghetto tax as "a cryptic collection of fees and charges paid by *quarantined* consumers" (emphasis added). To characterize neighborhood residents as quarantined pointedly defines the spatial boundaries of inequality writ in the built environment, whether or not there is malicious intent. Roy Brooks (2009) argues that public officials site noxious facilities in black and Latino communities not out of hate but simply because it is convenient. Indeed, racism makes it convenient to site noxious facilities because racism creates the lower property values and weakened political power that make it easy to site not-in-my-backyard facilities in black and Latino neighborhoods.

The same is true for fast food and alcohol marketing; several factors make it convenient for agent siting practices to center in black neighborhoods, whether or not invidious antipathy plays a role. In earlier work

(Kwate 2008), I argue that even in the absence of purposeful targeting, fast food is likely to proliferate owing to the downstream effects of segregation. These include economic and business conditions and land-use characteristics such as anemic retail corridors; concentrated unemployment and economic disinvestment, which provide available labor pools and increase community receptiveness to fast food restaurants; and weakened community political strength, thereby reducing possible opposition to siting. Racialized marketing inevitably invites questions about whether these practices are only about economics or are about something more sinister. But the answer is that even if it is "only" economics (which I would argue is not true), the fact that structural conditions make it more economically rational to concentrate on, and profit from the health risks of, quarantined black consumers is indeed sinister.

Cost is an obvious determinant of where fast food companies and franchisers choose to locate, and these are often lower in black neighborhoods. As one example, vacant lots are common; even middle-class black neighborhoods have higher rates of vacant and boarded-up housing than comparable white neighborhoods (Pattillo 2005). Vacant lots encourage placement of outdoor ads, perhaps because there is simply more available space for such uses in neighborhoods that are less well built up (Kwate and Lee 2007). Similarly, at the material level, vacant lots may present greater opportunities for fast food outlets. Physical decay in black neighborhoods may not only allow more fast food outlets to be built but also may foster more freestanding fast food outlets and varied signage; and for national franchises, neighborhood decay may also make it possible to meet ideal siting conditions (for example, for McDonald's, more than 35,000 square feet and additional room for parking).

Vacant lots are also prominent signs of decline in Northeast cities (Accordino and Johnson 2000), and thus at a social level, they may attract fast-food agents for other reasons. Social disorganization in the form of socioeconomic disadvantage and residential instability are associated with the prevalence of offsite alcohol outlets (Nielsen et al. 2010). Social and physical disorder are also associated with storefront advertising for malt liquor (McKee et al. 2011). It may be that similar processes operate to shape the prevalence of fast food restaurants. Because vacant lots suggest greater social disorganization, they may signal to fast-food agents that a community is weak in the resources that could be marshaled to resist the entrée of fast food. Affluent, predominantly white neighborhoods have been battlegrounds between fast-food companies and indignant community residents, with the spoils of victory often going to the neighborhood. Having been stymied in 1974 (Love 1995), McDonald's tried again in 1997, without success, to open a location on the high-income Upper East Side of New

York to penetrate an urban market that had heretofore been ignored (Allon 1997). In referencing incidents, practices, and marketing strategies involving McDonald's, I do not mean to equate this multinational fast-food chain with all fast food. But it is precisely because it is the oldest, largest, and most recognized chain that it is instructive in understanding fast-food operations.

To be sure, fast-food siting in black neighborhoods is not driven solely by external forces. For some black franchisees, locating in their own communities is an opportunity to buttress economic and employment conditions. Indeed, Dorian Warren's analysis of Walmart (chap. 3, this volume) reveals that corporate-owned big-box retailers may be welcomed, even if in the context of an uneasy tension, because of the possibility of increased employment opportunities. But for franchisees without such motivations, residential segregation still exerts irresistible pressure on the location of their operations. In real estate, a successful sales record depends on extensive knowledge of and social networks in target neighborhoods. Because most black people in the United States live in predominantly black neighborhoods, this is likely to lead black brokers to focus on properties in black neighborhoods (Krysan 2008). As with real estate brokers, black fast-food franchisees are likely to have knowledge, social networks, and other resources that make their own (or other black) neighborhoods best suited to operate a small business. Figure 10.2 maps the address listings as of April 2010 for residential Chicago–area black-owned franchises. With the exception of a few downtown locations, all the restaurants are sited in the overwhelmingly black South and West sides of the city (U.S. Census Bureau 2000). It is possible, but not likely, that the spatial patterning of these black franchisees reflects only individual preferences for black neighborhoods.

More likely is that black franchisees are deliberately steered to black neighborhoods. Black franchisees who seek out neighborhoods that are less saturated with fast food, more affluent, and predominantly white confront institutional racism in franchise allocation. Again, these kinds of resource disparities need not be motivated by invidious antipathy. In a critical race-theory framework, the assignment of black reporters to stories on the inner city rather than Wall Street is racist because it defines black journalists as equipped only to cover "black news" (Brooks 2009). The same filters may deem black-owned restaurants in white neighborhoods as risks, financial or otherwise. Individual and class-action lawsuits have been levied against fast-food corporations for denying access to neighborhoods that are not matched by race or racially driven employment prospects (Jerry J Stubbs v. McDonald's Corporation 2005; Quitmon Hartzol v. McDonald's Corporation 2006; Gladwell, Farhi, and *Washington Post* staff writers 1988).

Figure 10.2   Black-Owned McDonald's Franchises in Chicago,
               2010

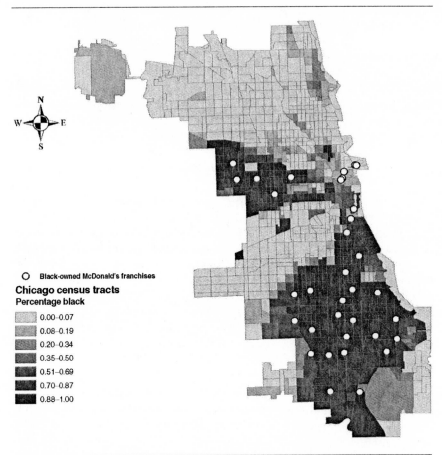

Source: Map created by author. Data from Black McDonald's Operators Association, "Our Locations" (www.bmoachicagoland.org/locations.php).

Remaking Fast Food as Black Food

When fast food emerged in the postwar era, McDonald's and most other chains studiously avoided central cities, concentrating instead on the suburbs (Levenstein 2003). Ray Kroc, the founder of the McDonald's franchise conducted location siting from a helicopter, looking for "schools and church steeples." He opened his first Chicago-area location in the far-flung suburb of Des Plaines (Kroc 1977), and chose as the image of the late-1950s McDonald's a tanned, hip, middle-class Californian (Kincheloe 2002). Mc-

Donald's represented a brash new concept in restaurant dining, and every U.S. town wanted one (Love 1995); when they received one, they felt that they had been validated and put on the map (Kincheloe 2002). Andrew Young argued that the coming of Walmart to Chicago's West Side meant that residents could live a middle-class lifestyle (chap. 5, this volume). Whether residents were middle class was another issue—discount, big-box shopping at least gave the imprimatur of the lifestyle.

Just as Walmart arrived in black neighborhoods only after twenty years of retailing to southern rural and suburban white America (chap. 6, this volume), fast food came late to black neighborhoods; and, when it did it, often it was not black owned. In the late 1960s, Cleveland saw black activists boycott McDonald's to protest the company's lack of black franchisees in black neighborhoods (Love 1995). Six years passed between the opening of Kroc's first restaurant in Des Plaines and a new franchise on East 35th Street on Chicago's South Side. The operator proclaimed that his aim was "to become a part of the South Side, a permanent community service just like the grocery or the neighborhood drug store" ("McDonald's Restaurant Opens on 35th Street" 1961). In the same vein, a West Side manager argued that "in the inner city, a McDonald's ceases to be a restaurant and becomes more like a supermarket. You see some of the same children five or six times a day, and adults, too. . . . The store is more of a necessity to the community than a place for treats" (Chapman 1974). Ironically and disturbingly, fast food has come to be just that in many black neighborhoods, one of few dependable commercial outlets that exist for food away from home and facilitate discretionary spending, social interaction, and entertainment.

In the 1970s the company debuted its first major television marketing campaign with the slogan "You deserve a break today," accompanied by a well-known commercial jingle. In the film *Ordinary People*, boisterous teens enter a McDonald's restaurant, singing the song loudly, thereby disturbing the patrons. One of these is the lead character, an affluent boy from the exclusive suburban Chicago enclave of Lake Forest, on his first date. This film scene portrays McDonald's as a site for conviviality and wholesome fun, a setting for rites-of-passage among all-American, suburban white youth. But as the fast-food industry grew explosively over the 1960s and 1970s, more and more franchises were located in black neighborhoods, planting the seeds for the connection between blackness and fast food. Industry documents made available to the public after the tobacco industry's 1998 Master Settlement Agreement shed light on corporations' marketing practices. For example, Lorillard specifically recast Newport as a black brand, using several programs in the mid-1980s such as Inner City Sales, with the stated goal of obtaining new smokers and maintaining current smokers among black and Latino young adults with a high school education or less, and the Van Program, which distributed free samples on the street. Without the kinds of documents brought to the surface after the Master Settlement Agreement, it is difficult to discern the extent to which the fast-food industry sought to specifically reposition fast food as black food. But an early 1970s McDonald's company brochure reportedly noted that although suburbs were well saturated and international sites were penetrated, "inner-city areas are virtually untapped" (Chapman 1974).

Regardless of the kinds of strategies fast-food agents employed to tap that market, while fast food became associated with blackness, it also came to be seen as an undesirable, "tasteless and offensive" (Davey 1998) retail segment that served only to destroy the character of upscale and white space. Fast food's prevalence in black neighborhoods stained the enterprise, rendering it inner-city culinary detritus. In 1974 residents of exclusive Brooklyn Heights expressed concern about the entrée of fast food in their community. When the neighborhood embarked on revitalization plans, one of the proposed changes centered on Montague Street, a key retail corridor. However, neighborhood residents had some concerns with this proposal, fearing "the intrusion of commercial uses serving only the [working population], particularly fast food establishments" (City of New York and Department of City Planning 1976, 7). Fast food was perceived, then, as a gauche product that catered to the laboring Other, who worked in but could not afford to live in the neighborhood. These thinly veiled concerns about fast food consumers were addressed more openly in skirmishes in Washington, D.C., and New York City, where residents cited fears of chicken bones, biscuit crumbs, and unwholesome people (Crow 2002; Levey 1980).

Progressive critiques of McDonald's also frequently veer into class-inscribed elitism and condescension toward those who work and eat there (Kincheloe 2002). But this elitist contempt is reserved for certain fast food agents—the large multinational chains and the fried chicken restaurant kudzu that dot the landscape in black neighborhoods. The products these agents sell—burgers and fries—are not themselves inherently problematic. Quite the contrary, within central cities, trendy burger joints currently enjoy gourmet culinary status, high sales, and media attention. In New York City, the Shake Shack describes itself as a "modern day 'roadside' burger stand," and the affluent Upper East Side welcomed the opening of a location there (Gregor 2010), a radical departure from the sustained resistance to the entrée of McDonald's. Other fast food restaurants proffer "foodie" versions of fast food, with organic ingredients and low-fat or homemade preparation methods (Better Burger NYC, Bark Hot Dogs). Fast food is not entirely absent from white urban neighborhoods—there are standard fast food outlets, and gourmet fast food locates almost exclusively in these

Figure 10.3   Ramshackle Fast Food Outlets in Brooklyn, 1980s

areas and attracts affluent clientele. But outside of gentrifying areas, foodie fast food remains largely absent in black spaces.

Ultimately, this discrepancy subordinates black people by designating fast food with higher perceived quality as compatible only with white space and by relegating the least desirable fast food establishments to black space. Moreover, many of the less desirable restaurants ply their goods with few frills; bulletproof glass, restricted seating, and rude kitchen facilities are commonplace. These ramshackle fast food outlets are often the only game in town for many blocks around, a condition that has persisted for decades (figure 10.3). Although the cheaper rents and other factors that make black neighborhoods attractive to fast food operators should be equally attractive to a diverse set of restaurant types, these areas are effectively redlined by retailers, particularly chain stores (D'Rozario and Williams 2005). In Atlanta, low- and high-income predominantly black census tracts had less access than predominantly white tracts matched to a number of resources, including restaurants that were not fast food (Hellig and Sawicki 2003).

Retail redlining results in part from industry characterizations about black neighborhoods as unsophisticated markets. Fergus (chap. 10, this volume) argues that the ghettoization of motorists in the 1970s was related to the wider trend of psychographics. Psychographics sought to profile the values and lifestyles of consumers and allowed marketers to target products to certain categories of consumer. Today, these consumer segmentation systems are widely used to describe the lifestyle preferences, spending habits, and favorite brands and products of neighborhood residents. It is argued that such systems enable businesses to capitalize on possible markets that might be missed when using demographics alone and are useful in identifying locations for new stores, selecting merchandise that matches consumer preferences, and targeting advertising with the right message (ESRI 2007). For example, one growing fast food franchise has used geodemographics to predict where other restaurants could successfully be opened ("Culver's Turns to GIS for Successful Franchising" 2008–09).

Applied Geographic Solutions' Mosaic system, originally developed by the credit-reporting company Experian, defines sixty market segments. In addition to narrative summaries of consumer characteristics, Mosaic also ascribes the names of a fictional heterosexual couple to each category, solidifying extant stereotypes about particular racial and ethnic populations (for example, "Jermaine and Keisha" to "African American neighborhoods"; "Jorge and Ana" to "Nuevo Hispanic Families"; and "Archie and Edith" to "Steadfast Conservatives") (Experian Business Strategies 2006, 2). Across all of these systems, African American neighborhoods fare poorly in retail reputation. As Fergus (chap. 10, this volume) argues, segmentation systems assume that neighborhood residence is a pure reflection of choice: "Segmentation systems operate on the theory that people with similar tastes, lifestyles, and behaviors seek others with the same tastes—'like seeks like'" (1); and "Neighborhoods are natural formations of people drawn together by their common need for a 'place'—for security and acceptance" (2). These assertions elide the fact that neighborhoods are strongly determined by institutional and other forces and that for black residents, the constraints induced by racial segregation make it unlikely that residential choices are made only on the basis of lifestyles and taste. The premise of community segmentation systems, that "like seeks like," assumes a free and unrestricted housing market and unduly privileges individual preference.

In the same vein, perceived consumer behaviors are described acontextually. In ESRI's tapestry system, "Laptops and Lattes" describes urban neighborhoods populated by cosmopolitan, single city lovers who shop at upscale apparel chains and buy organic and low-fat foods (ESRI 2007). The accumulated evidence shows that the reportedly predominantly white consumers in this segment can engage in these behaviors because they have access to goods and services that black consumers do not (for example, see Hellig and Sawicki 2003; Smiley et al. 2010). Black neighborhoods are generally depicted as unattractive and unviable retail markets where discretionary spending is minimal or absent and where residents are devoid of taste, cultural capital, and modernity. Residents in the "Top Rung" group are described as follows: "Health conscious, they exercise (do yoga and aerobics, play tennis, ski, ice skate, and snorkel), take vitamins and buy low-fat food" (ESRI 2007, 22). The implication is that individuals who do not engage in these behaviors are not health conscious. It may be that in black neighborhoods, residents do not engage in these kinds of physical and dietary behaviors simply because they lack the means (income or access to facilities) to do so. As a result, structural inequality is displaced onto neighborhood residents and interpreted as consumer preference.

Alcohol Advertising in Black Neighborhoods

Each day as thousands of persons visit the chain stores in their neighborhoods, their journey carries them past powerful messages advantageously placed on nearby poster panels. . . . These hundreds of thousands of buyers repeatedly receive up to the minute information concerning products necessary to their daily living. . . . Potential consumers are also reached by this all-inclusive medium. As purchase influencers, schoolchildren represent an active group of great value. Strategic locations ensure repetition, and repetition creates consumer remembrance, driving home a message. (Handy [Jam] Organization 1942)

Outdoor ads are nothing new. In 1937 outdoor ads on New York City's East Houston Street touted everything from hot Sunkist lemonade as a remedy for common colds to an operetta at the Imperial Theater. Notably, one of the largest of all of these ads showcased Trommer's, a local brewery. In the contemporary moment, high densities of outdoor alcohol ads are almost the exclusive province of black and Latino neighborhoods. In many U.S. cities, ad spaces themselves are more abundant in black neighborhoods. This is true in Chicago (Hackbarth, Silvestri, and Cosper 1995) and in New York City, where high- and low-income black neighborhoods were equally exposed (Kwate and Lee 2007). In Los Angeles, Austin, New York City, and Philadelphia, low-income zip codes had twice as many ads as high-income zip codes and three times the sheetspace (actual footage of ad space) (Yancey et al. 2009).

Research shows that once ad spaces are built, ads in black neighborhoods are far more likely than those in white neighborhoods to promote alcoholic beverages (Altman, Schooler, and Basil 1991; Hackbarth, Silvestri, and Cosper 1995; Mitchell and Greenberg 1991). Tobacco can no longer be advertised outdoors after the Master Settlement Agreement, but a review of the few studies done in the 1990s shows that black neighborhoods had 2.6 times as many tobacco ads per person as white neighborhoods (Primack et al. 2007). Alcohol, facing no restrictions, continues to populate black neighborhood ad space. In one study, although outdoor alcohol ads were more prevalent in black neighborhoods in Atlanta, this did not hold in a number of other cities (H. Moore et al. 2009). However, most research consistently documents a greater density of alcohol ads in black neighborhoods.

It might be assumed that high targeting reflects high demand for alcohol in these neighborhoods, but this is not borne out by health or consumer data. Drinking rates are lower in black populations for both men and women. In 2006, among black men, 58.7 percent were current drinkers, compared with 69.4 percent of white men; rates were 40.4 percent and 58.6 percent for black and white women, respectively (National Center for Health Statistics 2007). Indeed, black men have the same prevalence of drinking as white women.

Consumer expenditure data also reveal that blacks spend less than whites on alcohol. Figure 10.4 shows expenditures for liquor bought for home consumption in some New York City neighborhoods. As can be seen, expenditures for liquor were lowest in Harlem and the South Bronx, areas where alcohol advertising is dense. In contrast, on the affluent and predominantly white Upper West and Upper East Sides, where expenditures are high, alcohol ads are scarce. It is also true that alcohol advertising is not welcomed by black community residents. In the 1990s, cities across the country engaged in whitewashing campaigns, wherein alcohol (and at the time, tobacco) ads were painted over by residents and community activists. Figure 10.5 shows a more recent (2005) expression of such dissent to a Heineken ad in Brooklyn.

Industry pundits hold fast to the position that marketing practices are based purely on rational supply-and-demand models. Yet health data show low drinking rates, consumer data show low retail demand, and community responses to advertising are negative. In this case, it is difficult to dismiss arguments that intensive marketing in the face of such circumstances constitutes invidious antipathy, an attempt to actively foster black self-harm. At the very least, it has been argued, alcohol companies seek to profit from human misery in black communities (Weems 1998), if not to create it outright. In this regard, the representations of black people in alcohol marketing are important. The cultural commentary and specific messages that direct black audiences toward the palliative use of alcohol are important. Some research has been conducted coding ad content and tabulating the data in percentages of thematic categories (for example, see At-

Figure 10.4   Annual Expenditures on Liquor for Home Consumption
in Selected New York City Neighborhoods, 2006

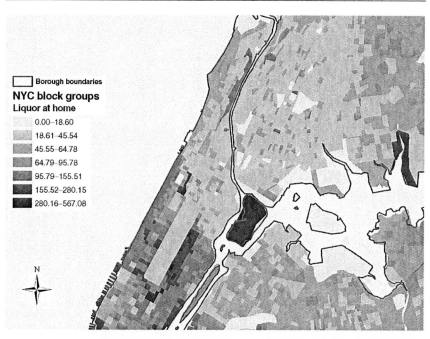

Source: The data in this figure, which are based on the U.S. Bureau of Labor Statistics'
Consumer Expenditure Survey 2006, were purchased by the author and form the basis of the
map, which was created by the author.

kin and Block 1981; Mastro and Atkin 2002; Schooler, Basil, and Altman
1996); findings suggest that certain themes such as sex and romance appear much more frequently in black than in white neighborhoods (Altman,
Schooler, and Basil 1991). Still, despite the volume of data on outdoor alcohol advertising in African American communities, little research has
closely investigated the semiotic content of the ads.

Representations determine not only how outgroup members view individuals but also how ingroup members think about themselves (hooks
1992). In the United States, representations of black people are overwhelmingly negative and challenge beliefs about their intrinsic worth. Black representations frequently depict primitiveness indicated by reliance on baser
instincts and sexuality, unusually strong corporeal constitution, and predatory violence. Also common are representations centering on less sophis-

Figure 10.5   Community Responses to Alcohol Advertising, Brooklyn, 2005

Source: Author's collection.

ticated psyches and inferior intellect (Guthrie 1998; Thomas and Sillen 1991). I focus on two themes found to be common in New York City ads: sex and romance and socioeconomic mobility. These themes, and the representations of blackness inscribed in them, make racial inequality and subordination a highly visible feature of the built environment in black neighborhoods.

Representing Blackness in Alcohol Ads

Lauren Rosewarne (2007) argues that sexist outdoor advertisements resemble "pin-ups," images that are forbidden in workplaces because they constitute sexual harassment. But audiences cannot avoid being exposed to sexist outdoor ads, which masculinize public space and make women feel out of place and excluded. Citing extant research, Rosewarne argues that a focus on women's bodies suggests they are merely bodies rather than somebodies. In black neighborhoods, the use of sexual imagery and themes has particular salience given the ways in which sexuality is connected to blackness in the dominant society. Black women are eroticized, stereotyped as sexually promiscuous and deviant. In contrast to the demure or moral posture that tends to be accorded to white women, black women are portrayed as lascivious and excessive (Roberts 1997; West 1995; hooks 1992).

Outdoor advertisements continue these narratives in public space. Ads suggest to black male viewers that alcohol is a means through which they can obtain or express power through sexuality. The ads objectify black women's bodies through the use of revealing clothing and an intense gaze (by both the viewer and the men in the ads). In this way, the ads position male viewers as able to simply step into and be admitted into the scene (Alaniz and Wilkes 1995). An advertisement for Colt 45 malt liquor (figure 10.6) aggressively markets deviant black sexuality, drawing on a previous campaign from the 1980s. The text, "Every time," is a shortened version of the earlier campaign's "The power of Colt 45. It works every time," a message once delivered by the actor Billy Dee Williams (Weems 1998). The shorter message is no less explicit: Colt 45 is associated with sexual potency and attractive women and will "get" women to have sex with men. In the 1990s, hip-hop celebrities were often spokespeople for malt liquor, connecting the product to a gritty, authentically urban, black masculine aesthetic. Ice Cube recorded a commercial for St. Ides, which then had the highest alcohol content of any mass-produced beer; the lyrics included statements such as "Gets your girl in the mood quicker, gets your jimmy [penis] thicker" (Alaniz and Wilkes 1998; Herd 1993; Scott, Denniston, and Magruder 1992). The continued use of such messages in outdoor advertising perpetuates representations of black women as ready and available sexual conquests and black men as sexual studs.

Today, malt liquor has a much smaller market share of alcohol sales; by 2001 it had suffered its fourth consecutive year of volume shrinkage (Adams Business Research 2001). In addition, advertising expenditures for malt liquor have shrunk compared with other beer categories. Distilled liquors such as brandy and cognac enjoy greater relative success: "The appearance of Courvoisier and Remy Red in popular culture . . . has garnered a hip image for the entire category. Much of the younger brandy and cognac market skews ethnic-urban African American consumers in particular" (Adams Business Research 2003). The advertising hip-hop artist Busta

Figure 10.6   Outdoor Advertising for Colt 45 Malt Liquor, Harlem, New York City

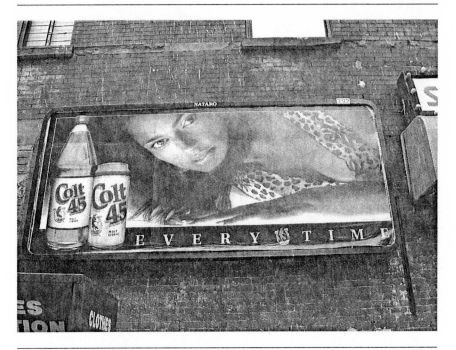

Source: Author's collection.

Rhymes, who released the hit song "Pass the Courvoisier" in 2002, was hailed by industry leaders as a catalyst in increasing cognac sales among black consumers. Indeed, in 1997 the percentage of white drinkers who consumed cognac was 8.6 percent, while it was 14.6 percent among black drinkers; by 2003, consumption had decreased to 5.6 percent of whites, and had increased to 21.1 percent among blacks (Adams Business Research 2003).

The promise of socioeconomic mobility undergirds racialized marketing for cognac. Marketing specialists recognize that black consumers can affirm their full participation and membership in U.S. society through their purchasing choices (Lamont and Molnar 2001), and alcoholic beverage companies are well aware of this fact: "It is difficult not to see these alcohol media entreaties as an invitation to participate in the 'good life' of the greater society. Admission seems to be available for the purchase price of the product" (Alaniz and Wilkes 1998, 447). Themes of upward social mobility, class status, and wealth accumulation are pervasive in advertisements in black neighborhoods, from blatant text such as "You've arrived" (Remy Martin) to more subtle messages suggesting that alcohol is part and parcel of black people's moving into social locations imbued with monetary reward, prestige, and legitimacy.

Courvoisier used a number of insidious messages to promote its XO ("Extra Old") product line, a cognac that retails for $148 a bottle. The price alone is suggestive of the ad campaign's underlying goals. To market such an expensive alcoholic beverage in communities where a significant number of the population live below the poverty line is to glorify conspicuous alcohol consumption as a means of performing an alternate socioeconomic reality. This is a dangerous proposition, with clear implications for alcohol-related health disparities: "The more drinks are used to signify selection and exclusion, the more we might expect its abuse to appear among the ranks of the excluded" (Akyeampong 1996, 4).

Ads in the Courvoisier series, such as the one shown in figure 10.7, feature a close-up of the bottle alone, accompanied by various taglines. To what "anything" does this ad refer? Given that it is directed at a black audience, long-standing and elusive struggles to achieve equality in almost every social domain certainly come to mind. This ad suggests that although a postracial republic may be an inchoate ideal, a sip of expensive liquor is not. An alcoholic drink might as well stand in for failure to achieve the American Dream; black people are invited to grasp the small part of the lifestyle to which they have access (Alaniz and Wilkes 1998). Another ad in the series reads "Upgrade." Here again, the viewer is encouraged to use alcohol as a means through which to move up the social ladder, to upgrade from the banality of life in the ghetto. Other ads in the campaign ("Don't Just Stand There, Get Rich," "You Wish," and "That's It, Look Up to Me") also tell black residents that though they may be distant from America's socioeconomic and cultural elite, alcohol consumption can close the gap.

Taken together, fast food and alcohol agents, marketing practices, and the black representations they disseminate work in concert to maintain black subordination. Many Americans believe the United States to be postracial primarily because they do not perceive blatant racial inequality on a day-to-day basis. But hidden from view are processes that are mundane and largely invisible, merely business as usual, literally and figuratively. Corporate agents at once highlight and attempt to deny racial inequity by targeting black audiences with the same subordinating filters that structure the rest of society. For that reason, racialized marketing constitutes an important health-destabilizing force among black populations.

Figure 10.7   Outdoor Advertising for Courvoisier Cognac, Harlem, New York City

Source: Author's collection.

Effects of Racialized Marketing on Well-Being in Black Neighborhoods

Racialized marketing acts as an institutional filter that sustains disparate resources. The disproportionate density of these commodities is essentially a spatial representation of racial hierarchy and marks neighborhoods as the ghetto, thereby furthering disinvestment. That is, an abundance of alcohol ads and fast food outlets are evident in a neighborhood perceived to be the ghetto; but it is also the case that the ghetto is perceived to be an area where those marketing practices are deployed heavily. As indicated in figure 10.1, racialized marketing negatively affects socioeconomic conditions in black neighborhoods, and the resultant conditions feed backward to incite further racialized marketing. Because investors and policy makers tend to infer community predilections from extant infrastructure in black neighborhoods, the marketing of alcohol and fast food mitigates against black neighborhoods receiving positive marketing characterizations. The end result is a vicious cycle in which negative street-level features result in negative characterizations and negative characterizations result in few positive street-level resources. Although black communities are abundant targets in fast food and alcohol marketing, research shows that they are lacking in the organizational resources used in day-to-day living such as hardware stores, pharmacies, banks, and restaurants (Small and McDermott 2006). Racialized marketing of fast food and alcohol contributes to the differential distribution of resources, goods, and services by creating negative retail reputations—marking some neighborhoods as less desirable or tenable than others as consumer markets.

A diminished retail environment is important not only because residents have minimal access to goods and services but also because neighborhoods without them are doubly saddled with compromised opportunity structures, which negatively affects health. Mary Pattillo (2009) contends that one common means of combating urban poverty is to increase the numbers of nonpoor people by luring them from somewhere else (through urban renewal, gentrification, and the like). In this regard, middle-class households are particularly valued because they attract taxpaying businesses. The poor retail reputation held by black neighborhoods mitigates against attracting business in the way that middle-class households do, making predominantly white, suburban and exurban spaces the default for savvy and eligible consumer markets. Retail reputation also affects asset accumulation because homeownership is the primary means through which Americans build wealth (Shapiro 2005). Retail and other organizational amenities are important determinants of neighborhood desirability, making the underresourced context in black neighborhoods a factor in lower home values. Together, the loss in money, power, and prestige (Link and Phelan 1995) wrought by an inferior retail reputation decreases health and well-being.

Physical Health

Racialized marketing directly affects health. At the most basic level, the promotion of fast food and alcohol and placement of outlets for their purchase shape health disparities because consumption of these products is associated with many of the conditions for which black populations experience significant morbidity. Fast food has been shown to be an important factor in adult obesity and chronic disease (Alter and Eny 2005; Bodor et al. 2010; Morgenstern et al. 2009), adult dietary intake (Jeffrey et al. 2006; Li et al. 2009; L. V. Moore et al. 2009), and childhood obesity (Currie et al. 2009; Davis and Carpenter 2009). Exposure to a marketing mix in which access to diverse food stores are limited and high-calorie foods are easily accessible or heavily promoted renders overconsumption normative and can override public health promotion efforts, which are less persuasive (Grier and Kumanyika 2008).

If outdoor alcohol advertising increases alcohol consumption, black residents are at risk for several negative health outcomes. Among youth, advertising is associated with more positive feelings about alcohol and increased consumption (Nyborn et al. 2009). Alcohol is the most widely used drug among black youth (Wallace et al. 2002), although use is low relative to all youth. In 2006, 45.3 percent of all high school seniors used alcohol in the past month, compared to 29.5 percent of black seniors (National Center for Health Statistics 2007). Youth drinking is associated with a range of negative health consequences. Risky sexual behavior is one of them, a critical factor in the incidence of infection from HIV/AIDS, which disproportionately affects young black males and females (Centers for Disease Control and Prevention and 2003). For adults, alcohol consumption is associated with hypertension, heart disease, and some cancers. Among black women in Central Harlem, neighborhood exposure to alcohol advertising was associated with greater odds of having a drinking pattern suggestive of abuse or dependence (Kwate and Meyer 2009). Intense marketing efforts to encourage black people to consume alcohol put them at risk of these and other negative outcomes.

The aesthetic quality of neighborhoods also affects health. Physical activity and well-being are lessened in environments that are less appealing (Diez-Roux 2003), and some research shows that black residents perceive their neighborhoods to be less pleasant and safe for physical activity relative to whites (Hargreaves, Schlundt, and Buchowski 2002). It is possible that an overabundance of fast food outlets and alcohol ads, in concert with other material liabilities, play a role in low assessments of neighborhood attractiveness.

Mental Health

Racialized marketing also has import for mental health and well-being. It increases race-related stress and reshapes norms around identity and health behaviors. With regard to race-related stress, one form is internalized racism. Black viewers may internalize the representations of blackness in outdoor advertising, which contains subordinating messages about the black community and its relationship to the dominant society. In the late 1960s and early 1970s, the sociopolitical philosophy prevalent in some sectors of the black community "came to identify blackness with the trappings of the ghetto . . . all of which appeared to mark a life lived close to one's black roots. . . . Eventually, poverty and ghetto life (sometimes the very degrading constraints imposed on Black America by White America) were frequently idealized and glamorized" (Bogle 1994, 236). The black sociopolitical climate is clearly different today, especially so with the election of Barack Obama. But the underlying processes of identification are still relevant, particularly because positive images of African Americans in the media remain few and far between and because the symbolic use of consumer commodities to express myriad social identities is significant. In this way, the images and messages used in outdoor advertisements themselves represent a toxic exposure. The disproportionate density of alcohol ads is racist not only because it represents unequal distribution in the marketing of health-damaging products but also because ad content frequently fosters negative representations of African Americans.

Indeed, Brooks (2009) argues that negative images of black people are projected into the homes of youth unfiltered, with no well-informed voice serving as a mediator. Youth may be particularly receptive to advertising imagery, but for all viewers, outdoor ads reify negative ideologies about black people and make them normative and authentic. This is particularly true given that the images promoted on alcohol ads are located in highly visible, outdoor locations that individuals must pass repeatedly as they move through their own communities. As was noted in 1942, repetition creates consumer remembrance, driving home a message (Handy [Jam] Organization 1942).

Racialized marketing can increase race-related stress not only through internalization of negative representations but through an alternative stress response to those representations. Some residents—perhaps those with greater sensitivity to race and racism—will perceive the disproportionality of promotion for these products as a deliberate and nefarious targeting scheme to harm black health (Furious Styles, "They want us to kill ourselves"). Thus to the extent that alcohol ads and fast food outlets are perceived as such, they represent a perceived exposure to racism, with all the attendant mental health risks of this stressor, including psychological distress and psychiatric symptoms (Paradies 2006; Pascoe and Smart Richman 2009). Similarly, some black neighborhood residents perceive alcohol ads as physical disorder in their neighborhoods—which typically comprises such elements as litter, abandoned cars, burned-out buildings, and graffiti (Sampson and Raudenbush 2004). Chronic stress derived from perceptions of disorder is associated with poor self-rated health, psychological distress, and impaired physical function (Steptoe and Feldman 2001), and feelings of personal powerlessness and psychological distress (Downey and Van Willigen 2005).

Finally, high densities of fast food outlets and alcohol ads affect the norms in the community. Fast food operators perceive black and Latino consumers as a valuable market (Arellano 2004; Bunn 1997; Perlik 2005; Wolf 2001), particularly children: the "youngest customer today is our buyer of tomorrow" (Moncreiff Arrarte 1997). Corporations know that young people's tastes and preferences are being formed, particularly through repeated exposure to certain foods. Thus if fast food is pervasive in the environment, children may view these choices as normative. Children going to McDonald's "know everything about it: how to deport themselves, how to stand in line, how to order, how to eat, and how to dispose of their garbage" (Kincheloe 2002, 20). In the same way that meals are routinized at McDonald's, the high density of fast food restaurants may serve to routinize dietary behavior in black neighborhoods. For children, a meal at a fast food restaurant may be a special treat, but for adults, these outlets become purely utilitarian aspects of the food landscape for cheap and convenient fuel. As noted earlier, many of these restaurants have little appeal, with cramped, institutional, and fortified structures (Vergara 1997). Simply by virtue of their spatial density, the restaurant landscape establishes norms about what dining is, can be, or should be.

CONCLUSION

Black consumers are at once a second-class and a sought-after market segment, and racialized marketing perpetuates racial inequity and contributes indirectly and directly to the maintenance of health and resource disparities. This chapter has focused on the agents that directly create racialized marketing. What about policy makers, who indirectly and directly create contexts amenable to racialized marketing? What kinds of policy levers are likely to be effective in redressing disparities, particularly when both the state and industry argue that consumers are free to make choices about how they will engage with available products? Resource-targeted policies (Yancey et al. 2009) include instituting municipal bans of undesired resources and are difficult to implement. For outdoor alcohol advertising, sheer volume presents policy makers with a daunting scope of marketing practices that require regulation. Anheuser-Busch alone spent nearly $100 million in outdoor advertising in 2009 (TNS Media Intelligence/LMR 2010), a disproportionate amount of which was most likely directed at black communities. Potential challenges to advertising are tempered by First Amendment concerns (Marin Institute 2007). Although advertising falls under the lower level of speech protections afforded corporations ("commercial speech"), public health advocates are frequently intimidated from using restrictions or bans on advertising, because corporations have been effective in using First Amendment lawsuits to scare off government regulation (Simon 2008). Yet the Master Settlement Agreement successfully banned tobacco ads in standard outdoor media, and bans on alcohol advertising have worked in specific contexts such as public transit (Marin Institute 2007) and in close proximity to areas where youth congregate (H. Moore et al. 2009).

Using resource-targeted bans for fast food outlets is also challenging, although some municipalities (for example, Port Jefferson, N.Y., and Calistoga, Calif.) have successfully implemented bans on "formula restaurants" for aesthetic and urban planning concerns. However, similar policy action based on health concerns (Los Angeles City Council 2008) has elicited strong outcries not only from industry but from public commentators as well—although these come rarely from the affected communities. Policy makers are much more willing to institute solutions that place the onus either on individuals, to modify health behaviors in the face of significant environmental challenges, or on communities, to monitor and counter racist industry practices.

A more appropriate framework might be to consider racialized marketing a civil rights issue. Dolores Acevedo-Garcia et al. (2008) argue that because residential segregation drives health disparities, antidiscrimination litigation could be invaluable in combating disparities in access to opportunity neighborhoods. Legal analysis is needed to determine whether this is possible for the racialized marketing of fast food and alcohol. It may be that such an approach allows the contestation not only of disproportionate spatial densities but also of subordinating representations. Otherwise, piecemeal and individual-level approaches are not likely to be successful and do not answer the broader question of why legitimacy is accorded to inequalities in health-destabilizing exposures in the first place. This volume has underlined the importance of this broader question. In the age of Obama, Americans are only too eager to pronounce the end of racism and foreclose race from serious discussion of American life. In so doing, the inequalities that remain embedded in day-to-day life either go unnoticed or are seen as the natural way of things (Loury 2002). In fact, inequalities in the marketing of fast food and alcohol in black neighborhoods are unnatural and unfair and harm black health, communal wealth, and well-being.

REFERENCES

Accordino, John, and Gary T. Johnson. 2000. "Addressing the Vacant and Abandoned Property Problem." *Journal of Urban Affairs* 22(5): 301–15.

Acevedo-Garcia, Dolores, et al. 2008. "Toward a Policy-Relevant Analysis of Geographic and Racial/Ethnic Disparities in Child Health." *Health Affairs* 27(2): 321–33.

Adams Business Research. 2001. *Adams Beer Handbook, 2001*. Norwalk, Conn.: Adams Business Research.

———. 2003. *Adams Liquor Handbook, 2003*. Norwalk, Conn.: Adams Business Research.

Akyeampong, Emmanuel. 1996. *Drink, Power, and Cultural Change : A Social History of Alcohol in Ghana, c. 1800 to Recent Times*. Portsmouth, N.H.: Heinemann.

Alaniz, Maria L., and Chris Wilkes. 1995. "Reinterpreting Latino Culture in the Commodity Form: The Case of Alcohol Advertising in the Mexican American Community." *Hispanic Journal of Behavioral Sciences* 17(4): 430–51.

———. 1998. "Pro-Drinking Messages and Message Environments for Young Adults: The Case of Alcohol Industry Advertising in African American, Latino, and Native American Communities." *Journal of Public Health Policy* 19(4): 447–72.

Allon, Janet. 1997. "McDonald's Withdraws, for Now." *New York Times*, January 5. Available at: LEXIS-NEXIS Academic Universe, General News.

Alter, David A., and Karen Eny. 2005. "The Relationship Between the Supply of Fast-Food Chains and Cardiovascular Outcomes." *Canadian Journal of Public Health* 96(3): 173–77.

Altman, David, Caroline Schooler, and Michael Basil. 1991. "Alcohol and Cigarette Advertising on Billboards." *Health Education Research* 6(4): 487–90.

Arellano, Kristi. 2004. "Pizzeria to Serve Up Latin Flavor in Denver: Four Restaurants Targeted Towards the Hispanic Market Are Planned for the Metro Area Beginning This Summer." *Denver Post*, June 6. Available at: LEXIS-NEXIS Academic Universe, General News.

Atkin, Charles, and Martin Block. 1981. *Content and Effects of Alcohol Advertising*. Report prepared for the Bureau of Alcohol, Tobacco and Firearms. PB82-123142. Springfield, Va.: National Technical Information Service.

Block, Jason, Richard Scribner, and Karen DeSalvo. 2004. "Fast Food, Race/Ethnicity, and Income: A Geographic Analysis." *American Journal of Preventive Medicine* 27(3): 211–17.

Bodor, J. Nicolas, et al. 2010. "The Association Between Obesity and Urban Food Environments" *Journal of Urban Health* 87(5): 771–81.

Bogle, Donald. 1994. *Toms, Coons, Mulattoes, Mammies, and Bucks: An Interpretive History of Blacks in American Films*. New York: Continuum.

Bonilla-Silva, Eduardo 1996. "Rethinking Racism: Toward a Structural Interpretation." *American Sociological Review* 62(3): 465–80.

Brooks, Roy. 2009. *Racial Justice in the Age of Obama*. Princeton, N.J.: Princeton University Press.

Bunn, Dina. 1997. "McDonald's Ads to Focus on Minorities." *Rocky Mountain News (Colo.)*, December 28, p. 5G. Available at: LEXIS-NEXIS Academic Universe, General News.

Centers for Disease Control and Prevention. 2003. *HIV Prevention in the Third Decade. Atlanta, GA: US Department of Health and Human Services.* Available at: www.cdc.gov/hiv/HIV_3rdDecade/(accessed July 15, 2011).

Chamberlain, Lisa. 2004. "The Residential Is Hot, but the Commercial Is Not." *The New York Times,* August 22. Available at: LEXIS-NEXIS Academic Universe, General News.

Chang, Virginia W. 2006. "Racial Residential Segregation and Weight Status among U.S. Adults." *Social Science and Medicine* 63(5): 1289–303.

Chapman, Lisa D. 1974. "Black Franchises under the McDonald's Arches." *Black Enterprise,* May. Available at: LEXIS-NEXIS Academic Universe, General News.

City of New York and Department of City Planning. 1976. *Montague Street Revitalization/City Options Grant/National Endowment for the Arts. A New York City Bicentennial Project.*

Cooper, Hannah L., et al. 2007. "Residential Segregation and Injection Drug Use Prevalence among Black Adults in U.S. Metropolitan Areas." *American Journal of Public Health* 97(2): 344–52.

Crow, Kelly 2002. "Is It a Fight over Fast Food or the People Who Eat It?" *New York Times,* March 3. Available: LEXIS-NEXIS Academic Universe, General News.

"Culver's Turns to GIS for Successful Franchising." 2008–09. *ArcNews* 30(4): 21.

Currie, Janet, et al. 2009. "The Effect of Fast Food Restaurants on Obesity." Working Paper 14721. Cambridge, Mass.: National Bureau of Economic Research.

Davey, Monica. 1998. "Area Aims for Quick End to Fast Food." *Chicago Tribune,* December 27. Available at: LEXIS-NEXIS Academic Universe, General News.

Davis, Brennan, and Christopher Carpenter. 2009. "Proximity of Fast-Food Restaurants to Schools and Adolescent Obesity." *American Journal of Public Health* 99(3): 505–10.

Dawson, Michael. 2001. *Black Visions: The Roots of Contemporary African-American Political Ideologies.* Chicago: University of Chicago Press.

Delgado, Richard, and Jean Stefancic. 2001. *Critical Race Theory: An Introduction.* New York: New York University Press.

Diez-Roux, Ana V. 2003. "Residential Environments and Cardiovascular Health." *Journal of Urban Health* 80(4): 569–89.

Downey, Liam, and Maeieke V. Van Willigen. 2005. "Environmental Stressors: The Mental Health Impacts of Living Near Industrial Activity. *Journal of Health and Social Behavior* 46(3): 289–305.

D'Rozario, Denver, and Jerome D. Williams. 2005. "Retail Redlining: Definition, Theory, Typology, and Measurement. *Journal of Macromarketing* 25(2): 175–86.

ESRI. 2007. *Community Tapestry Handbook.* Redlands, Calif.: ESRI.

Experian Business Strategies. 2006. Mosaic® USA Group and Type Descriptions [Last downloaded in July 2009; no current url for this document].

Fischer, Mary J. 2003. "The Relative Importance of Income and Race in Determining Residential Outcomes in U.S. Urban Areas, 1970–2000. *Urban Affairs Review* 38(5): 669–96.

Gladwell, Malcolm, Paul Farhi, and *Washington Post* staff writers. 1988. "Black Franchise Owners Sue Burger King Chain; Company Accused of Site, Price Deceptions." *Washington Post*, October 18. Available at: LEXIS-NEXIS Academic Universe, General News.

Gregor, Alison. 2010. "Long-Empty Plaza in Manhattan Lures a Popular Burger Stand as a Tenant." *New York Times*, January 20. Available at: LEXIS-NEXIS Academic Universe, General News.

Grier, Sonya A., and Shiriki K. Kumanyika. 2008. "The Context for Choice: Health Implications of Targeted Food and Beverage Marketing to African Americans." *American Journal of Public Health* 98(9): 1616–29.

Guthrie, Robert V. 1998. *Even the Rat Was White: A Historical View of Psychology.* 2nd ed. Boston, Mass.: Allyn and Bacon.

Hackbarth, Diana, Barbara Silvestri, and William Cosper. 1995. "Tobacco and Alcohol Billboards in 50 Chicago Neighborhoods: Market Segmentation to Sell Dangerous Products to the Poor." *Journal of Public Health Policy* 16(2): 213–30.

Hall, Stuart. 1998. *Representation: Cultural Representations and Signifying Practices.* Thousand Oaks, Calif.: Sage Publications.

Handy (Jam) Organization. 1942. "To Market, To Market," part 2. Video available at Prelinger Archives: www.archive.org/details/ToMarket1942_2 (accessed December 19, 2005).

Hargreaves, Margaret K., David G. Schlundt, and Maciej S. Buchowski. 2002. "Contextual Factors Influencing the Eating Behaviours of African American Women: A Focus Group Investigation." *Ethnicity and Health* 7(3): 133–47.

Hellig, Amy, and David S. Sawicki. 2003. "Race and Residential Accessibility to Shopping and Services." *Housing Policy Debate* 14(1–2): 69–101.

Herd, Denise. 1993. "Contesting Culture: Alcohol-Related Identity Movements in Contemporary African-American Communities." *Contemporary Drug Problems* 20(4): 739–58.

hooks, bell. 1992. *Black Looks: Race and Representation.* Boston, Mass.: South End Press.

Hurwitz, Phillip, et al. 2009. "Arterial Roads and Area Socioeconomic Status Are Predictors of Fast Food Restaurant Density in King County, WA." *International Journal of Behavioral Nutrition and Physical Activity* 6(46). doi:10.1186/1479-5868-1186-1146.

Iceland, John, Cicely Sharpe, and Erika Steinmetz. 2005. "Class Differences in African American Residential Patterns in U.S. Metropolitan Areas: 1990–2000. *Social Science Research* 34(1): 252.

Inness, Sherrie A. 2001. "Of Meatloaf and Jell-O." Introduction to *Cooking Lessons: The Politics of Gender and Food*, edited by S. A. Inness. Lanham, Md.: Rowman and Littlefield.

Jeffrey, Robert W., et al. 2006. "Are Fast Food Restaurants an Environmental Risk

Factor for Obesity?" *International Journal of Behavioral Nutrition and Physical Activity* 3(2). doi: 10.1186/1479-5868-1183-1182.

Jerry J. Stubbs v. McDonald's Corporation (United States District Court for the District of Kansas 2005). Available at: LEXIS-NEXIS Academic Universe, Law.

Kincheloe, Joe L. 2002. *The Sign of the Burger: McDonald's and the Culture of Power.* Philadelphia, Pa.: Temple University Press.

Kroc, Ray. 1977. *Grinding It Out: The Making of McDonald's.* Chicago: Contemporary Books.

Krysan, Maria. 2008. "Does Race Matter in the Search for Housing? An Exploratory Study of Search Strategies, Experiences, and Locations." *Social Science Research* 37(2): 581–603.

Kwate, Naa Oyo A. 2008. "Fried Chicken and Fresh Apples: Racial Segregation as a Fundamental Cause of Fast Food Density in Black Neighborhoods." *Health and Place* 14(1): 32–44.

Kwate, Naa Oyo A., and Tammy H. Lee. 2007. "Ghettoizing Outdoor Advertising: Disadvantage and Ad Panel Density in Black Neighborhoods. *Journal of Urban Health* 84(1): 21–31.

Kwate, Naa Oyo A., and Ilan H. Meyer. 2009. "Association Between Residential Exposure to Outdoor Alcohol Advertising and Problem Drinking among African American Women in New York City." *American Journal of Public Health* 99(2): 228–30.

Kwate, Naa Oyo A., et al. 2009. "Inequality in Obesigenic Environments: Fast Food Density in New York City. *Health and Place* 15(1): 364–73.

Lamont, Michéle, and Virág Molnar. 2001. "How Blacks Use Consumption to Shape Their Collective Identity." *Journal of Consumer Culture* 1(1): 31–45.

Levenstein, Harvey. 2003. *Paradox of Plenty: A Social History of Eating in Modern America.* Berkeley: University of California Press.

Levey, Bob. 1980. "Fighting the Battle of the Burger: Battling the Burger Franchise along Connecticut Avenue." *Washington Post,* June 12. Available at: LEXIS-NEXIS Academic Universe, General News.

Lewis, LaVonna B., et al. 2005. "African Americans' Access to Healthy Food Options in South Los Angeles Restaurants." *American Journal of Public Health* 95(4): 668–73.

Li, Fuzhonh, et al. 2009. "Obesity and the Built Environment: Does the Density of Neighborhood Fast-Food Outlets Matter?" *American Journal of Health Promotion* 23(3): 203–09.

Link, Bruce G., and Jo Phelan. 1995. "Social Conditions as Fundamental Causes of Disease." *Journal of Health and Social Behavior* 36(extra issue): 80–94.

Los Angeles City Council. 2008. Final Ordinance 180103. Available at: http://clkrep.lacity.org/onlinedocs/2007/07-1658_ord_180103.pdf (accessed March 1, 2010).

Loury, Glenn C. 2002. *Anatomy of Racial Inequality*. Cambridge, Mass.: Harvard University Press.

Love, John F. 1995. *McDonald's: Behind the Arches*. New York: Bantam.

Marin Institute. 2007. *The End of the Line for Alcohol Ads on Public Transit*. San Rafael, Calif.: The Marin Institute.

Massey, Douglas S., and Nancy A. Denton. 1993. *"American Apartheid: Segregation and the Making of the Underclass*. Cambridge, Mass.: Harvard University Press.

Mastro, Dana E., and Charles Atkin. 2002. "Exposure to Alcohol Billboards and Beliefs and Attitudes Toward Drinking among Mexican American High School Students." *Howard Journal of Communications* 13(2): 129–51.

"McDonald's Restaurant Opens on 35th Street." 1961. *Chicago Defender*, September 16. Available at: LEXIS-NEXIS Academic Universe, General News.

McKee, Pat, et al. 2011. "Malt Liquor Marketing in Inner Cities: The Role of Neighborhood Racial Composition." *Journal of Ethnicity in Substance Abuse* 10(1): 24–38.

Mintz, Sydney. 2002. "Food and Eating: Some Persisting Questions." In *Food Nations*, edited by W. Belasco and P. Scranton. New York: Routledge.

Mitchell, O, and Michael Greenberg. 1991. "Outdoor Advertising of Addictive Products. *New Jersey Medicine* 88(5): 331–33.

Moncreiff Arrarte, Anne. 1997. "Cable Firms Target Latino Children. *Denver Post*, December 21. Available at: LEXIS-NEXIS Academic Universe, General News.

Moore, Heather, et al. 2009. "Alcohol Advertising on Billboards, Transit Shelters, and Bus Benches in Inner-City Neighborhoods." *Contemporary Drug Problems* 35(2–3): 509–32.

Moore, Latetia V., et al. 2009. "Fast-Food Consumption, Diet Quality, and Neighborhood Exposure to Fast Food: The Multi-Ethnic Study of Atherosclerosis." *American Journal of Epidemiology* 170(1): 29–39.

Morgenstern, Lewis B., et al. 2009. "Fast Food and Neighborhood Stroke Risk." *Annals of Neurology* 66(2): 165–70.

National Center for Health Statistics. 2007. *Health, United States, 2007, with Chartbook on Trends in the Health of Americans*. Hyattsville, Md.: National Center for Health Statistics.

Neuhaus, Jessamyn. 1999. "The Way to a Man's Heart: Gender Roles, Domestic Ideology, and Cookbooks in the 1950s." *Journal of Social History* 32(3): 529–55.

Nielsen, Amie L., et al. 2010. "Racial/Ethnic Composition, Social Disorganization, and Offsite Alcohol Availability in San Diego, California." *Social Science Research* 39(1): 165–75.

Nyborn, Justin A., et al. 2009. "Alcohol Advertising on Boston's Massachusetts Bay Transportation Authority Transit System: An Assessment of Youths' and Adults' Exposure." *American Journal of Public Health* 99(S3): S644–S648.

Paradies, Yin. 2006. "A Systematic Review of Empirical Research on Self-Reported Racism and Health." *International Journal of Epidemiology* 35(4): 888–901.

Pascoe, Elizabeth A., and Laura Smart Richman. 2009. "Perceived Discrimination and Health: A Meta-Analytic Review." *Psychological Bulletin* 135(4): 531–54.

Pattillo, Mary. 2005. "Black Middle-Class Neighborhoods." *Annual Review of Sociology* 31: 305–29.

———. 2009. "The Mixed Blessings of Mixed Income Communities." Paper presented at Columbia University, Center for Urban Research and Policy. Seminar Series, April 23, 2009.

Perlik, Allison. 2005. "Minority Matters: Survival of the Fittest Means Rising to the Opportunities of an Evolving Foodservice Market." *Restaurants and Institutions,* March 15.

Primack, Brian A., et al. 2007. "Volume of Tobacco Advertising in African American Markets: Systematic Review and Meta-Analysis. *Public Health Reports* 122(5): 607–15.

Public Enemy. "1 Million Bottlebags." *Apocalypse '91: The Enemy Strikes Back.* Def Jam Records, 1991, compact disc.

Quitmon Hartzol v. McDonald's Corporation (United States District Court for The Northern District Illinois, Eastern Division. 2006. Available at: LEXIS-NEXIS Academic Universe, Law.

Resnicow, Ken, et al. 2000. "Dietary Change Through African American Churches: Baseline Results and Program Description of the Eat for Life Trial." *Journal of Cancer Education* 15(3): 156–63.

Roberts, Dorothy E. 1997. *Killing the Black Body: Race, Reproduction, and the Meaning of Liberty.* New York: Pantheon.

Rosewarne, Lauren. 2007. "Pin-ups in Public Space: Sexist Outdoor Advertising as Sexual Harassment. *Women's Studies International Forum* 30(4): 313–25.

Rothwell, Jonathan, and Douglas S. Massey. 2009. "The Effect of Density Zoning on Racial Segregation in U.S. Urban Areas." *Urban Affairs Review* 44(6): 779–806.

Sampson, Robert J., and Stephen W. Raudenbush. 2004. "Seeing Disorder: Neighborhood Stigma and the Social Construction of "Broken Windows." *Social Psychology Quarterly* 67(4): 319–42.

Schooler Caroline, Michael D. Basil, and David G. Altman. 1996. "Alcohol and Cigarette Advertising on Billboards: Targeting with Social Cues." *Health Communication* 8(2): 109–29.

Scott, Bettina M., Robert W. Denniston, and Kathryn M. Magruder. 1992. "Alcohol Advertising in the African-American Community." *Journal of Drug Issues* 22(2): 455–69.

Shapiro, Thomas M. 2005. *The Hidden Cost of Being African American: How Wealth Perpetuates Inequality.* New York: Oxford University Press.

Simon, Michael 2008. "Reducing Youth Exposure to Alcohol Ads: Targeting Public Transit." *Journal of Urban Health* 85(4): 506–16.

Singleton, John (writer and director). 1991. *Boyz N the Hood* (film). Columbia Pictures.

Small, Mario Luis, and Monica McDermott. 2006. "The Presence of Organizational Resources in Poor Urban Neighborhoods: An Analysis of Average and Contextual Effects. *Social Forces* 84(3): 1697–724.

Smiley, Melissa J., et al. 2010. "A Spatial Analysis of Health-Related Resources in Three Diverse Metropolitan Areas." *Health and Place* 16(5): 885–92.

Steptoe, Andrew, and Pamela J. Feldman. 2001. "Neighborhood Problems as Sources of Chronic Stress: Development of a Measure of Neighborhood Problems, and Associations with Socioeconomic Status and Health." *Annals of Behavioral Medicine* 23(3): 177–85.

Subramanian, S. V., Dolores Acevedo-Garcia, and Theresa L. Osypuk. 2005. "Racial Residential Segregation and Geographic Heterogeneity in Black/White Disparity in Poor Self-Rated Health in the U.S.: A Multilevel Statistical Analysis." *Social Science and Medicine* 60(8): 1667–79.

Thomas, Alexander, and Samuel Sillen. (1991). *Racism and Psychiatry*. New York: Carol Publishing.

TNS Media Intelligence/LMR. 2010. *Ad $ Spender Multi Media Service: January–December 2009*. New York: Leading National Advertisers, Inc.

U.S. Bureau of Labor Statistics. 2006–2007. Consumer Expenditure Survey, 2006–2007. Washington, D.C.

Vergara, Camilo Jose. 1997. *The New American Ghetto*. Piscataway, N.J.: Rutgers University Press.

Wallace, John M., et al. 2002. "Tobacco, Alcohol, and Illicit Drug Use: Racial and Ethnic Differences among U.S. High School Seniors, 1976–2000." *Public Health Reports* 117(S1): S67–75.

Weems, Robert. 1998. *Desegregating the Dollar: African American Consumerism in the Twentieth Century*. New York: New York University Press.

West, Carolyn M. 1995. "Mammy, Sapphire, and Jezebel: Historical Images of Black Women and Their Implications for Psychotherapy." *Psychotherapy* 32(3): 458–65.

White, Kellee, and Luisa N. Borrell. 2006. "Racial/Ethnic Neighborhood Concentration and Self-Reported Health in New York City." *Ethnicity and Disease* 16(4): 900–08.

Williams, David R., and Chiquita Collins. 2001. "Racial Residential Segregation: A Fundamental Cause of Racial Disparities in Health." *Public Health Reports* 116(5): 404–16.

Wolf, Barnet D. 2001. "Wendy's Ad Effort Will Focus on Sales among Latinos." *Columbus (Ohio) Dispatch*, September 9. Available at: LEXIS-NEXIS Academic Universe, General News.

Yancey, Antronette K., et al. 2009. "A Cross-Sectional Prevalence Study of Ethnically Targeted and General Audience Outdoor Obesity-Related Advertising." *Milbank Quarterly* 87(1): 155–84.

Index